A Commentary on
THE GOSPEL OF LUKE

UNLOCKING THE NEW TESTAMENT

A Commentary on THE GOSPEL OF LUKE

David Pawson

Anchor Recordings

Copyright © 2017 David Pawson

The right of David Pawson to be identified as author of this Work has been asserted by him in accordance with the Copyright, Designs and Patents Act 1988.

First published in Great Britain in 2017 by
Anchor Recordings Ltd
DPTT, Synegis House, 21 Crockhamwell Road,
Woodley, Reading RG5 3LE

No part of this publication may be reproduced or transmitted in any form or by any means, electronic or mechanical, including photocopy, recording or any information storage and retrieval system, without prior permission in writing from the publisher.

**For more of David Pawson's teaching,
including DVDs and CDs, go to
www.davidpawson.com**

**FOR FREE DOWNLOADS
www.davidpawson.org**

**For further information, email
info@davidpawsonministry.org**

ISBN 978-1-911173-21-2

Printed by Lightning Source

Contents

INTRODUCTION LUKE 1:1–4	9
1. LUKE 1	15
2. LUKE 2	53
3. LUKE 3	97
4. LUKE 4	123
5. LUKE 5:1–6:11	155
6. LUKE 6:12–49	173
7. LUKE 7	187
8. LUKE 8	205
9. LUKE 9:1–10:24	223
10. LUKE 10:25–42	255
11. LUKE 11	265
12. LUKE 12	293
13. LUKE 13	317
14. LUKE 14	327
15. LUKE 15	351
16. LUKE 16	373
17. LUKE 17	399
18. LUKE 18	423
19. LUKE 19	433
20. LUKE 20:1–21:4	455
21. LUKE 21:5–38	463
22. LUKE 22	473
23. LUKE 23	487
24. LUKE 24	499

This book is based on a series of talks. Originating as it does from the spoken word, its style will be found by many readers to be somewhat different from my usual written style. It is hoped that this will not detract from the substance of the biblical teaching found here.

As always, I ask the reader to compare everything I say or write with what is written in the Bible and, if at any point a conflict is found, always to rely upon the clear teaching of scripture.

David Pawson

INTRODUCTION

Luke 1:1-4

The Gospel of Luke has been called "the loveliest book in the world". A Scottish theologian, when asked, "Can you recommend a good life of Christ" replied, "Well, have you tried St. Luke?" All the world loves a story and it is full of the most wonderful stories. The account of Christmas is here, the story of the road to Emmaus is at the other end in chapter 24, and in between we have parables (like the Good Samaritan and the Prodigal Son) that are only to be found in this Gospel. Luke is a marvellous storyteller and the best thing is that all the stories are true. The author of this book was a doctor by profession and I am thrilled about that. I doubt if the Virgin Mary would have described the intimate details of her confinement to anyone other than her family doctor, and I have no doubt that was how Luke got the unique details that he has given us in the first two chapters. It has been said that a minister sees people at their best, a lawyer sees people at their worst, but a doctor sees people as they are. Certainly this is true of Dr. Luke, a companion of Paul in his missionary journeys, a man of culture, education, intelligence and sympathy, a man who has a tremendous heart for people. I am so glad God chose a medical man with scientific training to recount the mighty miracles recorded in this Gospel.

One of the things I am constantly being told by those who don't want to believe the Bible is that it is inaccurate. Have you come across this? As soon as you quote the Bible, some say, "How do you know it's an accurate record?" God knew that this would be an objection of the sceptic so he picked a man who would, with the same precise care with which he gave out his prescriptions, write down an account of what happened. He says in the prologue, "I went into it so thoroughly, so carefully." There are plenty of "lives" of Jesus about. Luke wanted to provide one that was absolutely accurate. Praise God that we have such an accurate account of the life of Jesus.

Here are two characteristics of this Gospel: first, it reaches up to heaven; and, second, it reaches down to earth. It reaches up to heaven in praise and prayer. There is no other Gospel of the four that is so full of the phrase "praising God", which occurs more times in Luke's Gospel than in the whole of the rest of the New Testament. Think of that as we go through this book.

You may have been through Luke many times before, but I will show you as we go along that this is the least known of the Gospels. Funnily enough, you may know some parts of it like the back of your hand but the rest of it is the least known. I sometimes ask people whether they think a quotation comes from Shakespeare, the Old Testament or the New Testament. Here is one such quotation: "If they do these things in the green tree, what shall be done in the dry?" It is what Jesus said as he carried his cross up Calvary, and it is part of Luke's account. Did you know that? Few people do. Most do not know this Gospel as they should, but as we go through it I hope the discovery of these unexpected things that you might never have realised were there will help you to praise God and lift your heart in adoration to him who planned it all.

INTRODUCTION

There are three magnificent hymns of *praise* here at the beginning, which have come to be known in worship as the Magnificat, the Benedictus, and the Nunc Dimittis, which have been used down the centuries by Christians.

It is also a Gospel of *prayer*. Luke includes more teaching on prayer than any of the other three Gospels and provides more examples of people praying. So it is a Gospel that reaches up to heaven in praise and prayer but it also reaches down to earth, to all sorts and conditions of people. For example, this Gospel has a place for *half-castes* — the Samaritans, the Good Samaritan and others. Luke also puts an emphasis on the Gentiles, people who were not even Jews. The genealogy is traced back not to Abraham (as Matthew does) but back to Adam – which includes us all. There are many references to Roman life. In fact it is written for a Greek, or a Roman with a Greek name. "Theophilus" means "God-lover". It is written for those who love God and want to know more about the love of God: "Theophilus" – Greek *theo*s = God; *philos* = one who loves. Luke himself was the only New Testament writer who was not a Jew himself.

This is also the Gospel for *women*. No other Gospel has such a place and tenderness for women as Luke. It comes out from the very first chapters. Think of the women mentioned here: the Virgin Mary, Elizabeth, Anna, the widow of Nain, the woman with the alabaster jar of ointment, Martha, Mary – they are all here.

Luke's is a Gospel for the *poor*. Time and again this comes up. Think of the words "Blessed are you poor" (in Luke 6). It is for poor people who don't have much in this world but who can still love God and praise him. Think of the parable of Lazarus the beggar and the rich man. It is only in Luke. The beggar is carried by the angels to Abraham's bosom.

Above all, this is the Gospel for *sinners*.

The four Gospels are not photographs, they are portraits.

Four portraits of one person will enable you to see that person in fullness, as each of the four artists have seen a facet or some quality of their character. You study the paintings or sculptures of Winston Churchill, every one of them brings out some facet of his character, but put them together and you get the rounded character that he was, physically as well as in other ways. In fact, this is what God in his wisdom saw was needed. So we had four portraits of Jesus and not just one account. You get the real Jesus by putting all four together. If Matthew looked through the eyes of a Jew, he saw the King of the Jews. His Gospel is full of the Old Testament and Jewish things, and if you are not a Jew, Matthew is probably the most difficult Gospel for you to read. Mark was a young man and he just saw the Son of Man and he saw a hero, he saw the suffering servant prophesied by Isaiah, and he painted a portrait by selecting the incidents. John, that aged, deep thinker, the man that got closer to Jesus than any other on earth, the man whom Jesus loved, looked and he saw the Son of God, and painted a portrait of the Son of God. But Luke, a Gentile "sinner", looked and he saw the Saviour of everybody. He painted a portrait of the Saviour. That is why, for somebody who was not a Christian, I personally would always give a copy of Luke's Gospel to read. I would not give John's Gospel – which is written for mature Christians, and we love it and think it is for everybody. Luke is the Gospel to give to somebody who is wanting to know something about Jesus and is one to start with.

This is the only Gospel with an author's personal pronoun "I". Matthew doesn't say "I", Mark doesn't either and nor does John. John, the "beloved disciple", refers to himself in the third person. Luke's expression is very personal, and in this prologue he says two things. First of all, he talks about his *authority* for writing and, secondly, he talks about his *accuracy* in writing. His *authority* is that Christianity

INTRODUCTION

(unlike all other religions except Judaism) is squarely based on history. The Bible is a book of history. It is not a book about philosophy or ideology, it is not a book of thoughts and opinions. It is factual, and I am thrilled about that. It gives my faith a solid foundation that you cannot have if your religion is just philosophy, thoughts and opinions. So Luke is saying this: I have delved into the facts; that is what makes me an authority.

We still use that word "authority" in this way. We say, "He's an authority on his subject." If he is, it means he knows the facts and you wouldn't argue with him. You see, Jesus was the kind of person about whom legend would quickly grow. Luke is writing thirty years after Jesus' death and resurrection. One Gospel had already been written – Mark. But Luke knew that there were other things going around about Jesus, and he wanted the truth, the facts, so he had looked into it, and his authority was that he had got the facts right. Many "gospels" written about Jesus were not included in the Bible because they were full of legend, myth and imagination. When any famous character leaves this stage of history, legends begin to gather very quickly afterwards and stories are told about them that are apocryphal. There are apocryphal gospels about Jesus. There was the "gospel of Hebrews", the "gospel of Thomas", and so on. But only those included in the Bible are accurate. They go back to the facts, back to firsthand testimony, and Luke is telling us: I have been acquainted with these facts from the beginning. He is an authority and therefore he has the accuracy. He is writing for intelligent people who want the facts, who want the truth about Jesus, the Son of God, the Saviour of the world. So this Gospel is the easiest to read. It assumes nothing. He doesn't even assume you know your Old Testament, so he hardly ever quotes it (though Matthew does all the time). So Luke starts from zero and he tells us that these are the facts and it is good news. If you are a God-lover and not a God-hater, this is good news. But if you are a God-hater, then Luke's Gospel will be bad news to you. If you want to know and love God, if you want to have a relationship with God, then, "O Theophilus", it is written down here.

1

Read Luke 1

Like the Gospels of Matthew and Mark, Luke begins with John the Baptist. John, the physical cousin of Jesus, is the person who is most ignored in the celebration of Christmas, yet the Christmas narrative belongs to two miraculous babies – John and Jesus, born within just a few months of each other. As you know, there is a gap of four hundred years between the Old and New Testaments. From the intervening period there came some interesting books called the Apocrypha, but we do not include them in the Word of God because they do not contain the phrase which occurs nearly four thousand times in the Old Testament, "Thus says the Lord", and the reason is that for four hundred years God never spoke. People studied what he *had* said but the last word of God in the Old Testament was from a man called Malachi and, if you read the last part of his book, Malachi says that God will send his Messiah, but before the Messiah comes he will send his messenger to prepare the way. The Old Testament closes with the promise of two people coming, one to get people ready for the other. That is why Matthew, Mark and Luke start this way, not with Jesus the Messiah but with John the messenger, the man who came to get things ready.

We should celebrate both births. For, humanly speaking, neither of them should have taken place. It is often when things come to a dead end that God steps in and starts what he wants to do. I remember the thrill when I read through

Genesis 11 – begat, begat, begat. I wondered what on earth it was there for and what you could get out of it, and then I suddenly noticed that all the begetting came to a full stop and Sarah was barren. Nothing was going to happen and the family tree would have had a line drawn under it. That was when God came to Abraham, Sarah's husband, and things began to move. This is how it happened here: one lady couldn't have a baby because she was too old, the other was a girl who couldn't because she was too young – not yet old enough for marriage. Yet in both cases they had a baby. It was a double miracle – there was God's foreknowledge of the events, and his prediction of them. Maybe you can tell somebody that they are going to have a baby, but in those days you couldn't tell it was going to be a boy. In both cases, God predicted a boy and it was God's power to accomplish it. He not only predicted what would happen, but he predicted it because he had planned it and because he was going to do it. That is why the predictions in the Bible are so accurate: because God knows perfectly well what he is going to do.

"In the days of *Herod*...." I wonder if that name sends a chill to your bone. It ought to. Herod was such a mixture— part of him was so good. He loved putting up buildings for people, though that could be said to be ambition. But whenever times were tough he used to reduce taxes. He actually melted down his own gold plate to give food to poor people. That was King Herod. Then what was wrong with him? He was a jealous man. He was a man with a chip on his shoulder. He was a direct descendant of both Jacob and Esau. He had the worst of both in him. He was a man who could not stand rivals, and he was cruel. He could have terrible tempers. The Jews wondered if they would ever have a decent king again. The Romans had planted this puppet ruler from a foreign nation – an Edomite, a descendant of Esau – on their throne. The Romans had given him the title

"King of the Jews" and it rankled. The whole nation was seething in the days of King Herod, but God knew what he was going to do: he came to two women. Isn't it lovely that when things look dreadful and you think you will never get through a bad patch – God has a way of quietly doing something that is going to change the total situation.

I will give what follows in this section two headings. First of all, we will think about the *similarities* between the accounts of the births of John and of Jesus, and then, second, the profound *differences*. The stories are so alike in ten features, yet they are so different in another six.

Similarities

Firstly, the *outline* is almost identical in both accounts: a description of the parents; a visit from a heavenly messenger – an angel; the prediction of a baby boy; an objection by the people to whom the prediction is made, and an explanation by the angel. It is almost like a carbon copy. People reacted much the same way. I guess you might if you had an angel come and say such things to you.

Here is the second similarity. We began with two things that were (humanly) impossible. We have already noticed that Elizabeth was aged and barren like Sarah and Rachel, and she was now way past forty-five. Mary was probably in her fifteenth year, to be married at sixteen. She was betrothed, which is stronger than our word "engaged". If the fiancé of a betrothed girl died, she was then treated as a widow. In fact, divorce was the word used to break a betrothal, even though the marriage had not been consummated. So she was in that position – more than engaged, less than married – but she would certainly not have known sex. Therefore it was impossible for her to have a baby boy. It is possible physically to have a baby girl under these circumstances: if a female egg begins to divide spontaneously in a kind of cancerous way, it can produce a female baby. But it can never produce a boy because the vital factor, the Y chromosome that is needed to turn that egg into a male, comes from the male and therefore it is impossible for such a woman to have a son.

The third similarity is that both were *firstborn sons* and this is rather important because, from the very beginning when they came out of Egypt, the firstborn son in each Hebrew family was saved from death by the blood of the lamb on the doorpost. The firstborn son was very precious to God, and when any Jewish mother had a firstborn son, the father was so excited he would rush out into the street and shout "David, David – I've had a firstborn son." It could be the Messiah. If you wanted to keep the boy for the farm you had to pay God, buy your son back and *redeem* him.

The fourth similarity is that they both had an *angelic visitor*. Angels are real. They are not just for supermarket shop windows at Christmas time. Though we may not see them all the time, they are around us and they have names. They are personalities. Gabriel is the angel who came to Daniel nearly five hundred years before these events. The angels do not die. They do not reproduce – their number is fixed. So they go on, and Gabriel is still around now, and he came to both Mary and Elizabeth. Twice that same angel had announced the coming of the Messiah to Daniel.

Fifthly, they were both *afraid* – and wouldn't you be? Can you blame them? There you are, and suddenly there is an angel! The angel appeared to Zechariah, the husband in the first case, and he was scared. One of the loveliest phrases in the Bible is, "Don't be afraid." Yet that is the very thing we are when God gets near. When the supernatural is around, when the Word of God is striking deep, we get worried about what it is going to do to us and we are afraid, and God says, "Don't be afraid." When Jesus came, he was always saying it.

Luke 1

The Bible says this three hundred and sixty-six times—once for every day, including leap year. Every day you can claim one "Don't be afraid" from the Bible. Fear is not a thing that God wants to inhabit the human heart.

Sixth is the fact that both children were *named by God* and their nature described. They were both to be under God's direct authority. Jesus was going to say of his cousin John: "He is the greatest man who was ever born". What a tribute from Jesus! When you study the life of John, you understand why.

Seventh, their careers are described. God *says* this is what he will do, and this is what he *will* do. God has planned it all out, and the lives that are going to be of greatest benefit to mankind are those that will be in line with God's predestination and fulfil his plan. John was planned for one kind of life, Jesus for another, but both were to live a planned life.

Similarity number eight: in both cases, Zechariah and Mary argued back with a question that began with the word, "How...?" Why didn't they say "Why?" You know they missed it all, and this is one of the frustrations you find: that people will ask how instead of asking why. They want to know how miracles can happen – and how this and how that. But the real question is "Why?". "Mary, you're going to have a baby boy and he'll be Jesus and he'll be great." "How?" Why didn't she say "Why"? It is interesting to know how the world was created and how things happened that did happen, but it doesn't affect your life. You might ask *why* the world was created, but science is concerned with the *how* questions and sometimes deaf to the *why* questions. How do the planets circle in space? How does a comet come hurtling through space? But why don't people ask why? That is the more important question. The Bible doesn't bother with many "how" questions. It doesn't say, "How did the blind see?" "How did the lame walk?" It says why. That is the big question, but these were typical human beings and Zechariah said, "How...?" and Mary said, "How...?" They had to have it all explained to them. There is something very human about this. Zechariah's expression of course implied unbelief, but Mary's was more positive.

The ninth similarity was that they were both given *confirming signs* to prove that it would happen. Zechariah was told: you haven't believed this but it is going to happen, and proof that it is going to happen is this – from now until nine months ahead, when it happens, you won't be able to speak a word. When he came out, he tried so hard to tell the others and he couldn't. He just had to point. That was the sign God gave Zechariah, to confirm the word. In the case of Mary, she says, "How...?" The angel said: you go off and visit your cousin Elizabeth. You thought she could never have a baby. You go and take one look at her, Mary. She's six months pregnant. So they both got a sign.

The tenth similarity was this. *In both cases there was an acceptance of God's will.* In v. 25, Elizabeth was so thrilled to be used. For her it meant a disgrace taken away, for I am afraid such was the society in those days that it was a disgrace for a woman not to have children. She could be divorced on that ground and her husband could take another to give him a son and heir. It still happens in the Middle East. Where a ruler doesn't get a son from one wife, he changes the wife and gets another who can give him this.

With Mary it was rather different. For her it brought disgrace, yet she was still willing. Of the two, I think we have got to hand it to Mary. There can be few more wonderful words than Mary's simple, "I'm your maid – if you say so, alright." Isn't that lovely – to be the Lord's maid? You don't get maids much now, do you? That is part of a bygone era but let me address every woman: the highest privilege you can have in life is to be the Lord's maid and to do what he tells you.

This was an extraordinary situation. Elizabeth could have worried about the confinement – how would she manage at her age? Would it be difficult? Mary had other things to worry about. For both of them it would be their firstborn, and they both accepted the will of God.

The Differences
Now let me run through the differences between the two baby boys. First, what *different backgrounds* they had. John came from a priestly family; Jesus came from a royal, princely family. John had blood in him on both sides from the Aaronic priesthood, but Jesus had blood in him from Mary, from the house of David, as did his foster father Joseph. So they were of priestly and princely background. In a sense, John's background was Jewish but Jesus' background was Gentile. Jesus came from the north – he was to live in Galilee, where there was such a mixture of nations, whereas in the south, where John lived, it was solidly Jewish. John was to come from a metropolitan background under the shadow of the capital city, Jesus from a little village up in the hills. John was from a rich background because the priests didn't starve then, but Jesus came from a home where one lost coin made a difference and where clothes were patched.

John came from a devout home, so did Jesus. But they *changed backgrounds*. John, from the rich metropolitan home of a priest, went to live in the wilderness. Jesus, from the little village in the north, made for the town of Jerusalem. So, in a sense, their backgrounds prepared them for different ministries. I never dreamt in my boyhood in the north of England that I would find myself ministering in the south. The Lord somehow takes us and puts us in a different setting or cultural/social arena in which to fulfil our ministry.

Second, *what a difference in the vision*! The vision about John came to the father in the temple. Every descendant of Aaron was a priest, and there were twenty-four shifts of priesthood at the temple in Jerusalem. The priests lived in the villages around the city, and when their turn came they would go up to the temple. They would all be there at Passover, Pentecost, and Tabernacles. One shift took one week per year and there were about a thousand priests. The possibility was that some priests would only have one chance in a lifetime to go and pray within the veil at the altar of incense. Can you imagine the big day? It is as if all the vicars in the Church of England were allowed once to go into Westminster Abbey and preach. Can you imagine how they would look forward to it and build up for it? Imagine the big moment – when the Vicar of Puddlecome-in-the-Marsh is going to preach in Westminster Abbey! It was done then by lot, so they didn't know if it would ever come up. It was such a scarce privilege.

One day the lot was drawn for this old man Zechariah – who had never had the chance, I believe – and he prepared to go into the Holy Place, beyond the first gorgeously embroidered veil, and say prayers for one hour. He went inside and it was lit by the fire on the little altar of incense, and as he put incense on the altar and saw the smoke rise, he knew that, outside, the people were praying for this hour – his big moment. Even that in itself would have been great, but suddenly there is an angel there. Can you imagine him all alone inside? Nobody would come in and join him. I can see him measuring his distance to the veil again, to get out. That is how the vision came. The old man Zechariah has reached the climax of his career and he is told, "You're going to have a son." Until this time, Elizabeth had not conceived and he had given up praying for a son because it was too late. But the angel's message is: the Lord heard your prayer.

Luke 1

The problem was that Zechariah had got the timing wrong. That's all. So often we have prayed for something for years and we think the Lord didn't hear. But the Lord did hear and he knew the right time for this. The name Zechariah means "the Lord remembers". What a lovely name to have. The Lord had remembered his prayer. The name Elizabeth means "my God is faithful".

The visit of the angel that came to the mother of Jesus came in the home. It wasn't in the temple. It wasn't in a religious setting. In fact, in the home where she lived, the kitchen and the bedroom and everything was one, so this time it was at the kitchen sink. How very different, and it tells you that God can visit you not only when you are in a place of worship but when you are washing up. Gabriel spoke to Mary and said, "O favoured one, full of grace." Some have thought that meant Mary was quite outstanding and spectacular in her own character. I think the emphasis of that statement is on what God is, not on what Mary is. For the glory of the meaning of the Bible is this: that God uses ordinary people and makes them great. That is why he chose the Jews. They weren't special. They were slaves but he chose them because he loved them. Mary was full of grace – not full of her own grace but full of God's grace. Mind you, she must have been a girl who had walked with the Lord. But we are not told that she was outstanding. We are just told that she was Mary, a young teenage girl, and she was favoured.

The third difference was in their *conception*. God can use a hundred and one ways to produce babies, and in one case he used a father, even though the wife was beyond normal childbearing age. In the other case he didn't use a father. It doesn't matter to God. He can use all methods, and I want you to realise this. We will tie God's miracles down to one method. We will say that God has got to work a miracle in *this* way. But no, God can use a husband or do without the husband. Their names were different. "John" means "grace of God"; "Jesus" means "Saviour; God saves." This is what is going to happen. The grace of God was to begin to appear with John but it was Jesus who would save. Names are very important indeed in God's book.

Fourth, their destiny and careers would be so different. On the one hand, John would be a total abstainer all his life. He would never touch wine. Something different would be true of Jesus. Jesus would be called a glutton and a winebibber because he was not a total abstainer. I want to emphasise this: *both of them were willing to accept the will of God the Father for them*—whether it meant to abstain or not. It was characteristic of the different lives that they were called to live. John was called to live in a desert as a hermit, with an old coat and eat locusts and wild honey. Jesus was going to go to parties and he ate and drank with tax collectors and sinners. The important thing is not that we should all be the same but we should all be doing the will of God. How easy it is for Christians to criticise each other: "Oh, he goes to parties and he drinks," and another person says, "Well they're narrow and they don't do this." If God has called you to be there, then you be there. If God has not called you to be there, then you stay away. The important thing is for you to find the will of God.

John, it says, was going to bring parents and teenagers together. They had their troubles then, I guess. One of John's ministries was to bring fathers and children together to get ready for the Lord. Think of that! We could do with a few John the Baptists around today to reform, to call people to get ready. If you knew the King of kings was coming to your house tomorrow, what would you do tonight? In the middle of the war, during the Blitz, a Cockney woman heard her doorbell ring and she went to the door and King

Luke 1

George VI and his wife, the Queen, were standing there on the doorstep! They had come to visit the people in the East End after a particularly heavy air raid. There she was with the dust around her hair and her apron on. Can you imagine it? Supposing she had known they were coming the day before – what would you do if the Queen was coming to your house? Well, John the Baptist said: get ready, the King is coming.

When Jesus came, he could build on his cousin John's work. Jesus could not have begun his work without him. They had such different careers. John's was temporary – only for a few years, just to get people ready and to fade out of the picture and go to prison and ultimately lose his head to a dancing girl's whim. But Jesus was to build on what was laid. Jesus said about John, when he had heard that he was in prison, that John was the greatest man who had ever lived.

Fifth, alone, selfless, filled with the Holy Spirit from his birth – and, instead of just gurgling and babbling as a baby, John would praise the Lord. Filled with the Holy Spirit, his tongue would praise God from the very beginning of his life. That is one of the things it means here. Fancy being filled with the Holy Spirit from your birth! From then on, John needed that, because he was going to have to go to school in the desert with no teachers and no other pupils. He was going to have to praise God by himself. He was going to have to learn, so God graciously gave him the fullness of the Holy Spirit at birth. Jesus was to be anointed with the Spirit when he was thirty years of age, at a baptism in the river Jordan.

Sixth, there is the difference in *knowledge*. Everybody knew about John's birth. The whole village was talking: Look at that – getting bigger every day ... Elizabeth, of all people! Everybody was thrilled. It was public knowledge and the crowd was there at the confinement. The crowd asked what the name of the baby was to be. Zechariah wrote: *His name is John*. Then Zechariah could speak! It was public, but the birth of Jesus was so private. People didn't speak to Mary in the village where she lived – no, she was having a baby before marriage.

One of the loveliest things in this account is that Mary didn't try to explain matters to Joseph. She didn't even say, "Look, this baby is not from another man, Joseph." She left it to God to look after that. She didn't try to justify herself. What trust, when people are going to misunderstand and say things about you – could you keep quiet? Mary did. For the birth, God took that little family seventy miles away. She had that journey, on a donkey or on foot, just before the baby came. It was in a little courtyard of an inn – probably in the open air by the manger, which was in the middle of the courtyard, open to the stars. Hardly anybody knew – a few dirty shepherds, and later a few brilliant men from hundreds of miles away. But the whole thing was so quiet, so unknown, just a girl having her first baby at sixteen in a courtyard. I want you to try to imagine this. Women, if God asked you if he could use your womb, what would be your reaction? Men, if God asked you to be a foster father for someone absolutely vital to God's plan, what would be your reaction? You can find out very simply. The Lord Jesus desires to use your heart. You can soon tell if there would be room for him if there is room for him in your heart. The rest of the New Testament talks about Christ being formed in us, until it becomes obvious to other people that we carry another life within us and they can see the signs of what I would call a "spiritual pregnancy" in which Christ is being formed within us. God have mercy upon us. We have sometimes been ashamed to carry the Lord Jesus in our bodies for fear of people, fear of consequences. You may have closed your life to Jesus and said, "I don't want him." That would be as if Mary had said, "No, I couldn't face it", and as if Elizabeth had said, "No, not at my age." But this lovely young girl and this aged woman both said yes. God's purpose was fulfilled.

1:39-56

One of the features I have mentioned that Luke brings out more than any of the other three Gospels is the place of women. For example, in chapter eight it is mentioned that apart from going around with twelve men as disciples, there were also women who travelled around with Jesus – a fact often forgotten and overlooked. Some of the women he had healed from physical sickness or demonic possession, but we are told that some of them were wealthy and ministered to Jesus out of their substance. In other words, he had a number of wealthy ladies who were able to provide clothes and food and do the cooking for the disciples. It is one of those insights that you tend to forget.

We see in this Gospel that Jesus used women with their unique gifts to do things that men didn't do then, just as he used men with their unique gifts to do things that women didn't do. It is this balance of seeing the differences of function, not differences of status. I think of the time after the burial of Jesus when the women came to anoint the body; men really were out of place in such a situation. The Lord called those women to go and lay Jesus' body out in the tomb and anoint it properly – a job that they could do – and therefore they were the first to know about the resurrection. Not only after his death, but before his birth, women had a vital part to play.

So this study is about these two women. They were related, they were probably first cousins, though we are not sure of the exact relationship. Socially, they were as far removed from each other as they were in age. One was married to a wealthy priest; the other was engaged to a humble village carpenter. Yet these two, spanning ages, spanning social classes, were to be related physically – in a remarkable secret, which they shared together for months before anyone else had any wind of it. One day, Mary, the teenage girl, went on foot over seventy miles to visit her elderly cousin. That could have been seventy miles as the crow flies, but no Jew walked in the line of the crow's flight because they crossed the Jordan, went down the other side, came up through Jericho and up to Jerusalem, up through the hills, to avoid going through Samaria and meeting any Samaritans. So the journey was even longer than it need have been. Up she came, up to Jerusalem and over the top of the hills, and westward down the hill to a little village which is still there today, called Ein Kerem, where Elizabeth lived.

Why did Mary come? Why did a fifteen-year-old girl make that long journey that she would make again nine months later – for Bethlehem is just a mile or two from Ein Kerem? She went to see if it could possibly be true that her elderly cousin, now in her late fifties or early sixties, was pregnant. If we can try and get inside that teenage girl's mind, she was thinking over a remarkable experience in which an angel had told her that she was going to have a baby boy without knowing a man. Since the angel disappeared, Mary's mind must have been saying, "Was that real? How could such a thing possibly happen?" But the angel had said something else. If she wanted proof, her elderly cousin was now six months pregnant. She could go and see her. If her elderly cousin could be having a baby with a man, then she as a teenager would find it possible to have a baby without a man.

So, as she went on that long journey and neared the house in Ein Kerem, she must have been wondering what she would find. Mary must have been getting more and more excited, more and more tense as she got near. She went through the little courtyard and knocked at the door. "Come in," said a voice. When she went in she took one look. There was Elizabeth, leaning slightly back with swollen tummy,

Luke 1

and Mary knew straightaway – it is not only possible, it is going to happen. The moment is dramatic. This elderly woman, maybe with grey hair, and this fifteen-year-old girl, staring at each other, and suddenly they are in each other's arms, kissing, and saying all the things you do say, "Nice to see you." "How are you?" "How wonderful!" Suddenly, in that moment when they have seen each other, Elizabeth springs back, steps back, looks at Mary, and joins the Pentecostals. That is what happened – I am using that phrase quite seriously. At that point she was filled with the Holy Spirit, and began to speak with a loud voice. I am so glad the scripture is accurate enough to include that word "loud". One of the things that keeps many people from being filled with the Spirit is that they are scared stiff they will develop a loud voice. They think that God only speaks in a still small voice – well, he only did once. On the other occasions when God spoke it was like a clap of thunder. God can be noisy. Somehow we got into this thinking that a thing is more spiritual if it is quiet and still, and if we are terribly whispery; that we should whisper in church. When the Holy Spirit really fills people, they get noisy. They use a loud voice and people will look around. Maybe what we are really afraid of is not using a loud voice to God, but we are worried about what other people will say.

But Elizabeth, thank God, was an elderly lady who let the Spirit fill her, and shouted with a loud voice and it came out like that, and that is likely to happen. Elizabeth was filled with the Holy Spirit. When we are, this is the usual overflow; when you are full up, that is where it will come out. Every time you read in the Bible of people being filled with the Holy Spirit, you find that is where it shows, that is where something happens. This happened to Elizabeth. So she stepped back, and there in that kitchen her voice rose, way above normal level. Out came the most wonderful things that she never thought she would say, and things that didn't come from her mind, because the things she said could not have been further from her thoughts. Up to this moment Elizabeth had no idea whatever what was happening to Mary. As far as Elizabeth was concerned it was her young cousin who had come to visit her. But now, through the Holy Spirit, she sees things she never saw before; she understands things she never understood before. Out it pours, and we are going to look now at the things she says.

She was doing what the Bible calls prophesying. But when God gets hold of your tongue the most amazing utterances become possible for anyone, for the most ordinary person. It is sheer poetry, but I want you to notice it was said, not sung, just as the "Magnificat" was said, not sung. But because of the poetry these words have become hymns of praise used by the Church for these two thousand years. She makes four statements. The first is a statement of *congratulation*. Now this is surprising, because really you would have thought that, when they met, Mary would have been congratulating Elizabeth. "Oh Elizabeth! You're going to be a mother after all these years. Congratulations!" But no, it is Elizabeth who congratulates Mary. The Holy Spirit has reversed their roles. Elizabeth is taking the initiative. To understand Elizabeth's excitement you have to go back to the Old Testament. For centuries the scriptures had promised that one day God would send a Messiah – a Saviour, a Deliverer, somebody who would fulfil the dreams of his people. Every Jewish girl had one ambition – to be the mother of that Messiah. They knew that one day a Jewish girl would have a baby boy who would be the Saviour, the Messiah, the Christ. "Messiah" is the Hebrew word, "Christ" is the Greek word. Now Elizabeth has been remembering something else the Old Testament says. Through the last prophet to appear, the last thing God had said was this: not only would he send the Messiah, but he would send someone just ahead of him as his messenger to prepare his way. Now Elizabeth knows that in her womb is that messenger.

Might she have had a little twinge of disappointment – "I can't have the Messiah now, because I'm to be the mother of the messenger"? But no, I guess that any disappointment, if it ever even occurred to her, was swallowed up in the excitement that she was producing the messenger. She and Zechariah must have wondered who would bear the Messiah. Things are moving after four hundred years. The messenger is on the way; therefore, somewhere in this land there is a girl who is going to bear a baby who is the Messiah. So they may have discussed it over meals many times. When Mary came in through that courtyard door, Elizabeth knew it was her own young cousin who was going to be the mother of the Messiah. Can you imagine the feeling in her heart? Her heart must have missed a beat. Now she says, "Blessed" – oh, how happy! She used the word "makarios" which means "blessed", "happy", "to be congratulated". Blessedness is not arbitrary. Non-Christians sometimes talk about "luck" but we don't. Blessing is in line with God's will and purpose and is not a matter of chance. So it is not "Oh, how lucky you are, Mary" but, "How blessed you are, and how blessed is the fruit of your womb." She saw all this by the Holy Spirit.

Her next word was one of consternation: "Why is this granted to me, that the mother of my Lord should come to me?" Once again the Holy Spirit has reversed the roles. It was the duty of a young girl to go and see an elderly relative, but now Elizabeth is saying that this was the wrong way around.

In these passages we get a balanced view of Mary. The Roman Catholics have too high a view; the Protestants have too low a view. The Bible has a balanced view. Some of the titles that the Catholics give to Mary are too high, and some of the titles we don't give to Mary we should do. We should call her "The Blessed Virgin Mary". This scripture tells us to do just that: "Henceforth, all generations will call me blessed." So, you can talk about the Blessed Virgin Mary, but "Mother of God" is not a title the Bible gives to Mary. That implies that Mary was there before God, which she wasn't. She wasn't even there before the Son of God. In the words "the mother of my Lord" we see Elizabeth realises Mary's son will be Elizabeth's King. The word "Lord" means precisely that here. Elizabeth was the first person in history to call Jesus "Lord". Do you realise that? It took those disciples three years to get through to saying "My Lord and my God". Later, the earliest creed of the Christian Church was three words: "Jesus is Lord."

Elizabeth has the same attitude to Mary as – thirty years later – John would have to Jesus, even though John was older than Jesus. When Jesus came for baptism, John had the same reaction as his mother had had, "Oh, you ought to be baptising me. I oughtn't to baptise you." Now do you see how the Holy Spirit was telling Elizabeth, thirty years earlier, the right attitude to adopt towards Mary? She was our Lord's mother, and therefore we must respect her as that. We must not give her titles the Bible doesn't give, or speculate about characteristics which she didn't have. But we must go as far as the Bible goes in respect for the Blessed Virgin Mary. We don't pray to her. We don't call her "Our Lady". We don't put statues up to her, but we respect her as "the mother of my Lord". That is a deep respect which we need to cultivate.

As Elizabeth talks to Mary like this, she sees an expression of bewilderment in Mary's face. Clearly, Mary's face is saying, "How did you know?" So the third thing that Elizabeth talks about is the confirmation – a beautiful sign, which God gave her, which was so suited to a woman and a

Luke 1

man wouldn't understand. She said, "When you walked in the door my son recognised you." They had been told that John the Baptist would be filled with the Spirit from his birth. I tell you now, the Holy Spirit was moving John *before* his birth. John the Baptist began his career three months before he was born, for his role was to point to Jesus as the Messiah. This foetus in the womb of Elizabeth was already pointing, and when Mary came into that kitchen then the unborn baby jumped, and Elizabeth knew. Fancy being guided like that – not just "a little child shall lead them", but an *unborn* child led Elizabeth. Once you know what God can do, and know that nothing is too hard for the Lord, the whole thing slots into place. So she told Mary of the moving baby. As Elizabeth told Mary about this sign, this confirmation, Mary's face became bathed in smiles; she was bursting – so happy. Elizabeth, in the Holy Spirit, had the gift of discernment to see why. So her final remark to Mary on this was: Mary, I can see that you are thrilled because you've believed that the Word of God will come true.

The happiest people are those who believe the Word of God will come true. Others might have a temporary and fleeting happiness, but the real secret of joy is faith. Mary has believed what the angel Gabriel said when he visited her, but now she has had tremendous confirmation: Elizabeth pregnant, and her baby inside her womb leaping. Mary knows it is true and she is so thrilled. Are you not thrilled that everything God says will come true? How do I know Jesus is coming again? I have nothing but his word for it, but my joy is based on my faith. Mary believed God's word to her and was happy. That word of God would be fulfilled. Elizabeth's prophecy is now over.

At this point Mary speaks. One lovely heart sets another on fire. One person filled with the Spirit moves others. Praise is infectious, and if just one person will praise God out loud, that will help others to do so. When Elizabeth was filled to overflowing with the Holy Spirit, and prophesied, and said, "Oh, how blessed..." then that sparked Mary off and she responded. Now Mary is full to overflowing. Out it comes from her mouth. We have what I would call in modern English, the "Magnificent". "Magnificat" comes from the first word of the Latin translation, "Magnify the Lord". To magnify means to get a bigger view, to enlarge your vision of God, to get bigger ideas of God – because for most of us our idea of God is too small. We ask him to do little things and we are petty about it. But magnify the Lord! Let us do that by looking into Mary's praise now.

For two thousand years the Magnificat has been sung. I think perhaps it has been sung a bit too often in some circles, and not often enough in others. So, it gets routine, but it is a magnificent song of praise. It echoes psalms and there is one Old Testament passage that comes out very clearly. It is the song of Hannah, another woman who didn't expect to have a baby and had one. You will find it in 1 Samuel 2:1-10. The same Holy Spirit inspired that and this, but it is all about God, not about Mary. Mary would be horrified if she knew how many people were praising her. She would say: follow my example in the Magnificat; praise God, it is all about God. She mentions God fifteen times in a short song.

There are four things here about God that I want to highlight. First, his generosity. That is a word that translates as "grace". I have said already that Catholics have too high a view and Protestants have too low a view of Mary. We have reacted against the abuse on the other side, and so we have gone to another extreme. There is a biblical balance; let's get the titles right. Number one, God is Mary's Saviour. Therefore, we don't need to try and say Mary had sinless perfection, or that when she was conceived it was an immaculate conception of someone who was perfect.

Luke 1

Mary was a sinner saved by grace. Therefore, God was her Saviour, and she recognised she needed a Saviour. That is the first thing we need to think of when we think of Mary: she was saved by God through grace. Grace was upon her, which enabled a sinner to be the mother of our Lord. That to me is far more wonderful than saying "if she was the mother of Jesus she had to be sinless". To think that God can use a sinner saved by grace to hold Christ – that is precisely what he does with you and with me. He plants the Spirit of Jesus in our hearts, and we sinners can say "God my Saviour".

The second title I want you to notice is the title Mary gave herself: "servant". It is incredible what titles have been added. One of the latest is "Co-Redemptrix". That means that she shared the work of redemption. No. Do you know what she would say? "Servant." We have seen this in the word, "maid; maidservant" or, literally, "slave". That is the title she gave herself, and what a title it is, and every true Christian should give himself or herself that title. When Paul writes an epistle he says, "Paul, a slave of Jesus Christ," and then calls Jesus the Saviour. Now Mary puts herself not at the front of the church to be worshipped, but among the congregation. Some years ago, a Roman Catholic bishop in Mexico was filled to overflowing with the Holy Spirit. One of the first things the bishop did was to go into his cathedral where there was a statue of our Lord at one end of the altar and a statue of Mary at the other, and he picked up the latter, took it to the back of the church, and turned it around facing the front. The people arrived and said, "What did you do that for?" He said, "In my Bible she is in the congregation worshipping Jesus." Isn't that wonderful? Now the tour guides point out the only Protestant Catholic cathedral in the world!

This is where we will unite. If we unite at all it will be on the truth of God's Word. Not on Baptist tradition, Catholic tradition or any other tradition – it will be on truth. Mary said: "God, my Saviour who has remembered his servant." That puts Mary with us. That puts Mary in the congregation in Acts 1 praying for Pentecost, and that puts Mary into the day of Pentecost as just one of a hundred and twenty men and women on whom the Holy Spirit fell. Once again she opened her mouth and praised God.

Then she said, "From henceforth all generations will call me *blessed*." The one thing about the word "blessed" is this: it always points to the blesser. If you say "blessed", that points to the God of all blessing. Therefore, when you congratulate someone, say, "How blessed you are," and that points straight to God. In fact, Mary would say, "Look to God, he has done great things in me." In fact, Mary did nothing marvellous; she did nothing other than any other girl who has a baby does. Carrying that baby for nine months and then going through labour – she did just what every other mother does. It was God who did the wonderful part, and, of course, caused that conception to take place miraculously. So Mary would say: he is the Saviour, I am his servant; he has done wonderful things for me, so, call me blessed and then you will think of the One who blessed me. Does that help us to get a true perspective?

Now she moves on from there to praise the *integrity* of God. One of the greatest mistakes being made today is to begin with God as love. You may be shocked by my saying this but I'm going to stand by it. I believe that we are getting a sentimental, soft, distorted view of God because people begin thinking about God by thinking about his love. That is not where godly people begin; it is not where the Bible begins. Genesis 1 doesn't say, "God is love". You have to work almost to the end of the Bible before you find that. Even in the book in which you find the statement "God is love", that is the second statement not the first, and the first is "God is light". The Bible begins here. Now I hope

Luke 1

you won't misunderstand this either, but because men and women are made differently, and men tend to be tougher and women are often more tender, it can make it more difficult for a mother to discipline children than for the father. The father can easily become over harsh, and the mother can easily become over soft; therefore, there is a temptation for women to concentrate on the love of God, and see the tender side rather than the strong side. But Mary is an example to all women. Where did she begin when she thought of the integrity of God's character? She said, "Holy is his name." Here is another who starts with the holiness of God.

Therefore, she goes on to talk about the *fear* of God. Thank God for mothers who believe in the holiness of the Lord and the importance of having a fear of the Lord. That is where Mary began. When you begin there, you then see his goodness as mercy – undeserved mercy because he is so holy that we don't deserve a thing except death and punishment. When you say "Holy is his name" when he does something good for you, then it is a mercy, undeserved. But, if you begin with the love of God you will regard his goodness as a right that you have. If you go around the streets today and ask people, "What do you think about God?" then, if they think anything at all, they will tell you, "Well, God is love." But very few will say, "Holy is his name and his mercy is on those who fear him."

Here is a woman with a balanced, strong view of God. Here is a woman, a fifteen-year-old girl, who knows the scriptures well enough to know that holy is his name, and those who fear him receive undeserved mercy. But if you don't stress his holiness, you don't use the word mercy. You just say "love" and then: "Well, he is bound to help us and get us to heaven because he loves us. There can't be a place called 'hell' because he is love." We argue like this, and we miss the mercy of God. But a person who starts with "holy is his name" and "fear him" will say, "God be merciful to me a sinner." I stress this because the integrity of God's holiness was something that Mary praised, and she rejoices that his mercy goes on down through the generations.

Then she praises his *equity* – a funny word maybe to use; you may never have thought of it in connection with God. Stanley Jones, an Indian missionary, once said this: "The Magnificat is the most revolutionary document in the world," and he was referring to the next three verses – the most revolutionary. God upsets all our ideas of human social importance and status; he reverses it all. Here we have a bigger revolution than any communist manifesto ever envisaged. What is the revolution? That God will take those who are proud and powerful, and have possessions, and move them to the bottom – even kings off their thrones. These are the things that people think are important. These are the things that people think will get them to the room at the top, life at the top. God will say, "If that's what you sought in life then back to the bottom." Then to those who are humble, those who are poor, and the nobodies and the have-nots – God exalts them. That is a revolution, if you like. It goes much further than everything the communists have thought. God is the greatest revolutionary of all, the great leveller, the great lifter and the great humbler. So the mighty kings and those who sought power, and those who have become proud (and pride is the deadliest of all the seven deadly sins) and those who thought they were the greatest – God brings them down to the bottom. Then he takes the humble and the have-nots, people you would not notice, and he says, "These are my important people." That is going to happen. The earth is the Lord's, and the fullness thereof, and Jesus said that the meek, the nobodies – the humble, simple people – are going to have the earth, not those who grab it, not those who want to develop property all over it, but those who are humble before God.

Now where did Mary get this revolutionary idea from? How did she understand? It is so simple; she must have asked this question a thousand times since the angel Gabriel spoke to her: "Why me?" Our pride is such that when God chooses us we look for a reason for the fact in us. The reason is not in us, it is in him. The reason is this: God chooses people not for what they have got, but for what they haven't got. It is why he chose the Jews; they hadn't got a thing. God loves to choose nobodies and make them somebodies; he loves to choose those who have nothing and then give them everything, for that will glorify his name and fulfil his purpose. Mary had realised this – the Holy Spirit had made it clear to her: God had not chosen Mary because she was special but because she was ordinary, and because she was just a poor little girl in the village, engaged to the carpenter. Isn't that tremendous? If any one of us had been given the job of arranging Christ's birth, we would never have thought of this. Can you imagine it? "Well, we'll have to get the red carpet out, and trumpeters that sound good." We are so good at ceremonies. But God didn't abide by human protocol. He chose a little girl who was poor and humble, and he said: you. Paul later wrote to the church at Corinth: not many great people among you, not many noble, not many wise, not many rich, not many clever, not many greats, just nobodies. But it is the nobodies who hold the future of our world in Christ.

So, finally, Mary finishes this magnificent song of praise by praising God's *fidelity*. She is saying to God: you remembered. She is referring to two things. He remembered his promise after two thousand years. We can forget a promise after two thousand minutes. After two thousand years he remembered what he had said, that he was promising to send a deliverer, and he said it to Abraham. The Lord remembered, he was faithful to his promise and to his people. You may forget God but he has not forgotten you. He remembers his people, Abraham and his descendants, forever; and if you believe in Jesus you are a descendant of Abraham. Read Romans 4 if you don't believe me. So, he will remember you forever. If you forget him, run away from him, he won't forget. When you are sensible enough to come back home you will find that he was looking out for you, and waiting to run and fall on your neck and kiss you.

So that is the magnificent Magnificat, praising God for his generosity, using a humble servant to be blessed, praising God for his integrity, the holiness of his name, and the fear of his name that produces mercy, praising God for his fidelity to his promise, praising God for that revolutionary equity by which he levels everybody out, and we become sinners before him, whatever our position in life.

Mary stayed for three months to help Elizabeth through the last stages of her pregnancy, and then she went. By this time Mary may have been feeling sick in the mornings. Now she has to go back and face her fiancé and face the village and the gossip. She doesn't explain, she just trusts God. Who would have understood if she had said, "While I've been south the Holy Spirit visited me, and I'm going to have a baby." No, she left it to God to do the explaining. She left just before the confinement of Elizabeth, presumably to avoid publicity, to avoid talk among the many relatives. She journeyed back. These two women, who as far as we know never met again in life, shared the most amazing secret: that within their wombs the future course of history was being determined. That is the way it has always been, that God comes down and chooses ordinary folk, and plants within them that which will fulfil his purposes.

Luke 1

1:57-80

We have looked at similarities and differences between the ministry of John the Baptist and that of Jesus. John's message may be summed up in one neat cliché: "Wash or burn." That kind of message isn't very popular at Christmas time. The sad fact is that fewer people become Christians at Christmas than at any other time of the year. That is because we have room for the baby Jesus, but we don't have room for the baby John. If you want to reach God you must come through Jesus, but if you want to reach Jesus you must come through the message that John proclaimed. John never appears on our Christmas cards, and there isn't a single carol written about him or Elizabeth or Zechariah. You might walk up the high street and ask people, "Have you heard of Joseph and Mary? Do you know who they were?" Some will be able to tell you, but then ask them, "Have you heard of Zechariah and Elizabeth?" See what they say! Mark begins his Gospel like this, "The beginning of the gospel of Jesus Christ the Son of God, a voice crying in the wilderness." That is the beginning of the Gospel, and the voice was not the voice of Jesus, but the voice of John the Baptist. Turn to Matthew and Luke, turn to John's Gospel, you will find they do the same thing. Where does the good news begin? With John. If you try and take a short cut past John, and try and get to Jesus without John, I will tell you what will happen: you cannot keep Christmas. If you want the real message of Christmas then listen to the message of John – a few months older than Jesus, and a cousin, and the one who got ready for him.

Look first, then, at Elizabeth's baby. I could call this "the other holy family". This section begins and ends in gossip. That is quite familiar to us – people talking – and they had something to talk about this time. People would have been chattering about Elizabeth, "At her age, having a baby!" We hear in the news these days of older women having babies.

But in those days it would have been a rare event. No wonder there would have been talk. "Have you heard?" Neighbours, relatives, and friends would have been debating whether she could carry it to full term, whether it would be born normal, whether she would survive the labour. So they talked and talked, and naturally a crowd gathered when Elizabeth's time came. The baby came and the baby was all right, and so was Elizabeth.

The only person who wasn't all right was Zechariah. He had been dumb and deaf for nine months. It wasn't the shock of becoming a father at that age, it was a little mild punishment for him for not believing God's word when the angel said, "You are going to have a son". When you are disobedient to God he has his way of correcting you. That poor man had been dumb for nine months, he had not said a word; it had affected his hearing too, so that when they communicated to him they had to make signs to him, and when he communicated to them he had to write it down on a writing tablet. We know that, three months before the baby came, Elizabeth was filled with the Spirit, and was filled with a loud voice and was praising the Lord around the house. That is not a situation that is unknown to us – a wife full of the Lord and praising him around the house, and the husband is strangely dumb – neither anything to say nor to hear. But, praise God, sometimes such husbands can catch up with their wives. Three months after Elizabeth was filled with the Spirit, something happened to Zechariah too.

Let us look at the birth of John. The thing that fascinates me is to see the swiftly changing kaleidoscope of emotion. The feelings surrounding this birth changed from joy to surprise and fear—all in one paragraph. Now what changed these emotions? Frankly, wherever God is busy these are the changing emotions of people today – just the same. Indeed, you may have experienced these three stages of emotion within your own family circle when you became a Christian, when you were born again. What makes people change from joy at God's activity, to surprise, to shock, and disturbance, and then to fear, and a desire to get away from the situation? Well, let's see.

The joy is easily explicable. Here she was having a baby and that is a happy event any time. We say, "When's the happy event?" With a new little baby coming into the world, we share in the joy of creation. We have been creative, we have helped to bring new life about, and God has shared his creative joy with us. There were two extra reasons in this case for joy. First, Elizabeth's age. She never thought she would have a baby, she had given up hope and long since stopped praying for one, but she had one now. And it was a boy. Now I don't mean to say that in the Bible days they were as harsh and cruel to girl babies as some societies have been, but the boy would be the son and heir and would be able to carry on the family name and the father's business. In this case, the father was a priest and so, in fact, they saw the boy as being able to continue what had been done. So the neighbours were thrilled, they all rejoiced, and Elizabeth said, "The Lord has been good to me." The neighbours were in a good mood, and they accepted that religious interpretation of events and said, "Yes, we rejoice with you." As indeed, if on such an occasion you say, "God has blessed me," you will find that most unbelievers would agree with you, and accept this and rejoice with you.

Now what went wrong? This other holy family stepped out of line and went against social custom, that's all. Eight days later it was time for circumcision and naming the child. Everybody came along with little presents for him, and it was a typical family occasion. Everybody expected it to go through just as it always does, just as all these occasions do. Then the time came when the rabbis said, "Now name the baby," and Elizabeth said, "John"– and there was a stunned silence. "Did you say John? You've got no relatives called John; it's not a name in your family." In fact, names were passed down to keep the identity of the family going. It was the custom; it was their tradition. There was nothing in the Bible that said they had to do it; it was one of those religious traditions that so easily gathers around occasions like this, and they went against it. Elizabeth said, "John." They were quite sure, you know, that this strange experience that she had gone through had just gone to her head. She thought she was so clever that she could be different in every way. So they turned to the father. He was the head of the house. They made signs to him. He wrote, "His name is John." Do you notice that word *is*? Not *will be* John – he is already named John. God has already given this boy the name.

Now it was then that there was great surprise. I remember the surprise with which some of our relatives greeted the news that we were not going to christen our children. People are happy for you when the Lord has blessed you, but as soon as you step out of line socially, as soon as you begin to behave not according to custom but in a different way, as soon as you begin to show you are now independent and that you don't accept religious traditions, however far they go back, but now you are free to do what God has told you, there is surprise and disturbance. Some young people come to Christ and their parents welcome it at first because they seem easy to get on with and help around the house. Then there comes a social or family custom that suddenly they can't join in, and they step out of line – surprise, shock, disturbance comes, and the joy of others begins to fade. "Oh, it's going to mean that you want to go to church on Sunday instead of the seaside." You begin to step out of line and the surprise comes.

Then as soon as they had named him John, because

Zechariah had been obedient to the Lord, he opened his mouth and began to speak for the first time in nine months. They had thought he had lost his voice for life. Now he was speaking and praising God, and suddenly now fear replaces the surprise. There is something not only unnatural about this birth, there is something supernatural about it. People are scared of the supernatural – any sign of strange things happening that they can't explain, can't understand, and they are on the run, measuring their distance from the door. The neighbours are off: "This is just getting a bit too near God." After all, you know, people who can't talk for nine months and then suddenly open their mouth at a family party – and praise God out loud...!

So we get the whole gamut of emotions. Do you see how it happened? This is what you find when you come to Christ and you are born again. People are happy for you at first because you are happy, and because you have resolved the disintegration of your ambitions and affections, and you are now centred on a new object of your love. They can see there is an improvement, and they are glad at first, and then they are a bit surprised – it has changed you, and you no longer laugh at the things you used to laugh at. You are stepping out of line and you are different. Then they sense that there is something supernatural happening in you, that God is there. Now they are a bit scared and they don't quite understand what is happening. "Is it religious mania?", they might say. But they will then leave you and talk. So the news of this strange experience spread out through the hills of Judea, and everybody was talking not about an elderly woman having a baby, but about an elderly man who had been dumb for nine months and was now speaking and talking about his boy. Those who had not been present at the occasion but who listened to the gossip would have said, "You know, I think that boy is something special. I think that he has got a particular part to play. Wonder what? What's he going to be?" Speculation would have spread. There was one man who knew what he was going to be, and that was his dad – Zechariah the priest. He knew exactly what John was going to be. While the others speculated, Zechariah opened his mouth and praised God.

Let us examine this song of praise from Zechariah's lips. It is called "The Benedictus", after the first Latin word, as with the Magnificat. This song has been used by Christians for two thousand years as an act of praise. It is one of those old hymns that is still as up to date as anything could be. There are many similarities with Mary's song. Again it is drenched in the Old Testament. It is all about God, about salvation and mercy; it mentions Abraham and Israel, and these points link the two songs. But they were composed by the same person, the Holy Spirit, and the similarity is explained.

Yet the Holy Spirit respects the person producing the song. In fact, if you looked at the Magnificat and the Benedictus out of context, and I asked you to pick out the one given out of the mouth of a woman and the one that came through the mouth of a man, you would have no difficulty. This is much more a man's song. It is less personal and more national. It is less subjective and more objective. It has less feeling and more fact in it. But that is one of those differences that we have in our make-up. The two belong together and we need both. That is the glory of it.

Is the Benedictus a benediction? There are four facts that Zechariah praises God for. First he praises God, mentioning the house of David. Now we have to go back a thousand years before Zechariah to the second king of Israel. The people of Israel said, "God, can we have a king? Everyone around us has got a king and we want to be like everybody else." They lacked the status symbol of a king. God allowed them to choose one. According to 1 Samuel 9, God chose

Luke 1

Saul in response to the people's demand. They thought he would be just the kind of king they would like. So God waited until Saul had messed things up, and then chose one for them. David became the greatest king they ever had. Peace and prosperity were the fruits of his campaigns, and he established that nation as it was never established before. Forever afterwards the people used to say, "If we could only get a Son of David on the throne; if we could only get another king like that!"

God said, "I'll give you another king like that!" The promised Messiah, the Saviour, the Christ, the deliverer, it doesn't matter what title you use, was to be a Son of David, of David's royal line, of the city of David. So the first thing Zechariah praises God for is this: God, you've done it! He must have known about Mary through his wife Elizabeth. He speaks of God having provided a Saviour already, even before the baby is born. Oh what praise, what foresight he had in the Holy Spirit. The Son of David has come. *God has provided a Saviour to set us free.* That is the first thing he praises God for.

The second thing for which he praises God is the divine *promise of deliverance*. Four hundred times in the Bible this Son of David is promised. Four hundred promises related to the Messiah, and God has been promising that for over two thousand years. Zechariah praises God: "You've remembered your promise, and you have kept it." Promises made to the prophets – now what were those promises? Those promises were to set them free *from*, and to set them free *for*. We often forget that freedom has two faces, two sides. We are not only set free from something by God, we are set free for something. We often forget that bit. We want to be set free from boredom and from suffering and from disease, and from death and from all the other things, but what do you want to be free for? That is the big question, and Zechariah got it right. So what did God promise to free them from? He has promised to deliver us from our enemies, and those who hate us. One thing God did promise the Jews was: you will have enemies and you will be hated. If anything has come true in history those two things have. The Jews have had enemies all their national life, and they have been hated more than any other nation by other nations. But God said, "I'll deliver you from your enemies and from those who hate you." That is one side of freedom, and the Jews had not really had it since King David. After David came Solomon. His grandiose building schemes meant that civil war broke out as soon as he was off the throne. They never again had a united kingdom; some were in the north, ten tribes with their king, and two in the south with theirs. Then the ten tribes were taken away into Assyrian captivity, and then one hundred years later the two tribes were taken captive to Babylon. So there they were, slaves of Assyrians then the Babylonians, then the Persians, but they came back under the Persians. Then they were overrun by the Egyptians, then the Syrians overran them. Then the Greeks came, and then the Romans came. By the time Zechariah was singing this song they had been under their enemies for centuries. But now Zechariah says, "You promised to set us free from our enemies."

But he got it right. Free for what? The trouble is that we so often want to be free for evil, but God wants to set us free for good. It is so often that we want to be free to indulge ourselves, but God wants to set us free to serve him. So, Zechariah got it right: you promised to set us free that we might serve you without fear in holiness and righteousness all our days.

Do you want to be set free? Not only from sin, but for holiness and righteousness all the days of your life? That is the kind of freedom Jesus came to bring.

Luke 1

The third thing that Zechariah praises God for is his own little boy. At this point he turns to his baby boy and says: you my child, you are going to help with this; you are part of God's plan, part of God's promise.

In those days whenever a king went anywhere he always sent before him, a few days before, his forerunner, the man who would even inspect the road down which the king's carriage would roll. If there were potholes he would order them to be filled up; every valley in the road was exalted and every hump was taken down until the road was level. He prepared the way of the king – that was his job. That is precisely how John saw himself, and how Zechariah saw his baby son, and how the prophet Isaiah, hundreds of years earlier, had talked in Isaiah 40 about, "A voice crying in the wilderness, 'prepare the way of the Lord, every mountain brought low, every valley exalted till there's a level road for the Lord to come straight in.'" How would John do this and get ready the road of the Lord? *By telling people to get ready to have their sins dealt with.* That is how. If you want to prepare people for real freedom you will have to talk to them about their sins, and tell them, "Those need forgiving."

The greatest news there has ever been is that God forgives sin. It is the one thing that our religion offers that you can't find anywhere else. A group of representatives of many religions of the world met together in Delhi to discuss the difference between the world religions. The chairman went around the circle and he said, "Each of you tell us what you think your religion offers that none of the others offer. Let us hear what you think is unique." They went all around, Hinduism, Buddhism, Islam – and they came to the Christian, and the Christian missionary was asked, "Now what does Christianity offer that no other religion can offer?" The missionary said "forgiveness", and nobody contradicted that. You see, forgiveness is not an easy thing, it is not just being let off; forgiveness has to be paid for, and Christianity teaches that it has been paid for.

But it doesn't work automatically. God doesn't wipe out all sins just like that with one stroke. He can only forgive those who repent. The message of John the Baptist was "Repent", and the message of Jesus was "Repent and believe", and the message of Jesus was forgiveness of sins. John had to get people ready because you cannot be forgiven until you have repented. This is the hardest part, and it is why so many people's sins go unforgiven. It is not that God doesn't want to forgive, but he can't do it until they repent. If you are desperately needing money I can hold a ten pound note out to you and wave it in front of you and say, "Here it is, here it is," but unless you will put out your hand and take it, there is nothing more I can do. God is saying: here in the name of my Son Jesus Christ is forgiveness, but the act of receiving it is the act of repentance, which is being sorry enough to stop. That is why John the Baptist went to the Jordan river, and called people to repent, to get ready for the King.

Here is the fourth thing for which Zechariah praised God. He felt he was coming out of a tunnel into daylight, or that the whole nation had been going through a dark night of spiritual blackness, and that now dawn had come. Have you ever been out at night and been wandering around and watched the dawn come up? Wandering around in darkness, you don't know quite where you are, and then the sun comes up over the horizon and you can see where you are and where you need to go – the path is visible. So Zechariah finishes with sheer poetry. He is saying that the dawn of salvation is shining upon us; we have been living under the shadow of the darkness of death; now the dawn has come and we can see our way. Their steps would be guided into the path of peace. It is poetry and it is reality, too. We live our days under the

Luke 1

shadow of death. It is all part of the darkness of this world. We have sinned so we must die. It is like walking through a dark tunnel to walk through this world, but Zechariah sees that the light is shining and we are going to be guided into the path of peace.

There is one more verse (v. 80) about John's boyhood – and what a strange boyhood he had. I have the feeling that Zechariah and Elizabeth died while John was quite young. They were elderly anyway, and I guess he was left an orphan fairly quickly. It is certain that his boyhood was a solitary one. The neighbours, still speculating about this strange lad, seemed to keep apart from him. He kept apart from them. His development was superb – physically and spiritually he kept pace. Thank God when someone develops together, body and soul. He grew up in both ways. But his development was due to his very strange environment – and he was a boy of the desert. Half an hour would get you to the edge of the wilderness, a narrow strip, fifteen miles wide, stretching from the deep Jordan valley and the Dead Sea, up the side of the Judean hills where rain never falls. The east side is a bare, craggy, stony, dangerous, empty area. The hyenas laugh at night still. In Bible days there were jackals, lions and bears roaming up from the Jordan jungle. It was in that place that this boy went to school by himself – alone with God. No man can have a better education than that. This boy grew up out there with just one suit of clothes made of camel hair. He picked locusts off the rock and he ate them. He slept while those hyenas howled, curled up under the shelter of rock. It was to take thirty years for this man to complete his education. He was in no hurry; he waited for God's timetable. In that time God prepared him for the moment when he would tell him to go and get the people ready for the Messiah.

We have seen how God has taken ordinary men and

women, and made them extraordinary in his Spirit. We have seen how he has already filled mouths with his Holy Spirit's words, and how in word and deed everything has been prepared. On the edge of the wilderness in which John had his education is a little town called Bethlehem.

2

Read Luke Chapter 2

The Historical Background

I want you to notice how carefully Luke dates the account. About this time Caesar Augustus, the Roman Emperor, decreed that a census should be taken throughout the nation. This census was taken when Quirinius was governor of Syria. Everyone was required to return to his ancestral home for this registration. Because Joseph was a member of the royal line he had to go to Bethlehem in Judea, King David's ancient home. Journeying there from the Galilean province of Nazareth, he took with him Mary, his fiancée, who was visibly pregnant by this time. And while they were there the time came for her baby to be born, and she gave birth to her first child—a Son. She wrapped him in a blanket and laid him in a manger because there was no room for them in the village inn. When we come to look at chapter three, thirty years later, in the fifteenth year of the reign of emperor Tiberius Caesar, a message came from God to John, the son of Zechariah, as he was living out in the desert. Pilate was governor over Judea at that time, Herod over Galilee, his brother Phillip over Iturea and Trachonitis, Lysanias over Abilene, and Annas and Caiaphas were the Jewish High Priests. Then John went from place to place on both sides of the Jordan river, preaching that people should be baptised to show that they had turned to God and away from their sins in order to be forgiven. In the words of Isaiah the prophet, "John was a voice shouting from the barren wilderness, 'Prepare a road for the Lord to travel on. Widen the pathway before him, level the mountains, fill up the valleys, straighten the curves, smooth out the ruts, and then all mankind shall see the Saviour sent from God.'" All of this is a matter of historical fact, and Luke sets out the facts very clearly.

At the risk of being misunderstood, I don't think Christmas is a time for children, I think it's a time for men. At least the actual nativity was. You study the story and apart from Mary herself, and Elizabeth her cousin, every character in the story is a man. Christianity is a religion for men, women and children – but I'm sorry if the men don't get their place in what was meant to be for them, and whether men work with their hands, as the shepherds did, or with their heads, as the wise men did, it was men who came to praise the Christ Child.

In Galatians 4:4 we read, "But when the time had fully come, God sent forth his Son born of woman." "When the time..."—what time? When what time had fully come? We never seem to have time to get ready for Christmas, yet God himself took centuries to get ready for it. I often used to wonder why he did not send Jesus earlier. The world needed him much earlier. Why did he come at that particular time? The more I have studied it, the more I have come to the conclusion that was the only time he could have come. It was God's time, it was the world's time, and it was everybody's time. God chose most carefully. Let us think about the way everything seemed to be converging on that time and that place for the coming of the Son of God.

Israel, the people of God, was ready for Christ four hundred years before he came. When you study the Old Testament you discover this: they were ready long before he came to Bethlehem. It took God sixteen hundred years to get them ready. Beginning with Abraham, going through Moses, then Elijah, Elisha and all the Prophets, and the Kings starting with Saul, and then David, and then Solomon and all

Luke 2

the others. Malachi spoke of the coming of the Messiah, the Saviour that they were all looking for. Then for four hundred years they had to live without a word from God – without any indication that he was coming. Twelve generations came and went, and every generation told the next one that the Messiah would come, and they kept alive this hope.

If they were ready four hundred years before Jesus came and there was nothing more that God had to do or to say to get them ready, why did he wait so long? The answer is very simple, and it is something that the Jews overlooked at that time – that the Christ was coming to be the Saviour of the world and not just the Saviour of Israel, and the simple fact is that the world was not ready, and it would not be ready for another four centuries. When Christ was born, the world was absolutely ready for the Saviour to come. I am going to divide this up into six headings: six simple things through which the world was prepared by God for the coming of Christ.

First of all, by the time Christ came, politically the empire was a settled world. It was the first time for five hundred years that it had been free from war, and it was essential to God's purpose that the Saviour come at a time of political peace. God was getting that ready for five hundred years. The dominating feature of the world of the Middle East when Christ came was that it was a unified world, one world. It was entirely civilised – the whole Middle East, from the Atlantic Ocean to the Caspian Sea; from the Sahara Desert to the Alps; from the Thames to the Nile; from the Rhone to the Danube; from Spain to the Euphrates. This world was one world at peace.

I am sure you have heard the phrase *Pax Romana*, meaning "Roman peace". This Roman peace had begun about seven hundred years before Christ in a village on the Tiber river, and from that little village it had spread to become a republic.

It had then spread to become an empire, down into Africa, through Gaul (now France). Rome, from a little village, had become a mighty empire. There had been wars on the frontiers, but by the time Jesus was born, and only by that time – it happened perhaps twenty years before he was born – there was one politically settled world and you could move freely through any part of it.

One of the reasons that we are told in the Bible to pray for those in authority – for kings and governments – is so that the world may have the peace that is necessary to the spread of the gospel. Do you realise that war prevents the spread of the gospel? I remember visiting a mission station on the Tana river in the northern part of Kenya. A friend of mine, who was then a missionary doctor in a lonely village, looked after hundreds of patients in very primitive conditions. He said it was the Germans who started that mission station and built this hospital, but when the war in Europe came they were interned and the missionary work stopped.

Not only was there the *Pax Romana*, there was the *Lex Romana* – the Roman law, and you cannot have peace without law. Roman law was built on one of the best administrations and one of the wisest systems of justice there has ever been – the laws of marriage and the family. Of course, for all this peace and law, the army and the administration had to be paid for, and therefore there were taxes. The whole world was taxed, and the whole world was registered, and it was due to this that Jesus was born in Bethlehem. But those taxes and that registration was the price that had to be paid for a world at peace, and a world that was united and settled.

Secondly, socially it was a small world. We know something of this in our day because in my lifetime the world in which we live has shrunk in that we now know everything that goes on. The media tell us as soon as there is a disaster. You can now go round the world in a matter of hours. Similarly, though not to the same degree, the world in which Jesus was born was a socially shrinking world. Take for example transport. Those Roman roads, fifteen feet wide and straight as a die, up hill and down dale, had linked the whole empire. Transport was easy—it was done for military purposes to send the army quickly to any frontier where there was trouble. Along those roads went commerce, culture, and there would travel Christian missionaries, and they did not need a passport to go anywhere.

Throughout that whole empire one language was known and understood. It was not Latin. Recalling my experience of Latin in my youth, I am not surprised that people didn't adopt that language universally. It was many years before Latin and Hebrew were used greatly in the Christian Church. The language they used in the beginning was backstreet Greek ("Koine" Greek). The New Testament is written in what I would call "Cockney Greek", not the beautiful classical Greek of the universities. It was the language that everybody spoke, a very common, ordinary language. If Rome conquered Greece militarily, Greece conquered Rome culturally, and her architecture and her language became known throughout the world. You can see Greek architecture all over England. It was the Romans who spread it, and they could speak Greek, which meant that missionaries could go out to any country in the then-known world without having to spend the first year grappling with the language, as our poor missionaries have to do today. They could go and preach the gospel quickly.

The third thing about this world is that economically it was a *suffering* world. The luxury and magnificence of Rome and Greece was just a veneer over rags. It was a poor world. It was in the middle of one of the greatest depressions that there has ever been, and the strata of society were sharply contrasted – there were the few rich and the many very poor. Two out of three people in that world were slaves who had been sold like chattels in a marketplace. The majority of people were poor. You may think that a strange thing to say, but Jesus said a great deal about affluence and a great deal about poverty. He taught that it is easier for the poor to understand God than for the affluent. Jesus said, "Woe to you rich," and when he said "rich" he meant anyone with more than a very modest amount. He said many things warning us about the danger of affluence, but few were in this danger. There are some countries today where there are both the fabulously rich and many poverty-stricken people.

Taxation was responsible for a large part of this. The plebs, the poor people, were taxed and taxed again. Their taxes were considerably higher than our taxes are today. Next time you grumble at your income tax, do a little research into the Roman world. They paid different taxes: capital tax, head tax, all kinds of customs taxes, and they were paying very heavily. So the rich were getting richer and the poor were getting poorer in that world, and that was a world where the gospel spread, and it spread among the poor, and the early Church was built up of slaves – it was built up of those who were not affluent. Quite frankly today, the Church of Jesus Christ is growing so rapidly you can hardly keep track of it in developing countries.

The fourth point is that *morally it was a sick world*. I know that some have accepted and swallowed the myth that the world was a very happy world until Christians came into it and they spoiled everybody's fun. The poet Algernon Charles Swinburne (1837-1909) once wrote this, "Thou hast conquered, O pale Galilean; the world has grown grey from thy breath", and many people think of Jesus as a killjoy. The Romans were enjoying themselves and then Christianity came and you couldn't do any of the things you liked doing and so it was all spoiled. That is a lie. The Roman world

Luke 2

was morally sick. There were men dying of old age in their middle years – worn and spent with sin. Do you know that of the first fifteen Roman emperors, fourteen were known homosexuals, including Julius Caesar? What was happening at the top was spreading right down through society.

As to honesty, there was an unscrupulous character about commerce – a corruption that was making the whole world morally sick. It was not a happy, lovely world such as people have tried to portray. It had been in the earlier days of the Roman Republic when divorce was almost unheard of, but, by the time Jesus was born, divorce was almost as common as marriage. If you want a picture of the Roman Empire in those days read Romans 1 – it is not overdrawn.

Fifthly, intellectually it was a *sad* world. Men had been trying for centuries to discover the truth: "Why are we here? How is life to be lived to the full?" And the world was full of intellectual philosophies: Platonism, epicureanism, stoicism, cynicism, scepticism. All these "isms" were systems of thought and they each had their answer, but people were mentally tired. They were sad because they felt that none of these philosophies had the answer. None of them had discovered the truth, and so the world intellectually was looking for someone to give the answer to the biggest questions of life: "Why are we here? What is life all about?"

I refrain from going through some of these "isms", but the more you study them the more you discover a note of despair. I draw a parallel with today. We live in a day of "isms" – existentialism, empiricism and so on. People are preoccupied with death. Our plays, our books are preoccupied with meaninglessness and despair, and so they have no story and they have no happy ending because people believe there is no happy ending and life doesn't work that way. We have the same kind of sad intellectual climate today as they had then, and into that climate Jesus was born as the hope and the light of the world with the truth that sets people free.

Finally, spiritually it was a *seeking world*. They were disappointed with their own religions. The Romans had built a large round temple, the Pantheon, the all-god temple – and they had put all the statues of gods in their niches round the temple, but they were all blown-up human beings. In the Greek temple at Olympus, the same thing was happening. There were the Greek gods, but when you looked at them they were just blown up human beings. The world was tired of worshipping human beings who had the same weaknesses as themselves. So the world was looking in two new directions for religion. It was looking to the east, and eastern mysticism was coming in. Isn't it remarkable that this is happening now? The so-called, "mystery religions" were creeping into the Roman world. The other direction in which they were looking was this: they began to deify the state and its leader, the emperor, treating a human as a god who cannot be wrong. They were doing that to the Caesar and they had begun to call the Caesar this phrase: Dominus et Deus, meaning "Lord and God". Spiritually they were barren and empty and they were seeking religious satisfaction.

All these factors I have mentioned converged upon the period 20 BC to 20 AD. All of them reached their peak at just that period. Israel had been ready for four hundred years, now the world was ready.

But just a moment. Why did God not get the world ready earlier? He could have done. He is in charge of human affairs. During those four hundred years God planned that two things should happen: that Israel should get into the world, and that the world should get into Israel. Israel was ready but she wasn't mixed with the world yet, and when you study the history of those four hundred years – as you can in the Apocrypha and in other books – you discover first of all that between 400 BC and the day Jesus was born, most of

Luke 2

the Jews had moved out of the land of Israel. Until the day when the baby was born in Bethlehem there were four and a half million of his fellow countrymen scattered through the whole known world – agents ready to spread the good news. Through many of those Jews who became Christians, through Paul's great missionary work, the gospel was spread.

It began, of course, when they were taken into exile, even as early as 721 BC and then 597 BC. They were taken away from their promised land into Assyria, and later Babylon. Only fifty thousand came back – the rest stayed and populated that area, and there were Jewish colonies right up the rivers Tigris and Euphrates, but it did not stop there. They spread and spread until by 4 BC there were eighty thousand Jews living in Rome in a colony on the banks of the Tiber. There were a million of them in Alexandria, and it was in Egypt that because Jews began to forget the Hebrew language and spoke Greek that seventy Jewish scholars took the Old Testament and translated it into Greek. We call that translation the Septuagint because it was done by seventy scholars. It meant that by the time Jesus was born the entire Old Testament was in the language of the whole known world. Can you see God's purpose in doing this?

So by the time Jesus was born, the Jews were scattered around the whole world. Over the four hundred years, ready as they were, with all the prophecies about the coming Messiah, they had taken on the language and lived in the towns of the then known world.

The other thing that had happened during the four hundred years was that the whole world had come to Israel. One of the most fascinating places you can visit if you go to the Holy Land today is the Dog river, up the coast in Lebanon. This short river running inland to the Lebanese mountains has to its side at one point a hillside, and on the cliff face have been carved various things. You will find, "Napoleon was here",

"Alexander the Great was here". You see, that little strip of coast is the only land link between Africa, Asia and Europe. Everybody has to come down through that corridor. So you had the Greeks under Alexander the Great, the Ptolemies from Egypt, the Seleucids from Syria, the Hasmonians, and the Maccabees who fought against them. At the time when Jesus was born, there were ten Greek cities in Galilee, called "The Decapolis". You will remember that Jesus fed four thousand people in Greek cities in the promised land. Then came the Herods, who were not Jews but descendants of Esau. Herod, bribing the Roman Emperor, was given the title "King of the Jews". Herod the Great was on the throne, not a Jew and calling himself "King of the Jews" when a baby was born who was the true King of the Jews. No wonder Herod was jealous.

During Jesus' earthly ministry, this whole land was divided up between foreign rulers so that when he came to the Sea of Galilee there were in fact three different countries bordering on that tiny lake. Philip was ruling one bit, the Greeks another, and a different Herod was ruling another part. Here you have the whole world around the shores of Galilee, and if you want to know why Jesus kept crossing the Sea of Galilee in a boat, he was doing it to get out of one person's territory into another's, to keep safe and have time with his disciples.

That is a very potted history, but the point is that it took four hundred years for Israel to get out into the world and for the world to get into Israel, so that when Jesus was born Israel was ready, the world was ready, Israel was in the world, and the world was in Israel. These circumstances had never occurred before and have never occurred since in the Middle East. When the fullness of time had come, God sent forth his Son, born of a woman. Isn't that an amazing text? It was the only time in the entire history of the human race when the promised land was in those relationships with the known world.

There is a remarkable parallel between those days and our days. The Church has been ready for Christ's second coming for centuries. Every generation of Christians has looked for the coming of Christ a second time. We are ready, we want him to come. The world is getting ready for his coming. Can't you see the things happening again that happened before his first coming? I cannot help seeing that the world spiritually is seeking, dissatisfied with its own religions. The world is intellectually sad and despairing. The world is morally sick, the world is economically suffering, and the world is socially small. All these circumstances seem to me so clear. If there is a gap now in which we must wait for his coming, it is solely that two things may happen. One: that the Church may get into every part of the world. Two: that every part of the world may get into the Church. These are the only two things now that delay our Lord's second coming. He said, "The gospel must first be preached to all the nations, then shall the end come." He will come back when we have done what he told us to do: go into all the world and preach the gospel to every person. Nine-tenths of the world has been entered by the Church, but there is still a tenth. There are people still going into new tribes, new countries, learning new languages. A few languages still remain to be turned into a written form so that the Bible may be translated.

It is God's intention and will that in his Church which he gathers in, in the Last Day there will be representatives of every tribe, every kindred, every tongue. Only when there are representatives in the Body of Christ of every part of the human race will he come. In the fullness of time God sent forth his Son, born of a woman. I believe that in the fullness of time God will send his Son again in glory. "Even so, come Lord Jesus. Amen."

2:1-20

The most striking fact of the nativity to me is the utter simplicity of it. If we had been writing it up we would have embellished it with so many adjectives and we would have been tempted to exaggerate. That is a temptation that no-one has been able to resist since. But God knew what he was doing when he chose a doctor for this. He was used to being precise, stating the facts. There isn't a word wasted. What a pity it is that we haven't followed Luke's example, for the truth of Christmas has become buried under an avalanche of myth, legends and speculation. We have almost got to rescue it from these other things. The manger has been turned into a stable, the wise men have been turned into three kings, and we have smothered it all in holly and ivy and covered the scene with snow, and Santa Claus, Rudolph the red-nosed reindeer – the lot. Dickens completed the job! Luke just told the simple, bare truth. There isn't a single adjective in this description. He just gives nouns, verbs and objects. It is so refreshing to turn away from all that other paraphernalia and just look at God's Word.

We will now look at three aspects of the birth of Jesus that come out in 2:1-20. The first is the *arrangement* of his birth. Who was responsible? The second is the *announcement* of his birth – that is a vital part of the baby coming to the world. The third is the *acknowledgement* of it—how many people actually realised what was happening?

Firstly, then, in the first seven verses we have the *arrangements* of his birth. When a baby is coming you start planning. Where are you going to have the baby – at home, at hospital – where? Someone has to decide these things. How did Jesus come to be born where he was, at that time, in the manner in which it happened? Who made the arrangements? There were at least five different people who were involved one way or another.

Luke 2

It started in an office about seven or eight hundred miles away. It started with an emperor who ruled over the Roman Empire from 31 BC to 14 AD. He was a good, wise organiser, a great administrator, and he brought peace to the whole Mediterranean world, because he was so well organised. The *Pax Romana* kept the whole area quiet during his reign. He could only do this with lots of money and lots of soldiers, so the two things he needed were tax and conscription. So every fourteen years he, in that office, made a decision which went out to the furthermost parts of the empire: another census, to catch two things. First of all, to catch people's income and tax it, and second to catch the young men of conscription age, so that he could keep the *Pax Romana*. So from Rome went out a decree, that would decide that Jesus would be born in the place that God said he would be born a thousand years earlier. A Roman emperor, without knowing anything at all about it, was arranging the birth of Christ. How God can use the most unlikely people, and unconnected people, to bring about his purposes! So the emperor was involved. The Jews as it happened were exempt from military conscription; they had religious objections to fighting on the Sabbath. They were given exemption from that but they still had to pay their taxes, probably a bit more heavily as a result. So, "Tax those Jews. Find out how many men there are, what their income is. Tell them each to go to the place of their family origin and we'll get them all tabulated."

The second person involved was a Roman governor at that eastern end of the Mediterranean, who looked after Syria and the Holy Land. Quirinius was his name, responsible for the governorship from something like 10 BC and then through to after the birth of Christ. Herod was the nominal ruler but Quirinius was the Roman power behind the throne. Quirinius said in the census, "We must have the names of everybody, we must have their property, we must have their occupation, and we must have their kindred, or relationships." Do you realise that the first time the name of Jesus was ever written on earth, it was written not in the Bible but in the Roman records of that day? We don't have the records now, they have perished. You would be astonished to find out how often Jesus is mentioned outside the Bible and in secular records. People who think it is all a made-up story have a difficult nut to crack when they come to those secular records. So there was a governor involved. But the governor decreed that only the male heads of each household need make the journey to the place of their family – the wives and children need not go. So the governor didn't make the arrangements fully – he would not be responsible for Mary being there, but he did require Joseph to be there.

The third person involved in the arrangements for Jesus' birth was the carpenter of Nazareth. He decided to take his fiancée, whom he had now married, though their marriage had not yet been consummated, so she was partly his fiancée and partly his wife, but she was very near her confinement. So he decided to take her along, eighty miles on the back of a donkey. You don't make that kind of a decision lightly. I am sure it wasn't because he wanted to be present at the birth. Why would he make such a decision – to take a girl in that condition on that journey? I'll tell you why—she was ostracised, nobody would help. A girl in that condition in the village life of those days would just be cut off by her relatives. She only had her husband. None of the relatives would have looked after her in her confinement. So imagine what this meant for Mary. She had to travel all that way to Bethlehem because there would be nobody else to help her with the birth, and it was her first, and she was about fifteen. So Joseph was partly responsible for arranging the birth of Jesus in Bethlehem.

A fourth person was also involved in the arrangements:

Luke 2

the innkeeper. I have the feeling that we are always a bit hard on him. You would have done precisely the same as he did, wouldn't you? If you were running a hotel and every room in the place was jammed, would you turn people out for yet another visitor? Of course you wouldn't. So let's not be too hard on him, or if we're hard on him let us be hard on ourselves. So the innkeeper had a hand in it. It may be that he was kinder than we think. He may have suggested the courtyard. For the inns of those days were built as stalls almost, around a square courtyard with one gateway into it. For security purposes at night that gate was closed, and all the rooms faced the courtyard. If you couldn't get a room then you settled and camped in the middle of the courtyard where the animals laid down around the trough in the middle and the well.

There were two words for hotels in those days. We could say that one was for one-star hotels and one was for five-star. They only had two classifications or categories. It is interesting that the word used here is for the one-star, not the five-star. So I suppose we ought to think in terms of a car park outside a transport cafe or the back yard of a public house, if we are to get the right kind of feel for the situation. So the innkeeper had something to do with the arrangements for Jesus' birth. Later in his life, Jesus was going to say to those who wanted to follow him and share his life, "Foxes have holes, the birds of the air have nests, but I don't have anywhere to lay my head." That was true at the very beginning of his life.

The fifth (and obviously most important) person to be involved in the arrangements for his birth was the mother. So we have an emperor, a governor, a carpenter, an innkeeper and a mother. Each of those five contributed to the arrangements and circumstances. What did Mary do? She had prepared something resembling a square of cloth, a long bandage, yards long, sewn to the corner. English translations of the Bible, I'm afraid, usually dress things up politely. Swaddling clothes are nappies (US: diapers). She wrapped Jesus in his first nappy. Now the significance of that statement may be lost on you – *she* did it. It was normally the job of the midwife or a relative. It tells me that there was no woman to help. Imagine that inn, how it would have been crowded with male heads of households, not families, but male heads – a real male do, a public house full of men, with no woman to help Mary. It was she who washed the baby. It was she who wrapped him in his nappy. It was she who put him in the manger. Joseph would do what he could to help, but what use is a man on occasions like that? I am just trying to paint for you the circumstances. Would you arrange the birth of your baby like this? Would you want your baby snuffled at by animals? Well, that is how God arranged the birth of his Son. For behind these five people was God. It was God who made the arrangements and it was he who made the decisions. It is so utterly unexpected, so different from anything we do, even for our own children, much less a royal confinement. The unexpectedness of God comes through in this story. The arrangements of his birth leave you breathless. Why?

One bit of it of course was done so that God's promise might be fulfilled. Six hundred years previously he had said through the prophet Micah, "You Bethlehem". Nobody noticed Bethlehem in those days. You had to say which Bethlehem you meant, there were three. So this was Bethlehem Ephrathah, the house of bread. "You Bethlehem, little village in Judea, don't think you're unimportant. Out of you is going to come the prince, the king, the ruler of all Israel." It came true and God made the arrangements in an apparently accidental way, in a way that the world would not realise, so that the cynic could say that it was coincidence.

Jesus was born in the very place where the King had to be born. This is how God operates when he does a miracle – people can say it's a coincidence.

Of the Red Sea dividing for Israel to cross, the cynic can say: coincidence. It happened occasionally at other times when a strong ebb tide coincided with a strong east wind. That is how God operates, so that the unbeliever can explain it away. So when Jesus was born in Bethlehem, to the believer that is proof that he is the Son of God. But the unbeliever says: it was accidental; it was an emperor, a governor and a carpenter. That is why so many people do not see what God is doing today. They dismiss it as accident or coincidence, but God is managing the affairs of men and working out his purpose, and the believer knows it.

Secondly, look at the *announcement* of his birth. When a baby comes we want people to know. I remember my father saying that when I came he wondered why the bus conductor didn't ask him about it when he got on the bus! In the nativity there was a very "proud" Father who wanted people to know. The "proud" Father was God, not Joseph. So he just had to have an announcement. The announcement is so beautifully organised. Imagine our heavenly Father, so proud of his Son for being willing to be born – because, remember, Jesus was the only person who ever chose to be born. It means, too, that Jesus had a hand in arranging the circumstances of his birth. He chose how to be born, and where.

We are not told which angel he sent; I guess it was Gabriel again, the one who had announced to Mary nine months earlier that she would have a baby boy. An angel came and the sky that was black above Bethlehem became bright with God's glory, and the angel said, "Good news! A Saviour's been born!" Look at the titles that pile up in the announcement, not just a boy, but our Saviour, Christ, the Lord, who has been born. "Great news! In David's town today, it's happened!" Some time during the night – that is when Jesus arrived. So the shepherds went to see. It surely must have been the most spectacular announcement: from the highest to the lowest. We have often overlooked the fact that to be a shepherd was not a dignified vocation in those days. It is in this country today. I worked on a farm and there were fourteen men who worked on that farm. The man that was superior to all the others was the shepherd – a man of age, and skill, and tremendous experience and wisdom. It was that shepherd, whom we looked up to, who said to us one night in the winter of 1947 when it was a lovely clear night, "Will you help me to get all the sheep down from the distant fields, the hills, down here?" So we worked late that night to bring them all down. During that night snow came. Neighbouring farmers lost hundreds of sheep but we didn't lose one because of this man's experience, age and wisdom. He felt it in his bones and he saved his flock. So we look up to shepherds, they are very difficult to get. In the Middle East it was just the opposite. The shepherd was the lowest of the low, despised and mistrusted. Most of them were robbers and petty criminals. Most of them had been in court. So one of the laws of that world was that no shepherd was allowed to give evidence in court. They took a job as night watchman of the flock because they were fit for nothing else and could not be trusted in regular employment. They usually had no home, they just slept in what they wore, out on the hills, watching their sheep. Maybe this is spoiling the romance of Christmas for you, but it is bringing reality into it. I want to tell you that when God chose to announce the birth of his Son, he chose to bring that announcement from the highest heaven to lowest earth. It is as if the news of a birth in the Royal Family was conveyed first in Guildford to the dustman working at the town's incinerator; that is the feel of this narrative. It is dramatic.

Why did God announce the birth of his baby to these shepherds? There are many reasons. One of them may be that he wanted to announce it to those who couldn't offer Jesus any other home but the manger. Could that be it, the one group in Bethlehem that couldn't take him into their homes? That is an interesting thought. But why? Is it because God sent Jesus to those who need a Saviour? Jesus later said to the religious people who didn't like what he was doing, "They that are whole don't need a physician. I've come to help those in greatest need." Is that the reason? There are two other reasons. One is that in the very fields where those young men were lying on the ground is where King David used to lie and look at the stars and say, "When I consider the heavens, the work of your fingers...." So he wanted to announce it in the same place where David, that great king of Israel, had slept on the fields, the youngest boy of the family, the one who was told to go and watch the sheep because all the others were too dignified to do so.

Or was it for one other reason? Do you know that Bethlehem is only six miles south of Jerusalem, that it is within sight of the Holy City? Therefore the sheep of Bethlehem were not used for war, and they were not used for mutton. Those sheep and lambs were sent to Jerusalem to be slaughtered for sin, to be made the Passover lambs. So was it God looking ahead to a day when his Son would be taken like those lambs from Bethlehem – the Lamb of God slain from the foundation of the world, to take away the sins of the world? Is that why? I don't know. I just know that when the announcement bridged the highest to the lowest, highest heaven to lowest earth, this was a symbol of what Jesus himself had come to do – to lift people like that into the glory of heaven.

So, thirdly, there is the *acknowledgement* of his birth. The shepherds were very curious; they wanted to see as soon as possible. They left the sheep; I don't think one of them stayed behind, they just ran to see. They went from one public house to another in Bethlehem, one courtyard to another, just taking a glance at the feeding trough in each. Then they saw one with a baby in it. They knew they had got to the right place. Verses 15-20 depict three different reactions. The first group are those who took a passing interest. It says when the shepherds told the others what they had heard, people were filled with wonder. But the verb "filled" in the Greek is a particular tense that means "filled once, but no longer". It means a nine-day wonder. It means those who were interested at the time and three days later had forgotten all about it. That is the biggest group in the account of the nativity and it's the biggest group in this country today. They acknowledge his birth but only fleetingly and then it is over and forgotten. The tragedy is this: so many sing about Jesus, talk about him at Christmas, yet they forget by New Year.

The second reaction comes from only one person in the narrative. Mary kept all these things and *pondered them in her heart*. The lost art of meditation – Mary had it. She kept thinking about what happened. Luke the doctor got the details from her, years later. Thank God that there are some people who will be so disturbed, so touched by God's Spirit, that they go on thinking about Jesus. From that will come such good fruit.

The third reaction is from those with a *praising* interest. The shepherds went back to their job, back to the daily round, back to the common task, back to the fields – praising God.

I am struck once again by the fact that God doesn't force himself on people. He came in such a way that the majority could sense the wonder of it and forget it. He never forces himself on anyone. How amazing that is. But I tell you this, the second time that Jesus comes it will not be like that. He will come then not quietly or helplessly as a little baby but in glory, in judgment, and every knee will have to bow then. If people had known at the nativity, they would have flung wide their best rooms. But they were not bothered. Jesus didn't want special treatment and never asked for it.

2:21-39

There are no carols, cards or children's plays featuring this part of the nativity narrative. Yet these events occurred between the visit of the shepherds and the visit of the wise men to Bethlehem. In most presentations there is a jump from the shepherds to the wise men, even though many months lay between those two visits. We turn now to the events that took place in between. They are part of the Word of God, and if we want the whole meaning we have to read them. Why is there this gap? Here are four possible reasons.

First: these events did not take place in Bethlehem but in Jerusalem. Though there were only six miles between the two places, the change of scene seems to produce a mental blockage because the wise men came to Bethlehem, then we jump straight from the shepherds to the wise men and stay in Bethlehem, but Jerusalem is also part of what happened.

A second reason why these events are jumped over is that they are not dramatic or sensational – there are no angels in the sky, there are no stars. There is none of the drama of the other events. All of us are guilty of loving sensation, something of which the media are well aware.

Thirdly, these events are the only part of the account that is thoroughly Jewish from beginning to end. Many Gentiles do not like to be reminded that Jesus was and is a Jew, and that Joseph and Mary were Jews, and that this is a Jewish family.

A fourth reason and I think the deepest one, is that these events are only understood and appreciated by spiritually-minded believers. The unbeliever can make nothing of them. The unbeliever likes the story of the shepherds and the wise men but not these events. They are spiritually discerned and therefore this part of our study is for the spiritually minded, and if you are spiritually minded you will rejoice in what we study. It is for those who let their souls be fed on the Word of God.

Apart from anything else, these events tell us a great deal about Joseph and Mary. They also introduce us to the third group of people who gazed on this baby – the shepherds were the first such group and the wise men the third, but the middle group is perhaps the most important group of all and the ones we overlook. This group consists of only two people, an old man and an old woman, and they are the most important group of all to have met this baby. In a sense a lovely thought struck me as I looked at this: just as when a baby is born, younger people come to see the baby, you take the baby to the older people to let them see, in the same way the shepherds and the wise men came to Bethlehem to see the baby Jesus, but he was taken to these two old people where they lived so that they might see the baby right where they were.

From Luke 2:21 onwards things are done with this baby that we do not necessarily do with our babies. It is vital to realise that these things were done not because of Jewish custom but because of the law of God through Moses. Mary and Joseph, being Jews, were under that law and Jesus was also a Jewish baby and was under the law. The first thing that happened was that Joseph, together with any male relatives he could gather in Bethlehem, and there must have been a few at that time in his own family, would gather and then the baby was circumcised, an operation which shed blood and was painful and sore. I often think of this when I hear the children sing the carol Away in a Manger – "the little Lord Jesus, no crying he makes". I say it reverently but I am quite sure he cried at this time. He was human and we must not forget the humanity of Jesus as we think of his deity. He cried later in life when he was in mental or emotional pain – and he was not ashamed of his tears.

Now they were doing what had happened to every Jewish baby boy for two thousand years. It was a little operation which was going to mark him forever as a Jew. Nowadays this surgical operation is sometimes performed for medical, social or hygiene reasons, but in those days it was for religious reasons – so what did it mean?

There are three reasons that I can think of. One I have already mentioned: it branded him a Jew. It was permanent and could never be disguised. Though it was not a public sign, it was there and it would be a constant reminder to a man himself that he belonged to the people of God.

Secondly, it was also a sign of a promise made two thousand years before and passed down through the male line from the man to whom it was made: Abraham. Since the operation was on the reproductive organ, it was a sign of a promise made to the inherited seed all the way down the line. This, too, spoke to a Jew so deeply of something wonderful in his history. So it was a sign that Jesus was in the line of this promise. What was the promise? That God would give a blessing to the Jews that would spread from them to every family on earth and all the nations. That promise came way down, accompanied by this sign which was the guarantee of the promise to Jesus. With Jesus, the sign stopped because with Jesus the blessing came.

The third thing that circumcision meant was that it put Jesus under the whole law of Moses. As a boy who had now been circumcised, Jesus now had to obey the law of Moses in every little detail. A boy who was circumcised was by that act made responsible for keeping the law of Moses in every little detail. Now of course a little baby can't keep laws, so the Jewish law was that until the age of twelve the parents were responsible under the law for seeing that every little bit of it was kept in the boy's life. Then, at the age of twelve, they would have to take him and present him in the synagogue or the temple, and from then on he was responsible for himself. It was a similar process to English law where parents are responsible for children's behaviour to a certain age and then, after that, the child is responsible.

Remember first that Jesus was and is a Jew. That should affect your attitude to every Jewish person you meet. Secondly, remember that Jesus inherited the promise of Abraham, and that if you want the promise of the blessing to Abraham, you must come right down the line to Jesus. When you get to know him, you will receive the blessing of Abraham. Thirdly, remember that Jesus was under the law so that he could lift it from our shoulders. Here I am into a very deep spiritual truth. If you have never studied Galatians, you will have difficulty perhaps in following me. Read Galatians through today. It is all about circumcision; all about the burden of the law. When you read the law of Moses, it is pages and pages of little laws, dozens of things you must do and you mustn't do – it is a most complicated way of life. If I had to keep that, I should never begin to be what God means me to be. It becomes a frightful burden. In fact, I find myself under a curse because there is a curse in these laws which says: "Cursed is he who does not continue in all the laws to do them." Jesus, when he was circumcised, got under the law. His circumcision was absolutely essential to lift the law off people's backs, and Jesus was the only man who kept every single precept of the Mosaic law all his life, and then smashed its curse by taking the curse of the law on his own shoulders.

When Jesus was circumcised it was the beginning of the cross for Jesus because that put him under the law, and he could only lift the law from people's shoulders – and the burdens the law's precepts demanded – by getting under it and by being circumcised. If I could put it quite reverently like this: this was the first occasion on which the Redeemer's blood was shed. If you do not see the connection between his circumcision and the shedding of the Saviour's blood at that point, and the cross thirty-three years later and the shedding of his blood at that point, then you have missed one of the vital parts of the birth narratives.

Now let me indicate straight away that I am *not* saying – as many people think I may be saying, and as many thought Paul was saying when he talked like this – that it doesn't matter how I live now under the law of Christ. Jesus has abolished the law of Moses and now, because he has been crucified for me, I am under the law of Christ; I am under his law alone, and that is the law of love. Jesus' circumcision was the beginning of the setting free, so that now instead of the law of Moses being my standard, the cross becomes my standard of life, as we see in Galatians. It was the greatest argument in the early church, and it was an argument – it nearly split the church from top to bottom. Paul was on one side, Peter was on the other. An argument that really caused persecution from Christian to Christian was the argument as to whether Christians were still under the law of Moses or not, whether they should still circumcise their baby boys or not. Paul, a Hebrew of the Hebrews, who was circumcised on the eighth day, said: It is finished. We are now under Christ. We are finished with all of that and if you go back to circumcision you go back to every law of Moses. And you are free. Christ has broken the chains and all those laws that bind Jewish families, all the laws that they have to keep in connection with their babies – those are broken and we are set free to love, and to love Christ.

Now that is what the circumcision of Christ says to me.

On the eighth day of our Lord's life, Joseph took the

little boy to be circumcised and said his name shall be Jesus. Isn't it significant that this is the point at which his name is first mentioned by a human being? I don't think the shepherds were told his name, but at this point, when he was circumcised, which was the beginning of setting people free from the law, "His name is Jesus for he shall save his people from their sins". Can you see the connection? Under the law to set people free – so his name is Jesus. The name Jesus means to me that I am not under Moses, I am under Jesus, and his service is perfect freedom.

So it was that Mary and Joseph packed up their few belongings, wrapped Jesus in a travelling shawl or something like that, and set off to travel the six miles to Jerusalem. Why did they go? Because he was circumcised they now had to do everything the law of Moses commanded. The law of Moses said that a mother had to go to God on the fortieth day after bearing a baby boy and she had to go through certain rites of purification and offer certain sacrifices and be clean. Until she had done this she wasn't allowed to go to the synagogue; she wasn't allowed to go to worship. When it was a girl, a mother had to wait eighty days. There was something more. If the child that opened the womb first was a boy then that boy was God's. Every firstborn male child was God's. That baby must be given to him completely.

The parents brought him up for the twelve years knowing that they would have to hand him over to the service of the Lord at twelve. When the Levites alone were priests, the mother and the father had to take the baby to the temple, present him to the Lord and, in recognition that he was the firstborn, they then had to pay five shekels to redeem the firstborn. That was the Jewish law. Because the first child Mary bore was a boy, she and Joseph had taken him to Jerusalem and presented him to the Lord, and in this case they did not buy him back. They didn't produce five shekels.

Luke 2

They said, "Lord, this is your boy," which meant: at the age of twelve you can have him completely. Isn't it astonishing that twelve years later they were so surprised when he stayed in the temple? They had given the boy; they hadn't bought him back. They had known they must leave him in the temple when he was twelve. Yet when he stayed there, they came and his mother scolded him and said, "Your father and I have been looking everywhere for you. What are you doing?"

How quickly we can forget what we have given to God. Did you dedicate your new home to God when you got it? Is it still God's? Did you give your life to God many years ago? Is it still God's? Last New Year did the Lord speak to you as he speaks to me and say, "Re-dedicate yourself." We do it, but a few months later we have forgotten that we did it. Mary and Joseph forgot what they had done and now they scolded him for staying in the temple.

There is one other little thing here that I find very interesting. Mary, for her purification, offered two little turtle doves or two pigeons. An ordinary family had to present a lamb. A very poor family was allowed to pay only two turtle doves or two pigeons. What does that tell me about Joseph and Mary? They were very poor. It was all they could afford, a couple of little birds which they would buy for a few pence. And what does that tell me about God? It tells me that God would rather have parents with little money who will do for a child what God wants doing instead of putting a child into a home where there is everything that money can buy but where the parents don't do what God requires.

Before we move on from this section, may I just remind you how much blood there is in it? Is this why people don't like this part of the Christmas narrative? There is the blood of Jesus shed when he was circumcised. There is the blood of Mary that rendered her unclean and for which sacrifice had to be made, and there was the blood of two turtle doves or two pigeons offered in sacrifice for the mother. We will never understand the wonderful story of our salvation if we miss out the word "blood". It is the scarlet thread that runs right through the Bible. It is there from way back at the beginning when Abel brought his sacrifice in blood and it is there right the way through to the very end: "These are they which have come out of the great tribulation; they have washed their robes and made them white in the blood of the Lamb." When we come to the communion service we take wine and it looks like blood, and it is meant to look that way. Our religion is a religion of blood. It is the blood of Jesus shed for the sins of the world that makes it possible for us to meet for worship.

As we have noticed, the baby was *brought* to Simeon and Anna – they didn't make a journey to the baby. Therefore the next difference was that they didn't have the kind of guidance that the others were given. The shepherds had an angel in the sky telling them to go to Bethlehem and see. The wise men had a star in the sky that guided them to Bethlehem to see. But with this old man and this old woman – no angel, no star. The Holy Spirit in their hearts said, "This is he." I feel at home with Simeon and Anna because I have never seen an angel in the sky and I have never been guided by a star, but the same Holy Spirit who said to Simeon and to Anna "This is Jesus" told me this too, and told you. This is how we receive the confirmation today that this is indeed the Saviour of the world. The Holy Spirit within us says, "That baby, that boy, that Man, that crucified body, that risen Lord – he is the Saviour of the world." It is the Holy Spirit who guides us now to Jesus, and he guided Simeon and Anna.

Consider Simeon: three things are said about him telling us that, even though he wouldn't have realised it, he knew the Trinity. He was righteous and devout towards God; he was looking for Christ, the consolation of Israel, and the

Luke 2

Holy Spirit was upon him. I can't imagine how people can read the Bible and not see the Trinity on every page almost – Father, Son and Holy Spirit all working together in the minds and hearts of young and old.

The most exciting thing about Simeon was that he was the only Jew as far as we know who knew when the Messiah would come. Others had been waiting eight hundred years and none of them knew when he would come. They guessed just as people today guess when the Lord Jesus will come again and say it may be this year and it may be that year, but nobody knows. Many have been proved wrong already. In those days, the Jews guessed but nobody knew. But one day this old man was worshipping God, and the Holy Spirit came on him, and he knew that it was to be in his lifetime.

Can you imagine the excitement of that knowledge? Now you know that Jesus is coming back to earth. You know that he is coming back again; don't you hope it will be in your lifetime? I do. Wouldn't it be thrilling? There would be no funeral for me. It would be so exciting, but I don't know. It may be in your lifetime, it may not.

Supposing God in his mercy said to an old man in your congregation, "It's going to be in your lifetime." Can you imagine the secret, the excitement of the mystery in his heart, and the older he gets the nearer he would know it was to the day when the Messiah would come. That is how Simeon felt. Every birthday he had, and every new year and old year that came and went, every year of his life brought him nearer to the Messiah.

Simeon not only knew *when* the Messiah would appear, he knew *where* because one day, as the old man said his morning prayers, the Holy Spirit told him to get to the temple. He realised in his heart he was going to see the Messiah come that day. What did he expect to see? Did he expect to see a great figure floating down from the clouds? Many Jews did, and the devil said to Jesus: why don't you throw yourself off the pinnacle and float down and everybody will know you've come suddenly to your temple as Malachi predicted.

Simeon came into the temple court and looked all around. Maybe he looked up into the sky first and there was nothing there; looked up at the pinnacle of the temple, no one there, and he looked all around. He saw a poor peasant and his wife and a baby, that's all. The Holy Spirit in his heart must have said, "That's the Messiah, that's the Christ everybody's been waiting for." I guess that he had a little battle in his head and in his heart, saying, "But Lord, that's just a little baby. I'm looking for the Christ." The Holy Spirit said, "That is the Christ." I think that Joseph and Mary must have been rather surprised when this stranger, Simeon, came up and said, "Let me hold the baby." Of course, elderly people like to do that, if not for too long. So Simeon held the baby and then he said those magnificent words which are sometimes sung on Sunday evening in Church of England services. The words are called in Latin the Nunc Dimittis ("Now dismiss me.")

> Lord, now lettest thou thy servant depart in peace:
> according to thy word.
> For mine eyes have seen: thy salvation;
> Which thou hast prepared: before the face of all people;
> To be a light to lighten the Gentiles: and to be the glory
> of thy people Israel.

It pours out, he can't hold it in. He praises his God out of his heart. What has he seen? He has only seen a little baby, nothing more. What tremendous faith this man has that that is all he wants to see. I'm afraid I would have been selfish enough to say, "Lord, let me live another twenty years and see what this little baby grows up to be. Let me see what he does. Oh Lord, can I not live with him?" But no, Simeon can say he has seen it all. That is faith. He didn't ask to see

Luke 2

anything more than just the beginning. He knew that if you have seen the beginning of something, if it is of God, it will happen whether you are alive to see the rest or not. Isn't it thrilling when elderly people can say, "I rejoice to see the beginning of things that will go on after I'm gone"? I can rejoice in the future even though I won't be here to see it.

It takes faith to rejoice in things even if you know you probably won't live to see them. This is faith: the substance of things hoped for, the evidence of things not seen. Abraham, Moses, Elijah, all the heroes of faith of old, didn't live to see the day of Christ but they rejoiced in God's unfolding purpose. As we get older, we should not have regrets that we are not going to live to see things. We should rejoice that we have seen the beginning of the purpose of God. Simeon was happy to go. How unselfish this man was. He called himself "your servant". He speaks of "your salvation", "your people".

Now that was on the positive side but then Simeon turned to Mary and Joseph, and maybe his face changed from gladness to sadness. He looked at this young couple and he blessed them. I don't know how he did it. He could have said: It's going to be tough; it's going to be hard; do you think everybody will welcome him as I've taken him into my arms? Do you think everybody will be thrilled that he's come? Do you think that when he reveals the thoughts of many hearts, they will all be so thrilled and excited? No, this child will split our nation down the middle. Some Jews will rise as they accept him and others will fall as they reject him. Some will live on a higher plane than they've ever lived before, because of this baby, and some will sink to the depths of shame and degradation because of him. Wherever Jesus comes, people rise or fall. You don't stay the same, you either rise to new heights or you rebel and you reject and you go down.

Therefore, Simeon said that there would be a sign which would be spoken against. Some would say, "Let this baby be gone" then, when he had grown up, "Let's kill this man, let's get rid of him." Then it would not be "I'm ready to die", but *he* is ready to die. So he turned to the mother and said, "A sword will pierce your own heart too." The cross shadow falls again across this baby. Christmas has the shadow of the cross all over it. Can't you see it – the blood, and the predictions of sorrow? Thirty-three years later Mary would be a widow watching her firstborn son cruelly done to death in a shameful manner. The sword would pierce her own heart too.

Now into the scene comes a dear old lady of eighty-four. I say old – today I would say "elderly", but in those days, the average life expectancy was twenty-nine. This lady had seen tragedy in her life at three levels. At the family level, she had only been married seven years and then she had been a widow for the other sixty or more years. She had seen tragedy at her tribal level. She was of the tribe of Asher which was one of the ten lost tribes taken to Assyria. Her ancestors had been among the few survivors of that tribe which had been just about obliterated. Anna had kept the family tree. She had seen tragedy at the national level. She had lived in Jerusalem and for the eighty-four years before Jesus' birth there had been one civil war after another. Jerusalem changed hands from one group of rulers to another – from the Hasmonean kings of Syria to the Roman emperors to the hated Herodians. She had seen nothing but bloodshed all her life. Jerusalem, the place of God, was filled with foreign people who had dominated and killed them.

What was her attitude in the face of such tragedy? Did she say, "How can I believe in God with so much personal tragedy all around me all my life?" No, she prayed, she fasted and she worshipped night and day, spending time in

Luke 2

the temple crying to God. That was the best thing she could do with her sorrow, the best thing she could do with all the tragedy that had trampled over her for so many years. She prayed that God would do something about it all. She came into the temple at that moment. She saw the baby and she knew, too, that God had answered her prayer. She had been praying sixty years for God to do something, and she went round and round the temple, talking to anybody who would listen who wanted to see Jerusalem redeemed, and she told them that the baby had been born.

Isn't it a tragedy that we forget Simeon and Anna at Christmas?

We have seen how God was weaving his purpose in history and how two elderly godly people saw it. As I look at Simeon with the baby in his arms, I see the Old Testament holding the New. I see the very finest representatives of the law of Moses introducing the One who came with grace and truth. I see the old passing on to the new.

2:40-52

Now we look at this amazing boy. Out of thirty blank years in the life of the most important person who has ever lived, the veil is only drawn back once at the age of twelve, and a tiny glimpse is given to us of the way that Jesus developed – an astonishing revelation. Our curiosity is aroused by what happened up to that moment and what happened for the next eighteen years until the next glimpse we have of the Son of God. We would love to know, and there have been plenty of people who have been willing to satisfy that curiosity with myth and legend. When you read the Apocryphal gospels and the incredible things they say about Jesus as a boy, you just know they are not true. Thank God you have got a true Bible in your hands. It has not got myths and legends in it, it has got sober fact.

A COMMENTARY ON THE GOSPEL OF LUKE

The Gentile doctor Luke, speaking to Mary the mother in her later years, got some of these stories from her. Of all the stories that Mary must have told him about her Son, this is the one he chose to put in his Gospel. Therefore, this is the only one that God wanted us to have. It is a very human story, very true to human emotions: a boy is absorbed in what he is doing; strong, and silent Joseph is standing in the background, not saying a word while the mother really lets him have an earful. It is an ordinary family, yet it is also extraordinary.

Think again of the little home in Nazareth where Jesus was brought up – somewhere that nobody would ever regard as important, a humble home where people had to work hard with their hands just to make ends meet. That was the perfect environment for this boy. It was the environment in which he developed and in which he grew.

Look first at his growth. It was so balanced. Every side of this boy's life developed, and all the sides developed together. It is the dream of every parent. Very few parents see this dream fulfilled. Most of our sons and daughters seem to go ahead in one direction and lag behind in another. It is always tragic when there is physical or mental retardation. Sometimes you meet a person whose intellect has developed enormously, but emotionally they have not developed and so they are still a child in their feelings. This is a real handicap in their later relationships. Sometimes you meet brilliant people who have developed intellectually but socially they are no good at all and they haven't developed in favour with other people. They just can't say anything when you put them in company and they haven't adjusted to relationships. But the greatest tragedy of all is where somebody develops physically, mentally, emotionally, intellectually, socially, and remains a spiritual three-year-old! I have met many like this. There are men who can write out a cheque for half a million pounds and think nothing of it; men who can grasp the affairs of big business, who can play the stock exchange; men of great talent and great gifts – and they can't pray as well as a kindergarten kid and they are spiritually underdeveloped. But Jesus, in this environment of a simple, poor home in Nazareth, developed in every way. What a joy he must have been to the hearts of Mary and Joseph. Here was Jesus and he grew in stature, in wisdom. Notice: not in cleverness, but in wisdom. That is far more important than being clever.

You notice that he didn't develop financially. How often parents say, "Oh my son has done well you know. He's earning forty thousand a year now and he's got five staff under him." Jesus didn't develop in that way. He didn't develop in social status. He didn't move up from a carpenter's shop to a nice suburb. He didn't develop in a whole lot of things that we count as important. He was not famous – not for the first thirty years of his life. He didn't develop in any of these ways but he developed physically, mentally, socially and spiritually – because of the home he had chosen, and the blessing of God was with him.

In other words, he grew up. Jesus at every stage of his development was always childlike but never childish. Even when he was a grown-up, he was childlike. He retained his boyhood name for God into his adult life. Forever afterwards in his prayers he called God the Father Abba, Dad. It was the childhood "Abba" equivalent to our "Dada" or "Daddy". He kept that in his adult prayers and he taught us to say the same.

I remember a man in hospital whom it was such a joy to meet. He had had a heart attack and he would die a few weeks later, but I saw him regularly during that time. What a privilege it was just to go into his room. His first sentence would always include the word "Father" and he would say some mornings to me, "Had a lovely chat with Father this morning." Another morning, "Father's been so good to me."

It was so Christlike. What a contrast to those who develop in other ways but remain childish even when they are adults – as easily upset as a little child. You want to say to them, "Grow up", but Jesus grew up and he discovered the secret of remaining childlike without ever being childish, and that is real growth.

The second thing I want you to look at is his initiation. All societies have their coming of age ceremonies, and the recognised age for becoming an adult among the Jews, as we have noted, was twelve. That is why the veil is drawn aside at this age – when a boy became an adult, morally and criminally responsible for his own actions; it was also the age at which a boy took full legal partnership in his father's business and was thenceforward to be found in his father's house. It was at this age that his parents went, as they did every year, to Jerusalem for the Passover.

They needn't have gone. The priests said that only if you live within twenty miles is the law incumbent on you to attend the Passover, and Joseph and Mary lived eighty miles away. They had to make it on foot, too. Whilst the priests excused them, Joseph and Mary didn't listen to the priests, they listened to God. God said, "You'll keep my Passover," so they went. Every year they trudged those eighty miles. They couldn't afford to ride and they would lose business while they were gone, but they went – God first. This year twelve-year-old Jesus went with them. I will never forget the sight I had in Jerusalem's main synagogue of seeing a boy of twelve with his skull cap on, proudly reading the law, and his doting father looking at the boy, so proud of him. He was coming of age, growing up.

The Passover was that remembrance of the greatest event in history – that means God sets people free. They use the word "redeem". We have got to drop that word now since pawnbrokers have ceased to be in an affluent society. It has

Luke 2

lost the only meaning it had for us, except, I suppose, those who redeem stocks and shares. But it means to set something free, and the God they celebrated was the God who set them free and got them out of Egypt and brought them to Israel.

I was once in North Finchley sitting at a table at a Jewish Passover celebration. They broke the bread and passed it round, and they poured the wine out and passed it round, and the elder next to me must have seen my face because he turned to me and said, "Very definitely the Messiah has not come." But when you break bread and pass the wine around on an occasion like that you can't but think of Jesus. For our Lord's Supper is the Passover but we believe in a freedom that is greater than the Jews got from Egypt. When we have communion it is to remember that God sets us free. We can sense something of this in the Passover in this passage. Mary and Joseph took him up and it was his coming of age. Then they set off home, and it is so easy to understand why they lost him. It wasn't neglect, it wasn't carelessness. This is how they travelled in those days: the wives would set off first with the luggage and the tents, and walk fifteen miles, and then they set the tents up and got the evening meal ready. Then the men came along later in the day, chatting and just in time for the evening meal. Totally unfair, wasn't it? I have exaggerated a little but the women went first at their own pace and the men came along later.

So what happened was this: when a boy was under twelve, he travelled with the women. When he was over twelve, he travelled with the men. But on this occasion Joseph would have thought that he had stayed with his mother; Mary would have thought he was now with Joseph, and when they met up at the end of the first day out, probably at Jericho, fifteen miles down through the wilderness they would have asked: "Where's Jesus?"

"I thought he was with you? No?"

"No."

"Well is he with some of the relatives?"

It took them another day to walk back. I can imagine Mary and Joseph chatting, and Joseph saying, "Now look, he's alright. He's twelve years old." Mary, I think, would have felt guilty. She had been charged with looking after the Son of God and she had lost him! But one day out, one day back, and the next day they spend looking everywhere but the right place. At last they found him in the temple.

Look now at Jesus' wisdom. What was he doing in the temple? Some of the artists who have painted this scene have got the whole thing wrong. They have pictured a scene of a precocious boy with his hands uplifted, preaching, and a crowd of learned elderly rabbis sitting on the ground gazing at him, awestruck. Actually, the normal method of learning in those days was by asking and answering questions. It is still the best method of teaching children. He was no more than learning. This is important. He showed a highly intelligent grasp of what was being said, but he was not a teacher here, he was the pupil. He was learning his Father's business. So let us get rid of these precocious images in which we think of Jesus teaching everybody else at this stage. He did later.

Now he is learning his Father's business in this very place and he has assumed that his parents brought him here for this. Maybe he remembered the account of Hannah who was given a boy when she could not have had one. She took that boy to the temple and left him there to serve God. It would have been a normal thing for Joseph and Mary to have done this. Jesus was the firstborn boy and, as we have noted, God had a right to him. This boy belonged to God and to the service of the temple, and Jesus just assumed it – that they brought him to leave him there, to learn his Father's business. So when they found him and Mary scolded him, it was Jesus who was surprised. He was amazed! Mary, bless her, told him of their

Luke 2

anxiety. Still Joseph is standing back there. He knew Jesus would be alright. Mary was so worried, so human. Where had Jesus slept? What had he eaten? Can't you imagine Mary asking that? "Where have you been? Where did you spend last night? Who has been feeding you?"

But, you see, Jesus is already finding out that his meat and drink is to do the Father's will. I don't know where he had been sleeping or where he had been eating, he had been learning his Father's business. It was he who showed the wisdom. It was they who were dull. So his answer tells us something more about him: his *vocation*. It is Jesus who expresses the surprise that they had not realised, and with his answer comes a shock to Mary. Mary had said, "Your father and I have been so worried." Jesus spoke of his Father's business. This is where he lives. Surely they would realise that. Had they been looking all over Jerusalem for Jesus? Why didn't they come to where they had brought him? I can imagine Joseph and Mary going on to say, "Jesus, we didn't bring you here to leave you here, we are taking you back to Nazareth." It was Jesus who was surprised, but at this moment he reveals one thing: that at the age of twelve he knew who his Dad was.

It reveals, secondly, that Mary had never told him, and neither had Joseph. They had allowed, as they thought, Jesus to be brought up as a normal boy. Maybe the villagers whispered that he was illegitimate, born outside wedlock. But Joseph and Mary treated him as their son and they never breathed a word of his origin. Now he says, "My Father". They had never told him but he *knew* – that is the drama of this moment. It is this thread that runs right through the life of Jesus, for these are his first recorded words: "my Father's business".

His last recorded words before he died contained the same lovely word in them: "Father, into your hands I commit my spirit." That came from a goodnight prayer which Jewish mothers taught their young boys. It comes from one of the Psalms. There you have it: the childlike Jesus at thirty-three saying the prayer that he used to say at Mary's knee – childlike, but never childish. Father, Father, from first to last, and that is why we believe that Jesus was and is the Son of God. He had no human dad; he had a heavenly Abba Father.

Now the next thing I want you to notice is so surprising. Since he is so wise and his parents so dull, what would you expect next? Would you expect this young adult (as he was in Jewish eyes) to say, "Right, I am now twelve, this is where I've got to be, this is where I stay; I'm sorry but I'm old enough to make my own decisions"? It says that his parents did not understand so he went back to Nazareth with them. There is an example for young people from Jesus – and it is for older ones of us too. What an example! He went back and was subject to them. Jesus, what are you doing? Do you realise you are turning your back on your Father's business and you are going to be stuck in a village shop for the next eighteen years because Joseph is going to die? You are going to be left with a family of maybe twelve others and you will have to look after them and you're going to be stuck in that shop for eighteen years. What are you doing? God's purposes are going to be thwarted and stopped. But he went back and was subject to them because they didn't understand. He was ready but they were not. Does that mean that the next eighteen years were wasted – that being tied down to those limited circumstances, those were lost years? Nothing of the kind.

What happened during those eighteen years? It is in the Bible; I can tell you exactly what happened. He grew. I know he was twelve, I know he was an adult. I know he developed in so many ways, but he went on growing. If we look back over a year, the important thing for you and for me is not what we did but what we became – whether your life was exciting and you went round the whole world and you did this, that and the other, or whether you were stuck in one little shop or office, or whether you had to stay at home and look after aged parents or whatever you had to do. When you are frustrated with your circumstances and hear about distant places and travelling around the world and exciting things that people can do in Christian service, and you feel, "I'm just stuck here," remember that Jesus went on growing – physically, yes, in wisdom yes, and in favour with men, yes. Jesus was very popular until he started preaching, telling them about their sins and that he had come to save people. Nobody would have thought he was the Son of God. They just said, "Jesus, great guy. Oh yes, a pleasure to go into the shop." But they never dreamed he was the Son of God. The Bible doesn't record a single miracle or a single sermon during all those years. It wouldn't have been possible. The Holy Spirit had not yet anointed him and he had to wait until his baptism and the anointing of the Spirit, and then he could say, in Nazareth, "The Spirit of the Lord is on me...." He could now preach the gospel to the poor, make the lame walk and set people free. When they heard that, they loathed him. Isn't this the carpenter? But for the time being he was popular and he grew in favour with men, and, above all in favour with God. I don't care whether you are rich or poor next year, whether you have a lot of friends or a few, whether you get a better job or not. If you are in favour with God, that is it – and so he grew. You might look back sometimes and reflect that it doesn't matter if nobody has heard about you – it has been worthwhile. But if you didn't grow, it has been a sheer waste of time.

Why did Luke include this one little passage about Jesus? When you study the life of Jesus, it is important that you begin with what he *was* before you study what he *did*.

Because if you study what he did without realising who he was, then you won't understand what he did. Let me explain. This passage is here at the beginning of the Gospel. It is before he began doing great things. It comes *before* he made the blind see and the deaf hear and the lame walk and the dead rise. There is not yet a miracle or a sermon, just a clear picture of who he is: Son of God and Son of Man. Everyone reading this needs to know one of those two things. If you are not a Christian then you need to be told that he is the Son of God. You may well believe that he was a great man and you may well have an admiration for his teaching, but all that is of no use to you until you realise he was the Son of God and not just a great man. In that he is unique, and you need to believe that before you study what he did because only then will you see its significance. You will see the significance of the miracles now. This was Jesus Christ, Son of God.

If you are a Christian, you need to be reminded that Jesus was the Son of Man. For if there is one mistake we Christians make it is this: that when we believe he is the Son of God, we forget that he is the Son of Man too. We forget the human side and so we have these anachronisms in our thinking about Jesus and we think that he was far more developed than he was at a certain age. If you look on the Christmas cards, it's usually a six-month-old chubby child in the manger. Then when we think of him as a twelve-year-old boy teaching all those learned men, we have forgotten that he had to grow. We have forgotten that he became so human that he wasn't lying in that manger looking up and saying, "Well, isn't it wonderful?" He was not conscious in that manger, I believe, that God was his Father.

Part of his incarnation was that he started at square one. At what age did he become conscious that he was the Son of God? I do not know. I know that by twelve he had come to that consciousness, but he grew and he learned obedience by the things he suffered. He had to go through life as I have gone through life – having to develop, having to grow; having to understand. The humanity of it is marvellous – that the Son of God who had all wisdom should come and be a baby and have to learn wisdom. Now that does not mean that he made mistakes. It does mean that he was ignorant of things and had to learn them. He admitted ignorance in his life. He admitted ignorance of the date of his second coming. He said that of that day or of that hour, knows no man, not even the Son, just the Father knows. He had to learn. There is a difference between making mistakes and having to learn.

We must grasp the humanity of Jesus, that he had to learn as well. He is still human. He is still the Son of Man. He was really down to earth. He was part of our clay. He ate and drank, he was tired, he was thirsty, and he went to the toilet as you have to. Are you shocked if I say that? You see we are so polite we don't mention it, but he talked about it on at least two occasions – he was as real as that. The Son of God was a man, therefore, we can now pray to him as a High Priest who understands our infirmities.

3

Read Luke 3

3:1-20
I suppose if John the Baptist appeared today, nobody would take any notice of him. His hair was long and he only had the clothes he stood up in. Having laid down in that clothing for some years now, it wasn't in very good condition. He scratched a living where he could. He was a loner, spent his days out in the desert, and yet, when this man appeared in public, his own cousin Jesus, the Son of God, said that John was the greatest man who had ever lived. He was a man who brought an entire nation to its knees. That is something that had never been done before and has not been done since. One of the most amazing statements about John the Baptist in the Bible is this: John did no miracle. No supernatural signs whatsoever accompanied his message. Yet the people believed what he said. He was filled with the Holy Spirit but showed no gifts of the Spirit – yet his words penetrated deep into the hearts of many men and women. They came to him by the thousand from all over. A prophet was a man who pointed forward to Jesus Christ, and there was no greater prophet than John. We are going to look at this man and there are several things I want you to consider with me.

First of all, I want you to look at his *moment*. There is a tide in the affairs of men, says William Shakespeare. There is no doubt that there is a tide in the affairs of God which John the Baptist took at the flood, guided no doubt by the Holy Spirit. The first few verses of Luke 3 may seem to you a bit boring – history. Why does he have to date this event in six different ways? Why doesn't he just tell us that it was in the year AD so and so and get on with it? Of course they didn't yet mark their years AD but he could have given us one simple date, instead Luke gives us six datings for John.

This is the beginning of the gospel; the gospel did not begin at Bethlehem, it began at the Jordan river. Mark tells us that clearly in the beginning of his Gospel. He says, "The beginning of the gospel of Jesus Christ, the Son of God – a voice crying in the wilderness." The good news begins with John the Baptist. It doesn't begin with Bethlehem and the birth of Jesus, and it doesn't begin with Jesus preaching, it begins with John's ministry. If we consider what we call "mission", we must begin with John. The word mission is the same as the word missile, it means *sent* and there was a man sent from God. He was a missile, a pretty devastating one and fully loaded with explosives, and when he was sent by God, things began to happen. Now this six-fold dating is fascinating because, if you read it carefully and read between the lines, you find that the whole situation has changed since Jesus was born. The result is that now the country is ready for Jesus to appear. That would not have been so when Jesus was born.

Let us look at these details of the historical background. For one thing, the Roman Emperor had changed. In the year AD 14, Augustus, who had been a good ruler, died. He had brought peace to the whole Mediterranean world. He had had to pay for it by taxes. He had to enrol people and have a census. It was his taxing and enrolling that brought Jesus unborn to Bethlehem to be born there. In AD 14 Augustus was replaced with Tiberius who was a bad ruler. With Tiberius, the moral rot began that ultimately brought the Roman Empire crashing down.

By the time that John the Baptist was preaching, the

Roman Empire, which had prepared the way for the gospel to spread through the world quickly, was beginning to wane. It was now that the gospel must get going. There had been political changes within the Holy Land itself. When Jesus was born, there was one kingdom of Israel and one king of the Jews: Herod the great. The country was unified, it was held together even if Herod wasn't popular. At least it was a unity and all the Jews lived under one family. But when Herod died in AD 6 the whole country was split up between four of his sons. The Roman authorities carved through the people of God and divided them into four pieces. There was one son called Herod – he was the worst, Herod Antipas – and he was given Galilee in the north and a strip of what is now called Jordan on the east of the Jordan river. Herod Antipas was going to be one of the greatest foes of the gospel. It was he who would kill John, and it was he who would want to kill Jesus. Philip, who was the best of the four sons, was actually the offspring of Herod the Great and Cleopatra, down in Egypt. Philip got the northeast corner up on the Golan Heights where battles have been fought in modern times between Israel and Syria. He had his capital there. He took over a little town called Paneas. He renamed it after himself and the emperor, calling it Caesarea Philippi. Whenever Jesus wanted to be safe and peaceful with his disciples, he would go up to Caesarea Philippi.

The other two rulers, down in the south, were not good. Samaria in the middle and Judea in the south were ruled over by bad sons of Herod. They messed it up so much that finally the Romans took them off their thrones and replaced them with a Roman governor in the year AD 26 –Pontius Pilate. So by the time John began preaching, the whole country was divided. Can you see the result? The decks were being cleared. There was now no king of Israel. Those four sons weren't given the title of king though they tried to take it for themselves. They were called "Tetrarchs" which means quarter governors.

There being no king of Israel, it was as if God had said: Out of the way, my Son is coming; behold your King comes to Jerusalem, meek and riding on an ass, but let's get all the other kings out of the way.

When Jesus was born there was a king of the Jews who was jealous of anybody else claiming to be the king of the Jews. But later it was literally true that the inhabitants were able to say, "We have no king but Caesar." Can you see the meaning of that phrase now? They really didn't – literally, the kings had been removed and there was only a Roman governor and he was an ex-slave and it was his first job. In fact, it proved to be his last.

The multitudes listened to John for he said, "I've come to get ready for the King." Isn't it strange how you can read a historical reference in the Bible and wonder why it is there, then you look at it more closely and the whole of God's purpose is there, written into history?

Two names are mentioned as high priest. In Israel there were many priests but there could only be one high priest. Annas was the high priest all through Jesus' boyhood and teen years but the Romans didn't like him. Annas was a man of strong principles, not all of them good. The Romans wanted a puppet priest they could push around. So they deposed Annas and tried four of his sons, one after the other, and none of them was quite what the Romans liked so they got rid of all four. Finally they took Caiaphas, the nephew of Annas, put him in, and said, "This is your high priest." Now the Jews knew that when a man became high priest he was high priest for life in the sight of God. So they never accepted Caiaphas. The Romans said he was high priest and you had this uneasy situation when Caiaphas was the front man and was the Roman high priest and they would only have dealings with him, but the Jews looked to his uncle Annas and said, "He's the power behind the throne." So in fact Annas and Caiaphas were high priests. Isn't it fascinating? Just one little detail in the Bible and it's all true and confirmed with history but do you see what this means? Somehow the proper high priest had been cleared out of the way. The man who was now high priest was not high priest. He was a puppet of the Romans as Pontius Pilate was. In other words, the decks are cleared for one to come who is both King and High Priest. So God prepared the stage for his Son. Everything was in a mess, and when chaos and confusion reigned over the little land of Israel, that was when John the Baptist knew the hour had come and he must get ready for the King. If it is any comfort to you, we are getting into greater and greater chaos and who knows what political chaos lies ahead. Don't worry. That is an opportunity for the Lord to step in. The decks are cleared when humans get bogged down in such a mess. God says, "Now John, tell them to get ready for the coming of the King."

On a global scale, when the world gets into more and more chaos and confusion, violence fills the earth and we wonder what things are coming to: Christians, lift up your heads; prepare the way of the Lord; make his highway smooth; let him come riding in; the King is on the way.

In verse 3 we look at his *mission*. Not in the main streets but out in the barren desert, a voice was shouting. At first maybe John shouted to the winds and nobody listened, and he shouted, "Prepare ye the way of the Lord." Then one or two shepherd boys heard, crept closer and heard him preaching. They told others, and they went out to see, until part of the wilderness which was normally deserted was full of people. I am going to go backwards through the verse. Look at every main word in it and you find that each one is important.

First of all, John's mission was about people's *sins* – that is where he began. He didn't begin with their fears, he didn't begin with their hopes, he didn't begin with their dreams, and he didn't begin with their sorrows. John's mission was concerned with sins. It was not concerned with sin but with sins, with the specifics. The old Puritans used to say, "Descend to the particular", meaning get down to the specifics. Get down to brass tacks. Don't just say, "Lord, deliver me from sin," say, "Lord, deliver me from *these* sins." That is what John's mission was concerned with. He was concerned with that which sin has produced – and that is the first note in his mission.

The second is this: he was preaching *forgiveness* of sins. Nobody else can do that; no other religion in the world can offer that. This is the good news: "forgiveness", which means blotting sins out, restoring the relationships they have spoiled, dealing with the past so that it will never more come up and affect the future.

Thirdly, he is preaching *repentance*. The meaning of that word in the Greek is to change your mind, to turn your thinking around; to see your sins as they really are instead of excusing them as faults or weaknesses or due to tiredness or pressure. You say, "They are sins." You think again, but if you have really repented, it will show not in your tears (which can be crocodile tears of regret or remorse) but in turning away. There is no repentance that doesn't do this. Repentance is not *feeling* sorry, it is being sorry enough to stop, and that was John's call.

Fourth, in his mission John *preached baptism*. Baptism is the new thing that begins the gospel. It is the new sign of a new covenant for a new people of God. It is a break. Baptism is never mentioned in the Old Testament. It is not a thing that has a history, it comes out of the blue. It is the sacrament of a new beginning and it belongs here to John. It is the seal of repentance, an outward expression of an inward attitude. It is a person saying, "I want to wash away the past, I want to bury these sins, I want to be rid of them, I want to finish with them publicly, openly, completely, permanently, finally." It is so expressive, and nobody can be baptised for you. You must be baptised for yourself, and that is the call. I don't believe that a person has properly begun with the gospel if they have not been baptised. It is part of the very first response to the call of God and the offer of forgiveness.

The next thing we notice in this verse is that he was doing it *by the Jordan river.* What is the significance of that? For one thing it was because there was plenty of water there, dirty though it was where John baptised. It was the nearest river to the city of Jerusalem. But I don't think that's the reason because there were pools in Jerusalem quite big enough to baptise in – the pool of Bethesda, the pool of Siloam. Why didn't he use one of the swimming pools in Jerusalem? Why did he go to the Jordan? Not just because there was much water there, as John 3:26 puts it. Another reason may be that it was the lowest point on the earth and the dirtiest river at that point. It is just before it enters the Dead Sea with all the foulness of that. It was from highest heaven that the Lord of glory came to the lowest, dirtiest river on earth to be baptised. There is something meaningful there, but the Bible doesn't say that. What does the Bible say about the Jordan? The Jordan river was the point at which the Israelites entered into the land of promise.

John the Baptist is saying: come right back to the place of entering into God's promises. Forget all the centuries you have been in the land of milk and honey, forget all the sins that have spoiled it and lost you that land; come right back to where the children of Israel started – and start afresh. Come down to this river and start again. That is what baptism calls a person to do. There is the river in front of you. It doesn't matter how religious you've been or how much God has blessed you. Leave your sins and come down to the river and start again with forgiveness. Now you can see the meaning of it all. That was his mission.

The next thing that is mentioned is his *mandate* (vv. 4-6). Where did John get his orders – his commission – from? The answer is that it was already nine hundred years old. For his commission had come nearly a thousand years earlier through the prophet Isaiah, who had talked about this. Have you ever noticed that Isaiah is a Bible in miniature? It has sixty-six chapters, just as the Bible has sixty-six books. In Isaiah the chapters are divided between thirty-nine chapters and twenty-seven chapters, just as the Bible is divided between thirty-nine books and twenty-seven books. Have you ever noticed that in the first thirty-nine chapters of Isaiah all the themes are Old Testament themes but in the next twenty-seven chapters, from chapters forty to sixty-six, all the themes are New Testament?

Have you ever noticed that chapter 40 begins with a picture of John the Baptist and moves on further to the life of Jesus and moves on to the cross of Jesus? You know Isaiah 53: chastisement of our peace was upon him; with his stripes we are healed. Then it moves on to chapter sixty-six which corresponds to the book of Revelation and talks of the new heaven and the new earth. It is as if God took the Bible and squeezed it down and put it in Isaiah's mouth. So if we go to Isaiah 40, we are at the beginning of the New Testament. There Isaiah said, "The voice of one shouting in the desert, get the way ready."

One journey I will never forget was a long ride at about four o'clock in the morning from Amman right down through the desert to Petra, hundreds of miles to the south. We did it in huge American taxis – down a new road that had been built through the desert by the Americans for Jordan. It was a straight, smooth road; the cars just kept a steady eighty or ninety and went all day to get down to Petra. What a journey it was: a highway in the desert, around us the hills, the sand and the basalt rocks, and the roughness of some areas that not even a camel can cross! Yet this road was smooth, straight, right through the desert. One often thought of King Hussein going down that road and one couldn't help but think of Isaiah and John the Baptist: get ready the road of the Lord. Make it smooth, fill up the potholes, pull the hills down, get a new road for the King. Or you could think of the kind of road that has been built from Jericho to Jerusalem. To go up it doesn't take long. It takes even less time to go down it – a lovely, smooth, wide road, and as you go down you can look up and down at the old rough road that Jesus would have walked from Jerusalem to Jericho.

Some people today know the Christian way is a rough road and there are barriers that go up – suspicions, doubts and fears. The Lord would love to come straight in but the road is not ready. Perhaps you haven't repented of your sins. Maybe you haven't faced up to the truths of judgment and the wrath to come, so there isn't an urgency in your heart to prepare the way of the Lord. The Lord is making very slow progress into your life because the road is not ready and it is so hilly and so rough and there are potholes. Can you see? Human nature is a desert without the King. There is a road needed through that desert right into your heart. It is picture language, but how telling it is, and John the Baptist said, "Prepare ye the way of the Lord." Why? Because the moment had come for all mankind to see the salvation of the Lord. Not just Jews – but all mankind.

Next, in vv. 7-9, his message is very direct. If you are going to prepare a road quickly, you need a bulldozer, and John was a spiritual bulldozer. He went right in and cleared the blockages out of the way. It is a stern theme. If I can put it this way: John dampened spirits as well as bodies. John really cut them to the heart. His theme was judgment. No playing to the gallery, no fear of losing his congregation. He didn't care that much about keeping a congregation. He wanted to preach judgment whether anybody would listen or not, knowing that those who would listen would have a smooth road for the Lord to come into their hearts.

John makes it clear that *race* has nothing to do with our salvation. I don't care what your family tree is. You may even have royal blood in you for all I know, or more particularly you may have Jewish blood in you. But John's message meant that it is not your race that matters. Don't say, "We have Abraham for our ancestor" – that is irrelevant. "God could take these rocks and make them into sons of Abraham as he took the dust of the earth and made Adam." But it doesn't matter. It doesn't matter if your parents were Christians and your grandparents Christians and your great-grandparents Christians. God has no grandchildren and that is not the vital thing.

Also, *ritual* doesn't help you. If someone goes through the form of baptism, the outward ceremony, it may do nothing for them. I will confess freely that once or twice I have baptised people whom later I certainly regretted baptising, for it was a ritual for them, even though they wanted it and they felt they had an emotional experience while they had it. I am comforted with the fact that the apostles made the same mistake. Do you remember Simeon in Samaria? – When Peter realised that there had been no repentance in his heart, he said, "You have neither part nor lot in this matter." Ritual doesn't save you.

What God is looking for is not race and not ritual, but *righteousness*. The axe is already at the root of the trees, and every tree that is not bearing good fruit is going to be chopped down. For in the last analysis, when you and I stand before God on the last day, the thing he will look for is not our race, not our ritual, but our righteousness. If you haven't got any righteousness of your own then God help you if you haven't got the righteousness of Christ. John says that God is even now judging, he is looking at the trees and he is saying there is no good fruit. Chop that tree down. Throw it in the fire. Yes, there is fire coming, and judgment.

In vv. 10-14, John's method was to tell his hearers what to do – not what to believe but what to *do*. He was so practical. When they came and said, "Can we be baptised?" he said, "Show visibly in your life that you have repented." They scratched their heads and said, "Repentance, that's a spiritual thing. How do you expect us to show that?" Then he got down to the brass tacks of it: "Listen now. If you've got two shirts, go and give one to someone who hasn't any." That is practical enough. He said that proves you have repented. My, what would John the Baptist say if he looked into our wardrobes and into our deep freezers and into our garages? You can hardly take it.

Then there came tax collectors. They weren't popular people – they collected taxes for the Romans. They were Jews but they were traitors in a sense, and the Romans used them at customs and tax offices. The Romans said, "Of course you can get anything for yourself you like. That is the pay. We are not paying you. You just line your own pockets. You add your commission." Of course many of them added a huge commission. They were on to a good thing. Nobody dared refuse them because they would go to jail if they didn't pay up. So these men took far more than their living wage. They were the newly wealthy, and so John said to them when they asked for baptism, "You just take what you're entitled to. Take your commission and no more."

Then came soldiers. They were occupying soldiers and they had the right to compel a person to carry their luggage one mile. Said Jesus: if any compel you to go one mile then go a second with him. That was out of grace. But any soldier could compel you to go one mile and carry his kit bag. He just had to touch you on the shoulder and say, "I compel you." That's how they made Simon of Cyrene carry Jesus' cross. They could therefore bully people so easily. They could push them and they could kick them and they could make them go further than a mile. So John said, "Stop bullying." Notice he didn't tell them to leave the army. The New Testament never told a soldier to stop fighting, but he told them to stop bullying – a very different matter. In these practical ways, what is John saying? He is saying: stop being so selfish. In other words, if you are ready for baptism, show it by stopping being so selfish. If you really want to be rid of your sin, if you really want to bury the past, then it is self you are going to bury. So start getting rid of self right now. Indeed, that was the practical demand that he made. Sheer selfishness showed a lack of love of neighbour.

Now the next thing I want to mention is John's *modesty* (see vv.15-17). This great preacher with huge crowds numbering thousands, with more baptisms than probably anybody else – it could have gone to his head so easily and he could have thought of himself as the greatest. He was called the greatest, and before Jesus was born he was the greatest man who was ever born of woman, but do notice his modesty. They thought he was the Messiah. They came to him and asked, and John told them that he wasn't even worthy to loose the sandal strap of the one who was to come. That is a very interesting remark because slaves had their own hierarchy. It was the second from bottom slave who had to tie sandals. The bottom one washed feet. Now just think that one through. John said, "I'm not even good enough to be his second bottom slave." When Jesus himself came, he took a towel and girded himself and washed feet. In other words, John was a very humble man but he was not more

Luke 3

humble than Jesus.

So John, in his humility, said, "No I'm not the one; there's somebody else coming." John taught them this: there are things I can do for you but there are things I can't do for you – much greater things – and he will do them for you. I can only deal with your past, but he will deal with your future. I can only baptise you with water to wash your sins away and get forgiveness, but he will deal with your future by baptising you with the Holy Spirit and with fire.

I wish I could baptise people in the Holy Spirit, but I can't. I have never been able to and never will be. I can baptise people in water if they are repentant and if they are ready to cut with the past and make a new beginning with Christ. That is all I can do. But to those I baptise I always say: "Will you ask Jesus to baptise you in the Holy Spirit, with fire?" That is something more. Baptism in water deals with the past only. Baptism in the Spirit deals with your future. So John the Baptist pointed forward to someone else. This fire of the Holy Spirit came at Pentecost. Tongues of flame sat on them.

There are chapels you can still go to see today where during the Welsh Revival they turned out to put the fire out because the roof was seen as burning – but the chapel roofs are still there un-charred. In the prayer meetings, the fire of God descended. Salvationists wear "blood and fire" on their uniforms. What does fire do? It destroys the dross and purifies the gold. Therefore, when he baptises with the Holy Spirit and fire, expect certain things in your life to be burned out but expect other things to get better and better. Fire can't destroy gold, it only makes it purer. That is the baptism which John said he couldn't give but Jesus can. You need to seek both baptisms, both ministries.

Sadly, we must come to the last thing mentioned here – his murderer. We are in vv. 18-20. It is tragic but John paid for his message with his life. If you accuse the immoral of sin, you cannot expect to be popular and welcomed. On the contrary, you will be put on an execution block. John the Baptist was fearless. Whose territory was he in as he stood on the far side of the Jordan and called Israel to come back over and start again? He was in the territory of Herod Antipas who lived in the great castle of Machaerus, up on the hills on the east side of the Dead Sea, looking down on John preaching – and from his castle Herod Antipas could see the crowds. Word came to Herod: "The preacher down there is talking about you. He is saying that you have sinned in the sight of heaven. You have seduced your wife from your own half-brother. She's not only your half-brother's wife, she's also another close relative – your half-sister. In other words he is accusing you of incest." That is the only crime or sin that every society on earth has always condemned as wrong. Did you know that? John the Baptist said, "That king in that castle up there is living in sin and he needs to repent just like everybody else." If you start accusing of sin the ruler of a country, then you will be in trouble, and Herod didn't like it. Josephus the historian says that Herod shut John up because he was a potential leader of a revolution. But John would never have led a rebellion. The reason why Herod shut him in prison was that he did not want those things said about him in public. So he took that man who had been brought up in thirty years out in the open air, the man of wide open spaces, the man of the hills and the valleys, the man of the clear sky, the man of the fresh air, and put him in a dungeon cell from where, through a little barred window he would be able to look down on the Jordan and across to the wilderness on the other side. That was a cruel punishment.

Finally, at the request of a dancing girl's mother, the head of John was brought on a plate to Herod. Herod now looked at that face and at that mouth which could no longer speak and at that skull. Herod must have known that one day he would have to answer to God for this. So within probably about six months of his beginning preaching, John's mouth was closed, his preaching was silenced but his work was done. Every one of the twelve disciples that Jesus got, he got from John. John had smoothed the highway into the hearts of those twelve men. Among the tax collectors who came to John were probably Matthew and Zacchaeus, and others watching.

I meet many people today who want to sing about Jesus, and watch films about him and talk about him, and be entertained about him – but do you want John as well as Jesus? Yet mission begins with John, with judgment, with repentance. It begins with facing up to the wrath to come. It begins with being prepared to have a moral examination.

If you feel really fit and you are convinced that you are healthy, you will be perfectly ready to undergo a medical examination. But if you have a suspicion that there is something seriously wrong with you, the last thing you would look forward to is a medical examination. If you feel you are alright morally, then you will be perfectly prepared for God to look into your heart and your mind and examine it. But if you don't feel that, then that is the last thing you would want to happen. We need to examine ourselves before God and ask him to help us to make a new beginning.

3:21-38

Jesus began his ministry at thirty years of age, though his work was to be done in less than three. But of the thirty years that prepared our Lord Jesus for what lay ahead we know next to nothing. As we have noted, only on one or two occasions is the veil drawn aside. Then, as he came up to the age of thirty, a tremor of excitement rippled through the country. More and more people began to take trips away from their home, deep down into that valley where, as we have seen, John the Baptist was preaching repentance, and baptising – preparing for the coming King.

I daresay in the little village of Nazareth, as groups of young people went to hear John the Baptist, and as groups of older people went too, and came back, they would have come into the shop in Nazareth saying things like: "You ought to hear him, Jesus!" "Have you heard him?" "Aren't you going?" As Jesus went on planing the wood, his heart would have been saying, "I know I am that King" – but not a word did he breathe in Nazareth at that time.

He waited until that wave of interest began to die down. He waited until more and more people had been and returned, and had come back, saying, "I've been baptised. I'm making a new start. I'm ready for the King." More and more went, and more and more came back, and then, finally, the interest began to die off. Then Jesus hung his tools up for the last time in the shop, and he went to be baptised. Now that was the beginning of his life's work. It says he waited until most people in Judea had been baptised. He waited until the rush was over because in fact their baptism was to get ready for him. One day the Father said, "Now you can leave the shop." No doubt there was a younger brother who could take over the family business, but Jesus put down the tools, and the next contact he ever had with a hammer and nails and wood would be when soldiers nailed him to a cross three years later. So he left the shop and trudged fifty miles southeast across the Jordan, just south of the Sea of Galilee, way down below sea level, right down into that hot, sticky valley – the Jordan Valley – to the lowest, dirtiest spot on earth. There Jesus asked for baptism.

There are two things I would like to say about his baptism by way of introduction. Firstly, nobody put him up to it, nobody egged him on; nobody told him he should be baptised. It was his voluntary choice at the age of thirty, in his prime, when he knew what he was doing. He had been through certain initiation rites as a child – he had been circumcised, dedicated, but now this was his choice. This is one of those profound insights which we believe very firmly was given to us for all time: baptism is to be the choice of the candidate. They must come in their prime to an acceptance of God's will when they are mature and responsible in his sight, and old enough to realise the need for repentance and faith. Then, as surely and as certainly as our Lord Jesus Christ decided for himself to submit to baptism, so should we. I have never yet in my ministry asked anyone to be baptised. I have preached baptism strongly, but a person must come to the point where God has said to them, "Be baptised" – the point at which they feel, "If I do not get baptised I am going to be disobedient to my Lord and I will sin by not doing so." So Jesus realised the moment had come. The second thing I want to say by way of introduction is this: it was his choice but it was not his need. If ever there was a person who could excuse himself from the rite of baptism it was our Lord Jesus Christ. If ever there was anyone who could have said, "I have a reason for not being baptised" it was he, because the reason for baptism is to wash away your past; to get rid of your sin; to finish with it; to make a clean break, and the one person who had no need of that was our Lord Jesus, which raises a very difficult question: why should he be baptised? What was in his mind and heart when he came to the Jordan and said to his own cousin, John the Baptist, "Take me into the water." First, of course, John said: No, you should be baptising me. Which reveals the rather disturbing fact that the first baptist was not baptised. That is quite a thought, but John said, "You should be baptising me." Someone had to start it, after all.

Jesus said, "No, you baptise me." Why? I'm going to have to speculate a bit because I have got no direct scripture for what I am going to say, except one, but I am going to give you four possible reasons. As I have thought about the mind and heart of Jesus I can see four possible motives for his baptism. First: the motive of *association with John*. John had begun something and Jesus was to continue it. John had been preparing for Jesus to come, and therefore in this way Jesus was saying: I link on to John. I'm following John. I'm coming after him. This was a lovely way of identifying with John and associating himself with John's ministry, but why did he have to do it by being baptised? He could have just gone there and preached and told the crowds: "I'm following on this man's work." Why be baptised? I don't think this is enough.

A second possible reason is that for Jesus baptism marked a separation from Nazareth. It is true to say that from his baptism onwards he had made a break with his past, and this is the meaning of baptism. He had left Nazareth. He had left his family circle. When his family came chasing after him a few months later because they thought he had gone off his head, and he was told, "Your mother and your brothers and sisters are outside," he said, "Who is my mother? And who are my brothers? And who are my sisters?" That must really have confirmed their suspicions. Had he forgotten all about them? No, he hadn't. He went on to say, "Who is my mother? Whoever does the will of my Father is my mother, my brother, my sister."

He didn't make a break at the age of twelve. He went back to Nazareth and was subject to them, but now he had made a clean break, and now for him the life at Nazareth in a family and in a shop was finished. Maybe baptism expressed for him, as it does for us, a break with the kind of life we have lived and a new kind of life coming on, a life that is going to be ordered by the Lord totally, and not subject to other necessities.

Luke 3

But I don't think I have hit the real reason yet. A third possible reason is that it was to be an inspiration to his disciples. To those who are going to be baptised, I can say: you are not only obeying a command of Christ, you are following an example; you are doing something he did, and in a sense, if he would be baptised for you, is it too much to ask that you be baptised for him? What an example he showed us. In fact, recorded in Matthew's Gospel, when John said, "You shouldn't be baptised!" Jesus said, "Yes, let me be baptised. It is right for us to do what is right." In other words, whether he needed it or not, he did it because it was right to do it. God the Father had commanded it and Jesus was one to be obedient. So maybe he did it as an inspiration to his disciples.

But, fourthly, I believe he did it as an *identification with sinners*. I believe this is the deepest note in his baptism: he wanted to be treated just like you, and therefore in your baptism you are being treated just like him.

Luke's account of Jesus' baptism misses a great deal out, but there are two aspects of it that I want to mention here: the heavenly blessing that came after his baptism; and the earthly background that came before his baptism. I am taking them in that order because Luke does. Of course Jesus was unique. Of course his baptism would be different, and yet the very different features of his baptism all point to something that can be associated with ours. After he came out of the water, Jesus went on praying. The reason was he didn't just want water baptism – he wanted far more than that so he went on praying.

Luke mentions our Lord praying on nine separate occasions and this is one of them. He went on praying, seeking more. So he got three things more. The first thing he got was an anointing. Six hundred years earlier, Isaiah had said: "Oh that you would rend the heavens and come down." On the day of our Lord's baptism that is precisely what happened. I think it must have been a wintry, cloudy overcast day, and after Jesus' baptism, as he stood praying, the heavens opened. I can only assume that phrase means the clouds parted and they saw through to a lovely deep blue sky, right up there with the sun shining. The heavens opened, and John, and maybe others who were there, looked up. John saw a little white fluttering thing right up in the sky. He thought, "There's a bird," and it came down, got larger. "Funny, I thought it was a dove but it doesn't quite look like a dove." Down it came and just alighted on Jesus. In our previous house we used to keep white doves. It was lovely to go out into the garden and see them wheeling in the sky and have them come fluttering down and land on your shoulders or on your head, and nibble your ear. There is something about a dove that is beautiful, lovely, so white. Having it coming and landing on you does something. I often thought of Jesus' baptism when those doves used to come down and land on our shoulders.

What looked like a dove came down – in fact this was the Holy Spirit. This was one of those rare occasions when the Holy Spirit became visible and materialised. Normally he is like the wind – you can feel him, you know when he is blowing, you know when you are being moved by him but you can't see him, yet this time he could be seen. Jesus had received the equipping that he needed to do all his work now, because even Jesus himself couldn't do his work without the Holy Spirit's power. He had been praying, and he went on praying, and years later he was to say, "How much more will your heavenly Father give Holy Spirit to those who go on asking him." He had proved the truth of it before he said it; he went on asking after his baptism until the Holy Spirit came.

Jesus came back to Nazareth not long afterwards, and it

is very interesting that when he went to the synagogue they asked him to preach. They never asked that before, and he got up and read his text from Isaiah to this effect: "The Spirit of the Lord is upon me because he has chosen me to preach the good news to the poor; sent me to proclaim liberty to the captive, recovery of sight to the blind, to set free the oppressed, and announce the year when the Lord will save his people." That was his text, and his sermon was one sentence long – the shortest sermon ever, I guess: "This passage of scripture has come true today as you heard it being read." What a sermon! Now he could preach, now he could perform miracles, now he could begin his earthly ministry.

You can receive the Holy Spirit, that is the glory of this. You can be equipped for service. You can be given an anointing from above – go on praying for it.

The second blessing Jesus got was an assurance: "You are my beloved Son; my dear Son." Now of course he knew that; he had known it at the age of twelve, but God graciously gives us reassurance, and how we need it in this life of ours. We need it again, and again.

The people standing around thought it was a thunderstorm – God's voice is pretty loud when he speaks. The word means: my special Son; my only begotten Son. Jesus had reassurance and the devil was going to attack that reassurance, saying: "If you are the Son of God prove it by turning these stones into bread." The devil will rob you of your assurance if he possibly can, but God will give you reassurance. God wants you to be sure that you are his child; he doesn't want you to be in any doubt about that. How does he give his assurance to us today? By a clap of thunder? No. Very often it is as we cry "Abba Father" – his Spirit is bearing witness with our spirit that we are the children of God.

The third blessing he got after his baptism was an *approval*. "I'm pleased with you." The actual word is "delighted" – "I'm delighted with you." The verb is in a peculiar tense which is timeless, meaning, "I'm always pleased with you." It's not just, "I'm pleased with you for being baptised." From way back in all eternity, God the Father has always been pleased with his Son. When Jesus was born at Bethlehem by his own choice, at his baptism, and as he grew up – mentally, socially, spiritually maturing – the Father was pleased with Jesus.

I'm afraid I have to say that the very fact that we come to baptism means that God has not been pleased with us. We wouldn't have anything to wash away if he had been pleased with us from the beginning, but he is pleased with you getting baptised.

The Father approved the Son by anointing him with the Spirit; the whole Trinity attended that baptism, and the whole Trinity attends every baptism.

We now turn to the genealogy in this chapter. I prefer the term "family tree". It comes as an awful shock to read that Luke put our Lord's family tree in connection with his baptism. Why did he not do it where Matthew did it – at his birth, far more appropriately we would think? Surely that is when your family tree is important, isn't it? Why are all these endless names put here in connection with his baptism? I puzzled and shook my head over this one for some time, but I am going to give you an answer which I believe to be appropriate, and you see what you think about it.

First, let me look at the family tree and notice one or two things about it in itself. Those who have read Matthew's family tree for Jesus, and then Luke's, have been struck by the fact that they don't correspond. There are differences between them. At least, it is all right between Abraham and David, but between David and Joseph they travel two different paths and people say, "Well now, here's a contradiction." I have seen this used by sceptics in a book

Luke 3

by the British Rational Association on biblical (so-called) "contradictions".

Well there are three possible explanations for it, all of which would explain the situation, and I am not sure which is the right one. If you are interested, here they are. One is that Joseph had in fact two collateral lines back to David, one of which contained royal blood and the other brought in priestly blood. You can trace your lineage back two ways if there has been intermarriage at a later stage.

That is one possible explanation, but I don't think it is the real one. A second concerns Levirate marriage. If a wife became a widow without children and her brother-in-law was free to marry her in place of the brother who had been her husband, he then married her and she brought up children with the name of the first husband. In other words, the brother brought up a son and heir for his dead brother. It is a bit complicated, but it means that one woman could have two family trees.

If this was so, then Joseph's mother must have been a widow and married the brother-in-law and kept both lines. That would explain the difference. But there is a third possibility, and to my mind it is the most likely explanation. This is that Matthew gives Joseph's family tree and Luke gives Mary's, and Heli was Mary's father, in which case the phrase "being the supposed son of Joseph" is a parenthesis and Jesus is referred to as the son of Heli. The words "son of" of course, in the Bible means, "grandson of" or "great grandson of". It means "descendant of". So that here, what would be the point of Luke telling us Joseph's family tree if he had just said, "Joseph wasn't his father" – no point at all. So if Luke is giving Mary's family tree here, as Matthew gives Joseph's, then we are saying that both legally and physically Jesus had a double claim to the throne of David; twice as good a claim as anybody else.

Let me now move straight on to the names that are included. Have you ever thought of digging up your family tree? My advice is don't. You never know what you will dig up. I received a letter from an elderly lady in Cornwall called Pawson, who has made a hobby of doing this, and she got us back to the fifteenth century – to a Richard Pawson way back then. It was a bit shattering when she described the characteristics of the Pawsons. There I was, just one of them, no question about it: fair hair, blue eyes, easily sunburned skin, and various other things about our temperament, which we needn't go into! She just described it, so I am a product of my heredity. I know I have a bit of Spanish blood in me and that may go a long way to explaining a number of things.

There was an American who came back to England, having used his savings to come and see his birthplace. There it was on the certificate: 1, Southall Street, Manchester. If you know Manchester you will know what he found. He found the jail. His mother had been a prisoner when he was born and he hadn't had any idea. He had saved up all his money to find that out. Don't dig up your family tree!

But the Jews used to keep their family tree very carefully, especially if they had a claim either to be a priest or a prince. They had to go right back through the priestly tribe if they were to be a priest, and they had to claim to be descended from royalty if they were to claim the throne. So Joseph and Mary both preserved their genealogical information carefully.

What a family tree it is! There are the names Zerubbabel and Shealtiel, those great figures who rebuilt the temple after the exile and led the people of Israel; and you go back through the names. Matthew's is even more fascinating— there are two women listed in the genealogy of our Lord who were Gentiles and one was a prostitute. Our Lord had a mixed family tree. Praise God for that. Go back through this list: there is David, and his great grandfather Boaz who married Ruth, the Gentile, the Moabitess. These names leap out. History is being written in his family tree, and you go back and you come to Abraham, Isaac and Jacob; and God was the God who identified himself with those three men. "I am the God of Abraham, Isaac, and Jacob."

When you get to Abraham, Matthew stops. That is as far back as he goes because he presented Jesus as the King of the Jews, but Luke goes further back. There is Noah who built that ark and saved his family and the animals. Noah was an ancestor of Jesus. There is Methuselah, that elderly man whose name meant, "When he dies it shall happen" – and he died in the very year of the Flood. Methuselah was kept alive as a kind of barometer of God's history. You go back and you come to Enoch, that wonderful man of God who went for a walk with God one day and never came back; he just stepped right into glory. These were our Lord's ancestors, and you go back to Adam. Do you notice how Adam is described: "son of God"? I am getting fed up with people who will write our family tree and get back to Adam and say, "son of Adam, son of Cheetah the chimpanzee", as if our Lord Jesus Christ came from the slime through the monkeys.

Adam was a creation of God. Man did not come from animals, he came from God. It was God who made Adam, son of God. Do you realise that is the second time that phrase has been used in this study? "You are my beloved Son" – that is a vertical line. Go back along the horizontal and you come to, "Adam, son of God", but how different these two sons of God were. One was obedient; one was disobedient. One pleased his Father enormously; the other was not pleasing in his sight. This is the contrast that I want to draw, because now I want to tell you why I believe that Luke put this family tree in connection with our Lord's baptism. I will put it this way and then explain what I mean: baptism is the crossover point between the two lines that have brought you to this time and place; between the heavenly vertical line which stretches from the highest throne of heaven down to this time and place, and the earthly line which stretches back to the dust of the earth.

It is extremely important to realise that we owe to both lines what we are at this point. The lines of space stretching up to heaven, and time stretching back through the centuries, cross. You see, with Jesus there were two threads. There was not only the heavenly blessing of the dove coming down and the assurance and the approval of his Father. There was the earthly line that had led him to this point.

Don't underestimate the human line. Every one of us has a family tree going back to Adam. So that is why Luke, I believe, shows the family tree of Jesus, and all the heritage of the Old Testament that was now becoming meaningful. The final thing I want to say in closing is this: all your heritage, and all your background, and all your breeding, and anything else, and all your temperament, and all your natural talents, mean nothing as a horizontal line until the divine line has met it. It is just a family tree otherwise, just a list in Somerset House, but when the divine meets the human, and when the heavenly meets the earthly, and the whole is caught up in a baptism, which is something God is doing as well as something you do, it is not just a human act of witness, it is a divine act of assurance, and the two meet.

If you don't yet know Christ: I don't care what your background is; I don't care what you can point to in your family tree; I don't care what talents you have inherited. Until God is pleased with you these are not meaningful, they are not significant, they cannot be used for eternal purposes, but when the divine and the human meet, all that has led you to that point becomes God's preparation for all that is going to follow.

4

Read Luke 4

4:1-13

"Then Jesus returned to Galilee and the power of the Holy Spirit was with him." The first event in the ministry of Jesus was the most private. Humanly speaking, it happened when he was all alone, which means that he must have told people later what happened. He must have shared this very deep experience with his disciples for their encouragement. For the first thing I want to say about the passage is this: *temptation is not sin*. Our Lord, in telling us that he was tempted, is making it quite clear that you can live a perfect, holy life and still be tempted. It is one of the things that will happen to you however far you progress in the Christian life. Until you are in your grave, you can expect to be tempted by the devil.

We are going to ask what we can learn from our Lord's bitter experience here, right at the beginning of his ministry; before ever he preached to the crowds and before ever he performed a miracle, he had to fight and win a private battle. He was now baptised, he was now full of the Holy Spirit, and I want you to notice that it was the Holy Spirit who led him into the place of testing, of temptation. When you say the Lord's Prayer you ask, "Lead us not into temptation," and people have said to me, "But surely, God the Father wouldn't lead us into temptation." Yes he would, and he did with the Lord Jesus. The Holy Spirit led him right into that place where he was going to be exposed to all the attacks of evil. He was led into that barren strip of territory about thirty miles long and some ten to fifteen miles wide, that is on the eastern slope of the Judean hills as they go down to that deep rift valley in which lies the river Jordan and the Dead Sea. It is a rain shadow – there are no showers here, so there are no trees, no grass, and there are deep rocky ravines and wild beasts. The hyenas laugh at night, and there, in the middle of that dreadful place, Jesus stood alone and yet not alone.

Notice by way of preliminary observation three things about this temptation: first, *the moment when it occurred* because that will tell you when to expect the devil to attack. The devil does not stay with you. Indeed, one of the things I want to make clear is that the devil, not being God, cannot be in more than one place at once. Some Christians talk to me as if the devil lives with them. If so, they are jolly important people because while he is with them he can't be with anyone else. We must get this quite clear: the devil is not God, and like any other angel, whether good or bad, he can only be in one place at a time – but he was in this place.

When are you likely to encounter the devil, or what is probably a much more common experience, one of his agents? In his book *The Screwtape Letters*, C. S. Lewis has this fundamental insight: that the devil stays in his office, and sends his agents to do his work, and they report back to him, and what we often call "the devil" may be no more than one of his minor agents sent to you. But here it was the devil himself. When did he attack Jesus? Because this is a clue to the moments when he will attack you. He attacked Jesus after a high moment of spiritual experience. Jesus had been baptised and it had been a great baptism. The Holy Spirit had come down, the heavens had been opened, there was a voice like thunder, and very shortly afterwards the devil came.

If you have a blessing today, I can tell you this: the devil will try in some way to arrange that you lose the blessing soon. If you have had a great time, expect trouble. If you have had a high moment of assurance so that you know you are a child of God, then expect the devil to say, "If you are a son of God..." and to cast doubts almost immediately on what you have been assured of in the Lord. Another thing is that this temptation came to our Lord after an exhausting period, after six weeks without food and in the extreme heat of the daytime and cold of the night. It is often when you are exhausted that temptation can come with greater force. The devil loves to hit someone when they are down. When you are tired, even just physically tired, when your body is crying out for refreshment, it is then that you need to be on your guard.

Let us look at the method that Jesus used to deal with temptation, because you can learn a lot from this. Do you notice that Jesus used certain weapons? He used the scriptures, and in fact, if you want to deal with the devil, do throw the book at him – literally. Martin Luther used to throw his inkpot at him, but the Bible is heavier, spiritually and in other ways. Jesus, the Son of God, who knew the Father so intimately, used the weapon of quoting the Word of God – taking a piece of truth and throwing it at the liar, for the devil is a liar, and this is one of the best ways you can use. Notice that it was the Old Testament that Jesus threw, and it was the book of Deuteronomy. If you want to be able to deal with Satan, do get to know Deuteronomy. What a book to deal with temptation! You try it. Read it through in the next week or two. Another secret of Jesus, in the method he used to combat the tempter, was to use the *power* of the Holy Spirit. He was full of scripture and full of the Holy Spirit. The two together enabled him to be invincible, even though the attacks of Satan were very deep and cutting. There are Christians who know the scriptures well, who can quote the text well, and have got the Word stored up in their heart, but who lack the fullness of the Spirit, and they lack the power that is needed to draw from that word the right weapon – for the belt of truth is the Bible, but the sword of the Spirit is that which the Spirit draws from it for the particular occasion of your battle. Therefore, we need the Spirit.

So there are those who are full of the Spirit, but who are not feeding on solid teaching from God's scripture, and they too will lack a vital dimension when the devil comes. But those who are full of scripture and full of Spirit are more than a match for Satan.

The third thing that we want to look at is the *meaning* of these temptations. Here I want to correct, if I may, a lot of misunderstanding. There are those who approach the three temptations of Jesus as though Jesus were sorting out his motives; as if he was primarily concerned with why he was going to do things in his ministry. If we approach the temptations with these spectacles on, we will say that he was being tempted to food without work, power without responsibility, and excitement without risk. Certainly those are three temptations that *we* are all prone to, but I don't believe that is the basic meaning of the temptations.

The second approach, which is more common and taught quite widely, is that Jesus was not thinking through his motives concerned with himself, so much as his methods concerned with others, and how he was going to do his ministry – that he is there in the desert, thinking out possible ways of doing it, and that his temptations come through this. According to this approach, the temptations are interpreted like this: that he was being tempted to use the material rather than the spiritual approach – bread rather than preaching; that he was being tempted to use evil means for a good end, or that he was being tempted to offer sensational proof to make people believe.

I still don't think that is the meaning of the temptations, for

Luke 4

both these approaches make one fundamental mistake which is that they are approaching the temptations through the mind of Jesus, but you will never understand a temptation until you approach it through understanding the mind of Satan. The question is not, "What was Jesus hoping to achieve?" but, "What was Satan hoping to achieve?" Then you will understand the temptations. We have got to see what the enemy was trying to do when he tempted our Lord. It is not so much Jesus thinking the thing through, it is Satan trying to think it through, and trying to gain an advantage.

Now for a few more preliminary comments. First: we are dealing here with real things, not imaginary ones. We are dealing with real places. I used to have the idea when I read this story as a child that it all happened in the mind, that it was a kind of series of pictures in Jesus' imagination, but when I went to the Holy Land I stopped thinking like that. I saw the places and they are real. That wilderness is so real, and in one part of it there is a special stone which the Arabs call bread stone, which just looks like crumbled bits of bread lying on the desert floor. A hungry man would see that almost as a mirage.

It is all real, and that pinnacle of the temple was real too. It towered ninety feet up, and from there you surveyed the whole area of the temple, with people like little ants running around in the courtyard. And that mountain is real – way above Jericho they still point to the traditional mountain. I daresay it is the real one, and in Jesus' day from the peak of that mountain you could see ten different kingdoms. I for one have no doubt that was the mountain that Jesus climbed up, looked out over those kingdoms and saw in them a microcosm of the kingdoms of all time and space.

We know we are dealing with reality because Jesus was a real person, but let me tell you that the devil is real, not a figment of the imagination. If you don't believe in a personal devil I honestly wonder how much experience you have of a personal God. The devil is not a little imp but a very intelligent being, far more powerful than I am, far more intelligent than any of us. He knows how to twist you around his little finger. You will never beat him on your own. The angels are real too. I have said that Jesus was alone, but he wasn't. It was quite crowded in the wilderness when he was tempted. There were wild beasts, there were angels, there was the devil, and there was the Holy Spirit.

So that is the first key to unlock what happened: this is not imagination and not picture language, it is reality. The second important key is this: to realise that Luke's Gospel is only a tiny bit of the Bible, and whenever you want to understand one part of the Bible, the best thing to do is to look at all the other parts of the Bible. The Bible is a self-interpreting book: one passage unlocks another. What other passages in the Bible would help us to understand the temptations of Jesus in the wilderness? I give you three. Firstly, John the Baptist went to school in the wilderness, that is where he learned. Now for six whole weeks the wilderness is to be the school in which Jesus learns something absolutely vital to fulfilling his mission: he learns obedience by what he suffers. The wilderness is a school. When you are going through the wilderness, God has sent you to school. When you are going through a dry patch, when you are going through an area that seems to have nothing attractive about it, remember that God has sent you to school. He wants you to learn something, and that is the first clue.

Let us look further back into the Old Testament. God sent the people of Israel to the wilderness for forty years. Why? To send them to school and to teach them things that would prepare them for a promised land. The wilderness was their school: the Sinai desert. That Sinai peninsula was their school, and the book of Deuteronomy contains the lessons they learned in an account of their schooldays. This is why Jesus, to beat the devil in the wilderness school in which he was now learning, went back to the old school textbook of Deuteronomy. He quoted the very lessons that Israel had to learn when they were hungry in the wilderness, and they lacked bread, and had to be told that there were more important things than bread – one of the hardest lessons we have got to learn.

The third passage of the Bible that helps me to understand this one is Genesis 3 – Adam and Eve in the garden. There is a clear link here. The devil sought to rob them of paradise, and by disobedience he achieved it – but you notice that the devil did it by offering food. When the second Adam to the fight and to the rescue came, the devil tried exactly the same tactic. He is not terribly original you know, and we are not ignorant of his devices: he started with food again, and tried to rob our Lord Jesus of his paradise and his obedience. So we are going to use the rest of the Bible to understand this passage.

Another key is that we must understand that these are the temptations that came to the Son of God.. Have you been tempted to turn stones into bread? Why not? Because you are not the Son of God.

We need to remember that Jesus' sayings are simply replies to what the devil thought up. These thoughts did not come from Jesus because Jesus was good, he was perfectly developing in his relationship to God and man, and therefore these evil thoughts had to come from someone else. Alas, I can be tempted from my own imagination, because it is not developed perfectly as Jesus' was. Therefore, these wrong thoughts had to come from outside and come inside, whereas for me they can often come from inside, and I mustn't blame the devil for what has come from me. We sometimes do blame him for things for which he had no responsibility.

Consider a man who forgets to set his alarm, he gets up late, he's in a bad temper, he argues with his wife about the way the breakfast is done, and he goes out to town in a foul mood, and he gets to the station and misses the train, and when he does get to the office he is in such a bad mood he tears a strip off a junior colleague, and he goes on all day. He comes to a fellowship meeting at night and says to a fellow Christian, "Oh, the devil had a good go at me today." The devil probably had nothing to do with it. He forgot to set his alarm and everything else followed from that. The irritability and all the rest came out of his own flesh. But that could not happen with Jesus – the evil thoughts had to come from outside him.

So if we are going to understand the temptations let us start with the mind of the devil and approach it through his evil imaginations. Think first of the first temptation. The devil is taunting him as well as tempting him. I don't know how long you have ever been without food. Do you fast? The Bible assumes you do from time to time, but I daresay you have never fasted for six weeks. We don't have to. We have plenty of food in this country. Jesus was without food for six weeks not by his choice, but by the Father's choice because he had told him to go somewhere there were no food shops, and where there wasn't even grass to eat. Jesus had been without anything to eat for a month and a half. There are a few streams running through that wilderness and so it obviously slaked his thirst – but bread? None.

So his body was crying out for something to eat, and the devil said: If you are the Son of God you can do anything; you can take stones and turn them into bread. Of course God can. The amazing thing is that a few weeks later, at a wedding reception, Jesus was going to turn water into wine. Why was it wrong to do such a miracle at this moment? The reason is very simple. The Father was going to teach his Son Jesus a most important lesson: no matter what need your body is crying out for, his will must be done first.

Now, you see, it is not much of a temptation to me to steal. I don't know why it is that wealthy people are caught so often shoplifting – people who don't need to walk out of the shop with something they haven't paid for. I am not tempted to do that in this affluent society, but supposing my three children had not had anything to eat for months, and I went round a supermarket and noticed there was nobody looking, and there was some food, what would come first – God's commandment, "You shall not steal?" or my family's empty bellies? That is the kind of situation that is terribly poignant, and we don't know what this pull is. We have not been in situations where we are as desperate as this, but Christ was desperately hungry, and the Father was testing him: Will you remain obedient to me even though your body is crying out for a little bit of bread? Will you put your principles before your appetite? Jesus was right up against this. If he had not fought and won the battle, then, three years later, when his body was crying out in agony to be free from the nails, do you realise he would have stepped off the cross? Because he could have done that easily. If Jesus had once allowed physical desire to have priority over the Word of God then he could not have stood the cross. It was only possible three years later because he had already fought and won this battle, but when the body is crying out for some relief – if God has told you to do something – you remain obedient.

So we know what the devil was trying to do. He was trying to break this, and therefore Jesus went right back to the experience of Israel in the wilderness when they were hungry and without food. God had said, "You leave Egypt and go to the promised land," and they were hungry and without food, and God had allowed the hunger to see if Israel would put obedience first and keep right on. But no, they talked about the onions, the garlic and all the tasty stew that they used to have in Egypt, and their bodily desires were pulling them back from God's will. We are physical creatures, our physical needs are sometimes so overpowering, but God says, "Will you remain obedient to me when your body is crying out for some relief? Would you still do my will?" You have to learn that, and there is only one way to learn it, and that is to be put into a situation where your body is needing something and God has said "Do that." Jesus had been led into the wilderness deliberately to put him away from food, to teach him through hunger that man does not live by bread alone.

However much bread you give anyone, he is going to die. Even though we have enough food to eat, we are all going to die. You can't live by bread alone. You can keep your metabolic rate going by bread alone, but you can't live – for that is not life, it is just existence. I pity and feel deeply for some poor people who are just living for just one thing: to keep body and soul together, just scraping to keep going.

Jesus knew that God the Father was testing him, and that obedience was more important than a square meal. What a battle – and he won it.

Let us look at the second temptation mentioned here. From the pull on the flesh, on the body, Satan now turns to a more subtle one: the pull of the world or of power. Here is the pull of wealth, the subtle pull that comes to us when the devil offers us this world and he says, "It's mine to give you." I am afraid that is true. The devil is claiming that he could give Jesus power and wealth, and he could, and he can give you power and wealth. If you want power and wealth, don't come to Jesus, he never offered it. Go to the devil, he will give it to you on his own terms, and they are terrible terms. So in the second temptation Jesus is being shown all that he wanted, and this was why it was such an awful temptation. Jesus had come from heaven to have all the kingdoms of the world. The Bible says that this is what he had come to do. The devil said, "I can give them to you if you will just bow down and let me boss you."

It was a bargain, it was Christ being offered the post of antichrist, and one day the devil will offer to a human being all the kingdoms of this world. The Bible predicts such a world dictator before the end of human history, and the devil will offer it to that man, and that man will get it by devilish means. He will be in the grip of Satan and that is the way Satan is increasingly going to control this world. At the moment Satan controls so much of it, but not on a world scale because there is no world government. Satan's ambition is to have one world government ruled by a one world dictator who is himself ruled by Satan, and in this way he will have totalitarian control over every member of the human race. Satan said, "Look, I'll give you everything on earth." What a temptation!

The tragedy is that on a much lesser scale the devil has said to some of his agents: "Go to that businessman and tell him, 'You can have the biggest business in this line in England if you'll do it my way. You can have that rise if you'll compromise my way. You can have this promotion if you won't let on that you belong to me, and if you don't let on that you have principles, you can have it!'" The devil can offer it to anyone, and we are led along – the power and the wealth that this world offers is something that our flesh desires. Jesus wanted all the kingdoms of the world, but he only wanted them to give them back to the Father. There is only one person that you are to bow down to.

I don't know if the day will come in this country when it will be as it was in Ancient Greece, where business was so tied up with pagan religion that you couldn't open a shop without bowing down to pagan idols; you couldn't join the

A COMMENTARY ON THE GOSPEL OF LUKE

Chamber of Commerce unless you did this. To be quite specific here is an illustration: freemasonry, with some of the rites and religious implications of that. I was once told by a senior man in freemasonry, "Why don't you join us? I could get you in, there are many ministers in, and it will help you on. You'll get the best churches, you'll get promotion, you'll get help, and you'll always have friends wherever you go. It's a great thing to be." He pressed me as a young minister to become a freemason, but I knew enough about the religious rites to say, "I can't bow down to that." You see, the tragedy is that if you are willing to compromise, if you are willing to go along a bit with things that are not Christian, you will get on. You will be helped. You will go up the ladder, but who wants to go up it without Jesus Christ? Who wants to go up it without God? Because if Jesus had got all the kingdoms of the world and the devil had given him this power and wealth, do you know that he would have lost it when he died? No matter what power or wealth you get in this world, if you get it Satan's way you will lose it very quickly. Two people were discussing a wealthy man who died and one said, "How much did he leave?" The other said, "Everything." All the human power you can gain just goes like that. It can end with a bullet or a germ, or just being born too soon – it has all gone. Jesus would not bow down to Satan and he would not dabble in anything of Satan's – and he came through victorious. The result was that later, when the devil came back, Jesus was able to deal with him. When the devil came through Simon Peter and offered Jesus victory without a cross, Jesus said, "Get behind me, Satan."

The third temptation is to appeal through popularity. The temple was not far from the wilderness – twenty minutes' walk would have got him there. The temple is now gone but you can still see the stone platform on which it stood, and if you stand on that platform, you look forty-five feet down to the Kidron Valley. On top of that platform there were the towering porches of Solomon's gateway and pinnacles on top of that, and every morning a priest used to climb up the tower to the very top of the pinnacle so that he was the first to see the sun rising over the Moab Hills to the east. He would then call down to the courtyard and they would offer the morning sacrifice.

Jesus climbed that pinnacle, and he stood at the top and the devil stood there too: Jesus, you know if you jumped off there when the crowds are looking up, and you just floated down, you would have them all in the hollow of your hand. Give them the proof they are looking for, give them sensationalism; give them something that will get them talking for months – the greatest publicity gimmick there has ever been. The devil was offering to be our Lord's PR man. Can you see this? Even more, do you notice that he used the scriptures? Oh, how subtle he is. Do you know the devil has studied them? He knows them very well and he can always quote out of context. If you study the text he quoted at this point, he missed out the most vital phrase that told us that in fact the promise of God – to protect his children and bear them up lest they dash their foot against a stone – would only apply if they were in line with God's will at the time. How important that is. In fact, if I took this text, I could just go to Beachy Head and walk straight off the cliff and say, "See you down at the bottom, we'll sing a chorus" – but I tell you it would not work. That is not because of any scientific law that states that gravity must always operate. It doesn't always operate – man can walk on water, but because I would not be in line with God's will to do it. The devil was using this text to say to Jesus: Give them what they want. Get the popularity; start with a great crowd that are hanging on every word; do an almighty conjuring trick."

There are still people who want to see miracles for this reason and this only. They say, "Go on, you perform a miracle and I'll believe." Don't you believe it – if a miracle was performed in front of their eyes they would say, "He had something up his sleeve." They would look for an alternative explanation and they would not be convinced. Do you know what would have happened if Jesus would have thrown himself down? They would have scraped his body off the paving stones of that courtyard. The promise would not have held because it was not in the Lord's will and Jesus would have been buried that day.

Now we are getting very near to answering the question "What was the devil trying to achieve?" Two things: our Lord's disobedience and therefore our Lord's destruction. King Herod, at Jesus' birth thought: I'm the King of the Jews; there's no room for two of us in this nation. When Jesus arrived and was baptised and began his ministry the devil realised, "There's no room for both of us." And there isn't – there isn't room for both in your heart. You cannot follow the devil and Jesus at the same time, and the devil knew that here at last was the one who would open the prison doors; the one who would set his victims free; the one who would open the kingdom of heaven to all believers. The devil knew that his days were numbered; that he was going to lose his power, that he was going to lose his kingdoms, and the his reaction was the same as Herod's: how can I get rid of this man?

Herod had tried it by killing every baby boy under two years old; the devil was more subtle. The devil knew that if Jesus disobeyed his Father, he would destroy himself. For that is what you do – that is what I do if I disobey my God in heaven – I kill myself, either quickly or slowly. "Whatever a man sows that shall he also reap. If he sows to the flesh, he will reap death," and it is written right through the scripture.

Do you know that the devil was trying to kill Jesus before he got to the cross and died on it? That is what he was after – he was trying to destroy him one way or another and bring him under the curse of God. Jesus was the very first person ever to be able to say no to the devil. Whether it was the power of the devil, the pleasure of the flesh, or the popularity of the world, Jesus said no.

The devil is so subtle, so powerful. His one aim is to destroy you, and he will do it by your disobedience. He does not bother with those who are not Christians. Why should he? They are no threat to him, they do not bother him, but the day you become a Christian, that day you are on his lists. You have got your name into two books. One is the Lamb's Book of Life, and the other is Satan's register. He will seek to do everything he can to drive a wedge between you and your heavenly Father. He will appeal through the needs of your body, he will appeal through the opinions of society around you, he will appeal to you through those incentives of power and wealth and all the glitter of a world that is fast passing away, and you will not be able to say no yourself, but if you call on the name of Jesus you can be sure that the devil will run. "Resist the devil and he will flee from you," and that is why we read, at the end of this temptation period, "The devil departed." Jesus left him.

As we noted earlier, the devil can't be in more than one place at a time. We sometimes talk of the devil as if he were divine, but he is not. He is only a fallen angel, a spirit being, but an angel can't be in more than one place at once. He is not omnipresent and he is not omnipotent. He doesn't have all power, even if he is stronger than we are. This means that the devil literally left Jesus at this point. He did not hang around. He came back some months later and I find that that is how his agents behave too. Temptation is not a constant in my life, and the devil is so subtle, he sends his agents to tempt me and then they go away again. They don't trouble me for quite some time until I have forgotten them, and then suddenly they are there again. Have you had that experience? You have had a big battle, and really been going through it, and the Lord brought you through it and you were victorious. Did the powers of evil go on trying? No, they just left you and you went on in victory, and you forgot all about it. Then, bang! That is why, for example, it says in the book of Job that God said to Satan one day in heaven, "Where have you been?" Satan said, "I've been going to and fro in the earth." You see? "I've been moving around." I wonder where Satan is right now. I wonder where he is concentrating his own personal interest. Like the evil supervisor that he is, he leaves it to his angels. He has one agent whose charge is Britain, another whose charge is America, another whose charge is Russia, another China, and he uses these princes of nations to go and do his evil will with the leaders of nations.

So he sends his agents, but where is he? If you ever have a personal encounter with the devil, you are meeting the man at the top as it were. It is a terrible encounter. I pray you never will. Jesus did on just four recorded occasions. The devil himself gave Jesus personal attention and Jesus said no.

I know that the enemy's forces are everywhere in our world. I do know that you will meet them. I do know that they have a personal programme to destroy you by getting you to disobey God, and I know that Jesus, who won that victory after the devil departed from him, came into Galilee full of the Holy Spirit. It is that personal, private victory you have against the forces of evil when you are alone that enables you to go into the public eye and there to have the victory for Jesus.

Luke 4:14-44
You cannot read this record of Jesus without realising that

Luke 4

it is an account of the supernatural. Many want to fit Jesus into a natural category and say that he was just a very gifted speaker and healer. But you can't do that with Jesus. The supernatural keeps bursting in, and this meeting of the natural and the supernatural is the key to understanding the whole narrative, and that begins at his birth. You can't understand the Christmas story if you rule out the supernatural element. There are angels to tell Mary that she is going to have a Son, that he is going to be the King of Israel; and angels in the sky singing "Glory to God in the highest!" That is all supernatural stuff. You don't naturally hear angels singing. This combination of the supernatural and the natural runs right through the Gospel.

The baptism and the temptations in the wilderness both have the mark of the supernatural on them. Many people get baptised and things don't happen as they did with Jesus. The first supernatural sign at his baptism was his Father's approval; and there came a mighty strong voice from the heavens, "This is my beloved Son in whom I am well pleased." Certainly there was a visible descent of the Holy Spirit on him. So here at his baptism, we have his Father approving and the Holy Spirit anointing him – that is the supernatural part. The human part is his cousin John baptising him in the Jordan. And then, immediately after that, the Holy Spirit led him into the desert to be tempted by the devil, and he has six weeks with no food, sorting out the methods that he was supposed to use from then on, and the methods he was not supposed to use which Satan suggested to him.

So now we have another supernatural dimension: Satan. If you don't believe in a personal devil, you will never understand what is happening, because there he is and he keeps coming back and leaving Jesus, and that is supernatural stuff. Furthermore, when the devil had stopped suggesting different methods for his mission, the good angels came and ministered to Jesus. No doubt they fed him and comforted him after the six weeks of nothing. Once again, if you don't believe in angels you will never make sense of the Bible because they run right the way through. Angels are created by God and they are above us and superior to us in so many ways. But they are divided into good angels and bad ones. There has been a rebellion against God not only on earth but in heaven, and it was led by Satan whose ambition it was to make this world his kingdom and he has led astray one third of the angels in heaven to work with him. They are what we call demons, the bad ones. They can inhabit a person and the results are horrific.

You can see how, from the very beginning, if you are going to study the life of Jesus you have to keep switching from the supernatural to the natural. Those who just see the natural – and there are plenty like that in our churches – see Jesus as a great teacher, a great healer, someone who did die for us on the cross, but the supernatural side has escaped them because, by and large, and I say this advisedly, the average church in this country never really encounters the supernatural. Natural gifts, yes. Supernatural gifts, no. I remember when the Holy Spirit began to work in our church in Chalfont St. Peter, and a dear old lady came to me and said, "I hope nothing supernatural is going to happen in our church." Considering why we go to church – to meet God Almighty – it was a priceless remark to make. I knew what she meant; she was scared of anything "spooky", and she associated that with the supernatural, though really it was a crazy comment to make.

Let us look at Nazareth, Jesus' home town. It is never easy to speak where you are known. You can be up against two things. There is familiarity, and "familiarity breeds contempt". Jesus was a man of habit, and he had the habit of going to the synagogue on the Sabbath – a good habit to have – and so he was attending a service in the synagogue in his home town where everybody knew him as the carpenter's son. Therefore they had known him for thirty years and he had not done anything striking except mend chairs and tables, and suddenly they are hearing that he is doing extraordinary things about ten miles away in Capernaum. So they are very interested to see him, and the leader of the synagogue says, "Would you read the scripture for us?" They handed over the big scroll of Isaiah. There is always a big cupboard with a veil over it in the synagogue and inside are the scrolls in Hebrew of the Old Testament. Jesus unrolled the scroll of Isaiah until he got to what we call chapter 61 and then he read the amazing promise that one day there would come to Israel a man who would liberate the oppressed, a man who would give sight to the blind, someone who would meet their dreams and would cause them all to come true. He read out the prediction. It is what we call a Messianic passage, which means it is one of those parts of the Old Testament that point forward to good new days that are coming and centre it on the Messiah. That word means "anointed" – anointed by the Holy Spirit – and therefore it also means "King", and it is the anointed King who is going to come and set them all free.

Now the word *anointed*. When the Queen was anointed with oil in the Coronation service, it was called the chrism, the Greek word for anointed. "Chrism" – "Christ". That is not Jesus' surname, it means King. Sometimes I have addressed him as "Your Majesty", and it is amazing what that does to you. People were looking forward to this King coming and they knew a few things about him. One was that he would be the "Son of David", who was the most popular king they had ever had. Jesus read that passage and then he sat down and said two things. He said, "Today this is now happening; you've lived to see this happen." They had waited for 600 years or more since Isaiah wrote this. Now he was saying: you don't need to wait any longer: I'm here! All your dreams are fulfilled because I am the person Isaiah was talking about. It is an amazing sort of announcement and it says they were not only amazed but the gracious words which he spoke really captivated them and every eye in the synagogue was fixed on him. Then it all went wrong; and he caused it to go wrong because, sitting in his seat in the synagogue, he could tell what they were thinking: let him do in Nazareth what he has done in Capernaum and we will believe. In other words, they were too familiar with him to believe that he was this magnificent miracle worker they heard about.

He knew what they were thinking. The proverb "physician, heal yourself" had been going through their minds. It must have shocked them that he read their minds so accurately. That proverb means: doctor, do it in front of us and then we will believe that you are the healer. Do your stuff here. And we are told in another Gospel that he didn't and that he couldn't – "because of their unbelief he did no mighty work there".

This is when things began to go a bit wrong, and it turned very nasty when he finished because he reminded them of their two favourite prophets, both of whom had been in the north – Elijah and Elisha – and he said neither of these were prophets in their own country. There were many widows short of food when Elijah stopped the rain for three and a half years. The widow whose food he gave miraculously so that her cruse of oil was always full of oil, and she always had the flour to mix and make bread – it was a sheer miracle, and she didn't belong to Israel, she lived in Sidon. So he said the great Elijah, your prophet, did not make a miracle for anyone except a poor widow in Sidon. Then he said there were many lepers in Israel in those days and Elisha didn't heal any of them; the only leper he healed was a man called

Luke 4

Naaman who belonged to Syria, and wasn't even an Israelite. So Jesus, I must say tactlessly, was virtually saying to them: I am not going to do any miracles for you. He backed it up by reference to Elijah and Elisha.

Nothing could have offended a Jewish audience more quickly than to point out that their two great prophets did their miracles for Gentiles outside Israel and virtually saying to them: so I am not going to do any here. A prophet is not without honour except in his own country, so, as far as what you have heard I am doing at Capernaum is concerned, I am not doing that here. This is my own country.

They were so indignant – they felt insulted; they had given him a good hearing, they had asked him to read the scriptures to them, he had expounded and said it is all about me, and I am here today and you have waited centuries for me to come. They had liked that very much, but when it came to doing something about it he had told them he was not doing any miracles, quoting the proverb back at them. That was an insult and they took it as that, and they were so angry about what he had said to them that they dragged him out of the synagogue. Nazareth is built on the edge of an escarpment at the bottom of which is the Plain of Megiddo and as a boy Jesus must have lain on the ridge at the top and watched passers-by. The local people now dragged him to that cliff, which you can still see today, and they were going to throw him off. At best, he would be injured for life. At worst, he would be dead. This is the first of five attempts on Jesus' life and it happened in the place where he was brought up and it happened with people who knew him – and there it was. But it was not the right time for him to die.. He knew he was going to die, but not in Nazareth. He knew it was going to be in Jerusalem. And so they had dragged him to the top of the cliff and were about to throw him down and he just quietly walked straight through them and went on his way. His presence must have paralysed them. It is an extraordinary account.

So his mission in Nazareth was a failure. They did not believe in him. He could do nothing good for them. They were too familiar with him and there it was. So Jesus escaped the first attempt on his life. Then he went back to Capernaum where he was very popular. Let me tell you the meaning of that place's name. "Caper" – nowadays "cupher" – means "village" and this is the village of Nahum, another prophet – 'caper-nahum', Capernaum, the village of another prophet. Here they really believed in him and he went into the synagogue, as his practice was on the Sabbath, and he preached. Unlike all the other preachers they had, he spoke with authority. What does that mean? It means he was very convincing. If you hear someone speak and say he is an authority on the subject, you mean he knows what he is talking about. That is what they meant, too. Jesus knew what he was talking about.

But there was more to it than that. When he spoke, he carried authority. In other words, they couldn't argue with him. It was just spoken. The interesting thing is they said he is so different from all the other preachers we get here. They don't speak with authority. They don't have firsthand knowledge of what they are talking about; they have got it out of books or in schools – they are scribes. All that they taught was secondhand knowledge of God, not firsthand. But they loved to hear this man because the tone of voice was so persuasive; he was compelling and he backed it up with action. Thus there were two aspects of Jesus' teaching – authority and power. It is because we so rarely have preachers who have got those two things that we go home and have the preacher for supper.

Jesus spoke with authority and power, and the power was visible in what he did when he preached, and here we

Luke 4

are up against demons – bad angels in heaven who rebelled against God's authority, and they are led by Satan, who is given many names in the Bible. They possess people and it does not happen by accident. It happens only to those who have been wrongly dabbling in things they should not be touching, and it does happen today. I have had to meet with demon-possessed people in some of my meetings.

In a meeting in Malven, for men only, there was a woman who came in dressed in black. She shrieked and said, "Why is this meeting forbidden to women? Who do you think you are?" And she went on and on. Fortunately, there were men in the meeting who knew what to do, and they cast the demon out of her. I received the most beautiful letter from her two or three days later, telling me how she got demon-possessed and how she came and shrieked at me in the meeting. It is a lovely letter. It had been really horrible to see her but she became a normal, friendly, quiet person.

In Australia, I remember another demon-possessed woman shouting at me at the end of the meeting. She had a man's voice and her twisted face was horrible to behold. She was there to do damage to what was going on. Or again, I was speaking at a youth camp in New Zealand on Christmas Day and we had 1500 young people including young Maoris from the streets – gangs. They were showing every sign of demon possession. We were meeting in a big barn, sitting on hay bales, with a straw-covered floor, and those young people were down on all fours growling like animals and eating the straw on the floor. It was pandemonium until some Christians decided to cast the demons out. I met a few of those young Maoris on the streets of the main city of New Zealand a week later, and they were transformed. Some of them had the letters H-A-T-E tattooed on their knuckles. One had OUTLAW tattooed round his neck. They had been really aggressive but now they were gentle, quiet – and in fact, I walked right past them because I didn't recognise them, and after I got a few yards further one of them said, "Are you not speaking to us?" And I turned back and asked, "Who are you?" It was the young man with OUTLAW round his neck, but now it had faded and he was now normal.

I hope you never meet a demon-possessed person because it is a horrible experience, but I am afraid our churches are not into the supernatural, so you don't see it often in this country.

Jesus always cast them out. Again, bear in mind they are fallen angels and therefore they are superior to human beings in strength. If it takes two or three men to control someone with mental illness, it can take up to ten to control a demoniac. One of the symptoms is that they have superior knowledge – the knowledge of angels. They began to taunt Jesus, saying, "Have you come to destroy us?" The simple answer is yes, he had come to deliver people from them. They then went on to say, "I know who you are, Jesus of Nazareth" and used the term "the holy one of God" – they knew he was human and divine! Later they would say, "We know you are the Christ" – showing their knowledge – and it was all true; every word they said about Jesus was true. They had all that knowledge when no human being had that knowledge. Jesus rebuked them and said, "Shut up; come out of him." And he did that because it was the wrong time and the wrong individuals. Jesus wanted human beings to realise who he was, and it would take three and a half years until Peter at last said, "I know who you are". But at this stage, in the beginning of his ministry, the demons knew who he was but nobody else did. The human beings welcomed him as a healer and as a deliverer from demonic possession, but they weren't welcoming him as the Son of God.

So that is why Jesus refused to let the demons speak, ordering them to shut up. That amazed the people. Who is

Luke 4

this man who can tell demons – order them – and they obey him? So that was another way in which Jesus spoke with authority and power. These demons were going to expose him too soon. That is why he shut them up and he exorcised them. It is interesting that later, when he sent out the disciples two by two to evangelise, he said: now you must show them the Kingdom and then tell them – authority and power. He said all you have got to do is go to a town, cleanse a leper, cure the sick, raise the dead and then you can tell them the Kingdom of God has come. Show and tell. Demonstrate, then declare. That was his pattern for evangelism.

The third section in this chapter continues the ministry in Capernaum, and Jesus is a guest of Simon the fisherman. Maybe that is one reason why he made Capernaum such a base. It was in fact the fishing base for the Sea of Galilee which is thirteen miles long and eight miles wide and full of fish, unlike the Dead Sea where there isn't a single fish. I have accompanied fishermen in Galilee at night when they go out to fish, and they hang a lantern over the stern of the ship which draws the fish who think it is the moon; and then they throw the net down and pull it back, and in a reasonable catch they might have eight or ten fish. Something very different from that is going to happen shortly. There was a problem. Simon's mother-in-law was sick (and I am afraid I am rather naughty, saying that means the first Pope was married). When Jesus came into a house, sickness had to leave. It happened again and again. So he healed her, and she immediately began to wait on him and serve a meal. It is interesting to note that the healing led straight to service.

Now let us leave the home and go out into the street where there are dozens of people sick and needing healing, and that requires explaining. Capernaum today is in ruins. There is nothing there except an empty shell of a synagogue and the remains of a few homes. Why was Capernaum so packed with sick people? The answer is that two miles south, along the west coast of Galilee, is a place called Tiberius, which to this day is packed with sick people, because in Tiberius there are hot springs springing from the depths of the earth and, like Harrogate or Bath, it has become a spa for sick people. There I have met Jews from all over the world who had come specifically all the way to Israel and to Tiberius to "take the waters", either by drinking or bathing in them. They are foul waters, full of sulphur – they smell, but they believe it heals, and here at the spa in Tiberius were hundreds of sick people, and they hear that up the coast in Capernaum there is someone who is healing and is successful every time. You can imagine the crowd rushing to Capernaum in the hope of being healed. That is why the street in any morning was packed with sick people. I like this: Jesus touched each one. There is a big crowd, the street was crammed, but Jesus didn't do any mass healing, he went to each one, touched him, and there was no failure, Jesus healed everyone. And once again, demons are on the scene.

Jesus didn't go looking for demons; they came looking for him. That is important because I am afraid there are some people looking for demons everywhere, even today. On this occasion they were shouting to get attention. "This is the Son of God," they shouted, and once again, Jesus wanted people to know that, but he did not want the demons to be the ones to tell. He was waiting until Simon Peter the fisherman would say: I know who you are. So with this demoniac man shouting at the top of his voice, Jesus silenced him because the demon knew he was the Christ, the coming King, the anointed one. Because he knew – and it was right, it was true – Jesus didn't want him advertising him.

The final section in this chapter I call: the privacy, popularity and priority of Jesus. First, the privacy. It was his habit at sunrise to get right away from the crowd, and to do this he had to leave Capernaum and go up into the hills by the town – to get away from the sick people, because if he had stayed in Capernaum that day he would have had to heal the sick the whole day. He wanted time with his Father and he had a need of those devotions. Jesus himself taught: when you want to talk to the Father, go somewhere private, go into your bedroom and shut the door. You need to be alone with God, and he knew that better than anybody else – to give the Father his whole attention, away from anything or anyone else. Secondly, he went to the Father alone to get direction about what he should be doing that day and where he should be going. We know, from the result of that private link with his Father, what his Father told him to do, and to anticipate it his Father said: I want you to stop healing people and I want you to get back to preaching because that is why I sent you there. Now Jesus could have had a successful mission for the rest of his life healing the sick, but he was convinced that all sickness is the work of the devil. My, how that is confirmed today. Our hospitals can't cope with the sick, they are full to bursting. Who is doing it all? Jesus' answer is that it is the work of the devil. It is Satan. This is a symptom of his control of this world. Having been tempted by Satan to do things the wrong way, he later said that you cannot spoil a strong man's goods unless you first bind the strong man. In other words, he had come to set Satan's victims free and therefore he had to deal with Satan first before he healed anybody. Before he delivered anybody from a demon he had to deal with him first, because he is the ruler of this world, the prince of this world; he controls this world. One of the ways he keeps control of us is through sickness, and Jesus could not deliver anybody from sickness until he had dealt with Satan. That is why the Spirit had led Jesus into the desert to be tempted by the devil before he was allowed to do anything else. Until his baptism and anointing with the

Spirit, he hadn't preached a single sermon, he hadn't healed a single sick person, he hadn't performed a single miracle. But as soon as he was baptised, and the Spirit anointed him, he was able to deal with Satan and set people free from him.

Now when the people followed him up into the hills, and found him all alone, it says they had one ambition: to keep him there, to keep him healing, and that was what they wanted. But Jesus said no, though he was terribly popular and though he could have had an amazing healing mission in Capernaum for years, because the sick were all coming there. But he had a different priority. His Father had told him not to go on healing but to go to other towns and preach the good news of the Kingdom.

What does it mean to preach the Kingdom of God? It is not just producing a sermon; he had orders from on high. He had asked the Father what he wanted him to do and he knew what that was: he was sent to preach the good news of the Kingdom of God. So he didn't stay in Capernaum, and he left a street full of sick people to get on with his priority which was to spread the good news of the Kingdom of God, which he did throughout the Jewish cities.

What is the good news about the kingdom of God which Jesus was sent to preach? For a fuller account of what the term means in the scriptures, please see my book *Kingdoms in Conflict* (Anchor), but it is essential for us to have some understanding of what a real, biblical kingdom is. In the UK we have a constitutional monarchy, and that is not what we mean here by kingship and kingdom. We don't want to live in a kingdom. We want to be free, to be our own king or queen and run our lives as we want to. We would be very resentful if the Queen started to *rule* us as well as reign. We would not like it and we would probably emigrate. There are very few absolute monarchies left in our world. Those which remain are what we call constitutional monarchies,

Luke 4

which means they don't have power over us.

A kingdom first of all has a king – that is what makes it a kingdom; and, secondly, it has voluntary subjects. A good king will live for his subjects; a bad king will live for himself, for his own power, wealth or status. When you study history, you find that there have been far more bad kings than good ones, and that is why we don't like the idea. Power goes to their heads. And I've news for you: I have found the perfect King, and his name is Jesus. My job is to go round nations telling them that they are not republics, they are Kingdom, and I have come in the Name of their King – not a very popular message in Muslim countries, but I have risked that, even in those places. So a kingdom is made up of a sovereign king who rules, and subjects who obey that rule. A true kingdom has no elections and no political parties.

When the Kingdom of God is talked about, it means *he* is the King and he is looking for subjects to be his Kingdom – because he doesn't have many. Indeed as I have mentioned before, whether you believe it or not, this world is not ruled by God. Satan is called the "god of this world", the ruler of this world and even the prince of this world. And looking at the mess we are in and never seem to get out of – with wars after wars after wars, with bad health after bad health – it is due to the fact that the king of the world of human beings is the devil. He has rebelled against the God, King of the universe. Traditionally, when observant Jews have a meal and thank God for the meal, they say "King of the Universe, thank you" and they are stating the truth. But he is not king of the world we live in. We know that Satan is the king of this world – by God's permission. When the human race said to God "We don't want you telling us anything, we don't want you deciding what's right and wrong, we'll decide for ourselves", it did not mean that we have total freedom, because God allowed Satan to step into the vacuum and, whether we like it or not, we were born into the kingdom of Satan.

There are two sorts of subjects in a kingdom – the voluntary ones and the forced ones. One thing God will not do is force anyone to be his subject. We are entirely free to rebel against him as King, but the penalty is that he allows another king to be our king. That is the explanation the Bible gives of the world that we live in, and I agree with that explanation. If you are a Christian, you should agree with it; if you follow Jesus, that is his outlook on the whole situation.

The good news of the Kingdom of God is this: God is going to take back into his own rule the world in which we live, and has sent his own Son who is the only subject he had, the only one who obeyed his Father from beginning to end, and who dealt with Satan right from the beginning of his ministry. He only sets free from disease because disease is part of Satan's kingdom, and he has come to demonstrate the superiority of the Kingdom of God – and that is why he cast out demons. They are fallen angels who possess people and do terrible things through them. But God delivers us from all these things because they belong to Satan's kingdom. But we are voluntary subjects; none of us was forced to be a subject of the King of Heaven.

That is the background to the good news of the Kingdom of God which one day will be established worldwide. Meanwhile, Jesus and those who trust him are anticipating that Kingdom, are enjoying the benefits of it, and are getting ready for the day when it will all become the Kingdom of God, and God will rule voluntary subjects. So in between, it is my job – and yours if you are a Christian – to get as many people as possible ready for the Kingdom that is coming, and to pray daily "Your Kingdom come on earth as it is in heaven", and so that gives you the whole picture of the Bible. The good news of the Kingdom of God is that you can enter it *now* and you can benefit from it *now*; and when you do, you are simply getting ready for the future when those who are prepared for it will enjoy the Kingdom worldwide, and those who are not will not even be allowed in. It is that future dimension which makes the Kingdom of God good news. To put it in Bible language: Jesus must reign until all his enemies are beneath his feet, and the last enemy he will destroy is death itself, which at the moment controls every one of us. Death has the last word on everybody, however great they may be. Poets saw this long ago.

> Death lays his icy hand on kings:
> Sceptre and Crown
> Must tumble down,
> And in the dust be equal made
> With the poor crooked scythe and spade
>
> From 'Death the Leveller'
> by James Shirley (1596-1666)

We are all under a kingdom of death. It will be the last enemy to be destroyed, and that is good news! Death, disease, demonic power – all that is going to go, and all Satanists will go with it; all mourning, all pain, all poverty is due to go.

5

Read Luke 5:1 – 6:11

Luke 5:1–35

There are four sections in this chapter and I have put the two that are concerned with healing together and the two that are concerned with the first followers of Christ together.

We are shown chronic conditions – two hopeless situations: two men who were so sick that no-one could cure them. The first was a leper, and to be a leper in those days was to be "unclean". They literally had to walk through the streets shouting "Unclean! Unclean!" so that people could step out of the way. Highly infectious, they were shut off from their families and friends. If they had any friends they would be other lepers; it is a horrible condition and a serious one, and until comparatively recently very difficult to cure. Now, thank God, there are medicines, and surgeons who can do something about it, but not in those days. It could have been a variety of skin diseases because the word "leprosy" in those days covered many things. The leper came to Jesus and said, "If you are willing, you can cleanse me." That is an amazing thing to say. Already the leper has faith and he knows it is Jesus' will that is important, because if Jesus is willing, the sufferer can be clean and go back to his family. Jesus said, "I'm willing"! Of course he was, and when Jesus saw a leper he had compassion and touched him. Now that would have made any person other than Jesus unclean, and meant that they would have to have gone through the streets shouting, "Unclean! Unclean! I've touched a leper." It is remarkable that Jesus didn't hesitate to touch him – and with that touch the leper was healed.

Now Jesus commanded him to be silent. Imagine how difficult that would be if you were a leper and you were now cleansed and you were told not to say a word. You would want to rush back to all your friends and say, "I'm clean now; you can come near me." Actually, he didn't tell anyone, he did obey the Lord there, but word spread because people who had known him as a leper now saw him back in society, and they did all the talking and the crowds came from everywhere.

But the other command Jesus gave was: "Go and show yourself to the priest." There is provision in the law of Moses for someone who believed he was cured to go to the priest, offer a sacrifice and give thanks to God, and the leper did obey Jesus in this. Whenever we had someone healed in the church where I ministered, we always told them: "Go and show yourself to the doctor." A housewife in our church called Bunty had been nine years in bed, crippled with anaemia and other things, and when she was healed the doctor came to her home on a Tuesday afternoon, as he always did, and found her sitting up in her chair. She could have done that if the neighbours had lifted her into the chair, so at first he didn't notice. Then she said, "Would you like a cup of tea?" She got up to go to the cooker to put the kettle on and the doctor couldn't believe it. He said, "What's happened to you?" And she simply replied, "The Lord has healed me." So the doctor made an entry in his notes – he put a line right across her file and just wrote, "The Lord has healed her." When she told the specialist, who had tried to help her all the way through, he had a nervous breakdown and couldn't cope. He was so sure his diagnosis had been correct and that she was incurable, and he couldn't believe it.

The BBC phoned me and said, "We're hearing certain

things about a lady in your church. Can we come and interview her?" We were very sensitive about this. We didn't want Bunty to become an exhibition, but we agreed to it – provided I sat in on the interview. The BBC reporter came down with his recording machine and interviewed her. At the end the reporter just sat there and said, "Wow! Wow! Wow!"

"What's the matter?" I asked.

He said, "I've heard of these things happening but I've never come across anybody to whom it happened."

He took the recording back to the BBC and we heard nothing more, and so after a few months I called them and said, "We did give you permission to record this story, what are you doing with it?" They replied, "We're not using it." I asked why, and they said it was because they didn't believe it. The religious department of the BBC could not believe what had happened to dear Bunty.

The next Sunday, though she hadn't walked for years, she ran all the way to church, refusing a lift in a car because she wanted to run. Six months later, as she came into church, she said, "The Lord has completed the cure." I asked her, "What do you mean?" She replied, "He's changed my blood, and I've been accepted as a blood donor." Now think of that – anaemia had been one of her main troubles. If anybody had known her background, they would never have accepted her blood, but there it was.

We now turn to the other *impossible* situation described in this passage, which concerned a man who had been paralysed for so long that he literally lived on a mat on the floor, and he could only go places when he could persuade four of his friends to pick up a corner of the mat and carry him somewhere. He lay on his side on that mat for years and his friends were determined to get him to Jesus, and when they carried him to where Jesus was, in a house, they could not get near – there were crowds all waiting to touch Jesus and get near him. You know what they did – they went up, they made a hole in the roof. I used to think of tiled roofs, really solid, and wondered how they got through that. But when you go to a house in the Middle East it usually has a flat roof with steps up the side of the house, and the roof will be made of rushes or twigs or even sods, very easily broken through. So the four friends carried the man on his mat, up the steps, onto the flat roof and then they literally dug through the roof. I often wondered what the poor man who owned the house thought; how much did it cost to put right? The result was that they got the paralytic to the front of the queue and right in front of Jesus. Then, when Jesus saw *their faith* – we're not told about the man on the mat, we're told about the people who carried him there and broke through the roof – he turned to the man on the mat and said, "Your sins are all forgiven." Now that raises a huge question. Does this mean that all sickness is due to sin? No! There are some people who have sinned and are now sick as a result, but not all by a long way. Sickness is part of Satan's kingdom and the most saintly people can be very sick in our world. Becoming a Christian doesn't mean you are immune to all the troubles in the world. Why did Jesus say to him "Your sins are forgiven"? Clearly, in his case there were sins in his past which had led to the condition. Jesus only said it once to this man and there were Pharisees there who immediately objected – "That's blasphemy." Why is it blasphemy? Because if a man says your sins are forgiven, he is claiming to be God. I can only forgive your sins against me, and if you did sin against me and offend me, I hope I would be able to forgive you. But to say I forgive you *all your sins*, none of which were against the person – that is claiming to be God because every sin is ultimately against God, and he knows them all and only he can deal with them all. You can forgive what has been done to you, but that is as far as

Luke 5:1 – 6:11

your forgiveness can go. How can you forgive something someone has done against someone else, or against God? Only God has that right. So the Pharisees present objected violently. Blasphemy deserved death under the Mosaic law. So that gave an opportunity to Jesus to talk about forgiveness, and he said: Which do you think is easier – to say to that man his sins are forgiven, or for him to get up and walk? He had said he had done this to prove to them that he had the right to forgive sins – and therefore he is saying: I am God; I am the Son of God, and you should have realised this. He proved that he could say both things to this poor man. "Get up", and he got up and he picked up his mat and rolled it up and walked out. No wonder the crowds were astounded! To see a paralytic walking home with his mat was astonishing. We have two healings of chronic conditions, both of them beyond human help. Now, in this passage, Luke is showing that nothing is beyond Jesus' control.

Here we encounter Simon Peter, a fisherman in Capernaum, on the shore of the Sea of Galilee. Now there was a time some years ago when Galilee was drying up. There wasn't enough water coming in, and the shores of Galilee shrank. I will never forget seeing that – it looked awful. It is a lovely lake but suddenly there were yards of mud. But something came to light when the water level in Galilee went down: a rowing boat emerged from the mud and so it was excavated and the timber was tested to find out how old it was. To the astonishment of many it was two thousand years old, and it could well have been Simon Peter's boat, or Zebedee's boat that his sons looked after. A museum was built – a modern building where you can go and see this wooden rowing boat which clearly belonged to a fisherman in that period. That is quite exciting!

Jesus came to Simon and asked to use his boat. Firstly, he wanted Simon (as he was known then) to push out into the shallows, and he did so. Jesus sat in the boat and taught the people who were on the shore. It was a very good device to avoid a healing mission because the crowd couldn't get near him and, acoustically, speaking above water is very good. They didn't have PA systems in those days, and if you speak above water your voice bounces over the surface. So Jesus needed the boat to protect him from the people who wanted to touch him, and to preach to them in a way that would enable them to hear. That was the first use of Simon's boat. The second was to use the nets: put the boat out into the deep, cast your nets and catch some fish. I have already mentioned that I have been on Galilee with fishermen throwing their nets out. It is a great experience, and those strong young men are really the sort that Jesus wanted for disciples. So they put out and Peter said, "Master" (that was the limit of his faith at that moment), "we've toiled all night and caught nothing, but if you say so, we will throw the nets a second time", and that is what they did, and they caught a huge number of fish. The catch was so large that the weight of it began to sink the boat and Simon had to call to the other boat, which wasn't far away, that was owned by the sons of Zebedee, with whom they had a partnership in fishing. James and John came out and joined them and took some of the fish into their boat, and they came to the shore with their catch. That would happen again after the resurrection, and then they caught 153 fish. That is an enormous catch on the shores of Galilee. If you catch a dozen at a time you are doing well. You would be amazed how many explanations there are about that number. The most common one is that it is the Trinity squared (9) plus the 12 disciples squared (144), $144 + 9 = 153$. You would be amazed what explanations there are, and my explanation is quite simple – that is an awful lot of fish. That is the meaning of 153 in my mind – somebody counted them.

Luke 5:1 – 6:11

Then Jesus says to Simon: I want you to catch *men*! He had shown him this miracle to encourage him to believe that he could. But there was something that Simon said before that. Simon, when he saw the catch, was filled with fear, as most people are when the supernatural gets a bit near.

So Simon Peter said, in effect: Lord, I'm a sinful man; you mustn't have anything more to do with me; you can have my boat or my nets but please get away from me. When you are right up against the supernatural, that is the natural reaction. But the Lord said: I want you Simon and you are to fish for men from now on. It says that Simon and James and John, in the other boat, all left their fishing immediately and followed Jesus. What an effect Jesus had on people – to say to them "follow" and they followed.

There was another who was called, and it was Levi. What was his job? He was a tax collector, and we have already thought about what that meant in those days. A tax collector was a hated man. I think of Zacchaeus. He was a tax collector and he managed to make four-fold. He was collecting for the tax and only some of that money went to the Romans. It was a horrible job, and bred hatred. They were betraying their own people. Jesus passed by in Capernaum, saw a tax collector in his booth and said: "I want you; follow me." Levi immediately left his booth and dropped everything, and said, "I'll follow you." The first thing he did was to throw open his house for a banquet and he invited all his pals, his colleagues – tax collectors – for a celebration. He wanted them to know what had happened to him. In other words, as soon as he followed Jesus, he wanted everybody else to – and that is still happening with believers.

Unfortunately, the Pharisees again criticised Jesus: "You're eating and drinking with sinners." Now a "sinner" was not a cannibal or a criminal; *a sinner was someone who had just given up on keeping all the laws of Moses* – that is what the word meant in those days. So Jesus was eating and drinking with people like that! Once again, Jesus was, as it were, drawing poison out of a situation into himself. When he touched a leper, he was making himself "unclean"; when he called Levi from his tax booth, he was making himself a traitor and coming under real criticism.

So at this stage Jesus had a few people following him. Now consider these verses:

> One of those days Jesus went out into the hills to pray and spent the night praying to God, and when morning came he called his disciples to him and chose twelve of them whom he designated apostles. Simon whom he named Peter, his brother Andrew, James, John, Philip, Bartholomew, Matthew, Thomas, James son of Alpheus, Simon who was called a zealot [and a zealot was a freedom fighter] and Judas son of James, and Judas Iscariot who became a traitor.

Twelve men. His Father had told him that night when he was alone praying: It is time you called some others to do the job with you, and train them and then you can send them out. Make them disciples first and then send them out as apostles. And so Jesus began to gather a group of men. Possibly five of them were his own relatives, but at least three definitely were. Among them he had a freedom fighter and a tax collector. Most were Galileans from the north, where they had been for a long time, but Judas Iscariot came from the south and he would become a traitor. It is amazing how Jesus chose such a sheer mixture of people and yet that was going to work.

5:33-6:11

If there is one thing that becomes obvious from studying any of the Gospels, it is that Jesus had a gift for making enemies. In fact, every time he spoke he divided the people – there were those who loved what he said and those who hated it – and therefore from the very beginning he made serious enemies who would plan to destroy him.

Next we are going to study three "rounds" as I call them, in the match between Jesus and the Pharisees, and they each get worse than the previous one. The enmity is building up all the time. It is amazing that he could make so many enemies so quickly. I have to tell you who the Pharisees were. They have had a bad press, and most Christian congregations have got it in for them. They have heard that the Pharisees were "whitewashed tombs" – that is what Jesus called them. Outwardly, they were clean and bright; inwardly they were horrid, deadly. It is this contrast between their outside and their inside which Jesus loathed. The one thing he cannot stand is hypocrisy – that is putting it on the outside for people when the inside is quite different.

Now what sort of hypocrites were the Pharisees and how did this all arise? The word "Pharisee" means "separated one". They were people who were isolated from the rest. They were only a minority; it is estimated that in Jesus' day only four to five thousand of the people were Pharisees. But there was a conviction that the nation had never been able to recover its political independence since the exile because they weren't keeping the law of Moses. Of course, by their day the Romans were occupying but they had been occupied by the Egyptians, the Syrians, the Greeks in the past – all since they lost their own country. Everybody was asking why this was happening. "We're God's people, why is God letting this happen?" The Pharisees came with the answer that it was because the people were not keeping the law of

Moses. The Pharisees kept it themselves religiously – but with them was a group of people called scribes, and they used to write out the laws of Moses in the Pharisees' way. The Pharisees' way of writing out the law of Moses was to split it up into different parts, and in particular the law of the Sabbath which forbade work on the seventh day. So the scribes, to help the Pharisees in their job, wrote out forty-nine separate chapters on the work you were not allowed to do on the Sabbath, and it reached ridiculous proportions. It became impossible to keep the law under the Pharisees' and scribes' interpretation – and that was to prove the greatest offence of Jesus towards the Pharisees. He would have nothing to do with all these little detailed laws which they were virtually adding to God's law. And they did become quite ridiculous.

The first difference the Pharisees noticed was that when everybody else was fasting and praying, Jesus' disciples were eating and drinking, and they couldn't line this up. They said, rather naughtily: John the Baptist, whom you have approved, taught us to fast, and we teach our followers to fast, but your followers don't. They eat and drink. They don't observe fasting periods. We all do – and you don't. Now that was a relatively superficial complaint. They were asking: Why don't you teach fasting?

But Jesus did teach fasting. If you study the Sermon on the Mount he said: When you pray, when you fast, when you give money – do it all secretly. Because far too many Pharisees were doing it to be seen. When they fasted they put some makeup on to look worse – some ashes usually. They rubbed it into their faces to make sure everybody knew they were fasting. And when they prayed, they prayed at the street corner so everybody knew they were praying; and when they gave money, they advertised their gift. I can remember as a boy attending a missionary meeting at our church and the chairman was a well-known man. When it came to his speech, he wrote out a cheque in front of us all for this missionary. Then he told us how much the cheque was for, and I couldn't help thinking back to Jesus' teaching in the Sermon on the Mount – your religious activity should be secret, whether it is praying, fasting or giving. Don't let your right hand know what your left hand is going to do. Because if you do it for people, if you do it to be seen and to get a reputation, that is the worst thing you could be doing in the name of religion.

This was the sort of hypocrisy that Jesus was tackling, and when they said, "Why don't your disciples join in the fasting when everybody else does?" he gave a little answer which is quite profound. In the defence that Jesus offered to the attack of the Pharisees, three times he gave very subtle teaching which you have to think through carefully to find out how he thought, and what his view of the thing was.

So he did not abolish fasting but he said that while the Bridegroom is with the guests, you don't fast – claiming to be the Bridegroom, which was a title for the Messiah again. He said: You've got the Bridegroom with you. His disciples don't feel like fasting – they've got the Bridegroom with them, they are *celebrating*. But he said there would come a day when the Bridegroom would be taken from them and then they would find that they would fast. He was teaching that it is not a matter of ritual, just because everybody is doing it. That doesn't make it right. It is when you fast for a reason that you really need to and you really want to.

Now this was a new religion, a new thought, especially to the Pharisees for whom fasting was an observance just as today people give up chocolate for Lent – they are just observing something that others are doing. They don't give anything up at other times in the year, but they do it *then* because it is a *custom*, a tradition. I am going to keep saying things like that because we need to realise there are Pharisees around today with whom Jesus would disagree.

Then Jesus goes on to bigger things by talking about the difference between new and old. And this is where we must struggle to understand what Jesus is saying. He is saying, I've come to bring a new attitude to religion, and it doesn't mix with the old. Tradition and truth don't mix. Ritual and reality don't mix. He says: Which of you, needing to patch an old garment, would take a patch off a new garment and sew it on the hole in the old? He said that if you do that you ruin the new garment and it won't match the old garment – it would be a mess. Then he goes on to an even more telling illustration. You don't put new wine into old wineskins. A wineskin of those days was simply the skin of an animal with the openings in it sewn up. If you put new wine in an old wineskin, it bursts. The new wine will ferment and split the wineskin and you lose both the wine and the skin.

Then he made another profound remark: If you have once been used to the old, you won't want the new. The new religion is one that has Christ at the centre and lets him tell you what to do. It is not about observing the ritual of a church or following old traditions, but the trouble is that once you have tasted the old, you have lost your taste for the new. Christmas is a case in point. Observing Christmas on December 25th is pure tradition, yet churches put up Christmas trees and fairy lights and think that is pleasing to the Lord. The Bible never says to celebrate Christmas. We thought that up ourselves. It is part of the "scribes' tradition" and we follow it like that, as if there is no problem, as if we are being good disciples by so doing. Jesus knew who he was talking to.

That was "round one" and you can see already that he is getting under their skin with what he says. He is making them think and, above all, he is putting himself at the centre of true religion. You can observe all the traditions, but unless

Christ is at the centre, it is old. When he is at the centre, you have the new religion that he came to bring.

In round one the Pharisees are criticising his disciples. In round two they get a bit stronger. One Sabbath, the disciples were walking through the corn field and they simply, without thinking, took some of the corn heads, rubbed them in their hands – and according to the Pharisees that was threshing, and you are not allowed to thresh on the Sabbath. Are you familiar with the word "threshing"? It means to separate the grain from the chaff. So they came down heavily on the disciples with their Sabbath law. Threshing was work and it was thought that was why they were in such trouble as a nation.

The rules had become ridiculous. If they had a safety pin in their clothes, they were sewing on the Sabbath in pressing the pin through the cloth. If they wore false teeth on the Sabbath, they were carrying a burden and that was wrong on the Sabbath – that's work. If they went walking with a walking stick and happened to trail the stick in the dust and it left a line, you were ploughing on the Sabbath and that was forbidden.

If you go to Israel today and stay in a hotel, you will find one of the lifts labelled "Sabbath Lift", and that is the only lift in which you don't have to press the button. It automatically goes up and down all Sabbath and you jump on quickly while it is at your floor (where it just pauses very briefly). So you jump in and jump out when it pauses. Pressing a button is considered work, and that goes back to the Pharisees.

When the disciples did "threshing" on the Sabbath, the Pharisees came down on that like a ton of bricks. Jesus' defence was very interesting. In effect he told them they didn't know the scriptures well. Had they never read about King David and his companions who were fighting for the nation? When they ran out of food and were hungry, he had no hesitation in going into the tabernacle; and in the outer part of the inner tabernacle there was a table with the shewbread on it, reminding people that God fed them in the wilderness. That shewbread was consecrated and only the priests were allowed to eat up what remained, and they changed it every day and put new baked bread on the table of the shewbread every day. And the priests ate up the previous day's shewbread.

I can remember in the RAF we shared a building with the Anglicans and the Anglican Chaplain was rather high church, and one day, after Communion, I had a lot of little pieces of bread left and outside were some hungry looking birds so I took the little bits of bread and scattered the bread to the birds who really loved it, and I'm sure were very thankful for it. But the Anglican Chaplain was horrified that I didn't eat up what was left. That is consecrated bread, he said. Now that is what Jesus is talking about here: Didn't you realise that King David ate consecrated bread from the tabernacle and gave it to his companions because they were hungry too? Now you're not going to argue with that, it is in the Word of God – and he was your greatest king. What Jesus is really implying – you've got to get inside his mind now – is that he, the Son of David, has every right to decide what to do with consecrated bread. The teaching was upsetting the Pharisees no end. By the way, 1 Samuel 21 is the scripture that tells about David feeding his soldiers on consecrated bread.

Jesus then gives himself two titles – Son of Man and Lord of the Sabbath – and both of those titles are very significant. This is the second time he has referred to himself as Son of Man. What did he mean? It is important that we realise what he was saying. If you read the book of Ezekiel straight through, you will notice that 84 times God calls Ezekiel son of man, and there is no doubt that in that context it means simply "human being". Your father was a man, you are son of man. But there is only one verse in the whole Old Testament where "Son of Man" means something entirely different and that is in the book of Daniel where it says you will see someone like a Son of Man coming on the clouds of heaven to re-establish the Kingdom of God on earth. And there is no doubt that that is why Jesus used the words Son of Man, because at his trial when they challenged Jesus about what his opinion of himself was, he said, "You will see the Son of Man coming in the clouds" referring obviously to his Second Coming, because his first was not in the clouds.

So Jesus saw himself in Daniel. But because there was such a general use, he could use it as if it was simply a human being and nobody would realise what he was saying. If they didn't know the prophet Daniel well, they wouldn't understand what he was saying. Once again, we have the firm impression that Jesus did not want people to know who he was. He had told the demoniac: Don't tell anybody who I am. And it was not until Peter finally realised who he was – which took two and a half years with Jesus – before they realised that he was using the term Son of Man in the one text that means "divine person" as against the 84 texts which simply mean a human person. It was a very clever title to use, and not until his trial did Jesus explain why he called himself Son of Man. Now that was one title.

The other title he gave himself in this context was "Lord of the Sabbath" meaning: I decide what's right to do on the Sabbath, not anybody else; you come to me and you say, Lord, is this what I should be doing or is it not? But that direct responsibility to Jesus is the mark of this new faith. And so he gives himself those two titles.

Now we come to round three. The Pharisees and scribes were in the synagogue on the Sabbath where he was teaching and they knew that there was a man who needed healing, a man with a withered hand, and they were watching Jesus very carefully – would he heal on the Sabbath? If he did, they had a direct accusation: he is going against the law. I can remember a youth meeting in New Zealand once where there was a girl with a withered hand – it was all screwed up, she couldn't use it. And she was right-handed in her brain, so it was a real handicap that she couldn't use her right hand. We had many healings that morning but one was this girl and an hour later, she wrote to her parents: "Dear Mum and Dad, I'm writing this letter with my right hand." You can imagine the thrill that was for her parents.

Jesus knew what the scribes and Pharisees were thinking: We've got him at last! We can accuse him of breaking the law on the Sabbath. The Jews did allow healing on the Sabbath on condition that the person would die if they were not healed. In other words, in an extreme case, in real need they would allow a doctor to heal someone, but this man had been like this for years and could easily have waited for the next day, so there was no need for Jesus to heal him on the spot. But Jesus knew their thinking. That is one of the things about Jesus which you learn – he knows what you are thinking. That is why he applied the idea of righteousness to the way we *think*. He agreed with the law of Moses that killing someone was wrong, but when Jesus read that law he said that if you have wished anybody dead, if you have ever been contemptuous of them, if you have ever thought them a fool, then you are in danger of hellfire. It is not the act, it is the thought; similarly with adultery. If you thought of it, you have done it. That is why he said that unless your righteousness *exceeds* the righteousness of the Pharisees, you won't get into the Kingdom of God. In what way could their righteousness be exceeded? Well, it would mean being righteous on the inside: in your thought life – that is righteousness. That is going way beyond the Pharisees. All they achieved was whitewashing the outside, but inside they

Luke 5:1 – 6:11

were full of dirt and death. So the Pharisees were watching, and waiting to accuse him. Will he heal on the Sabbath? – because it is not a necessary work. Jesus invited the man with the withered hand to stand at the front. The man came and then Jesus turned to the Pharisees and said: I've got a question for you – which is right to do on the Sabbath, to do good or to do evil? You see, in their *minds*, they were doing evil. They were planning to destroy him and he knew that, and in their thoughts they were abusing the Sabbath – entertaining evil thoughts about him.

Then Jesus poses another question: Which is right, to save life or to destroy life on the Sabbath? The Pharisees were thinking to destroy him and he knew all that. Those questions must have embarrassed them because he knew. Now his defence is fascinating. It was first the question – Should I do good or evil because it's the Sabbath? Should one save life or destroy it? He backed the question up with an action. He said to the man: Stretch out your hand. As soon as he stretched it out, he got it back, and being right-handed, that would give him his livelihood back. It was a real handicap removed.

So Jesus got out of all these attacks with brilliant argument, defending his view of the Sabbath, of healing, of everything; and he is putting religious observance second to human needs, and that is still his religion. I am going to ask you a question now which you can think over: Who are the Pharisees today? Where would you look to find them? It is so easy to prefer the old wine. Something new means you have got to change, and change in religion is very hard to make. Who are the enemies of Jesus? The Pharisees were the most religious group in Israel and everybody knew them for that, but Jesus was more critical of them than of anyone else. The most religious Jews were Jesus' greatest enemies and that is the extraordinary fact that this passage leaves us with.

6

Read Luke 6:12 – 49

We turn to a very practical part of scripture. Sometimes people say to me, "If everybody lived the Sermon on the Mount, that's all that would be needed." I agree wholeheartedly. There is just one snag: I have never yet met anybody who does live it. This sermon has to be one of the shortest ever to have been preached, but it is one of the greatest. An argument goes on amongst scholars as to whether this record in Luke is the same as the Sermon on the Mount in Matthew. Certainly it seems to cover the same ground, though Luke's account is rather shorter than Matthew's. Those who like to pick fault with the Bible, and those who like to try and find contradictions, point out that in Matthew this sermon was preached on a mountain and here it is preached on a plain. Once you see the place, the contradiction disappears. If you look at it from below, it is a mountain; if you look at it from above, it is a level place. Matthew was talking about the people coming up to hear the sermon and Luke is talking about Jesus coming down with his disciples to the level place to teach. So there is no contradiction; all the apparent "contradictions" that people have found in the Bible disappear as easily as that. But fancy wasting your time trying to discuss whether it is the same sermon – I am quite sure our Lord repeated his teaching many times. What he said was worth hearing again and again. So I don't mind if it is the same sermon or a different one; it is the Lord's teaching, that is the vital thing.

It is the Word of God coming to us now, giving us guidance for practical living. It is concerned with the three relationships that every one of us has to master: our relationship with ourselves, our relationship with other people and our relationship with God.

Before you consider a sermon, look at the congregation to whom it was preached, and you will realise why it was preached as it was. Jesus had a big congregation on this occasion. On the one hand, there were his disciples listening to him, and he had called them and chosen them. Out of the large band of followers he already had, he had just chosen twelve after a night of prayer. Look at those men: they were ordinary; there was not a single famous, rich or clever person among them. They were very mixed men – some of them were traitors to their nation and others were resistance fighters for their nation. At least four lots of brothers were among them. They were young men – it is not always realised that the twelve apostles began their ministry in their late teens or early twenties. Christianity began as a young people's movement, and wherever it is alive it still is a young people's movement.

The other group there consisted of people who had wanted to come because they had some need. Many were sick. In those days there was very little medical skill, no health service, no hospitals, and the thought of finding health anywhere must have been heaven to some people. Then there were the demon possessed – those who were racked with possession by an evil spirit. They came to find freedom.

The crowd could also be divided in one other way. There were rich and poor people, those in shabby clothes and others in good clothes. There were people who looked as if they had eaten well that day, and people who looked as if they could do with a square meal. There were people who were laughing and jolly for whom it was a great occasion, and there were others who were looking strained and sad. There were people there who were obviously popular and crowds around them looked at them and thought highly of them. Then there were others who seemed to be ostracised. The same two groups that I mentioned above correspond to these two groups. The ones who looked shabby, hungry and a bit sad and unpopular were Jesus' disciples. The ones who looked fairly well fed and well clothed were those who had come because they had chosen to be there.

Jesus looked at that congregation, made up of those groups and spoke to them all. In the first point, he is telling us the secret of true happiness. Do you want to know how to be happy? You won't like it, but here it is: How happy are you poor! How happy are you hungry. How happy are you who look sad. How happy you unpopular people are! That is how Jesus looks at life. It says he addressed that part of the sermon to his own disciples – a shabby, unhappy, poor, unpopular lot. He said, "Oh, you're the happy ones here today." Then he looked at the better dressed in his congregation and those who were laughing and chatting and his message to them was: How terrible it is to be rich and to be well fed and to laugh all the time and to be popular.

Here, right at the beginning of this amazing sermon, Jesus shows that his outlook is diametrically opposed to everything we think. The world says: if you can avoid being poor, if you can avoid being hungry, then do so if you possibly can. If you want to be happy you will need to be popular; if you want to be happy, you will need money; if you want to be happy, then go on watching TV comedy shows until you have laughed yourself silly; if you want to be happy, this is the way. None of that is what Jesus says. You see, his disciples had already been following him for some months and already they were getting poorer, already their clothes were shabby and their sandals were worn, with holes in the soles.

Already they were beginning to be unpopular, and already they were beginning to feel the burden that he had for the world, and to see the world through his eyes doesn't make you full of joy. On the contrary, he was a man of sorrows and acquainted with grief. Jesus taught: how happy you are if you are poor because you have followed me. That is the implication. He is not saying that everybody who is poor is going to be rich or everybody who is rich is going to be poor. He is speaking to his disciples, and these things have come because they are his disciples. So he is saying: maybe you are poorer than you were before. Some will read these words who are poorer financially than they would have been if they hadn't met Christ. Maybe you are hungrier; maybe you have burdens that you never carried before, and maybe you have lost a lot of your friends, but how happy you are. This tells me something very profound: that *real happiness is not dependent on your present feelings*. Real happiness is not related to the circumstances in which you are placed at this moment. Real happiness is dependent on your future, not your present. It is one of the hardest things in life to grasp. It sounds like a contradiction in terms, but Jesus knew what he was talking about.

Let me try to illustrate this. Some years ago, when I was living in Buckinghamshire, I read my local newspaper and discovered that a jobbing gardener in the county, who went around digging up weeds and cutting grass, had inherited a title, an estate and a fortune. He was now "Lord Somebody". Can you imagine it? It was a total surprise to him. He was the last surviving relative of some lord who had died. People were congratulating him. They were almost saying, "How happy you are." Yet he hadn't received a penny of it at that point. There would be a long legal process of probate and then it would be his, but people were already congratulating him. The real reason for Christian happiness is not how we are placed now, but how we are going to be.

Yes, Jesus promised that we would be poorer in this life. He promised us loss in this life. He promised compensations as well, but he promised trouble. He promised unpopularity for his sake. I read a quote from a wonderful Methodist preacher, Dr Russell Maulpe: "Jesus promised his disciples three things: that they would be completely fearless, absurdly happy, and in constant trouble." How about that for a promise? But at least it was honest. Happiness is not feeling happy, it is being in a happy position. Every Christian, no matter how low they get, no matter how they weep, no matter how hungry they may be, no matter how unpopular they may be, and men may insult them and say all manner of things against them falsely, they can say, "I'm the happiest man alive because of my future. I may be hungry now, but I'm going to be filled. I may be poor now, but I'm a millionaire's son. I may be weeping now, but I'm going to laugh. I may be unpopular now, but that puts me among the prophets in heaven."

So Jesus said *both* things: blessed are you poor, but woe to you rich; blessed are you hungry, but woe to you well fed; blessed are you who weep, but woe to you who laugh; blessed are you when you are unpopular – but woe to you if you are a disciple of mine and everybody speaks well of you. Of course, he is stating his own situation because this applied to him; this is how he was. He was not universally popular; he wept time and again. He didn't have a place to call his own, and he fasted and went hungry. He was poor – in fact, when he died he couldn't even leave his own clothes to anybody else; they were taken from him and he had nothing to leave but his peace. These are truths that no unconverted man would accept. A person who wasn't a Christian would laugh at such a suggestion – to go to the world and say, "Do you want the secret of happiness? Follow Jesus until it hurts, and oh how happy you will be." But that is the secret.

His message for those who seek their happiness in the things of this world, those who want to be rich now and those who want to laugh now and those who want to be popular now, is that you have had your easy life. In other words, which would you rather: go through a tough time in this life and look forward to glory and wealth and everything that lies beyond for those whom God loves, or have your good time here and do without it forever afterwards?

Now let us look at the second relationship: harmony with other people. There are two things Jesus talks about here: *concern* and *criticism*. These things will determine how you get on with other people. How deep is your concern for them, and how harsh is your criticism of them? First, the matter of concern. Jesus is here speaking of our concern for our enemies. Oh, what standards he sets! Not to those you like, not to your friends, not to those of your set, not to those in the church whom you like, but to those who hate you, curse you, mistreat you, hit you, rob or accost you. Your concern for them will decide whether you have learned relationships with people. Anybody can get on with those who love them. Anybody can relate to nice people – anyone can invite someone to their home who is in a position to invite them back. A woman said to me when I thanked her for a good turn, "Well, I always do a good turn to people because you never know when you are going to need one yourself." This was her philosophy, and a very common and practical philosophy you will find the world over.

There are plenty of good deeds done by people who are not Christians. There is plenty of love outside the church – in families and among friends. But Jesus teaches us that the kind of love that is the secret of real harmony is the love that can be concerned for those in whom there will be no response except abuse. It is a bit shattering to discover what human nature is like. I know a lovely lady who became a deaconess and plunged into the slums of a large city in this country. She gave her life for people, just gave them clothes, food, comfort, help. She was once in a rather well-to-do church, telling the ladies' meeting about her work. She invited questions and a lady said, "It must be lovely to see their grateful faces and to be thanked for all you do." The deaconess said, "It's not a bit like that. If the clothes don't fit, they come back and really tear a strip off me. If things aren't just right, I really get it. Do you think they always say, 'Thank you'? No." Then this lady in this well-to-do church asked a very significant question. She said, "How on earth do you manage to keep going then?" In that question she bared her heart. For, you see, she couldn't understand love that wasn't reciprocated.

What Jesus is teaching here is a love that expects nothing back whatever; a love that will lend to people and not even expect to get it back; a love that returns kindness for hate; a love that suffers long and is kind; a love that returns good for evil. What we call the golden rule comes in at this point. Have you noticed that most people who quote it do so wrongly? You ask somebody what they think the golden rule is and they will say, "Never do to anyone else what you don't want them to do to you." That is what Rabbi Hillel and some Greek philosophers have said, and you can find this golden rule in almost every religion of the world, but it is always in a negative form. Along came Jesus with something unique: do to others what you want them to do to you. That is just one of the differences between Jesus' teaching and the world's philosophy. The world's philosophy says, "I'm alright, I've never done anybody any harm." That is negative. Jesus' philosophy is: did you do them any good? The golden rule here is positive. Do to others as you would have them do to you – whatever they do to you. You see, love is not a matter of feelings here. Love is not a matter of falling in love. Love is not something that happens to you. Love is not something you can't help. Love is something you *decide* to do. There is a legitimate love, as between a man and a woman for example, or between close friends, which is reciprocal and responsive and which happens to you. You fall in love or you like that person and there is a two-way communication. But when Jesus spoke of love, he wasn't thinking of that kind of love at all, he was thinking of the kind of love that goes on loving whatever is done to it. That is a kind of love that you don't find naturally; it doesn't occur to us in our flesh. It is not a thing that happens to us. It is not a thing that we fall into; it's a thing that you *do* or don't *do*.

Let us move on now to Jesus' second point about our relationships – namely *criticism* of our friends. Funnily enough, criticism works this way: that you will always criticise those who are nearest to you. Did you realise that? You think through who you have criticised since last Sunday. Were they people in China? Or were they people who were close to you? The reason why we do it to people near to us is because that takes them down a peg or two and, therefore, lifts us up a bit. So, you don't criticise someone down the road in another church nearly as much as someone in your own – if you are doing things naturally. Alas, if you are not careful you become more critical of your own church than of any other without even realising it, because it isn't your enemies you criticise, it is your friends. That is why Jesus, speaking of our concern for our enemy, now goes on to speak about criticising one's brother. You see, this is the opposite of the world again. The world has deep concern for friends and criticism for enemies. But Christians need to go much deeper.

Let us look at what Jesus says about that. He gives two simple illustrations – one is very pathetic and makes you

Luke 6:12 – 49

cry and the other is so grotesque it makes you laugh. The pathetic one is of supposing you were out in the high street and you saw two people, each with a white stick. They were trying to help each other across the road and finished up in the ditch. That is sad, isn't it? But you know, when you try to help someone else you have got to watch jolly carefully that you are not so blind that you can't really see either of you properly. Your criticism may be just a blind man leading a blind man – you will both fall in the ditch together. It is sad but a lot of our criticism comes under this category. Since you can never get beyond your teacher, that means the blind leading the blind can't lead anywhere but disaster.

The other illustration Jesus uses here is very funny – at least it would be in the Middle East. It is not in our subtle, sophisticated Western humour, I know. Jesus said, "There's a man walking on the road with a roof joist stuck in his eye, he stops a passer by and says, 'Excuse me, there's just a little straw in your eye.'" Jesus could use humour as well as pathos. But when you have laughed at the joke, you have laughed at yourself. For, in fact, you can only really see the fault in your brother clearly if you have got rid of the faults in yourself first. How desperately deceitful the heart is.

Jesus is teaching that you are really going to learn relationships, harmony, concern for your enemies, and no criticism of your friends – and you will learn the secret. Now when he says, "Judge not, that you be not judged," he does not mean that you must renounce all critical faculties. If he meant that, if we were never to examine each other positively, then I would never write a reference for anyone, nor should anybody ever sit on a magistrate's bench, nor should there be any school or university examinations. What Jesus is now talking about is *condemning*. It means writing someone off, saying he is beyond redemption. It means saying he is hopeless – we can't do anything with him. Only God has the right to be such a judge.

One of the most frightening things that Jesus ever said is right here: that with what measure you judge, you shall be judged. In other words, in the Day of Judgment, when one stands before one's Creator, all he has to do is to play back a recording of the faults I have found in other people and said so, then to examine my life with what I have criticised in others. That is all, because he is saying: I judge you by your own outlook; if you condemn this in others, then it is wrong – I will therefore examine your life by what you believe to be wrong. Can any of us stand before God if that is how he is to judge? For we know we have condemned in others what there is in our own heart. This, then, is the secret of harmony with other people.

Finally, there is the secret of holiness before God. This is practical. Jesus spoke in pictures so that his hearers could see the truth. As his hearers listened to him they could say, "Oh, now I see." The last two pictures he paints are of a tree and of a house. It is a law of nature that a tree can only produce after its kind; what the tree is, that it will produce. It is also a law of human nature that what you are in yourself, that is what you produce. You can't produce anything else. What is stored up in your heart will come out of your mouth, which is why Jesus said on another occasion, "Every man will be judged by the idle words that proceeded from his mouth." What is so important about the mouth? Simply, when you open it, what is in your heart comes out unless you keep a very tight grip of yourself and you are one of those who speaks in a very reserved way and is careful and considerate in what you say. If you are really free and if you are really relaxed and if you let your mouth take over, it will reveal what is in your heart.

Jesus teaches: every man and woman, over the years, has built up a treasury in their heart. Thoughts are stored in your heart; all the experiences of life are there. Your heart has become more and more full of treasures, either of good things or of bad things. When you open your mouth, the treasures will come out – the things that you have stored. You might have someone to tea and just talk casually. The things that you have stored in your heart are what will come out. As a man thinks in his heart, so is he.

Jesus is saying a bad tree can't produce good fruit and a good tree can't produce bad fruit. But then he gives us a further warning. He says that the things that come out of the mouth can be unreal. In casual conversation, the things that come out will be from your heart; in formal and official circles, what you say may not be from your heart at all. This is the big danger in religion – that you say things that are not from the heart. "Why do you call me 'Lord'?" With a printed service our words are pretty well decided for us. The prayers are fixed. But halfway through the service I might say, "Just turn and talk to someone." Then you may wonder: what did he say? Some are frightened at letting things out of their heart and are very formal: "Good evening. Nice to see you."

So do watch language. When you are not consciously controlling your mouth, your heart is revealed. When you are consciously controlling your mouth, hypocrisy is only too easy.

Now for the climax of the passage: you will never get fruit without roots. Going deep down to the invisible, Jesus changes the picture from fruit to foundation. He tells us the secret of holiness before God, and makes it absolutely clear that the secret of holiness is not the number of sermons you have listened to. Everything rests on what you *do* with the teaching.

Jesus finishes this sermon with an illustration from his carpentry days. Looking back, he would have seen some houses built well and others built badly. I remember going to visit a family home many years ago. It was a beautiful house in the woods on a lovely residential estate. But when I got there, I couldn't believe my eyes. The whole place had been dug around – it looked as if they were going to put a moat in with great heaps of sandy clay in trenches around the walls. What was it? It was foundations which needed taking down. The builder had not made them deep enough. Jesus is teaching us that when you listen to preaching you are building something as you listen. If you enjoy that sermon, are moved by it, then go away and do nothing about it, you have built a house that looks alright, a life that looks Christian. You may live in that life for quite some time, but when the crisis comes, when the crunch hits you, your Christian life will collapse – it has no foundation. But if you listen to the sermon and listen to the word of God, and go away and do something about it, then it will be hard work; it will require effort – you will have to dig deep and get down to the bedrock of what you are really like and get down to the bedrock of what life is really like, and get down to the bedrock of what God is really like. Then, when a crisis comes, your Christian life will stand.

That is the secret of holiness before God: to listen to his Word and then do something about it. In your relationship with yourself, follow Christ until it hurts, then how happy you will be; in your relationships with others, have a concern for your enemies and refrain from criticism of your friends. The secret of holiness with God is to bear the fruit that comes from having roots and having a foundation. Isn't it strange that ordinary folk like us are builders for eternity?

It has been said that the sermon you read is a mirror to show the dirt, for it leaves you with a dilemma. When I read through the life and the teaching of Christ, I know that is right. I know it is the truth. I know that is the way; I know that is the life – but I just cannot do it. That is why I need a

Saviour and Lord. That is why people don't live the Sermon on the Mount – not until they find Jesus Christ. That is why it is silly to say, "If everybody lived like this, our troubles would be over." Of course they would be, but nobody does live like this until Christ forgives their sin, begins his work in their heart and begins to live his life in them. For all the good things we have read in this passage are perfectly true of Jesus. As they spat on him, whipped him, mocked him and laughed at him and nailed him to a block of wood, he said, "Father, forgive them, for they know not what they do." Not long afterwards, one of the early Christians who was stoned to death showed that he now could live the Sermon on the Mount. As the first Christian martyr breathed his last he said, "Lord, lay not this sin to their charge." It is possible to live like this, but not by yourself. You will only do it with Jesus.

7

Read Luke 7

Jesus was ministering all the time. People bumped into him or he was walking down a road at the same time as a funeral, or a soldier sent a message to him, or John the Baptist sent a couple of disciples along, or else he was invited out for a meal. Most of our Lord's miracles and most of his parables occurred in this casual, spontaneous way. It is a pattern for our ministry: to be on duty all the time and not just when we are in church or on official Christian occasions; to minister all the time as the Lord gives us opportunities in casual contact.

We encounter a great variety of people in this chapter: Gentiles and Jews, rich people and poor, good people (or at least those who thought they were good) and bad people who knew that they were bad. In all of this variety, Jesus steps in with just the right word or just the right deed. We are going to study four case histories.

God is interested in what happens inside us – what goes through your heart and mind. So we are going to look at each of these stories and ask what people were thinking about Jesus and what he was thinking about them.

I am presenting these as case histories of the Great Physician. It is as if we are reading his patients' medical records and looking up what Jesus did for them – his diagnosis, prescription and cure. History number one is the case of the surprising soldier. It is a remarkable background—he was equivalent in rank to a regimental sergeant major. You would not generally think of such a man as a deep, mystical, religious person, would you? If you have had any experience of RSMs, you will know that they are often the backbone of the army – utterly reliable, men of strength and character.

This man is a most unusual soldier. As well as being a strong character, a leader, a well-trained military man, he has tremendous sensitivity. First, he is sensitive to his slave. Do you know what they used to do with worn-out slaves in those days? They would put them in a room and shut them in with no food, or put them out in the yard to die. A slave was no more than a tool, and when a slave was worn out he was discarded – not worth feeding. But here is a man who says, "My slave is sick" – and his concern was not only for the soldiers beneath him but for the slaves. That was almost unheard of in the ancient world.

More than that, here is a man who is in the position of trying to keep the peace and who out of his own back pocket builds a needed place of worship for people in an occupied territory. That is unusual – yet he had built a synagogue. You may have seen the ruins of a synagogue in Capernaum that stand there to this day. That is not the actual synagogue referred to here, but it is built on top of the one that the centurion built, and to this day the ruins that you can see are Roman architecture with Hebrew symbols worked into the stone, and bear testimony to this man who paid for an architect to put up a lovely synagogue right there in Capernaum – for the Jews, who were normally despised by the Romans. Their religion was thought odd. What a remarkable soldier.

I want you to notice one little thing. Nowhere in the New Testament is a soldier told that to be a soldier is a dishonourable profession for a believer in Jesus. On the contrary, centurions seem to stand out as fine men. There is one at the cross saying, "Surely he was the Son of God."

Luke 7

There is another called Cornelius in Acts 10. These were men who stayed in the army and who were never told to stop being soldiers, even by John the Baptist, when they said, "What do we do to repent?" They were told to be just, honourable soldiers. So it has been ever since. Some of the finest Christians in our times have been soldiers who have understood Christ well. This man was going to understand Jesus Christ very well because of his military training and background.

Notice his humility, again remarkable in such a character. The Jews said he really was worthy for Jesus to do this thing for him. But the soldier's message was: I am not worthy either to come and speak face-to-face to you, a Jewish rabbi, nor to have you come into my Gentile home. What a man! He stands out as having the right scale of values. But let us ask what he thought about Jesus. Let us get inside his mind and heart. Here is the most incredible fact of all: he believed that Jesus could do anything by word of mouth alone, whether he was present or not. That is astonishing faith.

You see, Jesus had already been healing people by laying his hands on them and touching them. This man affirms that he didn't even need to come and touch the slave. Wherever you are, just say the word. Most people needed the touch of Jesus or needed to feel the hem of his garment or to have some tangible sign of Jesus' presence so they might believe in his power – but not this man. He was in the same position that a believer is in today. We can't see Jesus. We can't touch the hem of his garment. He is at the right hand of the Father in heaven, and the faith that is required of us is the faith this centurion had, which is to believe that he only has to say the word and it is done. Of course, we have far more reasons for having that faith than this soldier did. He had not met Jesus, he had only heard about him. Jesus had not yet died and risen again as we know he has. This centurion is outstanding, and he had the utmost confidence in Jesus.

The reason he did was this: the key word is "under". He recognised Jesus as a man under authority. Now that is the opposite of what you would have thought. He said, "I also am under authority, and because I'm under authority I can tell people what to do." Now if that centurion had not had the rank he had, if he had not been in Caesar's army, if he had just been an individual, he could not have told another man "Go!" and had the man go. But he had taken a commission.

I remember the time I took a commission, and still have the certificate. The Queen, bless her, gave it to me. I don't think she did it personally but there is her name on it anyway. The commission put me straight in at the rank of Flight Lieutenant. This was quite unusual for me. I had been used to a voluntary society of a church where you ask somebody to do something, hoping that they would feel that the Lord was leading them to do it. But now suddenly, as an officer I could say to someone, "Go!" and, lo and behold he did. It took quite a lot of getting used to at first! Now that was no power in myself, no power of personality. I was under authority because the Squadron Leader above me could say to me, "Go." I was now in a chain of command, so with the Queen's commission, I could give an order to anybody below my rank. Because I was under authority, it was as if the Queen was telling that person to do something.

Now this soldier, when he heard about Jesus, saw this: That man is under the authority of the King, under the authority of God. Therefore he can order this disease to leave my house. He can say to it: "Disease, quick march!" and the disease would have to go right out of the house, right out of the slave. That is how he came to his faith. That is how many soldiers have come to their faith – they have recognised authority. Since conscription ended, a generation of young people has grown up that finds it very difficult to recognise

Luke 7

authority, and that makes it hard to accept the authority of Jesus. But in a society where you recognise the chain of command and accept it, then you recognise the power of the Lord in people. So this centurion was declaring: "I also am a man under authority, and I tell slaves what to do and soldiers what to do, and they do it. So when you are under the authority of God, all you have got to say is, 'Disease, quick march!' and it's done." What faith!

So what did Jesus think of the soldier? He was surprised, and that shows the true humanity of Jesus – he could be surprised by something. He was delighted, and he said, "I haven't found this kind of faith among any of the Jews." The word "marvelled" which is used here is only used twice in the ministry of Jesus. The other occasion was when he had preached in Nazareth, and it says, "He marvelled because of their unbelief." Do you remember that? He could do nothing in Nazareth; he was helpless to help people. You can imagine the thrill in his heart: he had never expected a Roman soldier to have the kind of faith he had expected in his own people and had not found there. That is what Jesus thought of this soldier.

So I challenge you in this way: the trouble with Nazareth was familiarity, and the great blessing that came to the centurion was due to faith. These are opposites. Jesus marvelled at Nazareth because through their very familiarity with him, they could not believe in him—"Isn't this the carpenter's son?" But a total outsider with no such background said, "Jesus, just say the word and it's done." Those of us who have been brought up in Christian churches, in Sunday school, in Christian family homes – one of the perils of that is the familiarity that can't believe things can happen. You will be shamed and embarrassed from time to time when someone with no background, no church upbringing, comes to Jesus and says, "Jesus, say the word," and things happen that you have never seen before. Do you expect Christ to do something? Do you expect him to touch lives? Do you say to him, "Jesus, just give the word"?

The next history is the case of the weeping widow, and it is a very sad scene: a woman who has lost all her menfolk. She had a husband once, and he is dead. She had an only son and he too is dead. There are no pensions, there is no support for her. She is alone, and she must be a beggar from now on. There is a funeral – probably a very poor one, yet all funerals would have professional wailers, and, unlike this country, when in a terribly unhealthy way we try to hide our feelings of mourning, in the Middle East, in a much healthier way, they let it show and they don't mind weeping and howling on such an occasion. Any psychologist will tell you that a person who is ready to weep openly will get over it better and more quickly.

We used to hear funerals like that. It has to take place within a few hours of death, and they don't use coffins – they can't afford to use all that timber. They simply have a long, open basket on poles with the body lying in it, and they tip the body into the grave. Imagine the scene in the Gospel. That procession of death on the narrow country lane meets the Prince of Life with his followers, and one group is going to have to give way and get off the road for the other. Until recently in this country, if a funeral procession came along, people used to get out of the way. The procession of death takes priority. But on this occasion, it was the funeral that got out of the way. When the Prince of Life met the procession of death, it was death that had to get off that road. It is the most dramatic scene and your heart begins to beat quicker just trying to picture it. The tragedy of it is that every death is ultimately the result of the fact that we live in a sinful world, and therefore a world where there is disease and darkness and death. Here is the Son of God meeting a scene that God never intended. So something had to give way.

Jesus' attitude to the mourners was one of pity and compassion. Time and again in these case histories, our Lord's humanity is the first thing you notice and his deity is the second. Have you noticed that? As a real Son of Man, as a human being, his heart went out to this party, and he felt full of compassion. That is a very deep word. It is translated in the Authorized Version as "bowels". In modern, rather cruder language, it is a gutsy, real, deep-down feeling and Jesus had it. But I want you to notice that his feelings were translated into practical help. Compassion is of no use unless it is turned into action. So his pity and compassion turned into action, and he did a number of surprising things.

First he ordered the woman to stop crying. A very strong word is used here in the Greek. "Stop crying! Stop it!" It is almost like: "Stop hurting me; you're hurting me too much in crying like that; I can't bear it; stop crying." Second, Jesus touched the coffin. Now if a rabbi touched a coffin he would be defiled and unable to say prayers that day. Then Jesus said something to the young man – to a corpse. Jesus said, "Get up young man. Sit up."

Luke uses a medical term for what happened next. He says, "He sat up in bed" – the medical term for "began to get better". What would you have felt in that moment? What do you suppose the mother felt? What do you suppose the young man felt? He began to talk, but there is no record of what he said. In fact, although in the Bible there are a number of instances of people being raised from the dead, in not a single case is anything recorded in which they said anything about what it was like to be dead. That is very significant. It would not help us to know, so we are never told.

What did the people think about Jesus? They were scared stiff, frightened out of their wits. Fear came on them all. Why? You need to remember where it happened. On the

Plain of Esdraelon there is a hill, on the northern side of which is a village called Nain. That is where this happened. Nearby, there is a village called Endor where had lived a spiritist medium, the witch of Endor, who claimed to be able to contact the dead. A thousand years earlier, King Saul had consulted this medium, and the spirit of Samuel had appeared to Saul and told him that because he had consulted a medium he would die. And die he did, on the mountains of Gilboa within sight of that place. Also in that region there is a village called Shunem, where Elisha laid his body on the body of a young boy and raised him back to life nine hundred years earlier than the scene in the Gospel. The whole hill was a place where people spoke of the dead and being raised from the dead and contacting the dead. There was all kinds of local folklore going around this area, and now here was a man doing the same as Elisha had done. Is it the power of evil spirits or the power of good spirits? Certainly it is supernatural, so which is it? You can imagine the fear.

Out of that fear came the conclusion that it is another Elisha – a prophet. God is doing something. It is God who has done this. You know, when God is as near as that, and as real as that, you are scared stiff. There may be a deeper reason for their fear and this would be it: for many people the thought of resurrection from the dead is a fearful thought. I know that at funeral after funeral where somebody has been buried who is not even a Christian – who doesn't know God, who has never had their sins forgiven – because the facial muscles relax in the moment of death the face always looks more peaceful than it did in life. I have heard so many relatives look into the coffin and say, "They're at peace. They're safe. They're beyond disturbance now. No one can touch them now." This has brought a lot of false comfort to many people because the fact is that a dead person can be disturbed, and a dead person can be called to be given an account for themselves.

A dead person can hear the voice of God.

In fact, in John 5:28-29, Jesus says that the hour is coming when those who are in the graves will hear his voice [the voice of the Son of Man] and come forth – those who have done good, to the resurrection of life, and those who have done evil, to the resurrection of condemnation. You know, the possibility of resurrection is the thing that would produce fear in people. The reason why most people today in Britain don't fear death is that they think death is the end and that you are safe beyond recall and you won't have to pay your bills after death and you won't have to account for your life after death. But when Jesus raises the dead, he is saying the dead can be called back. That produces a very deep fear in people because they know that death is not therefore the end and not therefore an escape. It is not a way out.

Remember that these mourners had no idea who Jesus was. He was a total stranger to them. But those to whom Jesus is no stranger have no fear of death or of resurrection – no fear of being called back to life. Ask yourself in your heart: does the thought that dead people can be disturbed disturb you? Does the thought that they can be called out of their graves by the Lord fill you with joy and excitement? Or does it fill you with a horrible sense of foreboding? That will depend on whether Jesus is a stranger or a friend to you. I daresay that woman got over her fear, and the joy of being with her son banished the fear. But Jesus is the Lord of life and death; he has the keys of death and Hades in his hands. So Jesus says to us, "Weep not." Paul says, "We do not grieve as others do who have no hope."

Now consider the case of the puzzled prophet. The ripples of fame at what Jesus had done spread out through the country, and they spread far south, down the deep rift valley of the river Jordan. The ripples reached an ugly fortress castle on the east cliffs on the hills of Moab as they sloped down to the Dead Sea. The place was called Machaerus. There in solitary confinement, in a dungeon, with the little barred window looking out over the vast wilderness that he had roamed for thirty years, was a young man, the cousin of Jesus, John the Baptist.

I want you to try to imagine how John felt as he lay there, knowing that he had nothing to look forward to but death. He heard the amazing accounts of what his cousin Jesus was doing in Galilee. I want you to realise that this man is under physical, mental, and spiritual stress. He is under physical stress because if you have lived in the open air all your life, out under the clear blue sky, and slept in the fresh air, and suddenly you are in a tiny cell, that is a physical strain: no exercise, little food, and John is suffering. As to mental strain, there must have been one question torturing his mind: Jesus was raising the dead, doing all kinds of things, why doesn't he get me out? Can you imagine the torture of that question? For you have to remember that Jesus didn't help everybody. The Bible states quite clearly that he didn't heal all the sick who wanted healing from him. He didn't raise all the dead and stop every funeral that took place – only two or three. You have to remember that he left John in prison. That is not easy. When other people are being set free, it is not easy to stay in a cell for Jesus. So John had mental torture.

Then there was a spiritual stress. You see, he had said, "When the Lord comes – when this coming one arrives on the scene, he will baptise with fire. He will judge the nations. He will separate the wheat from the chaff. He will throw the chaff into the fire." He preached about a king who would come and judge sins – and here is Jesus helping people.

There are many, you know, who would say this: "John was quite mistaken; Jesus came just to be nice and do good; in fact, John had the Old Testament idea of the Lord, and he was quite mistaken." Actually, John was not mistaken except

Luke 7

in timing. For the simple fact is that when Jesus came the first time he did not come to condemn but to save. But when Jesus comes the second time he will come with the fire of judgment and his winnowing fork will be in his hand. He shall come to judge the quick and the dead.

John the Baptist wanted to be sure. Was Jesus the one coming? Disciples visited John and came back to Jesus. For anybody who has questions as to whether Christ is really the one you thought he was – take your question to Jesus. Don't take it to anyone else, go straight to him. The glory of it is that Jesus didn't give a straight answer to John's question. He says, "Go back and tell John what you've seen and heard. Blind see, lame walk, dead rise, and poor people are hearing the gospel." That is perhaps the biggest of all – nobody thought the poor people had any chance. Jesus is appealing to John's knowledge of the Old Testament in Isaiah 35 and Isaiah 61. Isaiah had said when the Messiah comes the blind will see, the lame will walk, the dead will rise, and the poor will have the gospel preached to them. If you have doubts about Christ, the reason may be that you have got the wrong idea of Christianity. It is important not to be offended by Jesus as he is. We need to take the Bible as it stands and not say: "This bit doesn't fit with my ideas and that bit doesn't." God's ways are so much higher than our thoughts.

So we see what John thought about Jesus, and off went the disciples. The crowds who overheard this may have been saying, "John's not much of a man, is he? Doubting already, and he was the big preacher we all went to hear – the revivalist, the prophet." Jesus springs immediately to the defence of his cousin so that there is no suspicion, no doubt about John. Jesus is so understanding. Believe me, when people point at you and say, "Doubtful kind of Christian there," remember there is Jesus to defend you, and that whatever they may think about you, Jesus will stand up for you if you belong to him. He had no doubts about John. So Jesus' message means this: What did you think you were going out to see? Did you think you were going to see a reed of grass that is easily shaken in the wind? Did you go out to see a man who was lining his own pockets and getting fancy clothes and a man who was just interested in himself? Never! You will find those men in palaces. But you went out into a desert, and what did you see? You saw a man of God, and you saw a prophet. You saw more than a prophet. Because John the Baptist was the only prophet who was himself the fulfilment of a prophecy. All the other prophets pointed away from themselves, but many of the prophets in the Old Testament pointed forward to a prophet who would come. John was a prophecy as well as a prophet.

Of all those born of women, he is the greatest there has ever been (other than Jesus). Then Jesus adds a surprising thing: "But the very least in the Kingdom of God is greater than he." Commentators have argued about what that phrase meant. Some have pointed out that John the Baptist was never baptised. That is true, but it is deeper than that. Some have tried to say he was not born of the Spirit – but he was filled with the Holy Spirit from his birth so I don't think that one washes. In what way are those in the Kingdom greater? I think in this way: you are further on than he was. Even though John is in the New Testament, he is the last Old Testament prophet – the last of the preparation. We need to get our perspective right.

You see, when John the Baptist came, the greatest there had ever been, he didn't please everybody. Some accepted his preaching and were baptised in water, but some were too proud and too religious to do so. You find that you can never please some people who are too proud to humble themselves before God, and be baptised and believe in Jesus – people

Luke 7

who will find fault with everything. To put it very simply: a person may come to one service and say, "That was too long," and someone comes to the next service and says, "Well, that was much too exuberant, and much too shallow and superficial; it was like a concert." Then they come to the next service and say, "The preacher was far too mournful. I went away quite depressed" – and so on. Sooner or later, you know that they don't want God. The service will be too sad, or too happy, or too this or too that, and you will never get through. Jesus said, "You who refuse John's ministry are childish; you're like kids in the marketplace." Sometimes we are taught that Jesus had a high view of children and thought of them as very innocent and good, but he didn't. He was the eldest of a large family. He knew what children were like and how petulant and sulky they can be.

He said, "You're like kids in the marketplace." They played weddings and funerals – trying to be grown ups. So you would see them all marching around wailing in the marketplace, playing at funerals. Then they would play at a wedding, and a little boy and a little girl would be marching up, with everybody cheering. There would always be one on the outside of the crowd not playing – "Don't want to. Want to play funerals today, and you're playing weddings." Then the next day, "Want to play weddings today, and you're playing funerals." Can you imagine that kind of thing? The trouble is that grown-ups can be childish, and when the Pharisees refused John the Baptist's ministry, they were being childish. When you just can't get a service right for someone it is because they are childish; because they are not seeking God. Even if there are things in every service that you don't appreciate, if you are seeking God you will go away with a blessing. That is the important thing. "Oh, you childish generation...." I might paraphrase what Jesus was saying: "You just can't be pleased. John the Baptist came, and he was an ascetic, a total abstainer; he wouldn't have a drink of wine with you; wouldn't go to parties, he lived in the wilderness – so unsociable.... I have come, and I'm totally different. I come into parties, and I drink and eat with you. All you call me is a glutton and a winebibber...." Then Jesus said a lovely thing: "But God's wisdom is recognised by those who are wise." John called for repentance and Jesus went around doing good. All of it is God's wisdom, and it is a narrow, childish mind that says, "You've got to be this, and you've got to be that – you've got to line up with my ideas of what a Christian should be."

God's wisdom is the important thing. Jesus deals with honest questions, but where a person is criticising and questioning because they are childish, you can't do anything with them. Here then is the lesson of the case of the puzzled prophet. There may have been times when things haven't fitted into your understanding of the Lord. You may have been puzzled, wondering why he did something the way he did it. Have you ever grumbled and criticised childishly because it didn't fit in with your ideas?

Finally, we have the case of the heartless host. Simon the Pharisee invited Jesus to lunch. Why? They obviously did not have a lot in common. Simon was a Pharisee and not a very nice chap at that. Did he do it out of curiosity to try to get to know Jesus better having heard about him or having heard him preach? Did he do it out of suspicion to try and trip him up in talk? Or, most probably, did he do it simply out of pride – that he was the one who always entertained the preacher or the visiting celebrity or whoever it was?

Whatever the reason, Jesus accepted. He must have known he wouldn't get a very warm welcome, but he went into the house. In those days they ate on a veranda or in an open courtyard with archways around. There was a table in the middle, and they would lie at it with their feet out, heads in towards the circle, leaning on their left hand and eating with their right. Around would be gathered all the villagers. They used to love this. The host would like the village to see what he had put on his table and who he had with him for lunch. I found that in the Shetland Islands this kind of practice was still occurring. We had some very embarrassing moments when my parents came to visit me there, and the local chapels, bless them, put on a real spread – covering the communion table with the meal. My parents and I had to sit up there and eat that food while the congregation (without any food) sat and watched us eat! As we took a bite you could hear someone saying, "That's one of my scones." You can imagine our feelings. In the Middle East that would have been welcome – you want the village to see the important guest and what lovely food you provide. So there they all were, crowded round the archways, watching this (probably) Sabbath midday meal.

Then suddenly the whole thing is spoiled, for Simon at any rate. The most disgusting thing happened. A known immoral woman, whom everybody avoided except a few men, came pushing through the crowd and went straight up to Jesus. We can imagine Simon thinking: "Dear me – my reputation! Does he think this woman comes to my house regularly?" She knelt down and did something no woman should ever do in public – she unwrapped her hair. We still have a relic of this act. We might say about somebody who has lost their dignity at a party that they had "let their hair down". To let your hair down in public was degrading. Then she brought out the only tool of her trade – perfume. She poured it on Jesus' feet and then she began to stroke his feet with her hair. Simon would have thought it obvious what she was trying to do. Didn't Jesus realise? If he was the sort of man he claimed to be, he would understand who this is. If he was a prophet, he would discern this and not let her do it.

Jesus' thoughts about Simon now come out. "Simon, I want to tell you a story...." Our Lord now told the parable of the eccentric moneylender. Did you ever hear of a moneylender forgiving people? That sounds really eccentric. Simon, being a Pharisee, probably knew many moneylenders and he may have been one himself but he had never heard of a moneylender like the one Jesus talked about now. It was, of course, fiction. It is not true to human life, but it is very true to divine life. "Simon, there was a moneylender. One man owed him five hundred denarii and the other owed him fifty. They had nothing with which to repay him, so he cancelled their debts." What a parable – two sentences and it is all over. "Now Simon, which do you think will love the moneylender most?" Simon, in an offhand way, said, "Oh, I suppose the man who...." Now why did he say, "I suppose"? Well, he is implying that no moneylender would ever behave like that anyway. So it is a hypothetical issue, but I think there is a deeper reason why he said "I suppose". He was getting the message, and he didn't like it, and he wanted to turn the conversation as quickly as possible.

Jesus sees that Simon is getting the message, and he does what in society today would be considered a very rude thing. He criticises his host's hospitality. But Jesus has holy boldness here and he points out that the woman had washed the filthiest smelliest part of him with her tears and wiped them with her hair. She loved in a way that Simon did not understand – because her sins were many, and they had been forgiven.

Jesus is saying here that to do the minimum shows lack of love; to do the maximum shows the presence of love. You can divide Christians into two groups: those who do the minimum – once on Sunday if they can manage it; and those who do the maximum and who will give and give again everything they can – time, energy, effort – whatever it costs. What is the difference between the minimum and the maximum Christian? The answer is very simple. The minimum one has obviously had very few sins forgiven and loves little. The maximum loves much.

In other words, what the Lord wants from us is not the kind of service that is a duty, which says, "How little need I do?" but the kind of delight that says, "How much can I do?" Love is a reckless spender. A person who loves the Lord will become a big spender. Your love for the Lord is in direct ratio to the forgiveness you have received. You know you should love him with all your heart and soul and mind and strength, but that is hard if you have not been forgiven much. When you have been forgiven, and when you have felt the breathless wonder of leaving a thing behind you that has been wrong, knowing that God will never bring it up again – that is when you love. So this is the lesson of the heartless host. He gave adequate hospitality. There was a meal on the table. It was adequate, but it wasn't loving; it wasn't reckless.

Our Christian service can be adequate, fulfilling the minimum responsibilities of church membership or what have you, but that is not loving, and the Lord wants love.

Jesus turned to this woman and said to her, "Your sins are forgiven." How did that woman get her sins forgiven? Was it because she had washed his feet? No, it happened before that. That was just an expression – the effect, not the cause. It was the fruit, not the root. It was the consequence, not the condition. Forgiveness was the cause, and love was the effect.

When had her sins been forgiven? I am going to guess now, but Matthew's Gospel gives me a little light on this. Both Simon and the woman had obviously been listening to Jesus preaching that day just before he was invited to the meal. Do you know what his teaching was that day? It was:

"Come unto me all you that labour and are burdened. Come to me and I will give you rest" – and she came. When she heard where Jesus was, she came and she had found rest.

8

Read Luke 8

8:1-21
Now we have a very different approach and some big surprises. The first thing which may be news to you was that Jesus had female followers. He was leading a whole bunch of men and women around the country – twelve men whom he had chosen and many women, most of whom had benefitted from his ministry. Among others there was Mary Magdalene. Jesus had cast seven demons out of her, and she was cured and asked if she could follow him. There was Joanna, the wife of Chuza who was Herod's butler in his castle. A very well-off woman, she had also benefitted from Christ's ministry and asked if she could follow. The women ministered to Jesus and to all the twelve men, out of their substance. In other words, those women supported the men. I was brought up to think of Jesus walking around the country with just twelve men and the tendency is to forget that there were also many women. That tells you quite a lot about Jesus. They were not the wives of the twelve; they were other women, and you can imagine how, in that sort of society, he was running a huge risk of accusation of immorality. But he took them with him to town after town and village after village, which meant that there was quite a big team that had to be accommodated and fed, and they paid for it out of the resources of the women.

Here we have a balance which we must keep today. He was not training the women to be apostles. They had their particular function and ministry which he benefitted from, and so did the other men, but he never got male and female confused. Paul, likewise, led a team of people with women included – people he referred to as deacons, servants. So this balance which Jesus had and which Paul had is to have both men and women together ministering, but with distinct ministries. There is a balance there which runs right against the contemporary spirit of the age, but nevertheless, Christians need to follow Christ in that. He would send out the twelve men as his deputies.

The bulk of this passage consists of two parables and I find it fascinating that one parable is for the men and the other parable is for the women, and Jesus made sure, while he was teaching, that he had words for the men and for the women. He was not biased towards men – that is a libel on Jesus – but he included men and women in his teaching and when he did that, he always took a parable from outdoors for the men and a parable from indoors for the women. For example, when he wanted to speak about what it means to be lost, he gave the parable of the lost sheep for the men; and the parable of the lost coin for the women. He had this real balance of outdoors and indoors.

Let us take the two parables – first of all, the one for the men: an outdoor story of a farmer sowing seed. It is an observation of something that happened each year. When a farmer went out to sow the seed, the seed was good but three quarters of it was wasted and there is this difference between the wasted seed and the seed that produced a harvest. The farmer was not bothered about the wasted seed because from the good seed he got a harvest. If you see a sower sowing seed in the traditional manner of the Middle East, you realise what Jesus was describing. They didn't have fields to plough and grow corn in as we grow it, they had pretty rough areas full of rocks and weeds. The farmer could not sow all his

Luke 8

seed in good soil as we can. He just had to scatter it. Three out of four seeds fell on bad soil. Some fell on a path where there had been too many people treading already – it was hard and the seed wouldn't go in, and the birds of the air just came and had a good feed, or secondly, it was very shallow soil on the hard rock and while it grew for a time, it didn't last and it usually died off fairly soon. Then there was also the seed that fell among weeds - which choked it as soon as it grew up.

But, here and there, as he scattered the seed, it fell into good soil, and that is when it germinated and produced even a hundred heads of corn for the one that had got in. So the farmer reckoned it was all worthwhile, even though a lot of it appeared to be wasted. Jesus said: if you have ears to hear, then hear. He didn't draw out the moral. It is very important to realise that Jesus, when he used a parable, didn't explain it. He left it to people to work out what he was saying. So it was not a big surprise that the disciples, when they got him on his own afterwards, asked him what that was all about. Jesus only explained his parables to those who asked him afterwards what they meant. Before he told the disciples the meaning of that parable, he first explained why he spoke publicly in parables.

Now I was brought up to think of the parables as sermon illustrations, little stories that would enlighten the people, but that is entirely wrong. Jesus said that he spoke in parables to hide the truth, not to make it more obvious – but to hide the meaning so that only those who have got the clue would understand. The rest will hear but not understand; they will see, and not see. Now here is a very important point. He is quoting the prophet Isaiah. In chapter six, Isaiah is called by God to be a preacher and he is warned that people will not listen to his preaching. God says: Isaiah, you will teach and teach and preach and preach and they will see but they will not see. They will hear but they won't understand. So poor Isaiah was called to a lifetime of preaching to people who wouldn't understand, and that is an awful calling. He had to do that until he died and no-one understood what he was getting at until long after he had died.

So, like Isaiah, Jesus was hiding the truth in stories so that people will not understand because God does not want people to understand and get converted and healed. Now there is a truth about Jesus' teaching that many Christians don't even try to understand. Yet this is crucial because Paul also quotes the same verse from Isaiah when the Jews don't accept the gospel. He observes that it is just what Isaiah found – he preached, but people didn't see the point.

What was the point of just telling us about something that happens every day and which is normal? Because there is nothing abnormal about the sower going forth to sow. When the disciples got Jesus on his own, they asked him to tell them the meaning. He explained that to them was given the secrets of the Kingdom. He gave them the meaning so that they would understand the story. He said that the good seed the farmer scattered is the Word of God – and when you scatter the Word of God among people, you will find different responses, not because there is anything wrong with the seed but because the soil is different.

I have found that whenever you talk about the Word of God you do get different reactions, depending not on what you are saying, which is perfectly good truth, but depending on the soil in people's hearts. Then he taught that the trodden path stands for those who have had a lot of other people's views pass by, gone through their minds, and their minds have got harder and harder and they don't take the Word in – they can't, they are too hard. The birds of the air stand for the devil, and when you are sowing the Word of God in people's hearts and their hearts are too hard, the seed is wasted. It doesn't come to anything. Furthermore, the devil will make sure that he comes and takes that seed away. They go away and forget everything they have heard. There is no fruit from it.

The shallow soil are people who eagerly accept the Word and say, "That was great stuff, thank you, I enjoyed that" – but when troubles come, then the seed doesn't develop. It doesn't grow, and as soon as a bit of pressure is on those people, the Word just disappears, dissolves. There are those who have too many weeds in their life, too many riches, too many interests, too many pleasures – there is just too much crowding into their hearts and the seed can't get room to develop. It will be crowded out very quickly by the other interests in life.

Now that happens enormously today because, with televisions, computers and so forth, we have so much wanting to get into our minds and hearts that to get the Word of God germinating and with room to develop often doesn't happen. I am afraid that is probably one of the main reasons why it is so difficult for British people to listen to the Word of God and let it grow. There are too many interests, too many calls on our time, too many things that choke out the interest in the Word, and we are not used to sitting down and thinking about what we have heard. Even reading books seems to be on the way out. So this choking effect is very common indeed today.

But when the seed of God's Word goes into good soil, and the heart is ready to receive it, to think about it and to put it into practice, then you get a hundredfold harvest and it was worth it for that one person. Every preacher knows this, and here is Jesus thinking about the ministry that he is having – very popular ministry, but with many people it is not going to last. With some, it is going to be choked; with others it is just too shallow – it hasn't gone right in. But when you get good soil, the joy of a really good harvest is worth it all, however much seed appears to be wasted. You can delight in the good soil.

Looking back over my ministry, there have been overseas trips when I have come back and told my wife that there was one person who really got it, and that trip was worth it for that one person, and they have produced a harvest that was worth the whole trip. So I know exactly what Jesus is talking about here and it is a sheer joy when you get a good bit of soil.

He immediately goes on to a second parable about a lamp and light. At first sight, it doesn't look like the same message at all. What is there in common between sowing seed and lighting a lamp? Bear in mind, as I told you, that he now had an indoor version of the same truth for the women – a story that they would understand, because the lamps were clay with a big hole to pour oil in and a little hole at the end where you had a wick. You light the wick and you pour the olive oil in the bigger hole and, having lit the lamp, what do you do with it? You put it as high as possible. The one thing you don't do with such a lamp is put it under something, either a jar or even a bed.

There is a village on the Golan Heights which has been built in exactly the same way as village homes two thousand years ago, and they are dark. They have mud walls and a thatched roof, or even a roof made of sods and they need lighting if they are to be of any use at all. Now once you have lit the lamp, what do you do with it? You put it on a stand. Light is always best when it is high. That is why we have lights up in the ceiling and why you put a lamp stand near your reading desk. You put the light up and then it shines down and illuminates the house. Now that is a parable. It is a very ordinary thing, and every woman knew that is what you do with a lamp. You don't light it and hide it – that would be crazy. You light it and lift it up, and then the whole house benefits from the light.

There is a parallel between planting seed by scattering it and lighting a lamp and putting it up at a height. The connection is that there is going to be an influence on other people. Jesus, for example, said, "I am the Light of the world" and it is the life of Jesus that has exposed people for two thousand years. Jesus also said, "You are the light of the world." It is one of the few things he said about himself and about us. He teaches: once you have the light, lift it up where people can see it or where it can see people. Because one of the main effects of lamps or a light is to expose things, and of course, if you haven't dusted the house lately and you put a strong light up then everybody is going to see, and you are going to expose your dust. So Jesus said in the Sermon on the Mount: let your light shine before men so that they may see your good works and glorify your Father in heaven.

Nothing hidden will be kept hidden but will be shown up, nothing concealed will be kept concealed, and one of the things about the light that Jesus brought into the world is that the worst of men have been exposed – and comparing anybody with Jesus, they will be exposed for what they are.

Jesus promised that what was whispered in the bedchamber will be shouted from the housetops. That is a disturbing thought if you think it through. So the effect of light is to enlighten – show up, expose. It is here that he says something that really fits the parable of the sower rather than the parable of the lamp: those who have will get more and those who have not will get less. Sure enough, again I have found in practice that when you are preaching the Word of God, those who have got some understanding will get more and those who have none will lose even what they have. So whenever you listen to the Word of God you will either get more or less. So the key verse in both parables says the same thing.

In the first parable, the key verse is, "Anyone who has ears, let him hear." And the key verse in the second parable is, "Consider carefully how you listen." In both cases, you either go away with more or less understanding, you can't stay the same. The Word of God either gives you more understanding or you have even less than you started with.

Finally, we have what I call Jesus' family. We had a surprise with his followers at the beginning – that he had men and women followers. Now we have a big surprise about his family. He is in the middle of the crowd and somebody says, "Your mother and your brothers are outside and they want to see you." We know why they had come. We don't hear it in this Gospel, but in one of the other Gospels they were convinced that Jesus was suffering a mental disease – schizophrenia. They said, "He's beside himself" – two people; someone in public and someone in private, and the poor man is ill. They had come to take him home and to persuade him to stay at home and leave all this public ministry and come back to the carpenter's shop and recover his normality.

Jesus did two surprising things. First, he disowned them as his family. He said they were not his mother and brothers. They didn't belong to him. That must have been very hurtful, cutting, especially for his mother. Then he said: who is my family, who is my mother, who is my brother? My mother and my brother are those who hear God's Word and put it into practice. Very simple. In other words, you are Jesus' family if you listen to God's Word and put it into practice – that is all, whether you are a man or a woman. It is amazing how anybody who becomes a serious, obedient servant of God will be called crazy. Become sincere, become obedient, and you are a maniac! But you are Jesus' family and in the long run, it is only those who are Jesus' family who are going to live with him forever – and many who think they are his family will not.

After the resurrection of Jesus from the dead, his brothers were convinced that he was who he was. His mother was convinced all the way through and she quietly believed in him. So it was that his mother and some of his brothers – one called Jude, another called James – did change their minds about him and they knew that he was not mad but totally sane. When you get to know Jesus, you get to know someone who is totally sane. And the more you follow him, the more you are convinced.

8:22-56

Luke recounts miracles of healing and what we call nature miracles. The disciples are left in complete bewilderment by the calming of the storm. Who is this man that even wind and waves do what he tells them? They were so near the truth there. He was God! That was how he could control the weather, and they could have guessed even then who he was. The demons had already told people who he was but Jesus had told them to keep quiet. Now the disciples were seeing for themselves.

The Sea of Galilee is a beautiful lake thirteen miles long and eight miles wide, surrounded by steep hills on all sides, so it is in a hollow and below sea level. People don't realise that; they know the Dead Sea, further down the Jordan, is way below sea level, but Galilee is 600 feet below sea level. During the day what happens is this: the sun heats up the water of the Sea of Galilee and in the afternoon the hot air over the water rises and sucks in cold air, down all the valleys around, from every direction. So if you are in a little boat in the middle of that, you are stranded in the wind and you can't move anywhere. I have been in a larger boat in the middle of an afternoon squall on the Sea of Galilee and it is frightening. In fact they forbid anybody to go out in open rowing boats in the afternoon in Galilee because there is real danger. Suddenly, this beautiful still lake is in turmoil and the wind is blowing at you in the middle from every direction and you just can't escape. Furthermore, the boat was a bit overloaded – all the twelve disciples were in it, water was coming over the edge and they looked to be in real danger of drowning. For fishermen to be afraid of drowning means they were in real danger. It must have been very frustrating that Jesus slept through the whole thing. He was up in the stern of the boat (see Mark's Gospel), fast asleep, and not troubled, so they woke him up and said, "Don't you care? We're drowning!" Now what they expected him to do I don't know, except they expected him to drown with them! But he didn't. He just stood up and rebuked the wind and the waves. Our Bibles have a wrong translation here. Have you heard the words "Peace, be still"? That is not what he said. He said, "Get muzzled!" It is how you would talk to a puppy dog that was jumping up at your guest.

As soon as he said that, all was calm. Then, having rebuked the wind and the waves, he rebuked the disciples and said, "Where's your faith?" Didn't they have any faith in God to believe they would be okay? He could sleep through it because he trusted his Father, but they obviously didn't trust him yet. It was a very sharp rebuke to the wind, the waves and the disciples. It is then that they asked who on earth this was. They had lived with him for two years and they were still perplexed. It is no wonder they were perplexed. They should have realised who it was – this must be the Son of God who can talk to the weather like this.

I have talked to the weather in the name of Jesus on three occasions in my ministry, all of which were necessary to the Kingdom of God. One was on the Northumberland moors where we had an open-air meeting and people were sitting

Luke 8

on hay bales – there must have been quite a few hundred – out of sight of any house. I had agreed to go and speak because the local farmer up there had said: "Please come." In fact, he said, "I know you're free on that date because the Lord has told us you're the one to speak" – and I was free just on that Saturday. But when I arrived at the farm, miles from anywhere, the farmer presented me with a complete fisherman's outfit – a conical hat, a big cape, waterproof trousers and waders! I asked, "What's all this for?"

He said, "Well, the weather forecast is just the worst it can be; there's a band of heavy rain crossing Northumberland this afternoon right when you're due to speak." And he had gone to such trouble.

I said, "Why did you spend all this money on this outfit? It won't be necessary." But my faith began to waver: they had no platform, they had a big truck with a little generator for the electricity, and, as I got up to speak, I saw this black cloud moving straight towards us, and, at my first words, umbrellas went up everywhere in the crowd. I am afraid I got angry with the Lord and said, "Lord, you arranged this and I've been obedient to come, what are you doing sending rain like this?" I remember saying, "In the name of the Lord, split that cloud." You can believe what you like about this, but that cloud divided and it rained – it poured – on fields to either side of us – and in the middle I had sun and actually got sunburnt lips!

The national magazine for farmers, *Farmers Weekly*, reported the miracle. The *Methodist Recorder* recorded the meeting but not the miracle. Even the local press had the headline "Miracle" because many local people saw it happen.

I would not do it because we were going to have a picnic but if it is for the kingdom, and if the kingdom is at stake, I am prepared to do that. I mention things like this because I want you to realise that Jesus is still the same and he can still control the weather and still does, for he is God himself.

The stilling of the storm was not the first time in the Gospels that Jesus controlled nature. The first time was at the wedding at Cana in Galilee when he turned the water into wine.

The second miracle we are now considering was when they got over to the other side, and I want you to realise that the eastern shore of the Galilee was not in Jewish hands and it specifically says that they crossed the lake according to Jesus' request, and they entered the country of the Gerasenes. There were Gentiles living there, so you could cross the lake from one race of people to another. On the far side, the eastern shore, was the Decapolis which means ten cities, which were not Jewish at all but were largely Greek. Strange that you could cross a small lake and be in a different country and among different people, but that is an important clue to what happened, because they were immediately met by a demon-possessed man.

I want you to realise that demon-possession is quite different from mental illness. There is a sharp difference in symptoms. Here are some of the symptoms of the former, and this man had them. First of all, he had a very loud voice. In every case of demon possession we have looked at, they cried with a loud voice. Their voice was not a human voice, it was the voice of a fallen angel, and that is loud. More than that, he had supernatural strength. Now a mentally ill person might need two or three people at the most to control them, but, for a demon-possessed person nine or ten people may be needed to hold them. Supernatural strength is another clear symptom and this man had it, because as fast as they had chained him, got handcuffs on him, he broke them. So there is the second mark of supernatural strength. He is possessed by a fallen angel.

Furthermore, a mentally ill person may be confused in

speech but a demon-possessed person can be addressed rationally and hold a proper conversation – and then they reveal supernatural knowledge. Every demon-possessed person we have found in Luke's Gospel knew who Jesus was and was able to say: I know who you are, you're the Holy One of God; or, you're the Son of God, but showed that they had known Jesus before he was conceived and born. They knew where he had come from, and again and again a demon-possessed person felt threatened by Jesus. "Have you come to destroy us?" "Please don't torture us." They are defensive against him.

Dr Kurt Koch has specialised in demon-possessed people and it is interesting that he visited a mental home in Germany (where he came from) and its head challenged him, asking, "What's the difference between mental illness and demon possession?" Kurt simply said, "I will demonstrate. Let's go into a private room in the home with a list of your patients and we'll pray for them individually." Those who were mentally ill were calmed by the prayer and behaved themselves more normally, but about a quarter of the people in that mental home went berserk when they were prayed for in the name of Jesus. My friend Kurt said, "Those can be cured instantaneously. The mentally ill will take time." He then went to those they had prayed for who went berserk and healed them in the name of Jesus – and they became normal immediately.

Most churches don't have any experience of demon possessed people and therefore they have no idea what the symptoms are, but the symptoms are all there in these cases mentioned in scripture. I hope that you don't meet any demon-possessed person because it is pretty frightening.

Here was this man, naked, living in a cemetery among the tombs; nobody touched him, nobody went near him, and he had a reputation as you can imagine. They were scared of him, and when he met Jesus, he opened the conversation and said, "Are you going to torture us? What do you want with us, Jesus?" And then he said: "Son of the Most High God". So the demons knew the truth about Jesus long before the disciples did, and Jesus was waiting until the disciples realised who he was before he could move any further in his ministry. It would take a little longer before Peter said, "I know who you are" – the first man ever to do so; and Martha, who was stuck in the kitchen, was the first woman who ever realised who Jesus was. As soon as they knew, he said: now I can go to Jerusalem and die. He had been waiting all those years for that to be realised because until you know who Jesus is, you will never understand why he volunteered to die and why he came to die. But that is another story – it will come up later in Luke.

You would have thought when they saw the man who had been demon possessed "clothed and in his right mind" and behaving perfectly normally, that the local people would have wanted Jesus to stay. On the contrary, there was something supernatural going on which they didn't like, and they asked him to go away, and he got in the boat to leave. They were not Jews, they saw this Jewish man come and deal with this demoniac, and they were scared. At the same time, the man himself begged Jesus to let him go with him back to the Jewish side. He didn't want to stay around where he had been known for his past. But, contrary to all his advice on the Jewish side, Jesus said, "Go and tell everybody." They had known the demoniac in the past and they could now see what he was like.

This is the interesting thing: Jesus didn't want to be talked about on the Jewish side, but he wanted to be talked about on the Gentile side. It was safe for him to be talked about there but on the Jewish side, where they had wrong expectations about the Messiah, it would be very dangerous to let it out prematurely. So he went back to the Jewish side, where his orders were: silence; don't talk! This is further proof that he had gone to a different country, different people and a different situation.

Now we come to the third miracle. Jesus returned to Capernaum. Jairus, the ruler of the synagogue, came to him and said, "Please come, my daughter is dying." She was only twelve and he loved her so much, and Jesus was the only one who could help her. So Jesus set off to go to the house of Jairus but they were some way away and he was some time going, and something happened on the way which delayed him a long time. You can imagine how Jairus was feeling, wanting to get him to the little dying girl quickly when a woman came in the crowd and she reached through and got hold of Jesus' clothes and knew immediately she was healed. She had suffered from continuous bleeding for twelve years. It was the normal monthly period gone completely wrong and she had spent a lot of money on doctors, it says, and no-one had been able to cure this. Then she got the shock of her life. She thought, having come in the crowd, and reached through between the people who were pressing him on every side, and touched his clothes, she had managed to get away with it and that no-one knew she had been healed, and she was safe. Jesus stopped, turned round and said, "Who touched me?" He said that goodness had gone out of him. This tells us something about Jesus. Whenever he healed someone, it cost him; goodness went out of him and he knew it. That is why he used to retire for prayer with his Father regularly – to get topped up with power again. He knew that somebody had touched him, and he only had to look around to see who it had been. Here was this blushing, trembling woman who thought that she had got away with private healing. The disciples saw that people were crowding him from all sides. Then the woman confessed that it was her. It wasn't his clothes, it was Jesus; her faith in him had cured her – his goodness flowed out when she had reached out and touched him.

Now all this took time and we can imagine poor Jairus tearing his hair out – his daughter was dying, and dealing with this woman must have seemed like a delay. Even as Jairus spoke, some friends from his home said, "Don't bother the teacher any more. She's dead." Imagine his sheer disappointment. He had persuaded Jesus to come and now this woman had delayed the whole thing, delayed it long enough for his daughter to die, and people had already started wailing and mourning. But Jesus said one thing to the parents and one thing to the mourners. To the parents he said: "All you've got to do is believe" (go on believing, meaning: go on trusting me). But to the mourners he said, "She's not dead; she's only asleep." Now from one point of view that was not true, but from another point of view it was, because the Bible often says, when a person dies, that they have "fallen asleep". That is what it looks like, as if someone has just "gone off". The important thing is that if someone is asleep, they can be woken up, and Jesus is preparing the mourners for what happened. Instead of wailing and mourning, they are laughing at him. She's dead – you can't do anything now!

It is one of the few occasions when Jesus didn't want even all the disciples in the know. So he carefully chose Peter, James and John. It was the first time he picked out those three, but he would do so again later. Out of the twelve, those three were the closest to him. He took the three in, shut the door, then took the little girl by the hand and said, "Get up." That is all! She got up, and he said two things to the parents. First: give her something to eat; she would have been hungry, not having had anything since she had died. Second, he told them to tell no-one what had happened. Once again, Jesus is protecting himself with silence.

Luke 8

When you read the Gospels and you read things about Jesus and you are tempted, with your Western sophistication, to say, "Oh, I'm not sure about that; that is a bit far-fetched, that's pushing it a bit" – well, the people who have a childlike faith and say, "I'll just believe it" are those who benefit from Christ today – and only those. Those who are too sophisticated to believe it all remain with their sophisticated ideas and they never see the Jesus of the Gospels. But those who come with simple faith say that it is the truth. These people were reporting the truth – what they saw and what he did. There is no exaggeration here. They were just simple fishermen, and they said: that is what he did. Jesus told the wind and the waves and they obeyed him. He is the one we are prepared to follow.

9

Read Luke 9:1–10:24

9:1-17
I call this the "Providential Picnic" because the Lord was providing the food. We are now looking at the closing of his ministry in Galilee, and then we move on to the great turning point in his ministry. The early ministry, for two and a half years, was in the north and then it all changed and he set his face to go to Jerusalem – and certain death.

This last bit of his ministry in the north consists of summary of what he did with his disciples, what Herod began to think about him, and then the Providential Picnic. This was a real turning point, where disciples became apostles which means "sent ones", and those who had been called to be with him, having studied him, were now called to deputise for him. They were sent out to do what Jesus had already been doing so they were first commissioned and then he commanded them to do certain things. In commissioning, he gave them power and authority, and they needed both. He told them that they were to preach and to heal exactly as they had seen him do, but without him. That was the crucial changeover. The commissioning must have been done with something like the laying on of hands. That is how it was usually done in those days. He gave them certain commands which they were to follow, and the first was to take nothing for themselves – no money, no spare clothes, no bread. Why were they sent out with nothing? The answer must be that they were to depend on the people they went to for food, for a change of clothing, for any money. They were to go with nothing at all and I can imagine that was quite a test for them.

They were to stay in the first house that welcomed them. That was a very subtle thing to tell them, and I am quite sure that it was because if they were in a rather poor house at first they would be tempted to move to a bigger or better house as they got known in a town, and they were not to do that. Jesus was being very sensible. He knew what can happen. And then he said: if they receive you, well and good, and you must receive anything they give you. If they give you food, receive it. But he said that if the people didn't receive them, they were to shake the dust off their feet as they left, as a testimony against them. That, of course, was a well-known sign of disapproval.

So off the disciples went. They duly came back and reported everything that had happened – what they had done, how they had got on, and on the whole, they had had a good time. They were excited. "Even the demons do what we tell them." Jesus told them not to be excited about that but to rejoice that their names were written in the book of heaven. That is more important than being able to tell demons to get out.

Now let us move on to the second section. Curiosity got hold of Herod. He was one of the four kings left in charge of parts of the Holy Land, and therefore he was called a tetrarch, a fourth part of the government. Herod's butler, in charge of all his palaces, had a wife called Joanna and she was one of the women following Jesus around. So she would report back to her husband what Jesus was doing. Herod was curious because people were speculating as to who Jesus was, and he was already doing such incredible, great things at 29 or 30 that some thought he might be a reincarnation of a great person – John the Baptist, Elijah or one of the other prophets. When Herod heard such rumours they stimulated

Luke 9:1-10:24

his curiosity. He would have loved to find out the answer to the question "Who is he?"

It is interesting that his first answer was: it couldn't be John, I chopped his head off. He could not accept any of the rumours, and we simply learn that he longed to see Jesus. Being a king, he wouldn't go to see Jesus; he would expect Jesus to come and see him, if invited, which Jesus never did. If I jump ahead in the Gospel of Luke, firstly, Herod became an enemy of Jesus and wanted to kill him, and Jesus said, "Go and tell that fox..." – which is one of the most remarkable things Jesus ever said about someone. A fox is a sly, cunning creature. Jesus saw him when at his trial he was forced to go. When Pontius Pilate discovered Jesus came from Herod's territory he had him transferred in chains to Herod, and Herod was thrilled. He thought: I've longed to see this man; I want to see the magic that he does. Jesus had nothing to say to him.

Let us get on to the big miracle, the feeding of the five thousand, and see how it happened. When the disciples came back after their mission, they were exhausted – goodness had gone out of them and they knew it. Jesus knew it, and, wanting to restore their resources he took them to Bethsaida, a tiny village up the hills in the wilderness. But somebody saw them go and spread the word, and crowds followed them, and when they arrived at Bethsaida he had thousands of people – five thousand men; I don't know if that means there were women and children with them. We know there was at least one boy because he figures in the story. But Jesus found that, instead of a rest, instead of a retreat, instead of retiring from the crowd, they had thousands of people.

What would have been your reaction? A human reaction would have been: we've come here to get away from you; we don't want a crowd, we've been ministering to people. We need a rest, and I've planned this for my disciples so

225

get away – we don't want you. That would have been a very human reaction. But Jesus' reaction was: we've got a crowd; let's minister to them; let's preach and heal. He welcomed them.

When you have planned a holiday and you are going away to get some rest and you find that people who know you are going and have gone there before you, it takes a lot of grace to welcome them and say "I'm so glad to see you". But Jesus wanted to help them. They had followed him because they wanted something. He preached the kingdom and healed all the sick, and it took most of the day. So their day off turned out to be a pretty full day of ministry.

When the sun began to go down – that was the time when they would all want and need a meal; that's the time when most of the people then had their main meal, after a working day. But they weren't at home, they were miles from anywhere, so the disciples said to Jesus: send them away. Jesus replied, "You feed them." And here is a kind of deadlock. The disciples' reaction was: how can you say that to us? There are five thousand people here and the only food we've got is five loaves and two fishes. They didn't say they had pinched them from a boy and that was his picnic he had brought. They wondered how they could possibly feed that crowd. But Jesus knew what he was going to do, and that is when the miracle happened.

He took those two fishes and the five loaves and began to break them up; he got them to sit down in groups of fifty. He organised it. There would be a hundred groups of fifty if my mathematics is right. He said: now you feed them and here's some food. By implication, he is literally making food in his hands, multiplying those loaves until there are hundreds of them. He is multiplying the two fish and he goes on handing the food out. He got the twelve people to act as waiters and to take the food from his hands and put it in the hands of the people.

Then comes the final verse and it says they all ate and were satisfied! To satisfy five thousand appetites with a handful of fish and bread is a miracle – something that God can do but man can't. I think the funniest comment is that they gathered up twelve baskets of fragments that remained. Now I think that's so funny, don't you? Let me explain. I'm always asking questions of the Bible, and the two questions I asked of this last verse were: (a) whose were the baskets? and (b) why were they empty?

Now as soon as you say that, you realise that the twelve empty baskets they used to fill with what was left over may have belonged to the twelve disciples. When they had known they were going away for the day with Jesus, they had packed lunch. They had got little baskets and filled them with food – for themselves. Now these baskets were empty. Quite simply, they had gone and hid in the bushes and emptied those baskets earlier in the day. They had eaten all their lunch – they hadn't shared any of it so they were now holding twelve empty baskets. The funny thing about that is that, first, Jesus is saying there is enough left over for you as well, but secondly, when he had said to them why don't you give them food, he was challenging them because they had already emptied their baskets. They had already eaten secretly and never let the crowd have a crumb. I think that's quite funny – to tell the disciples "you feed them", knowing that they had already fed themselves and that they had taken a boy's picnic for the crowd. Jesus was rebuking them.

Jesus was not doing anything new in scriptural terms because Elijah had already done it. If you know your Old Testament, you know that Elijah had caused a famine for years by praying for the rain to stop, and that Elijah himself had fled out of the country to a widow's house, and asked if she could put him up. She said that she could put him up but she didn't have any food for him. She only had a little cruse of oil and a little flour left – enough for one meal. The Bible records that, as long as Elijah stayed there, the more oil and flour kept appearing. The widow had cooked a good meal for Elijah every single day of the drought. So that was one occasion where it had already happened. The other was when God provided bread for a crowd of hundreds of thousands when he sent manna from heaven for the people of Israel as they wandered through the wilderness. Manna – the word means "What is it?" Every day there was enough manna on the sand to gather up and feed all those Israelites. The children got fed up with it and said, "What's for supper? Oh, not what-is-it again!" They had manna which kept people alive for forty years, but the day they got into the Promised Land the manna stopped and then they could produce their own food and get enough from others.

So this was not an unknown thing to happen. Of course, the question now becomes: does it happen now? Does Jesus multiply food and other physical things today? I am going to give you two stories that answer a glorious "Yes!" to that question. Come with me to the Mexico/US border. You may never have heard of the Mexican border until Donald Trump arrived on the scene, but if you look at an atlas, half way along the border there is a large American city called El Paso, and on the southern side of the same border and next to it is a Mexican city called Johannes. The two cities are so close, you would think it was one metropolis, and in between them is a gigantic garbage dump serving both cities. On the edge of the big landfill (as we would call it) were shanty houses made of cardboard and corrugated iron where lots of Mexicans made a living out of recycling rubbish – bits of metal and paper.

Now on the El Paso side – the American side – was a small Catholic church. When the Charismatic renewal hit the

Catholics, the priest and the two nuns who ministered there got filled with the Holy Spirit, and that changed their lives and the lives of the church. From then on, the Holy Spirit told them what they should be doing. When it came nearer to Christmas, the Holy Spirit said to that priest and the two nuns: I want you to take a Christmas dinner to the garbage pickers on the garbage dump. So they did that. They made enquiries and they were told that there were 120 people living on the rubbish, so they prepared that number of bags with a pork pie and a piece of fruit (the members of the church had cooked the pies), and they set off in an old van for the garbage dump. When they arrived, to their horror, they found there were three to four times as many people living on the rubbish as they had been told. So they prayed and said, "Right, we'll just have to distribute the bags we've got" – so they opened the van doors and the people queued up very quickly and they gave out a hundred and twenty Christmas lunches. But there were still bags in the van and they thought they had made a mistake and must have prepared a few more. So they decided to go on giving them out, and they went on giving until three or four hundred people had Christmas lunch – and they came back to the church to praise God.

They wanted the Pope to know what the Holy Spirit was doing in their church and they sent a video of the whole thing to him, and the dear priest, at the beginning of the video, says, "Holy Father, you ought to know what the Holy Spirit is doing in our little church." My wife and I have seen the video and watched it, fascinated – because this is really happening and it is the Holy Spirit telling a church to give a Christmas dinner to far more people than they thought, yet they had enough. That is one example.

For the other example I am going to Holland – to one of the saints of our times. She is dead now but her name was Corrie ten Boom, a wonderful lady. I first encountered her in Berlin at a conference. To me, she was just a name then. Billy Graham made a film about her called The Hiding Place, and I have seen the actual hiding place; it is in Harlem, Holland where Corrie, her sister and her father (who was a watchmaker) lived. When the Germans occupied Harlem, Corrie's father who was a saintly man, said they must hide Jews from the Nazis; and they built, in one of their bedrooms, a false wall about 18 inches away from the real wall and made a little cupboard, and through the back of the cupboard was a door into this very narrow place – the hiding place. They hid a family of Jews in the house because there were no windows overlooking. When the Germans came to the house, they put the Jews in this hiding place behind the false wall. It is an amazing story.

The family was betrayed by some neighbour who told the Nazis that there were Jews hiding in the house, and told them about the hiding place, and the whole family were arrested and taken to concentration camps. The father was taken to a men's camp and they never saw him again. Nobody knows what happened to him. Corrie and her sister Betsy were sent to a women's camp and of course, when they were first brought to the camp, they were stripped naked, given a shower, then given prison clothes. Betsy suffered from a serious deficiency and the doctors had given her a liquid to counteract this, and Corrie managed to smuggle it in – in her hair. She had long hair in a bun and she managed to hide this bottle for Betsy in her hair when they were taken to the shower.

When they got into a big hut in the camp, to her horror, she discovered four or five other women suffering from the same deficiency. Corrie was faced with an awful dilemma. Either she gave this medicine to her sister alone for perhaps a week or ten days or she shared it with half a dozen women with the same deficiency. She prayed about it and decided to share it. So she told the other women who needed it, and on the first day she tipped some into a spoon and gave a dose to each of the women. She did that for a week, and for two weeks, and for three weeks, and for a month.... and for two months. Still the bottle produced the medicine that was needed – and the women in the camp hut gathered every day around what they called the "magic bottle" to see it happen. God multiplied the medicine in that bottle every single day until one day, months later, Corrie tipped the bottle up and nothing came out – and she had a real crisis of faith. She said, "Lord, why is there no medicine in the bottle now? Have I weakened in my faith?"

But, later that very day, a Red Cross parcel arrived in the camp with many medicines – including the one that was needed, so they had enough. Now God did that. He multiplied the medicine in the bottle until the whole camp knew about it.

I have drawn those two examples from our day – to show that the Lord still multiplies what is needed. He can multiply a physical thing like medicine. He can multiply lunch boxes for the garbage pickers of Mexico. He is still the same Lord. Jesus is just the same as ever he was.

9:18-45

Up to now, Jesus has been preaching, healing, casting out demons – but all up in the north, in Galilee. From now on, he will set his face to go south to Jerusalem and to his death, so this marks this great turning point, and it all happens in one spot.

One of the great advantages of going to Israel is that you realise how connected everything in the Bible is with where it happened. There is a geographical dimension to Jesus' ministry which you don't fully realise until you are actually there and see the place and you think: so that is why that happened here. The background to this passage is that in the north of Israel there is a snow-capped mountain, the tallest in Israel. The Israelis can now ski down it, but in Jesus' day it was virtually inaccessible. Wherever you are in Galilee you can look up to the north and see this mountain. You can see palm trees at Galilee and you can look up and see a snow-capped mountain; it is amazing.

Until this point, Jesus has not been near that mountain but everything recorded in this passage took place up there and that was quite deliberate. What he wanted to say to them had to be said up there, and the first scene we are looking at is at the foot of Mt. Hermon, at a very unusual spot, because at the bottom of Mt. Hermon is an extraordinary sight. There is a red sandstone cliff, vertical right at the foot as if somebody has chopped it off; and from the foot of that cliff there comes a river twenty or thirty feet wide – straight out of the rock. That is the beginning of the River Jordan, and it is because the snow on Mt. Hermon melts and goes down a big crack inside the mountain and comes out at its foot. The opening of the crack is below the water so it looks as if a whole river starts from nothing and comes straight out of a cliff, and goes all the way down to the Dead Sea.

You can imagine that that would be a very religious place because of its unusual appearance, and it is the most exciting part of any trip I have led, because carved in the cliff face are alcoves shaped like an archway. They are carved out of the cliff and in those alcoves there were little statues; people worshipped there. In one of those little alcoves was an image of Pan, a Greek god who was supposed to appear as a man on earth, so they worshipped Pan at that very spot. Even today the village nearby is called Panias after that deity; in the first century it was called Caesarea Philippi after both Caesar and Philip, one of the relatives of Herod who governed that part of the Holy Land. In another of the alcoves was a statue of Caesar, who was a man whom people thought was a god.

Luke 9:1-10:24

Jesus took the twelve disciples to that spot where there were gods who appeared as a man and men who thought they were gods – and you can understand now why he took them there and said, "Who do people think I am?" He was giving them clues by taking them there. That is the most important question anybody could ever ask – what you think of Jesus determines your whole life and makes such a difference.

So that is the place where this first thing happened which we call The Great Confession. I took my daughter there once and it was pouring with rain, and we were miserable because even the coach windows were covered with mud. But we got out and walked through the rain, in the mud, to the foot of the cliff and I read this passage. Just as I read that Peter said, "You are the Christ", lightning struck a tree just by us with a great crash of thunder and, before we knew where we were, we were lying face down in the mud. It has always been a special place and everybody I have taken there has been profoundly moved.

Jesus asked them first, "Who does everybody else think I am?" – and the answer came in an unusual form: they are sure that you are a reincarnation; some say you are John the Baptist who's come back to life. Remember that Herod chopped John the Baptist's head off for the sake of a dancing girl. The second person they said it might be was Elijah. Then they said: most people are sure you have been one of the prophets before.

"Who do you think that I am?" – that was the big question. He had waited two and a half years to ask it. He had taken them with him and preached the Kingdom and healed the sick and delivered people from demons. He had done all that and given them clues. He had fed five thousand people with five loaves and two fishes, and he had stilled the storm. He had given them clue after clue, and now he asked them what conclusion they had come to. Peter said, "You are the Christ of God". He said more than that, and the other Gospels tell you what more he said, but what Peter was declaring was: You have lived before, but not on earth; you have lived in heaven before; you are the Son of the living God – that is the only explanation for what you say and what you do; we have watched you for two and a half years and we are convinced that you are the Christ, the Son of the living God.

Jesus had waited for one of the disciples to say that. He commanded them to tell no-one. Now he could go to Jerusalem; now he could die. At the age of thirty-three he says that now he can die. It is amazing; and from that moment he set his face to go south into his worst enemies' camp in Jerusalem. They knew what would happen to him. Above all, he knew. He said the Son of Man must suffer many things and be rejected by the elders and the scribes and be killed and be raised on the third day. That was the first time he had mentioned either his death or his resurrection. It wasn't the last time; he is going to tell them again and again what is going to happen to him in Jerusalem – and they can't face it.

Now we don't know the sequel from this Gospel. We know it from Mark. Peter wasn't having it – "far be it from you Lord to die" – you can't do that, I won't let you. Jesus said: Satan's put that into your mind. My Father put the truth into your mind; now Satan's got hold of you. "Get behind me Satan" – I've got to die, and I'll be raised from the dead on the third day.

The next paragraph is a little difficult. It is obviously little pairs of statements and each one of them would make a sermon. All I can do is to affirm that as Jesus walked with the disciples, wherever he was, he was teaching them, talking to them, telling them things they needed to know – and they remembered. In verse 23 to the end of that paragraph, you have at least five little sermons, and each of them is important. He has told them what is going to happen to him; now he is going to tell them what will happen to them.

The first thing he says is: if you are going to follow me it means a cross. You will need to take up your cross every day and deny yourself and live as if you are dead, and follow me. In other words, it is tough to be a disciple. It is tough to be a Christian. It involves a daily crucifixion.

The next thing he says is that if you want to keep your life – if you want to save your life – you are going to lose it. But if you lose it for his sake, you will save it. That has comforted many Christian martyrs over the centuries. It doesn't sound like anything other than a contradiction, but it is true, and Christians have found it to be true.

Then he says: what good is it if a man gains the whole world and loses himself?

Then Jesus told them: "If anyone is embarrassed or ashamed of me and my words in this world, when I come back to this world, I'll be ashamed of him." There is a thought. Have you ever been embarrassed to admit you are a Christian, that you belong to Jesus, that he is alive today?

Then he said, "I tell you the truth, some of you standing here will not die before you see the Kingdom of God." They were still alive in the days of Acts when they saw the Kingdom of God come with power.

Well those were just a few sermonettes on the way up the mountain, because they were climbing Mount Hermon, above the snow line, to the top. That would be an exhausting climb because Hermon is just short of 10,000 feet. It says that when they got to the top the disciples were sleepy, and I am not surprised after that big climb. The first thing they saw was what I call a heavenly fluorescence, the most wonderful sight. Jesus' face changed, his clothes changed, and as Peter told Mark later, Jesus' clothes were brighter than any soap on earth could get them. The secret was this – the light was shining inside his clothes, through them. In other words, Jesus himself became a blazing light, his face shone, his body shone through his clothes. If you have ever shone a torch behind your shirt or blouse, you know what that would look like.

Luke said his clothes looked as if there was a flash of lightning going through him. They were being given a glimpse of who Jesus is. I think it is so interesting that, after they had guessed who he was, Peter, James and John were given a glimpse of his previous life in heaven. Later they would write down: "We beheld his glory, glory as of the only-begotten Son of God." Peter, in an Epistle, talks about this – how they saw his glory with their own eyes. It must have been an unforgettable sight and it is how Jesus will appear when we see him. It is no wonder that Paul was blinded by that. It was too bright for his eyes.

I have a picture painted in 1916 by Charles Butler, called "The King of Kings", and it appeared in the Royal Academy in London. Mine is only a rather poor copy of it, but here is Jesus, King of kings, and surrounding him are portraits of all the kings and rulers of the world – one hundred and sixty of them. Each of them is painted in the attitude he had towards Jesus. The interesting thing about the painting is that Charles Butler was able to make Jesus' clothes shine from the inside. No-one has ever been able to repeat the luminescence of Jesus' robes in this picture. Butler never told anybody how he did it, but it was his great work. In the picture, there is Edward the Confessor offering his crown to Jesus; Napoleon, aloof and looking at Jesus as if he has contempt for him; behind Jesus can be seen the prince of this world, the devil, dark and forbidding, and he is shrinking back from Jesus. But the luminosity of Jesus' robes! In the original oil painting they shone out as if a light was behind them.

The disciples were amazed at what they saw, and to their astonishment, when they became fully awake, they saw not one but three people covered in glory. With that instant recognition which we will all have in heaven, they recognised two people who had been dead for centuries – Moses and Elijah. It says that Jesus discussed with them – then my Bible says the "departure" that he was going to fulfil in Jerusalem, but in fact the Greek says the "exodus". Moses was saying to Jesus: now you are going to do an exodus in Jerusalem; you are going to set a lot of people free by your death. Moses and Elijah represented the Law and the Prophets.

Then Peter put his foot in it. I have a lot of sympathy with Peter because I put my foot in my mouth frequently, and he sometimes said the wrong thing. This was the most wonderful experience of Peter's life. Let's put up three shrines, three shelters for the three of you. Let's capture this moment and keep it. That is what he was saying, and it says he didn't know what to say – well, he sure didn't, because immediately after he said that, they were enveloped in a cloud and a voice came out of the cloud – "This is my beloved Son. Listen to him." Then the cloud went away and there was only Jesus left. The message was a rebuke to Peter with his silly suggestions. That moment could not be captured and embodied in three shrines on the mountain. It was a glimpse into heaven, into the life that Jesus had in heaven before. To put it quite simply, others were saying Jesus was reincarnate – reincarnation was a popular idea then, and it still is. However, Peter was not affirming reincarnation, but incarnation – the incarnation of Jesus. Jesus had lived before, but in heaven. "You're the Son of the Living God" – that was right. Peter, having said the right thing, sometimes said the wrong thing a few minutes later.

When you go to Israel, one of the things that does put you off are the buildings that Christians have put up to enshrine big moments in the life of Jesus, and they have spoiled it.

Some can't pray without a church building around them. That is why so many of the Gospel events are commemorated by buildings. If you go to the place where the Sermon on the Mount was given there is a beautiful church called The Church of the Beatitudes, and it was built by Mussolini – the Italian fascist dictator, equivalent to Hitler. He put that up so that Christians could pray where the Sermon on the Mount was preached – what a tragedy. But when the Christian pilgrims began to go to the Holy Land, they put up shrines wherever something had happened, and covered the Holy Land with shrines and churches, and the pilgrims used to go from church to church to pray.

Thankfully, they didn't build one on top of Mount Hermon. They built a church for the Transfiguration on the top of a hill in the middle of the Plain of Esdraelon, Mount Tabor, some thirty miles from where it happened. But if you care to climb the 10,000 feet and get above the snow line, you are at the right place. I haven't climbed up there, haven't even taken the ski lift, though you can do that now.

So there those disciples were. They were left speechless, and temporarily they didn't tell anybody what they had seen – they couldn't.

For our third event, we are back down at the bottom of Mount Hermon, so you see how this mountain played such a part. I label this third event "Treachery" because for the first time the disciples were going to let Jesus down, and one of them was going to let him down badly.

When they came down from the mountain, there was a huge crowd waiting and there was a man in the crowd who called out, "Jesus, please can you do something for my only son." He pleaded, "Look what's happening to my son, he's being destroyed by an unclean spirit." This spirit was causing the boy to foam at the mouth and have convulsions, throwing him on the floor. He added, "I brought my boy to your disciples and they couldn't help him." Yet Jesus had given the disciples authority and power and sent them out. They could have dealt with it and they didn't. In another Gospel we are told why. Jesus said, "You can't do this casting out of demons without prayer and fasting." That is as much as to say: that is what you're missing, so don't try and do this in your own strength – you will fail. Then Jesus demonstrated frustration, saying, "How much longer do I have to put up with you, this perverse and unbelieving generation?" A very human reaction. His disciples should have been able to deal with this, but they just hadn't, they couldn't.

"Bring the boy to me," Jesus says. Even as they brought him, the boy convulsed and the evil spirit took hold of him and threw him on the ground and he foamed at the mouth. Jesus said, "Come out of him", and the evil spirit came out. Jesus gave the boy, healed, cured, back to his father – a lovely moment. The crowd were amazed. They had seen the boy on the ground, flinging himself around, and they saw Jesus tell the demon to come out, and they saw that the boy was perfectly normal, and was given back to his dad. But the interesting thing is that they didn't say "Isn't Jesus great?" They said, "Isn't God great?" Now that is very interesting – they realised that it was God in Jesus who was throwing out the evil spirit.

Now we come to something very serious. Peter, James and John were special disciples and were given special experiences, and they came down to meet the nine apostles who had failed to help this boy, and so already there was a failure among Jesus' twelve apostles, but worse was to come. Jesus told them all to listen very carefully and told them that he was going to be betrayed. This was the first time he said this to the apostles among whom was Judas Iscariot, the man who was going to do it. You can imagine Judas's shock, because he was already a bit too fond of money. He was the treasurer and he kept the cash that they were given to pay for their food and so on, and he helped himself to that cash. Jesus, predicting the betrayal, says he is going to be betrayed. That meant it was going to be someone close to him.

Later, at the Last Supper, Jesus said the same thing; only this time he said, "One of you will betray me", and their reaction was to ask, "Lord, is it I?" They asked a question. But this time, being the first mention of betrayal, it says they didn't understand what he was saying, and they didn't dare to ask him anything about it. All this is so true to life, isn't it? You can imagine them so shocked that no-one said anything. Later, it was almost as if they had got used to the idea. But this time they didn't grasp it and were afraid to ask him about it.

One day we shall all see Jesus in his glory and, like Moses and Elijah, we shall be glorified. That is the final stage in discipleship. We are justified, then sanctified, then glorified, and we shall share his glory. Whether you can cope with this in your imagination or not, one day your clothes will shine like lightning, for we shall share his glory and reflect his image.

9:46-10:24

Again we focus on those passages that are peculiar to this Gospel. Our subject now is discipleship, which means learning or discipline, which means education. In the twentieth century it was realised that the method of education whereby one person stands up at the front and passes knowledge on by writing it on a blackboard, or dictating it, or simply speaking it, is not the only method of learning. Personally, I believe that this method will never be obsolete. But I believe it is only one third of our process of learning. If, for example, you can find your learning of the Christian faith and discipleship by listening to my talks you will only be a third of a disciple. There are two other methods of teaching which Jesus himself practised with his own pupils. There is the formal method of education – preaching, teaching, in which you are listening to someone speaking. The second is what I would call the casual way of teaching, in which as you go through life you pick things up; you learn them in an almost off-hand way. Your children learn a great deal from you in this way.

The third way is the practical way when you do a thing yourself. For example, I learned both farming and flying both those ways. Take farming: I did go to college, I did sit through three years of lectures on the subject, and got a head start with facts and with knowledge, and managed to scrape through some exams at the end. That was my formal education, but ever since I was a little boy I would spend one holiday each year on a farm, and when I was evacuated in the early years of the war it was to a farm. So casually I picked up a great deal just through living there. That came in very useful later. The other part of my education in farming was to do it and to look after sheep and to milk cows, and to do all the thousand and one jobs that are done on a typical mixed farm. Do you see the three kinds of education? If you are going to be a true disciple of Jesus Christ you must learn at all three levels – never despise education; never despise training. There is one outlook among Christians that thinks as long as you are filled with the Holy Spirit you need no training and you can just go straight out and do the job. But it took our Lord three years to get his disciples ready, and they were not wasted years – far from it. During those three years he didn't sit them in a lecture room all the time. There were moments when he gave a formal discourse. We studied one in Luke 6 – the sermon on the plain. In that, he gave a formal lecture if you like, though it was an exciting one. That was the formal teaching but we are now going to see in this passage all three methods being used to train disciples.

The first section, which covers the last part of chapter nine, is what the disciples learned casually as they moved through life and encountered one kind of situation after another, and as Jesus corrected them as they went along. That was casual learning – the correcting of their motives and getting their attitudes right. The second style of education comes in the first part of chapter ten: the formal education when he gave them a lecture on how to be missionaries and how they were to conduct themselves when they went out to preach the gospel. This was the commission of their ministry. Then they also learned from actually doing the job – the practical side of education. After a number of weeks out doing the job they came back and they said, "We've learned this and this," and they had learned the practical way. Swimming provides another illustration: you may have read books on swimming, you may have picked up a lot of casual tips, but you will never swim until you get into that water sooner or later, and do it. If you want to witness for the Lord you can read all the books that have ever been published on witnessing, but half an hour on the streets is worth ten hours of reading books on that subject.

It is always preferable to have formal education because you don't have to do anything but listen. But it is the casual plus the formal plus the practical that will make you a true disciple of Christ. So let us look first of all at what they learned in the casual way. They had to learn the right attitudes, the right motives: it is not only *what* you do, it is *why* you do it. You can even be a Christian for the wrong reason; you can be a Christian minister for the wrong reason; you can be a Christian missionary for the wrong reason. They had to learn attitudes, and Jesus had to teach them the right attitude and the wrong attitude as they went along.

The first little lesson they learned casually was on

humility. They were having an argument. It is a little bit of a comfort that there were arguments even among the disciples of Christ, though we mustn't excuse arguments on that ground. It was a very interesting one: who was the most important disciple? Before you condemn them, have you ever thought that yourself? Who is the most important person in the church? Who is the most important person in your missionary society? As if some Christians are more important than others! It is the besetting sin of the church to construct hierarchies. We are forever developing a hierarchy, and, if you want to know what that is, spell it "higherarchy" and it means that some people are higher than others. This produces ambition leading to status. This is totally foreign to disciples of Jesus Christ. It is a hard lesson to learn, and Jesus taught them this lesson quite casually. He said two things about who is important among his disciples. He took a little child and he gave two lessons from this child, and it is very important to grasp them both.

First, he explained that the important disciples are those who give time to unimportant people like that child. Now, think that through first. The important disciple is the one who has time for unimportant people, and a child symbolised someone who was unimportant to the world. This world of ours is an adult world, and on the whole the decisions are not referred to children. Jesus taught: if you welcome this child you are welcoming me; if you are welcoming me you welcome my Father who sent me.

The second point about humility that he taught from the child is this: the important person is the one who considers himself unimportant – who is like this little child and looks up to everybody else. A child has to because they are small, and if you put a child in a bunch of adults the child has to do this all around. The important disciple is the one who has time for unimportant people, and the one who considers himself unimportant. What a lesson in attitudes!

A second kind of lesson that came in this casual way was about charity. Some disciples were telling Jesus they had heard a man who didn't belong to their group casting out demons in his name. Notice what the problem was: it was another man who was using the name of Jesus and using it effectively. This was not the problem of our relationship to Christian groups that are not being effective in the name of the Lord. It is the question of relating to groups or individuals who are clearly preaching the gospel, using the name of Jesus, casting out demons, converting souls, and doing the work of the Kingdom, and yet don't belong to your group. It is very easy to drop into this. "Can any good thing come out of the..." – and then you supply a denomination or name that is not your own. It is very easy to think this way. I shudder, I am afraid, when I hear somebody talk about "our church" or "our denomination" or "our missionary society". If our church is only ours it is not worth the soil it is standing on. If our missionary society is only ours it is not worth keeping going. This must be *his* church, *his* missionary society, it is not ours. But it is so easy to get into this kind of denominational sentiment and pride.

When I was a Methodist minister I heard this phrase so frequently, "Oh, he's a good Methodist", and then when I switched I heard the same phrase, "Oh, he's a good Baptist." I began to ask what is this "good"? I felt like saying, like Jesus, "Why call me good?" It is a silly word to use in that context – as if our group, our denomination is all-important. Jesus was teaching them to have a mind of charity. If the man is doing effective work for Jesus he is not your enemy, he is your ally. He is not against you, he is for you, and you must recognise that. He didn't say that you must unite with him or try to get in the same organisation with him. Sometimes there is the most unlikely source of something good. Where Christ is being preached, and where the gospel is saving souls, and where demons are being expelled and the devil defeated, it does not matter what label it is under, we must rejoice and accept it. It is a very different situation where the gospel is not being preached and souls are not being converted. That requires a different approach and attitude.

The third casual lesson is to take the blows that come to you as a Christian. You see, if you are a Christian and you are universally popular you are not a very good Christian. Whoever would live a godly life in Christ Jesus will suffer persecution. That is a spiritual law. This is a godless world and you will be badly treated. You may be socially ignored and it may be even worse; you could be beaten up, you could be put into prison, all kinds of things can happen. It is absolutely vital that a disciple of Jesus can take it without wanting to hit back. Jesus was going to Jerusalem and the quickest way was due south from Galilee straight through Samaria, but the Samaritans had a centuries-old feud with the Jews, and they did not welcome them. Anybody going to Jerusalem was not allowed to pass through; they had to go all the way around by Jericho. Jesus sent his disciples on to try to find lodging for the night and they came to a Samaritan village where, having been rejected, James and John were furious. You could say, "Jesus why did you send those two? Look at the nickname you gave them when you first met them." He nicknamed them "Boanerges", which means "Sons of Thunder". Jesus didn't give nicknames without a reason. The disciples were ready to blast the villagers off the face of the earth by calling down fire from heaven. They got all excited, but Jesus rebuked them. So again the teaching came out quite casually. A disciple of Jesus has to learn to take it all, and never want to hit back in any way. Force should never be used in the Christian cause. If that lesson in discipleship had been remembered, many of the "holy wars" would have never been fought; the crusades would never have been held; the Inquisition could not have taken place.

The fourth lesson was to give priority to Jesus. It is a hard lesson this, and it came out again quite casually. A man rushed up to Jesus and said, "Lord, I will follow you wherever you go." This man was saying something he had not thought through, but you have to be very careful that you have counted the cost; you must not say things you haven't thought through. Jesus could see that this was one of those enthusiastic but shallow dedications, and pointed out that he himself had no place to lay his head. As long as you follow Christ you have no abiding place on earth; you can be uprooted at any time. He can uproot you; the world can uproot you. We have no abiding city here, we have to go where he is, even if it means no home at all.

In another case, Jesus took the initiative and said, "Follow me." The man wanted to bury his father. This doesn't mean that this father was already dead. What he wanted to do was to look after his father until he was dead, and then come. In other words, he had a prior loyalty. But when Jesus calls, the prior loyalty is to *him*. "Follow me" – if you are going to be a disciple of Jesus it has got to be Jesus first and others second, yourself at the bottom, and there is no alternative. You can't say, "Lord, I'll follow you, but I have one other loyalty first." Young person, are you deeply in love with someone who doesn't belong to Jesus? Then Jesus has to come first, that other person second. It is the only way to be a disciple.

A third person is encountered. "Lord, I will follow you, but..." – here it is again, "but first...." Again, there are to be no "buts", no "firsts". "But first let me say 'goodbye'." Well, what is wrong with saying goodbye? Jesus knew this man's heart. When he went back to his family, their pressure and his own slight wavering would mean that he would sit down and discuss it with them, and he would never come back. Have you ever seen somebody plough and look back? You think you are getting on great the first time you plough, especially with horses. You think, "Oh look at that," and you look back. Then you go on a bit further and you look back. I heard of one boy who did this and he finished up all over the place. So the farmer said, "Look, fix your eyes on something ahead." So he did, and when he finished it turned out that he had kept his eye on a cow in the next field! So it is not just looking back that is a problem, but looking at something that isn't fixed, and that means keeping your eyes on someone other than Jesus. Looking back – in other words, do you look back fondly at the life you had before you were a Christian? Do you ever look fondly back at something you once had that you have had to give up? Then you will find, as soon as you look back, you will waver. It is fatal to live in the past, and too many Christians do. We can't live in the days of church even ten years ago. For whoever is going to follow Jesus it has got to be straight on with him, forgetting the things that are behind and stretching forward to the things that are before. There is a lesson in discipleship and priority.

The disciples' formal education came in the form of a lecture before Jesus sent them out to do the practical. He chose seventy more (other than the twelve) to be "John the Baptists" for him and to go everywhere he was about to go. He gave them a magnificent lecture in missionary work. First of all, in 10:1–2, he gave them the situation in which there are three outstanding features: a large harvest; few workers; many dangers. If you are going to go out for Jesus you must remember all three. There is a large harvest and you must *expect to be successful*. There are few workers and you must *pray for more*. There are many perils and you have got to *be on your guard*. He said, "I send you out as lambs among wolves".

There is a large harvest. Some sermons I have heard on this text have said, "The *field* is large," and pointed out the population. But Jesus didn't say the field is large, he said the harvest is. This should make you optimistic, thinking, "I'm going to bring some back," not, "I wonder if I'll get anybody." There is a large harvest and there are millions in that harvest. We mustn't go out pessimistic, thinking that hardly anybody will be won for Christ. Let's think big; believe big. There are hundreds waiting for us to go out and pick them – they are ripe for reaping. I believe that is truer today than when I began my ministry. The harvest is there, but the workers are few. Even so, if you've only got a few workers you should still send them out *two by two*. Maybe this is why so many of us fail to do much reaping: we try to do it by ourselves. Here is a practical suggestion: consider getting hold of one other Christian and saying, "Let's together pray for some people, and let's together try and win them for Christ." Husbands and wives have an advantage – you can do it together.

Many missionaries are labouring on their own, but God wants them in at least pairs – teamwork. When Paul was called to be a missionary, God sent Barnabas with him, and then later Timothy, or Titus, or John Mark, or somebody, but there were always two.

Jesus told them it was a tough task, and then how to integrate within it. They are to travel light and take no resources with them, not even a spare pair of shoes. They are not only to travel light, they are to be sparing in their use of time, and not pass the time of day with people – that is literally what the translation means. "Don't greet anyone on the way" doesn't mean "Don't just say 'Good morning' and walk straight past, it means don't pass the time of day with them. How much time you waste passing the time of day with people. Get on with the job; concentrate.

Luke 9:1-10:24

It is very interesting how he told them to be supported. I am not sure much missionary teaching has really given careful heed to this. His principle is that you must take your support from those to whom you go. This is the scriptural principle. It is in 1 Corinthians 9: "He who lives for the gospel should live by the gospel." You should take your support from those you help. So you are in a two-way relationship with the people you are helping: you are giving them spiritual benefit and they are giving you material support. Just as Jesus with the woman at the well of Samaria said, "Give me a drink," and he gave her the truth.

That is the basic principle and I sometimes wonder if better work would be done on the mission field if missionaries lived by this principle, so the people they are trying to help could feel that they are helping the missionaries rather than having all the support sent from some other country. In other words, you are prepared to listen more to someone whom you are supporting. This was Jesus' principle: when you get to a town, eat what is set before you; let them support you; take what they offer and don't pick a better house if you find one; stay in the house you started in; tell them about the Kingdom; heal their sick; do everything you can for them with my power, but let them do everything they can for you. That is a basic principle when you are trying to witness to somebody. Have you ever thought of asking their help? Have you ever thought of letting them support you in some way? You will find them far more open to the gospel if they are supporting you. It is an extraordinary fact, but to say, "Give me a drink of water" is to open a person's heart so that they feel there is something they can give to you, and then they are prepared to receive. But if we go out saying, "No thanks, I've had a cup of tea", and, "I've had my meal – now, I've come here to tell you about this; here is a tract" – can you see how that sounds? Instead you should say, "Look, I've been knocking at all the doors up this street, you couldn't get me a cup of tea could you?" You would be amazed what that would do. This is the method that Jesus chose for his missionaries: Let the people you're helping support you; have a two-way relationship with them.

He did not expect everyone to accept their ministry. "Tell them the Kingdom of God is near" – but he expected many of them to reject it, and now he said some of the most terrible things, which almost make you shudder to read. Do you realise that if you send a missionary anywhere you make some people worse off than they were before that missionary arrived? Some will be better off, but many worse off. The tragedy is this: if you have brought a person to a church service you could have pushed them nearer hell. We have to face this unpleasant truth, that when you preach the gospel to someone you haven't left them as they are. You have either brought them nearer to God or you have pushed them nearer to hell. Every missionary we send out makes some people more guilty than they were before, and therefore ready for greater punishment than they were due for. You can't remain neutral with the gospel. When you hear Christ preached you either come or you go. You either take a step nearer or you pull back – you cannot remain the same. The tragedy is that there are some things even worse than moral degradation. Jesus is teaching here that to reject the gospel is a far worse sin than anything that happened in Sodom and Gomorrah. We tend to think those are the worst sins in the book, but no, Jesus is saying the worst sin in the book is when somebody rejects you when I have sent you to witness, because in rejecting you they have rejected me; in rejecting me, they have rejected God. This makes us representatives and ambassadors when we witness, and that is a frightening thing. To be a disciple of Jesus and to meet other people is to put them in the position where they must either come nearer to God, or draw further from him.

There is a parable Jesus told, which is widely misinterpreted and misapplied, about the sheep and the goats. In that parable if we are not careful we draw from it the conclusion that the people who will be saved on Judgment Day will be those who have done most good deeds for their neighbours. The parable says nothing of the kind. What Jesus teaches in that parable is that when the nations stand before him on the Judgment Day he will say to some people: "You are coming to heaven because of your attitude to me." They will say, "Our attitude to you?"

"Yes, you did a lot for me when you were on earth."

"For you? You weren't even on earth when I was on earth."

"Oh yes I was. Inasmuch as you did it to the least of these my brethren, you did it to me."

Then he will say to others, "You are going to hell because of your attitude to me."

They will say, "We're not against you, Jesus. We never attacked you."

"You did. I was sick and you didn't come and see me. I was in prison and you didn't visit me."

"When were you in prison?"

"When my brethren were."

In other words, your attitude to the brethren of Jesus is your attitude to Jesus and is your attitude to God. If you laugh at Christians, you are laughing at Jesus; if you are laughing at Jesus, you are laughing at God. It is a sobering thought, but my attitude to God the Father of Jesus Christ will determine my attitude to Christians, and my attitude to Christians will reveal my attitude to God.

In Israel, one of the things that struck me afresh was on the north side of the Sea of Galilee where I tried to locate the site of Chorazin – it has gone! There were just a few black basalt blocks of rock. I tried to spot where Bethsaida was and it has gone. They were thriving, crowded towns and Jesus said, "Woe to you Chorazin! Woe to you Capernaum! Woe to you Bethsaida! If the miracles that had been done in you had been done in those dreadful places you talk about – Tyre, and Sidon, and Sodom – they would have repented, but your judgment in the day of judgment will be worse than Sodom."

Not one of those three towns in which Jesus did his miracles has survived. Whereas just down the lake there is a town that was there in Jesus' day that is still there. It is called Tiberius. Why is it still there? I'll tell you: because Jesus did no miracle in it, and they didn't reject him. When you stand and you can see this before your very eyes, and you realise that Tiberius is better off because Jesus didn't go there, it makes you tremble. What we are realising here, and it is a profound principle, is this: there are degrees of punishment in hell as there are degrees of reward and glory in heaven. When you go out to witness to somebody who was already going to hell, they will suffer a severer judgment because they have refused what you gave them. But on the other hand, why do you go then, if sending missionaries abroad is going to make the situation worse? It is because if we go and tell people the gospel, at least some will get to heaven as a result. I realise, as I preach, that people are either coming nearer to the Lord or hardening their hearts against him. It is a sobering thought, and whenever one preaches, it is at the back of one's mind. But there is the joy of preaching too. Why must one preach? Why must one go on preaching? The love of Christ constrains us. We have got to preach. We have got to go on drawing people nearer to Christ – the harvest is large even though the workers are few.

Now let us turn to what the disciples learned practically. They came back very different: they went out reluctant; they came back radiant. You can imagine them going out, two of the disciples trotting down the road hoping they won't meet a sick person or a demon-possessed person. They weren't looking forward to it, but when they came back they were so excited. It works! All the things you hear in formal sermons and all the formal education of the Christian life doesn't bring you the joy that will come to you when you go out and try it and come back and say: "It works; I've tried it, and the power of Jesus can change a life, and I've seen it happen."

A church member told me of a close friend who had just come to the Lord Jesus Christ. As she told me this, her face was alight – radiant.

The disciples came back and they were thrilled. There had been a large harvest and it worked. They could even tell demons what to do and they did it. Jesus just saw a little danger. He was thrilled with the defeat of Satan. "I can see Satan's finished, he's fallen like lightning from heaven." Here are seventy ordinary people and Satan was no match for them. The power Jesus had given the disciples was even more than they realised. Nothing could hurt them when doing Jesus' work. They could step on snakes and scorpions and be all right. All the power of the enemy can't hurt you when you are doing Jesus' business. But be careful: don't get so thrilled about the power. Don't get so thrilled about what you've done for God, get thrilled about what God has done for you. This is very important – you must be more thrilled about the grace of God than the gifts of the Spirit. You must be more thrilled that he has written your name up there than with anything you have managed to do in his name. When you have been successful in Christian service, when you come back rejoicing, be thrilled that your name was written. Don't be thrilled with the power, it will go to your head; don't be thrilled with the success, it will go to your head. Be thrilled that you are in the harvest.

So they had success but they had to learn what true happiness was. Then Jesus rejoiced in the Spirit and prayed a beautiful prayer to the Father. Things had been revealed to ordinary men and women which had been hidden from the wise and learned. Prophets like Moses, Elijah and Jeremiah, and kings like David and Solomon, wanted to see this happen. Do you ever thank God you were born AD and not BC? Why don't you? Praise God that we live now, for we have seen things that prophets and kings wanted to see and hear.

Are you a *disciple* of Jesus? I mean: have you begun to follow him? Have you begun to learn? If not, I tremble for you because I think you are going to be further away from him after this teaching unless you begin to be his now. Second, to those who would say, "Yes, I am a disciple. I'm learning of Jesus" – are you getting an all-round education? I hope you don't just listen to formal sermons. That is part of it, but it is not all the teaching you need. You need the casual teaching you get in everyday life. Wherever you are in the casual education, are you letting Jesus correct your attitude as you go along? Above all, are you getting the practical education? Are you prepared to go out and gather in this harvest? Are you prepared to do it with someone else?

10

Read Luke 10:25–42

It is interesting that the two best-known parables in the Bible both come from Luke's Gospel. One is the parable of the prodigal son, the other the parable of the good Samaritan. There are many who believe that the parable of the good Samaritan contains all we need to know about Christianity – that Jesus came simply to tell us to try to do good deeds for each other, to try and help each other when we are in trouble, and that if only the world was full of good Samaritans we wouldn't need anything else. We wouldn't need church, we wouldn't need the Bible, we wouldn't need worship – all that would be quite superfluous – but the vital thing is that we should go out and help our neighbours. One has a certain sympathy with this outlook. But those who take this view that Christianity is a kind of grown-up Boy Scout movement doing good deeds every day have never really read the parable of the good Samaritan. Certainly, they have not looked at the context in which this parable is set. For when you read a story that Jesus told, you always have to ask why he told it on that occasion. When did he tell that story? To whom was he speaking? What was the point he was making? Then we find that this parable may have a very different message from the one that most people assume it teaches.

It started because Jesus was asked a question – the most important question that anyone can ever ask, and the tragedy is that nine out of ten people never dream of asking it: "What must I do to be able to live?" Because most people just exist, they get by, they keep body and soul together; they scrape along, they get up and go to work and come back and go to bed; they get by for seventy or eighty years – that is not life. Real life has both quality and quantity. It has quality in that this is real living, and it has quantity in that it doesn't last only until old age but goes on. The most important question you ought to be asking now is: "How can I really live?" I think most people want to know that. If only they would ask the right question in the right way! How can I really live forever? That is eternal life – of a unique quality that is really alive, and life that will never come to an end. Would you like life like that? Then you ought to be asking this question.

It was a religious teacher, who ought to have known the answer, and ought himself to have had the life he tried to teach to others, who asked Jesus what he needed to do to get this everlasting life that even death can't affect. He asked the right question but for the wrong motive. We read that he didn't ask Jesus because he wanted to know, he was trying to trap him. He was trying to prove that Jesus was a heretic – unsound. He was a religious teacher to the Jews, and Jesus was suspect to him because he felt that Jesus had come to teach a new kind of religion, which was perfectly true.

Jesus asked him what his answer was first. Jesus, the Son of God, the one who knew the Father so intimately and had all the answers in his mind and heart, takes him to the scriptures. That is the only place you will find the answer to this question. If you want to know how to live forever, you will find the answer in the Bible. If you want to know how to have real life, you will find the answer in the Bible. I passed a church and I was thrilled with the poster that I saw displayed outside. It read: "You can have life before death" – not just after death, but before death.

That religious teacher had been asked the question and

Luke 10:25-42

he had given his answer. Incidentally, this shows that Jesus accepted the Old Testament as God's Word. He accepted it as true from beginning to end. The teacher put his finger right on the spot. There are 613 commandments in the Old Testament. There are ten big ones. The teachers of the law wanted to summarise the fundamental things. This teacher had summed it all up – you have got to do two things: love the Lord your God with all your heart, mind, soul, and strength (using a text from Deuteronomy); and, from Leviticus, love your neighbour as yourself.

Jesus told the man he had answered rightly – and notice some subtle points about Jesus' answer. First of all, it does not just say: You must love God and you must love your neighbour. Both those commands are qualified with a total claim. It is not just loving God, it is loving him with *all* your heart, *all* your mind, *all* your strength, *all* your soul. That is a big qualification. The second point, "You shall love your neighbour..." has another qualification that is pretty big. You must love your neighbour *as much as you love yourself.* You must be as concerned about their needs as you are about your own. Then there is something else rather subtle that doesn't come out in the English. When the lawyer asked, "What must I do?" the word "do" is in a peculiar tense there, such that the sentence means: "What single action must I do to live forever?" When Jesus replied, "Do this and you will live," he used the word "do" in another tense which means "continuously – all the time". The lawyer was clearly asking, "Give me some grand noble gesture, some specific thing that I could do, and I'm in." Jesus was saying: do it all the time, all your life, every moment of every day, and you will live. Now you can see what Jesus was doing here, can't you? He was starting where the lawyer was with his own thinking with the scriptures, and he was trying to press him to the point where the lawyer would say, "That's impossible" – but the lawyer wasn't going to be trapped himself. He had set out to trap Jesus, and Jesus just about trapped him, and he wasn't having any of it, he was going to wriggle out of this. He had a legally-trained mind and he saw a loophole. Why did he not say straight away, "Well look, if that's the way to eternal life I don't stand a chance." That is the only honest thing to say because if what Jesus says here is true there isn't one person who ever stands a chance of getting real life.

Could you say: "I love God with all my heart, all my soul, all my strength, all my mind, and I've always done so" and, "I've always cared for my fellow men as much as I've looked after myself"? You couldn't say it! This lawyer couldn't say it and he should have admitted that right from the start. The tragedy of those who are trying to get to heaven by being good enough is this: they will never make it. It is an impossible standard. But the lawyer wasn't going to admit it because it says he wanted to put himself right. Here is the pride in our heart that gives us a stiff neck when we face God, pride which says, "I don't want you to put me right God, I'm going to get there and do it myself, under my own steam if it kills me." It is this "DIY" religion that is the most common religion in this country: "I'll do it myself if it kills me" – well, it will. That way of trying to be good enough to reach God leads to certain death.

You can see how the lawyer had such pride that he wanted to put himself right. He tried to cut the requirement down to manageable proportions: if you tell me who my neighbour is, I'll try. When you define a thing you limit it, so when you define your neighbour you limit your duty. Now most people would be very relieved if the Lord said, "Well, your neighbour consists of the people on this side, and the people on that side, and the people over the road." Wouldn't it be nice if that is all we had been told to do? But you see the Lord will not define.

Luke 10:25-42

To the question "who is my neighbour?" Jesus told the familiar story of the Good Samaritan. You know it backwards, don't you? The actual setting is an extraordinary place – it is a real road that winds down through the most barren area with steep ravines, caves and rocks. It winds down something like four thousand feet in the fifteen miles between Jerusalem and Jericho. It starts way above sea level and finishes way below sea level. There were bandits on that road. They used to hide in the caves, and if you went down that road alone you were asking for it. It could have been said of the man who fell among thieves that it was his own silly fault. What was he walking down that road alone for? He should have gone with a group of people. It is a terrible road, especially at night. The characters were real too – a priest, a Levite and a Samaritan.

Let us look at the points that Jesus is making. First, his definition is utterly practical. The "neighbour" is not someone who *feels* something about someone else, but someone who *does something about another's need*. Second, you must never limit the term "neighbour" to the people next door. The word "neighbour" means anybody in the entire world who is in need and whom you are in a position to help. Third, the question this man should have asked was not "Who is my neighbour?" but "Whose neighbour am I?" That is totally different. Fourth, the act was an act of mercy, which means an act that was totally undeserved.

The lawyer couldn't even bring himself to say the word "Samaritan". That was his prejudice. But he at least acknowledged that it was an act of undeserved mercy. So Jesus' words "Go and do likewise" meant: off you go; do that all your life, to those who hate you, to those who despise you for doing it, to those who don't speak to you, to those who curse you – and you'll live. Once again, Jesus has pressed this lawyer to the very brink of admitting that he can't do it.

But the man is still so proud and we don't know what he did. Presumably he went away, and I don't know how he got on.

So the parable of the good Samaritan is not just saying, "Do a good deed now and again to someone up your road who is in need", it is showing us an attitude of mind towards those who are your natural enemies, those who are totally different from you, those who do not deserve your help – you go and do good for them; let your compassion show itself in action. My, that takes some doing! If we are honest, every one of us would have to admit we can't live like that.

Notice that the lawyer never even bothered to ask Jesus what loving God meant. He was so keen on getting his neighbour defined, he thought, "Well I can tackle that one, and at least I can say I've done one of them." But what is loving God with all your heart, soul, mind and strength? The Holy Spirit inspired the written Word, and we are now told what loving God is. You can be so busy being a good Samaritan, so busy helping your neighbours, that the Lord gets none of your time. You can be so busy doing what to you is a good deed that you never love the Lord.

This happened the very next day. Jesus and his disciples were going through a village and a home was opened to them and they were made welcome. Here are these two sisters Martha and Mary, and we say, "Well, the real difference between them was one of temperament." Don't you believe it; that is not the lesson of the incident. It is not a question of temperament. People say, "Well, I'm a Martha," or, "I'm a Mary". "The world has to have both, and the church would be a sorry place if there were no Marthas or no Marys. You know it's just the way we're made." If it is just the way we are made, why did the Lord rebuke Martha? You don't rebuke someone who can't help being what they are. Jesus rebuked Martha because she got so busy doing good for people that she wasn't loving the Lord. How important it is that we get

Luke 10:25-42

the balance right. The first step on the way to life is to love the Lord. The second is to love your neighbour. Some people are so busy loving their neighbour that the Lord doesn't get a look in. Here is Martha in the kitchen, and there is an unexpected guest, and a very important one – a real chance to show hospitality, to lay on a wonderful spread. Oh, she was so busy, and there was her sister. Do you notice how, having taken one wrong step, she takes another? She begins to be resentful towards other people, and then, worst of all, she begins to rebuke the Lord himself – all because she was trying to do a good deed. What a lesson there is here for us. If you think the whole of life is doing good deeds for your neighbour, just stop and remember that the Lord would like your time, and would love to chat with you, and that if you love someone you will spend time with them. Jesus did rebuke Martha, quite rightly. Her attitude towards Mary was wrong. Her attitude towards Jesus was wrong. Her attitude towards herself was wrong. Yet she is a picture of all of us when we are so busy trying to do good deeds and trying to do what we think is the right thing for someone else.

Now what Jesus said about Mary ("She's chosen the one thing needed") is variously interpreted by the commentators. It is almost as if he had said: I only needed one dish, and you are trying to prepare a seven-course dinner for me. But it is deeper than that. It is as if he is saying that he only wanted one thing when he came in – someone to talk to. Sometimes that is the deepest need of a person. If you are so busy getting a meal ready, you may be missing that one thing. Bear in mind that Jesus was on his way to die. Bear in mind that he was already burdened with his coming death. Bear in mind that he wanted to get this off his chest.

I heard of a woman who goes into a hospital ward where there are serious cases, and she scrubs the floor. Patient after patient in that ward talked to her and said, "You know, I'm going to die. The doctors won't tell me. My relatives won't tell me, but I'm going to die and I've got to talk to someone." They talked to the women scrubbing the floor beneath their bed because they needed to share it. Jesus was going to die and he wanted to talk to someone about it. One of the fruits of that conversation was that Mary anointed him for his burial before he even died. She would never have thought of doing that if she hadn't sat at his feet. I am sure he talked to her about the cross, and the fact that nobody would be able to anoint his body afterwards. So she did it beforehand.

Martha and Mary – it is not a difference of temperament. It is a difference between a person who wanted to help a neighbour and a person who wanted to love the Lord. The person who was sensitive to the Lord realised the Lord likes to have time with you.

This, then, is love for the Lord, and, "Mary has chosen that good part, which will not be taken away from her," Jesus said. She had chosen the one thing needful, and it was the better part. That meant that not only was it the better thing for Jesus, but the better thing for herself. Let the world criticise if it wishes. Let those who simply want to love their neighbour criticise if they wish. Those of us who want to spend some time with the Lord, listen to his Word, and sing to him – it will not be taken from us, the love that is prepared to spend time with the Lord. Now do you see how those two commands were put together beautifully? It is important for a Christian to love their neighbour; it is important to do good. It is important to help. It is also important to love the Lord and to listen, and to spend time with him and listen to his Word.

But even so, it is still absolutely impossible for me or any of us ever to love our neighbour enough, or ever to love our Lord enough, to have eternal life. The proof is this: find someone who is trying to get eternal life this way and say

Luke 10:25-42

to them, "But have you got eternal life?" They will have to say, "I don't know."

The lawyer had understood his own scriptures, but he needed to be pushed to the point where he would admit that way was closed, and that you can't do it. It is perfectly true that in theory any man or woman who will love the Lord with all their heart, soul, mind and strength, and love their neighbour as much as himself or herself, and do this for their lifetime, will go straight to heaven at death. But none of us will succeed in all that. Only one person who has ever lived managed it, and his name is Jesus. He loves his heavenly Father with everything; he loved everybody he met who was in need, no matter who they were. Jesus has eternal life. The Bible teaches that eternal life is *in* Jesus. It is in the Son of God. He is the only person who has ever really lived. When they put him in the grave they could not end that real life. He rose from the dead and he is alive for ever.

Where does that leave us? He managed it, I have already failed, and nothing I can do now can undo the fact that I have not loved God in this way, and I have not loved my neighbour in this way. Is there no other way, Lord? If only the lawyer had asked that question! I can sum up the way in two words: admit; accept. Admit you don't love God like that, and admit you don't love your neighbour like that. Admit you never will, no matter how hard you try. That is the first step. The second step is to accept the life that is in Jesus by accepting him as your personal Saviour and Lord, and washing away that past of your unlovingness, making a clean start. Not to *try* to love God, and to *try* to love your neighbour, but to let the love of Jesus in your heart reach out to the Lord and reach out to the neighbour – to accept Jesus' righteousness, *his* life, *his* eternal life, as a free gift, and stop trying to work your passage. Those who do this are really living *now*, and they are going to live forever – not because they have tried, but because they have admitted they could never make it. That is the gospel.

When people are baptised, in washing their bodies we are saying so clearly they have *not* loved God with all their heart, soul, mind, and strength. They have not loved their neighbour as themselves. Therefore, they deserve to die; they do not deserve eternal life. But that past is washed away. They make a new, clean start – not to try to do these things, but by resolving to let God do these things in them and through them.

11

Read Luke 11

Many years ago I spent a few days with a number of others at Ashburnham Place in Sussex. Early one morning I went out into the grounds to walk around the lake, and I suddenly heard some very sweet singing. It was the song "How Great Thou Art". A few yards further on, I looked across the lake and there in a clearing in the trees was a girl in her late teens. She was standing there pouring out her soul to God, alone and singing praise to the Lord from her heart. I am afraid I listened to the end of the song which was so beautiful, and then I crept away because I felt I was on holy ground. Indeed, you get this feeling whenever you accidentally overhear somebody talking to the Lord. You feel you are intruding and that you shouldn't be there.

One day the disciples got up early. They were staying in Capernaum. They were crowded into a room, maybe in the home of Simon's wife's mother, or her neighbours. They got up and there was an empty bed, which was the bed our Lord had gone to sleep in the night before. So they hurriedly pulled their clothes on and rushed out to find him. They couldn't find him anywhere in town, so they thought they might spot him by climbing the nearby hills and seeing if he was walking by the lake. Up they went, and when they came over the brow of a hill they found Jesus in a little dell, talking to his heavenly Father. They had never heard anybody pray quite like this.

As far as we know, Jesus would usually have prayed aloud. That is always a good thing to do if you are on your own. We are told that he usually prayed with his eyes open; especially when he was in the open air, he lifted up his eyes to heaven when he prayed. They listened, and when he had finished they said, "Lord, teach us to pray, just as John taught his disciples." They knew how to say prayers; they had been brought up to – they were Jews and they had been to the synagogue. They could have recited certain prayers very meaningfully and sincerely, but when they listened to Jesus talk to his Father they were moved to ask for teaching.

Look at how much Jesus taught spontaneously. When somebody asked a question or made a criticism, out came a gem of wisdom. He is a standing example to us to be ready to speak about the things of God, not just when we are in a church or house group, but when somebody asks a question or when somebody makes a comment – there is a glorious opportunity to pass on the truth about God. So Jesus taught them a little prayer they could use, and for the last two thousand years Christians have used it. I am sure he didn't mean us to use it like parrots, but on the other hand this prayer is so ideal that no other prayer has ever matched it, and it is lovely to use other people's prayers – it broadens your own praying. It helps you to stretch your spiritual life to use other people's words as well as your own. Use your hymnbook; use the book of Psalms. Use the Lord's Prayer with meaning and sincerity and you will never pray a better prayer. We call it the Lord's Prayer, but the Lord would never use it because there are some things mentioned in it of which he had no need. He never needed to pray "Forgive us our sins". He had no sins to be forgiven, though he could have said that he forgave those who sinned against him. "Father, forgive them, they know not what they do." So it is a prayer for *us* – we call it the Lord's Prayer but it is really the Lord's people's prayer, and when you look at it, it is marvellous. Let's just analyse it briefly, and realise that it is a model. One of the things I notice is that it is brief. I don't know why we still hang on to the idea that prayer has to be long to be deep. In fact it is the depth, not the length, of a prayer that matters. It is the quality not the quantity, and Jesus warned his hearers: don't think that by heaping up long prayers you will somehow get God to listen. This prayer is brief and to the point. It is simple yet comprehensive. A child can use this prayer, yet even the deepest saint will still not understand its full meaning. This masterly prayer is even shorter here in Luke's Gospel than it is in Matthew; it is given on a different occasion. Here in Luke it is boiled down to the absolute bare essentials of prayer, yet you have everything here.

Here is the first thing I want you to notice about this prayer: pray about what God wants before you pray about what you want. That is a very simple lesson in prayer, and one that we ignore at our peril, and one that we need to learn often. The prayer begins with God, not ourselves. Too often we rush into God's presence with our shopping list – the things we want. Somebody has said that much Christian prayer is little more than giving God advice and telling him what we think he should do and what we think he should want – but in fact the prayer begins by saying, "God, Father."

There are three things we are to think about our God when we pray. First of all: his *Fatherhood*. It is amazing to me that Jesus didn't say, "Now when you pray, heap up all the adjectives you can: eternal, ever-blessed, holy and merciful and slow to anger God. He said, "You just say, 'Father...' It is so much simpler; more direct. Jesus taught: if you want to talk to God like I talk to God, just come straight into his presence as a child would come into an earthly father's presence and say, "Father...." Prayer is climbing on the Father's knee – that is beautiful, lovely.

Secondly, think of his *purity* because you have never known an earthly father whose name was holy, and you need to remember that this is our Father in heaven, which means our Father in holiness. He is not like an earthly father who has his own faults and weaknesses. He is the heavenly Father who is holy and his name is holy. God's name should be held in awe. But people use the name of God and the name of Jesus Christ as swear words to relieve their own feelings – and it hurts. May your name be reverenced; may people never refer to it except with reverence and respect.

The third thing you think about God is his power, his kingdom – which means his reign, his power to govern; his power to control – and it is patently obvious that this world is not under his government. My hope is that God's kingdom will come on earth as it is in heaven, and that his power will be manifest in every department of life. Your kingdom come! We want to see it on earth. We want him to be in charge of the situation. If only our nation would pray that prayer.

Now we have prayed for what God wants. He wants his parenthood to be enjoyed by sons; he wants his purity to be reverenced by people on earth, and he wants his kingdom to be entered so that we become his subjects. In other words, you think of God as Father, Judge and King – and *now* you are ready to bring your own needs to him. If you think of the things you have prayed for and compare them with the list that Jesus gave you, it is a little embarrassing. There are three needs that you have every day of your life. They are not always the things you pray for. Health is not mentioned here. Physical safety is not mentioned here either. Wealth is not mentioned here. There are three things that everybody needs every day, and they are all in this model prayer: food, forgiveness and freedom.

You need *food*. It is hard for us to pray the Lord's Prayer because you have food in the freezer and fridge, and there are well-stocked supermarkets. If things were beginning to run out we might very soon get to the point where we would pray this petition with meaning again, and say, "Lord, give us enough food for the next twenty-four hours." The prayer is telling us to live a day at a time. Lord, give us day by day the food that we need. We will spiritualise things you know, but we are physical creatures, and when we read "Man shall not live by bread alone" it means that we need at least bread to live. We need more than that, but if you were living in many countries in the world today you would pray this prayer and mean it: "Lord, I need food."

Secondly, I need *forgiveness* every day. I know that when you became a Christian your sins were all forgiven and taken away, but subsequent sins require repentance and God's forgiveness too.

There is one clause in the prayer that has a condition to it. As you confess that you have sinned today, in using this prayer you also confess that you have forgiven others today. It is patently obvious that you cannot be forgiven unless you forgive others. May I put it this way? It is like an electrical circuit, and it is only completed when your hand is in the hand of God and your hand is in the hand of someone else, and the current of forgiveness can only flow into your life on this daily basis – if it is flowing out of your life at the other end. You cannot have God's forgiveness if you are holding grudges or resentments against others. So the circuit must be complete, and then your daily need of forgiveness can be met by your heavenly Father.

The third need that you have is *freedom*, not freedom politically but freedom spiritually and morally: freedom from temptation, freedom from the evil one, and freedom from the worst slave master of all – yourself. That is the worst slavery, to be a slave to your old self with all its horrible desires. You need freedom from that, and so you pray, "Don't let me be tempted above what I can bear. Don't let me be pushed too far. I want to be free from shame, free from guilt, free from fear." In the other version of the Lord's Prayer in Matthew it finishes, "Deliver us from evil" – but we never say it correctly. Jesus said, "When you pray, say, 'But deliver us from the evil one.'" If you begin your prayer thinking about God, end it by thinking about Satan. That is quite a thought, isn't it? Pray against Satan as you leave God's presence, because you are going from God's presence into Satan's realm. You are going into his world, and you need to be delivered from it; to be in the world yet not of it.

One disciple asked for this prayer, one disciple was given it, but he was told always to say "Our...." It is a revolution in your private, personal prayer when you say "our" and "we" and "us", because there is no need that you have that other Christians don't have at precisely that moment. You think you are unique, I'm afraid you are not. Every need you have, every sorrow, every burden, every frustration – there are others of God's children in the world who have exactly the same thing, and so when you pray for that, to be delivered from selfishness, pray "our". You might pray: "Lord, I'm feeling terribly sorry for myself, I'm very sad, I've had a bad knock today, but Lord there must be other children of yours who have had knocks today. Lord, help us. Deliver us from resentment or bitterness. Set us free from this." You are linking your prayer with so many others around the world, so that God is listening not just to a lot of individual prayers, but many people who are praying together as a family, as brothers and sisters all climbing on his knee together.

The Lord's Prayer is a beautiful prayer that puts the language of humility on your lips and teaches you to come before God and acknowledge his name, and I want you to notice that all of that prayer is *asking* for something. I have met some people – usually they have been studying other religions or eastern mysticism – and they have told me that asking for things is a very childish and low form of prayer, and that as you mature in prayer you come into the heights of meditation when you stop asking for things and only think about things. I don't believe it. You study our Lord's prayers and he was always asking for things. Prayer is asking – that is the heart of it. We should say please, thank you and sorry. A child's relationship to his parent includes asking for things the child can't do for himself, and this is the relationship: asking. Therefore never be afraid or ashamed to ask. Never let people say that is a low form of prayer. Come to God and ask, but ask for the right things.

Which brings us to the second part of this lesson on prayer: *if you ask you should expect an answer.* We can easily rationalise this and say that prayer is simply meditating and therefore you shouldn't look for answers. But if we pray we should expect answers and be able to say to each other: "Do you know what happened as the result of our prayer time?" It is vital to have answers to prayer because it is a two-way thing. We are asking God, and this is not just auto-suggestion; we are not just trying to condition ourselves to accept things as they are. Prayer changes things. We are asking, and we should expect things to happen as a result.

We should look to God to give us food and forgiveness and freedom, and thank him when they come. We should look to God to send his kingdom on earth and to answer our prayers. When we ask God to demonstrate his power, we should expect him to do something about it.

In other words, unanswered prayer is a problem to the Christian, and we must never evade that problem. It is a problem because the point of praying is to get an answer. We are now going to look at the reasons why some answers don't come, and Jesus gives us the conditions. He has talked about the contents of our asking prayer, and now he is going to speak of the conditions for God answering our prayer. One condition is on our side, the human side, and the other condition is on his side. The condition on our side is very clear: persistence. Persistence doesn't mean long prayer but it does mean frequent prayer, and going on until you get the answer. This is a vital part of true prayer. We will come to the reasons why in a moment, but Jesus tells a funny story.

In the Middle East in those days they went to bed fairly early. They didn't have electric light and oil was pretty expensive; the sun went down at around six and they went to bed shortly afterwards. They didn't have separate bedrooms; the family all slept on a raised part of the floor, and the animals slept on the lower part of the floor. The people baked their bread fresh every day because they had no deep freeze to keep it in. So you used up the bread by nightfall and then you baked some more in the morning. You travelled at night because of the heat of the sun at midday, and most people making a journey would travel late at night. Here is this poor chap and suddenly a visitor had arrived – a relative or a friend having come from some distant part, having had no supper, and in the Middle East hospitality is a sacred duty. There is the situation. Neighbours who borrow things are not unknown, and so the householder goes to a friend's house: "Have you got some bread?" At midnight, mark you, and the friend who is being asked is thoroughly fed up. The family had gone to bed for the night. It is not the best way to win friends and influence people, to wake them up at midnight for some bread, yet the man shamelessly went on knocking on the door—not the slightest bit embarrassed, not sensitive to the householder's feelings. He went on knocking on the door until he was given the bread.

Jesus is not saying that God is a reluctant giver – that he is someone you have to persuade to give you something – but what he is teaching is that the human side of this story is true of prayer. If you really mean business with God, you will go on until you get it. Of course you may be asking for the wrong thing, and you have to test what you are praying for by the Lord's Prayer. If you are praying for the right thing it will come under one of those six heads that we studied. So you can always check whether you are praying for the right thing, and thank God he doesn't spoil us as children; he doesn't always give us what we want. There is a horrible text in the Bible about God's judgment in the Psalms: "He gave them their desire and sent leanness into their soul." But if your prayer checks with the Lord's Prayer and is legitimate, you go on knocking at God's door until you get it! Therefore, let me bring out the hidden meaning of the tenses that Jesus used. In one of the greatest promises on prayer in the Bible, he said: "Keep on asking and you will receive. Keep on knocking and the door will open." Keep on – that is the significance of the present continuous tense he used. Not just ask once and that's it, but keep on until you get it. Persistence in prayer is a vital part of prayer on the human side, and I suppose the reason that God has ordained this is not because he is slow to give, not because he is like that neighbour in bed who didn't want to get up, but because we need persistence. After all if my child asked me for something and then didn't get it, and they never asked for it again from me, I would say, "Well, I don't think they really wanted it, you know. Just a passing phase, something they thought of in the moment." But if my child goes on and on and on, I'm afraid they might get it. But the promise is, "You keep on asking God." This is about human persistence.

Then, to balance up the story so that people don't think God is reluctant to give, Jesus now talks about divine providence – his willingness to provide you with good things You know, one of the things that stops people praying and asking God for something is that they are afraid of what he might give. I have known people who are afraid to ask him to fill them with the Holy Spirit and they have said, "I'm afraid I might get a demon." Jesus says, "You earthly fathers are evil people." That gives us Jesus' understanding of human nature. He never said that people were basically good. He always taught that all of us are basically evil people, and yet he was saying: even you evil earthly fathers, you are sinners, you are evil people – and yet you wouldn't give your child something harmful, would you? If they asked for an egg, would you give them a scorpion?

Now a scorpion is a horrible little oval beast, and when it is curled up it looks just like an egg, and eggs in the Middle East are not usually washed. It looks just like a dirty egg. The sting of a scorpion is the greatest pain that a man can stand without dying; it is horrible. Those with weak hearts would die from it. Would you give your child a scorpion if he asked for an egg? Then comes the greatest argument in prayer. When you pray, think of these three words: "How much more...." How much more will your heavenly Father give you something good, something helpful? Do you think that God would give you something harmful because you are wide open to him? Never. There was a minister whose ministry was languishing, who was not seeing fruit for his work, and he got to the point where he felt he should resign, but he went into his study, locked the door and said, "Lord, if you don't fill me with your Spirit, I'm leaving the ministry." The Lord loves a challenge like that and gave him the filling he asked for.

There may be persistence but a reluctance to receive. We are sometimes afraid of what might happen. "Lord, I'll go anywhere in the world but Africa." You can bet your boots it will be Africa! We are afraid of what it will mean. "Lord, I want to dedicate myself to you, but Lord, let me stay here." Do you think he will give you a scorpion? Never!

Luke 11

Here, then, is our Lord's teaching on prayer for the Holy Spirit. This is a prayer that the Father loves to answer, because that is the greatest gift he could give you, next to the gift of his only Son. To give you Jesus to die for you is a very great gift. To give you the Spirit to live in you is as great a gift, and it is a gift that you should pray for. Go on asking and go on knocking and go on seeking.

As soon as that prayer for Holy Spirit is answered, you will become aware that there are such things as evil spirits. Until you have really experienced the power and presence of the Holy Spirit, you will not be troubled much by evil spirits. Though God will not give you a scorpion, the devil has a sting in his tail, and I am afraid you will become aware then that this world is a battlefield – not between people, but between intelligent evil spirits and the angels of our God. I wish I could persuade people of the reality of this. I find two extremes. There are those on the one side who say there are no evil spirits, no demons at all, and that this is just an old-fashioned way of talking of psychic disorders, or even physical complaints. At the other end of the scale I meet an alarming number of people who find a demon under every gooseberry bush and try to exorcise a common cold.

There are real physical complaints that are not demonic, and there are real psychic disorders that are not demonic, and it is very important that we discern. It is important that when supernatural powers are being exercised we discern whether these are divine or demonic: healing can be either. Jesus was exercising the power he received through prayer, and it is no coincidence that Luke puts together power prayer for the Holy Spirit and power over evil spirits in conjunction in this passage. The one leads to the other. The wind whistling around is the picture that Jesus gave of the Holy Spirit: invisible power, you can hear the sound of it, you don't know where it has come from, you don't know where it is going, but you know when it is happening. Jesus used the power that he had gained through prayer to cast out a demon who was dumb. Therefore the person whom the demon inhabited was dumb. The tragedy is that evil spirits cannot operate in this world except through human beings. They need the hands, mouths, eyes, ears and feet of people. Therefore they are restless, wandering around, looking for someone they can use. God is looking around for those who can become the temple of his Holy Spirit, and whom he can use. So this is the spiritual warfare in which we are engaged. In this particular case a demon had struck a man dumb.

The devil does all sorts of horrible things to people: anything that will spoil them for being a good Christian. There is a dumb spirit that can get hold of us. In fact, you know, the devil controls our tongue as much as any other part of our body, either by making us dumb when we should speak or making us speak when we should be dumb. When the Holy Spirit takes hold of you, one of the first things that will show is your tongue. It has always been so.

Here was this man and his dumb spirit inhabiting him kept him from praying and praising. He couldn't have prayed the Lord's Prayer. Jesus set him free – not easily, it took power – tremendous divine energy. It says, "He drove him out," and as soon as that happened, the critics of Jesus who were malicious and prejudiced said that it was not by divine power but by demonic power. They could not have been further from the truth.

Have you read William Golding's book *Lord of the Flies*? It is a profound religious allegory of our day. The storyline has an aeroplane crash on an island. The crew are killed, and all that are left are a bunch of young schoolboys on a school trip. On the island, evil gradually takes over these boys, and before they are rescued they have had war, committed murder and done unspeakable things. A parable, it is a marvellous

Luke 11

book. The author is saying this: put a group of innocent little schoolboys on an island and there are powers of evil that will do to them what has happened to our whole world, and do it in a matter of weeks. It is compelling and so true to our nature. Do you know what "lord of the flies" means? In the Hebrew language that phrase would be: Beelzebub. That is one of the strange titles given to the devil in the Bible, and these enemies of Jesus said, "Don't touch him. It's the lord of the flies who is giving him this power. It is evil; don't touch it!" Jesus defended himself – he is talking about the dynamics of demon possession. You need to understand the dynamics before you get involved. No Christian rushes into this situation if they can help it. The dynamics are that only heaven can overcome hell. "The devil is a strong man," says Jesus. He is stronger than anybody you can see and he has weapons and he holds people in his sway. Don't tackle the devil in your own strength. You'll never win.

Jesus now teaches: "The strong man, as long as he has his weapons, can keep his goods safe, but when the stronger man comes...." It is interesting that in the English it is usually translated, "A strong man keeps his goods in peace, but when a stronger man comes he is able to take his weapons and spoil his goods." In fact, in the Greek, Jesus said, "The strong man" and "when the stronger man comes," for the strong man, being the devil, is only one devil, though he has many lesser demons with him, but there is only one stronger man than the devil. The stronger man is Jesus. You will never beat the devil unless Jesus is with you. Call on the stronger man. You are no match at all for this kind of thing. Stronger man Jesus, come. Lord of Hosts, come.

That is the dynamics of it all. Only heaven can overcome hell, and Jesus points out how ridiculous it would be to say this was being done by the power of the devil – that he was beating the devil by the devil! A nation divided like that would soon collapse. If Satan has started fighting himself, he is finished. Once you have brainwashed yourself into believing that the demonic is divine, and the divine demonic, you will never be able to tell the difference between right and wrong, and you will never be able to repent. That is the only sin that is unforgiveable, and it is what these people were doing to Jesus.

Then Jesus spoke of two awful dangers in this spiritual warfare. You see, the battle in Britain is not between political groups but between the forces of good and the forces of evil who are not human but supernatural, and who are just wreaking havoc in our country at the moment. The first danger is that of remaining neutral. You can't! So many of my fellow countrymen would say, "Well, I'm not against Christianity and I'm not against God," but Jesus would say: you are, because you are not for me; you have not decided for me, so you are against me.

You can't be neutral in this. You can't sit on the fence and say, "Look at those Christians at that end, and look at those terrible people at this end, and look at us nice folks in the middle." There is no fence to sit on, no middle ground, no neutrality. Sweden and Switzerland could remain neutral in World War II, but in this war they can't, and nobody in Britain can either. The sad truth is that if you do not decide for Christ, you are against him. Unless you line up with him, you have lined up against him. It is not that you have consciously chosen to help evil along. It is that you were born into the evil world, you were born with an evil nature, you are part of it before you start, and if you don't make any decision for Christ during your lifetime you are not neutral, you are against. "He that is not for me is against me, and he that is not gathering with me is scattering." If you are not seeking to be filled with the Spirit, if you are not lined up with Christ, then frankly you are on the side of evil forces, whether you are conscious of it or not. There is no neutral ground.

The second danger Jesus warned us against was being only negative in this warfare – the tragedy and danger of an empty life. Chalmers, the great Scottish preacher, began a sermon on this text with these words, "You've got to fill a man with something. Human nature abhors a vacuum. We can't remain empty." Some people are against evil; they have emptied their life of this and that and the other, and they have remained empty, and the last state of that person will be worse than the first, as Jesus taught. Because a man doesn't do this, and doesn't do that, and doesn't do the other, do you think he is any better a person, or any safer a person? Far from it! The tragedy is that when you have cast out some crude thing, some rather sophisticated thing comes in its place. When you have cast out the things that the world would call sins, the things that God calls sins come in: pride, hyper-criticism—all sorts of things come in when you have got your life cleaned up.

Don't think you can clean your life up alone. Don't try and get rid of evil out of your life and then leave it empty. In place of degrading things you will just be dull. Emptiness – there are few people so empty as those who go to church but have never been converted. You know they have cut out many crude sins and many things that are evil. Maybe they don't do a whole list of things, but how dull, and how dangerous. The pride, the Phariseeism, the legalism and the criticism of others that can come in, all because a person's life has been cleaned up without being filled with the Holy Spirit.

It is not just getting rid of evil out of this nation. If we cleaned up this nation and got rid of the things that we call evil from it, and left the nation as it was, it would be in a far worse state than it is now. There is only one hope and that is for people to get filled with the Holy Spirit of God, and for the emptiness to be replaced with divine fullness, and for the evil to be replaced with the good – the expulsive power of a new affection. So it is no use going to church and getting *reformed*. What you need is to be *regenerated*. It is no use getting the wrong things out of your life and leaving your life empty. I have seen this happen and I have seen people try to turn over a Christian leaf, and try to live a Christian life, and they have managed to get rid of certain things, but when the emptiness gets filled up with other sins they are far harder to reach with the gospel than they ever were when they were outright sinners. The respectable have always been the most difficult to bring to conversion.

So Jesus finishes – what a sermon! What a challenge: prayer for the Holy Spirit, power over evil spirits; heaven and hell are in conflict, and then there is a woman in the crowd who shouts out from the congregation, "Blessed is the womb that bore you, and the breasts which nursed you!" Is she talking about Mary? She is really saying something about herself. She envies Jesus' mother for giving birth to such a wonderful preacher, the man who is the Son of God.

He says, "More than that, blessed are those who hear the Word of God and keep it!"

Which is more blessed: to give birth to Jesus or to receive the Spirit of Jesus? True blessedness consists in listening to God's Word, obeying it, and finding that this is the victory.

11:29-54

If I were asked to give a title to this passage I would call it "How to Lose Friends and Antagonise People". This is the death blow to the kind of sentimental view of Jesus that so many of us picked up from some of the things that were said to us as children. The sentimental picture of Jesus I hear so often is that he was such a nice person, that he never said a hurtful thing to anyone, and that he went through life looking for the good that was in people. That kind of picture is totally removed from the truth, and this chapter tells us why. That kind of sentimental picture of Jesus leaves one with a gigantic question: who one earth would ever want to crucify a person like that? On the contrary, it seems as though Jesus went out of his way to rub people up the wrong way, to antagonise them, to upset them. There isn't one word of commendation here. He is dealing with three different groups of people and he slates every one of them.

Let us look at the groups. First, he spoke to the people at large, the Jews. He said, "How evil are the people of this day." Jesus said, "No one is good but God" – and his opinion of human nature was always summed up in one word: evil. "If you then, being evil," we read earlier: "If you then, being evil, know how to give good things to your children" – this was his summary of human nature. Everybody he met he regarded as evil. That is extraordinary, isn't it? One of the most amazing texts which I've never heard preached on comes from John's Gospel where it says that, "Jesus would not trust himself to any man, for he knew what was in man." Don't tell me that Jesus went around with a rosy view of human nature, saying, "Everybody's fine if you only look for the good things in them." That is just the opposite of what he did.

Now, what do you think they were doing to deserve that word? Who would you call an evil person? What would they have to do to merit that adjective in your mind – or, as another translation puts it, "Wicked"? Jesus' definition of an evil person would be someone who will only believe what he wants to believe, will only hear what he wants to hear, and will only see what he wants to see – that is evil and devastating. That kind of evil is what is responsible for all the other troubles in the world. That is the kind of evil that is running right through us and right through our nation.

First, there are those who will only believe what they want to believe. Somebody said to me when I was talking to them about the Christian faith, "Well, I think everybody believes what they want to believe." I said, "I think you're absolutely right – that doesn't decide what's right though. That doesn't decide what's true, but it is true that if you want to believe in Jesus now, you can believe in him. And if you don't want to, there's nothing I can do to convince you." Whatever objection you raise against the Christian faith, if I answer that objection to your satisfaction, you will immediately produce another if you don't want to believe. We all believe what we want to believe, and we don't believe what we don't want to believe, and that is the problem.

If only we could consider evidence with an open mind – but none of us can. These Jews had been prepared and they knew two thousand years of the history of their nation. They were all ready and Jesus came to them, the Son of God, with the truth and he gave it to them, and they wanted him to prove it. They wanted to see a miracle, some sensational proof; they were not prepared to take his word for it. Then he challenged them with a story from scripture – one which many people today refuse to believe because they don't want to believe it – the story of Jonah.

Unbelief keeps millions out of the kingdom of heaven. It is the unbelief that says, "I don't want to believe and I'll find every excuse. I'll believe it on my terms and if you can persuade me on my terms that it's true, I'll believe it," but they are still not believing it on God's terms; they are not believing it because God said it was true. You know that Jesus said that one day the very people that Jonah preached to would confront you. So Jesus believed in Jonah, and Nineveh is a real city and you can go today and see its ruins, and Jonah went to that city. Notice that the people to whom Jesus was speaking had not seen the miracle of Jonah. They had not seen the miracle of his survival, they had only heard about it. Yet that vast pagan city, which had a boundary sixty miles in circumference, a city with 250,000 people living in it (nobody living there now, it's a ruin), at the preaching of one man, believed the word of God and they cleaned up the city. It was a pretty rough place. If you have studied any of the bas-reliefs in the museums that tell us what went on in Nineveh, they cleaned up the city at the preaching of Jonah. Jesus was reminding his hearers of those Gentiles, who unlike Jews had not had the Old Testament, had never had the Hebrew history, yet at the preaching of one man they believed – and you won't.

The second characteristic of an evil person is that there is something wrong with their ears too – they only hear what they want to hear. I have deep sympathy for deaf people. It shuts them off more from social contact than other handicaps do. I have never heard it said of a deaf person, "Doesn't he cope wonderfully with his handicap?" We have known in our own family what a handicap it can be. But sometimes you meet people who are not physically deaf but you wonder if they hear what they want to hear. Have you had that experience? And in some cases what they want to hear is evil. The things we like to hear, of course, are the things that are nice and complimentary. The things we don't like to hear are the things that are critical. So there is something wrong with our ears and we select what we hear.

This is what Jesus was teaching people of that generation: you have deaf ears, not just doubting minds. You only hear what you want to hear and you don't want to hear. In the judgment day, when you stand before God, there will be a woman standing there, the Queen of Sheba, and she was a woman who travelled halfway round the [then known] world to hear the word of God from the mouth of Solomon, and you won't even walk down the street. You just don't want to hear what I've got to say – that is evil.

It would have been a mighty journey for the Queen of Sheba. It would cost a lot of money and it would take a lot of time. Yet that Queen of Sheba will stand – she was real, she is not just a character in a fictional story. She will stand in the judgment day and say, "You wouldn't go down the road to hear the Word of God. I went a long distance to hear it. I wanted to listen to what God was saying through his servant Solomon."

Jesus is now teaching this: one greater than Jonah is here; Jonah was a weak, unstable prophet who ran away; I am the Son of God, I am the Prophet; Solomon was a king, but he made his mistakes and he had his folly; I am the Wisdom, a greater than Jonah, a greater than Solomon, and you will only believe what you want to believe and you will only listen to what you want to listen to.

The third dimension of evil is only to see what you want to see. For a gathering of blind people the Lord gave me an extraordinary word from the Sermon on the Mount, "It's better for you to lose an eye and go to heaven, rather than go to hell with all your members complete." I said to those people, "Will you pray for those of us who have got sight. If the ear is the major channel of God into your soul, the eye is the major channel of Satan. The lust of the eyes, the pride of life, coveting – all these things come in here. Will you pray for those of us who are sighted?" It was the first time one old woman had pitied those who could see. Through that, the Lord removed resentment from her heart and she became the Lord's. She became radiant and she went to glory a week later.

The eye is the light of the body, and what comes in through the eye will determine whether your whole body shines or lives in the shadows. You look at what you choose to look at. Jesus is teaching this: there is not only trouble with your mind, doubting minds, there's not only trouble with your ears, deaf ears, there's trouble too with your eyes – darkened eyes. You only see what you want to see and that can either fill your body with light or shadow. Here is what an evil, wicked person is in Jesus' sight. A wicked person is someone who will only believe with their mind what they want to believe, who will only listen with their ears to what they want to hear, and will only look with their eyes at what they choose to look at. That is evil. God wants to put truth into our minds, speak to us through our ears, and show us himself through our eyes. Evil people can't get any of it; the three channels are closed because they are selective. Well, that's pretty tough stuff. I am afraid it finds a lot of us out, too.

The second group he turned to were the Pharisees, thought to be the holiest people in the Jewish race. They were not liked, but respected, and people used to say of them, "Well, I'm not very fond of them but if anybody deserves to get to heaven, they do. They really have gone hard at it." Calling themselves the separated ones, they followed their religion right down to the last ditch. They tried to be as separated to God as they could, they tried to be as holy as they could, and they got a long way further than most of us have ever been. They prayed five times a day, without fail. They gave something like a quarter of their money to the Lord's work. They knew their scriptures backwards.

Jesus said to his followers: "Unless you can do better than the Pharisees, you'll never see the kingdom ... unless your righteousness can exceed theirs." You can't exceed something until you have got up to it. Some of us have never got near the righteousness of the Pharisees, it was pretty good. Yet Jesus turned on these people who devoted themselves to being religious, who had separated themselves from ordinary life. He said, "You Pharisees!" Now, he begins to curse them for three things. First of all, he says, "You are too bothered about externals." He had actually gone to have a meal with them and they noticed that he didn't wash his hands before the meal. That wasn't just a matter of hygiene, it was a matter of religion. They had a ritual: you washed your hands down from the elbow, not only before the meal but between the courses. It was a religious ritual. They kept it assiduously. Jesus walked in, and without washing his hands he sat down and started eating. They were horrified. He said, "You Pharisees, you're far more bothered about the outside than the inside, that's one of your troubles."

You see, if we get the idea that we are only in the presence of God when we are in Sunday clothes then the next time you are gardening you will not think of God. It is thinking that the important thing is the clothes you wear when you go to church, but God looks on the heart, not the outward appearance. I sat in the bath early one Sunday morning and thought about this, and the Lord said to me, "Have you washed your heart? You're starting Sunday clean." He said that so clearly right there in the bath.

The second thing Jesus criticised the Pharisees for was that they were so concerned with details. Not just externals, but details. They got tied up in petty regulations. The first tenth of their income they gave extended to this: when they planted a row of herbs in the window box outside the kitchen, they would carefully measure it and divide it into ten and make a little gap, and there was the little tenth for God. They were so careful with details, but they neglected the larger matters of justice and love for God. You can get all the details of a service right, and get every note in an anthem right, and get every note in a hymn right, and you can get it all just perfect. Jesus would say: what about love for God? He would rather that someone loves God even if they miss every note and sing flat the whole way through. The love is the bigger thing. He says you ought not to neglect the details, but don't make them so important that you neglect the weightier matters. Love of God is first, and we are to be merciful, and we must be flexible about rules and regulations. The bigger matters are more important. The Pharisees' righteousness was petty and detailed; they were forever making it a matter of rules and regulations.

The third thing Jesus said about them was, "You like to parade your piety. You like the chief seats in the synagogues so people can see how you pray."

Jesus teaches us not to parade our prayer. We are not told: "Let your light shine before men that they may see your good *prayers*"! No, the Word of God doesn't say that. It says, "... that they may see your good *works*...." Those are things to let shine, but as to your piety, keep it secret. Keep your devotions private – that is between you and the Lord; you don't pray as a witness, you pray as communion. It is easy to start letting people see our religion. The Pharisees loved people to see that they were good pray-ers, and Jesus tore them to shreds for doing this. Now Phariseeism is not dead, there is a little bit of it in all of us. Our religion so easily becomes a matter of externals, a matter of details, and a matter that is to be paraded in front of others.

Can you cope with the third part of this? I am finding it increasingly difficult because the third part is all about those who teach the Bible. They called them "scribes" in those days, teachers of the Law. They had produced the Pharisees with their teaching and so they said, "Jesus do you realise that you're insulting us? These Pharisees are our pupils, we taught them to do these things." Jesus said, "Woe to you too, you teachers of the law!" All those of us involved in teaching the Word of God to others are going to be spoken to now: ministers, Sunday school teachers; in fact, all Christians are teachers of the Word of God – as parents, as friends, whoever you are. If you seek to teach another the Word of God, then there are three things here for you. First: don't make it harder for people. Don't just keep loading them with a higher and higher standard and never lifting a finger to help them to reach that standard. The scribes did this. They multiplied the laws and the rules and the regulations until people said, "I give up!" It is so easy to teach the Word of God like this.

Jesus lifted the standard higher than anyone else. He made the commandments not only a matter of action but a matter of motive and thought as well. Jesus set impossible standards but I will tell you what he did. He said, "Learn of me for my yoke is easy and my burden is light." The normal yoke in the Middle East is made of a block of wood with four smaller sticks thrust through holes and jammed there. This fits over the necks of two animals – two oxen, or an ox and an ass, or whatever. A yoke is always double. When Jesus said, "Take my yoke on you," he was saying: link yourself with me and I'll pull with you. Isn't that lovely? I know he gave us an impossible standard – by ourselves it would be impossible – but then he is teaching this: take my yoke, clip it on; come on, let's pull through this together – my yoke is easy and my burden is light. Jesus has the highest moral standards of any teacher, yet he will help us. The teachers of the law laid it on thick and then did nothing to help.

The second message to teachers was this: you pretend respect for the great teachers, protestors and prophets of the past, but in reality you are so thrilled that they are dead that you are happy to put a monument over them. One of the strange laws of human nature is that when a man is doing good in this world he is hated for it, but as soon as he is dead they will put up a monument. I have seen this happen again and again. I always cringe when I go into the Baptist Union headquarters in London and see a gigantic bronze statue of C H Spurgeon with his arms outstretched and his mouth open, preaching the Word of God, as he used to preach it to a congregation of five or six thousand in the Metropolitan Tabernacle at the Elephant and Castle. His sermons were read the world over, and from him the Word of God went forth, but he was fearless and therefore he told the Baptist Union, "You're departing from the Word of God." The controversy that followed killed him, and he was out of the Union before he was dead. Men who deny the deity of Christ walk past that statue. We do it still.

When I was a Methodist I heard so many Methodist people speak with bated breath of John Wesley. Then I discovered that if John Wesley came back and preached those very doctrines today, here and now, he would not be welcome.

William Booth was turned out of the ministry because of his unorthodox evangelistic methods. Now those who turned him out would be first to say, "Great man!"

So we go on. As soon as a man is dead we are safe, no longer can he protest, no longer can he challenge us. So we now say what a great man he was and we erect the memorial. It is so easy to do that but the real test is not what do you think of the man, but what do you think about what he said? What do you think of his message in the Lord? The real test is not what you think of Isaiah or Jeremiah, what you think of Augustine or Martin Luther. If Martin Luther were preaching today, his crude language, his blunt expression and his devastating rhetoric would make him a very unpopular preacher.

You teachers – beware of saying you love all that the Bible says and then not letting the challenge of the words of the prophets eat into your own soul. What do you think Amos would be saying now in London? Whatever he would be saying would be terribly unpopular. How do I know that? Because men are saying the same thing today and the world will not listen.

The third thing that teachers are warned about, you

teachers of the law, is this: you have the key to knowledge and you suppress it. You should be the people who are encouraging others to read and search the scriptures. The effect of your teaching is to bottle up the scriptures. Shall I tell you how we preachers do that? We parade scholarship, we bring in theoretical theologies and funny philosophies, and we make ourselves out to be such brilliant people that our listeners say, "Well, I can't read the Bible. I'll have to leave it to the pastor." That is how we do it. That is how they did it here. They made the scriptures so complicated and difficult to understand that people said, "Leave it to the scribes, leave it to the scholars, we'll never understand it." The result of being trained in theology for so many men is that their preaching stops people reading the Bible, because the congregation says, "I'll never understand it unless I have that same subtle theological training." I'm speaking to my own heart here. I must so teach that you will say, "I can understand the Bible too; I can get truth from it too" – so that you can have the same exciting discovery that I have in my study when I see something new. I get so excited that I walk up and down and say it to myself again and again – some new truth. I want you to have that excitement; I want you to share it. Forgive me if anything I teach about the Bible makes it more difficult for you to understand it and more difficult to dig into it for yourself.

Do you wonder that they put Jesus on a cross? Do you wonder that they hated him? Why was he so critical of these three groups? After all, he could be very kind and gentle to little children, to prostitutes, to crooked tax collectors. There is just one simple reason: it is because they were *religious*. Of all the nations in the world, the Jews were given the true religion, the true revelation of God. For them to be as they were was criminal. Within that nation, of all the groups of people there was one group professing to be holier than all the others, namely the Pharisees. They had no right to be as they were. Those who had taught those Pharisees had no right to be as they were either. In other words, Christ has no room for religion if this is the kind of religion it is. It is one of the reasons that the poor, the sinful and the down and out have got on better with Christ than respectable, religious people. Those of us who have put on a veneer of religion are the most uncomfortable. With a devastating accuracy Jesus pinpoints the weakness of religion when it is a prop or a cloak. He strips it off and says it is full of deadness and rottenness inside; it is like people walking over tombs without realising it.

This chapter is preparing us for the cross. It is stripping away the veneer so that we may have reality and come as we are to the foot of the cross. It is knocking us down so that God may build us up properly, in reality. It is removing the veneer so that we might be clothed with the righteousness of Christ. It is helping us to be honest about ourselves, that we may be in a position to believe the truth about God. So Jesus was doing it out of kindness. It is at the cross that you find the whole truth about yourself, because he had to die for you; about himself, because he didn't need to die, and they hated him because he was so good; and about a God who gave his only begotten Son that whoever would believe in him should not perish but have everlasting life.

12

Read Luke 12

12:1-34

The earliest name for our religion was not Christianity but The Way. Right through the last two thousand years, people have likened the Christian life to a journey down a long road. I suppose the most famous of such pictures would be Bunyan's *The Pilgrim's Progress* but there have been many others. It all started with Jesus who talked about a narrow road that leads to life. Like every other road there are pitfalls and dangers and we need warning signs to tell us when there is a steep hill, a sharp bend or a slippery surface. It is not an easy road to travel. In this chapter it is as if Jesus is travelling the road ahead of us and putting up signposts to tell us where the dangers lie: the things that can cause you mishap; that could slow you down; that could hinder your journey, your pilgrimage – because you are not here to stay, you are just passing through this world. You have got a journey to make to a heavenly city.

So we are going to look at four of the major dangers along the Christian road, any one of which could bring us to a halt in our journey. I think it may be true to say that these hazards are so common that every one of us has been halted by one of them. Most of us will have had problems with all four. They are hypocrisy, fear, greed and worry.

The first is hypocrisy. The word itself means to put on a mask. It came straight from the stage of the ancient theatre where many of the plays were performed not with makeup but with masks tied on. So you put a mask on to represent the character. At first, the word "hypocrite" simply meant "actor" – to play a part. So if you went to the theatre you would walk away saying of the lead actor, "My, he's a good hypocrite isn't he?" In those days he wouldn't have been terribly upset but the word has now come to mean putting on a front. Jesus is warning us to beware of play acting. Beware of putting on a front. It is one of the easiest things to do when you become a Christian. It is one of the most common things in our Christian journey to fall prey to. He says it acts like yeast. I have never made bread but you may have done and will know what yeast is like and what it does. You know that there are three characteristics of yeast which are also true of hypocrisy. The first is that it only needs a little to affect the lot.

The second characteristic of yeast is that it spreads very quickly indeed, especially in a warm atmosphere. The third thing about yeast is that it works invisibly and secretly and silently, so you are not even aware that it is happening. Jesus said, "Beware of the yeast of hypocrisy." Then he went on very boldly to hold up certain people in his presence as an example of the very thing he was warning against. Only Jesus, who is perfectly holy, could have such courage, and only a person totally free from play acting could point to another and warn against being like them.

Then he highlights a particular form of hypocrisy to which we are more prone than others. Not hypocrisy of conduct, though that is possible, but hypocrisy of speech. He singles out this as the particular danger to which his disciples will be prone because the one part of us that we use more than any other in our religion is our mouth. When we come to church, this is the main part of the body that we use. I know we sit and stand, but by and large you can do with your hands and feet much what you like during a service. Your mouth is going to be doing particular things. We take upon our lips as Christians many wonderful and holy thoughts

I recall one fine, very decent-living man who attended church but wasn't a Christian. He came to services to accompany his wife, who was a Christian. I noticed that during the hymns he would stand, he would read the hymn, but he would never sing. I asked him once why he didn't and he said, "Because it would be dishonest of me to say those things, I don't believe them yet; they are not true of me." So I felt he was right in not singing. You can imagine the thrill when one day I saw him throw his head back and sing his heart out, but I knew that the previous Sunday at the end of the evening he had given himself to Christ. I take my hat off to that man. He was honest and it could be that for some of us the honest thing may be not to take Christian things upon our lips for we are not ready to do so.

On the other hand, Jesus is thinking of those who can and do and should take Christian words on their lips, and it is what they say when they get home that is the kind of hypocrisy he is most concerned about. It is the hypocrisy of speech. In other words: is what you say behind people's backs the same as what you say to their face? Is what you say to God's face the same as you say when you think you are behind his back? Is the kind of language that is on your lips in church compatible with the kind of language that passes your lips at Sunday lunch as soon as you get home? This is the hypocrisy of speech. Our Lord warns us that it operates like yeast in a fellowship – silently, secretly, so that you never hear it in the open. There it is, permeating the whole lump and destroying it and spreading its own influence. Here is the first warning sign: beware hypocrisy. As we are in pilgrimage along this road we need to look at that sign and take appropriate action.

The second hazard to which he points is fear – one of the

great inhibitors of the Christian life. Fear paralyses our words and our deeds. Fear grips us, preventing us from doing what the Lord wants us to do. We are in a little prayer meeting and would love to pray and the Lord wants us to pray, but fear chokes us up and we get a dry throat and a throbbing heart. We just can't get it out and fear has crippled us. Or we are in a situation where people are chatting and religion comes up. We know there is an opportunity for witness and we are afraid of saying the wrong thing or worry about what they may think about us or do to us afterwards, and if they will laugh at us or if we won't have the answers to their questions. Fear closes our mouths and it is a terrible inhibitor: fear of man and what men may say or feel or think or do to us.

This is a warning that Christians need as we go along the Christian road. Fear of man is a hazard that could stop your travelling. That is why the Bible says 366 times, "Don't be afraid" – once for every day including leap year. After all, what is the worst thing that a person could do to you? Well, the very worst thing is they could kill you and rob you of life itself and put you out of this world forever. That's all. Jesus taught us to think like this, saying that is the worst thing that can happen. Well, it happened to him. The worst thing that man can do to you is to kill your body and that is all they can do because the truth is that if they kill your body, they haven't killed you. All they would have achieved for a disciple of Jesus would be to rush them to heaven early.

We are all sensitive on this point and we all have our hesitations about what other people will think or say if we behave in a certain way or express our beliefs openly. What is the cure for fear of men? The cure of a small fear is a big fear. You can only cast out one fear by putting another in its place. Think about some occasion in your life when you have been afraid, and then suddenly some greater threat has entered the situation. Your new fear has totally swallowed up the old one. I can only think of a thoroughly ridiculous illustration: if I were standing on the edge of a motorway and needed to get to the other side and the cars were whizzing past at full speed and I wondered if I would get across. I would be afraid to try – but if a lion appeared behind me, I would get through that traffic like a shot! Do you see what I mean? It is a silly illustration but gets the point across. If you are afraid of man there is only one thing to deal with it and that is to be more afraid of God. If you are more afraid of what God will think of you and say to you and do to you, then your fear of man will disappear. When we are afraid of people, at that moment it is true to say we have lost our fear of the Lord which is the beginning of wisdom. Do you realise that God can do far worse to you than that person you are afraid of? The worst that other person can do to you is to kill your body, but do you realise that God can judge you eternally? God can send a person to hell. There is a place for fear of God in Christian discipleship. I have heard it said that for the Christian there is only love now, and no place for fear. There is a place for godly fear, it is a vital part of Christian discipleship – not the terror that is afraid of God and shrinks from him, but the fear of grieving a holy God and forcing him to chastise you as a child, and that is a healthy fear.

To get rid of the wrong sort of fear of God, Jesus says that God cares for you very much and knows all about you, using some illustrations. Take sparrows, ordinary little brown birds. They were sold in those days for very poor people to use as a little sacrifice. God knows about each one and you are of more value than many of them.

Even if people killed your body and nobody knew you had been martyred and you were flung out or buried in an unknown grave; if everybody forgot about you – and there must be hundreds of martyrs unknown to anybody but

God – he sees the sparrow fall. God knows how many hairs there are on your head. Do you know roughly how many hairs that would be? If you are blonde basically you have approximately 145,000 when you start life. If you have dark hair you probably have about 120,000. If you are a redhead, you have probably got about 90,000. God has counted every one of those on you and could give you the exact number. That is astonishing, isn't it? God knows all about you, but there is still a place for fear of God.

This theme of what the right fear of God is like is now developed. It is vital to look at the situation not from the point of view of what men will say or think but from the point of view of God. Here is an illustration. Somebody says to you, "Are you a Christian?" Or you are in a situation where you know you ought to declare yourself and say that you are a Christian. People in the office are discussing what religions there are in the world and what religion each one favours and you are present. You're saying to yourself, "I'm awfully afraid to confess I'm a Christian because maybe I don't live up to it very much, and you know, I'm a bit embarrassed to acknowledge it." That is thinking of men, but if you think of God, this is what he would say in that situation, "If you don't admit you belong to me, I can't admit you belong to me. If you are ashamed to admit it, I am ashamed to admit it." When you are the coward and you don't say, "I'm a Christian," when you should, if Christ is asked at that moment by the angels, "Is that one of yours?" He will say, "I can't acknowledge him, not at this moment. One of mine would acknowledge me." On the other hand, the moment you acknowledge publicly to others, "Yes I do belong to Jesus Christ. I know him and I love him" – then at that moment Christ can say to the angels, "That person is mine and I acknowledge them openly. They belong to me." Now that is the direct consequence of what we do on earth. It is what the Lord says about us and thinks and feels, not what the other people do, and that will alter you tremendously.

So next time you get a chance to nail your colours to the mast, remember that Christ can acknowledge you in heaven too, and say, "Look at that person – one of mine, openly acknowledging it." But if we deny him, he has to deny us because we are not being true to him at that moment. Another thing that he looks at is rather puzzling at first. He says, "You can say anything you like against the Son of Man and it could be forgiven, but you speak against the Holy Spirit and it can't be forgiven." Many have been puzzled by this: that the worst blasphemy that a man can make against our Lord Jesus can be forgiven, but the same thing against the Holy Spirit can't. People have said, "Well, why?" The answer is very simple. It is true to history too – many of the Jews said horrible things against Christ. Some called him a blasphemer, and dreadful things, and wanted him put to death as a criminal. But seven weeks later, three thousand of them repented of that and were converted by Peter: "You crucified this man who is the Son of God. God has made him both Lord and Christ, this Jesus whom you crucified." They repented, and they said, "We're sorry we said it." They found forgiveness. The reason is that the Holy Spirit convicted them of sin. So the Holy Spirit can convict us – if we listen to him – of the wrong we have done to Jesus, and, when we see that, we can repent and be forgiven. If you sin against the Holy Spirit in this way, who is going to convict you of that? Who will tell you that you have done wrong then? The answer is no-one, because there is no-one else to help you.

You see, Jesus came to those who had spoken against God and then the Holy Spirit came to those who had spoken against Jesus but there is going to be no one more. If I will not let the Holy Spirit speak to me and if I deny his voice and if I speak against the Holy Spirit, then frankly I have come to the end of the road, there is no one else to help me. Can you see that? Therefore, we must be careful when we speak before man. We must have a great fear of speaking against the Holy Spirit. Jesus said the blasphemy against the Holy Spirit is to look at what the Holy Spirit is doing and say, "That is of the devil." When you say that there is no hope for you, then you have reached the end of the line. If the only person who can convict you of sin is the one you are calling the devil, then who will now do so?

Then Jesus teaches that when you are in a tight corner, when you have been arrested, when you are being tried for being a Christian, that same Holy Spirit whom the world is blaspheming is going to be your greatest help. Don't be afraid, you may find yourself in a court of law. You may find yourself in the dark because you belong to Jesus. This does not cover being in the dark because you have committed a sin which is also a crime, but if you are there in the name of Jesus don't worry! You may not be a preacher, they may have taken your Bible from you, and you may not know what to say, but don't be afraid of man, because the Holy Spirit will put words in your mouth. There are such amazing examples of this. Read the life of Stephen, read the life of Paul, Peter, James, John; when they appeared in court they always had the right word from God. It is true through the ages: Wycliffe, Hus, Luther – you find that whenever they stood on trial, the Holy Spirit delivered them from fear of man and put words in their mouths. So here is the second great danger on the Christian road – fear of man. Let the fear of the Lord take that away. In every situation you will find the Holy Spirit will help you.

The third danger is greed. It is quite extraordinary that a man came to Jesus to ask him to settle a domestic quarrel over a legacy. The cynics say ,"Where there is a Will there's relatives!" I have seen that break so many families. I have seen families begin to break up at the funeral itself. Before the deceased is under the ground, families have started arguing about that favourite item of furniture which mother said I could have. It is tragic that death is often divisive among the remaining relatives and leaves bitterness behind. This man following Jesus was in such a situation. He was saying that it was not fair; he should have had a share in his parents' assets. His brother would not share the property with him but was keeping the money. Jesus was concerned about the heart of this man himself and he deliberately kept out of the dispute, but the very way in which the man asked for help showed there was something very wrong. Greed was there. Jesus taught that riches are one of the greatest handicaps there can be to living a Christian life – even to starting it. It is very hard for a rich man to enter the kingdom, easier to push a camel through the eye of a needle, though with God all things are possible.

The minute you die, every pound you possess loses one hundred percent of its value, and Jesus now tells the story of a rich man whose greed for wealth had done a number of awful things to his character.

Firstly, greed had tied him entirely to this world. He couldn't even think beyond this world. He only thought of his business. Secondly, greed had made him only concerned with himself. "I wonder what I should do – I will pull down my barns, and I will take it easy." I, my, mine – do you see how he thought? His greed has tied him down to one person and that makes a very small bundle of life. Thirdly, his greed had deluded him into thinking that he was going to live here forever. The way many people are planning their future you would think they were going to stay down here on earth eternally. The way they planned the bungalow that they are going to retire to, the money they are going to need when they retire, and all the countries they are going to visit, you would think they were going to retire for an indefinite period. All the statistics are against this. Life on earth is not certain but death is. This wealthy man's whole life was spent thinking through his investments and wondering how to increase his business. God says, "You're a fool." With all that man's cleverness, all his business ability, he was still a fool. That is a strong word – it means somebody who is without sense; capable of doing a good thing but silly enough not to do it. When Jesus said in the Sermon on the Mount, "Don't call anybody a fool," the word he used meant someone who can't help it. When Jesus said "fool" here, he is using a different word which means someone who can help it and is being utterly silly: you fool, tonight you are going to have to leave every bit of it; tonight you are a pauper; tonight your business is gone; tonight you have got nothing and you are bankrupt. So it is with those who are rich in things and poor in soul.

We turn from material plenty to spiritual poverty. We live in a world obsessed with acquiring material goods and it is very difficult not to let it rub off on you. How much is there in your account in heaven? If you were going to live in another country, you would arrange with a bank to send some money on so that you would have some support there, wouldn't you? That's the kind of investment we ought to be considering. Otherwise you will finish up making the last long journey of life on your own from this life to the next and you will have no luggage in advance, no transferred bank account, nothing going on ahead – all through greed in this life.

The fourth hindrance to the Christian life we come to in this passage is worry. If greed is the hindrance that tends to come into those who have a lot, worry is the hindrance that tends to come to those who have a little. So whether you have a lot or a little, there are still hazards. Many of those who don't have enough to make ends meet are tempted to worry. What a waste of nervous energy it is, and what harm it can do to the physical system. First of all then, let us realise that God does know the basic needs which we do have, such as food and clothes. Did your children have to go out and find their own food and clothing or did you provide those things for them? Do you think your heavenly Father doesn't think of his children? If you are worried about what you eat and what you are going to wear, then frankly you are libelling God. You have a heavenly Father who sees that your expenses are met; it is as simple as that. "Worry," said Jesus, "What does it do for you? Can you live any longer with worry? Can you add one span to your life?" Far from it, you will shorten it considerably. If you are worried, your arteries will harden, you will soon shorten your life; worry never lengthened anybody's life. Then why worry?

The unbeliever has every reason to worry. He has no heavenly Father, he is an orphan and he is left alone. The unbeliever should be worried stiff about the present state of their finances. The unbeliever should be really worried about their investments, they have got everything to worry about, but you are a child of God, and your heavenly Father knows you have need. Look how he cares for birds and flowers. Do you think you matter less to him? The argument is unanswerable. It adds up to one simple thing: worry is sin.

Whatever sin you mention, we all have different temperamental proneness to certain ones. You may be more prone to worry than others but that doesn't make it less of a sin. Again you could say, "Well, somebody has got to worry about the family." Have they? Have they got to worry about the family with a heavenly Father? We have got to work, there is no excuse here for laziness, sloth, indifference; there is no excuse here for not managing things properly. We are talking now about worrying about it, and does worrying do any good at all? No, but what a testimony it is when in straitened and needy circumstances, a child of God has learned godliness with contentment, whether they have much or little.

Worry is a terrible hindrance, it saps nervous energy and it denies God. What is the antidote? Is there a cure? Yes, there is. Just as the cure for the wrong fear is the right fear, the cure for the wrong worry is the right worry. Get worried about God's kingdom; seek his concerns, then you needn't be worried about food and clothes. Do you see? Cure one concern with another. Seek first his kingdom, his righteousness, and all these things shall be added. In other words, when you are in Christ's service, you can run an expense account on heaven. Notice there is a condition here. He is not saying, "Every one of my children needn't worry." What he is saying is: you needn't worry because I know you have needs and I will provide.

So, finally, Jesus finishes up by teaching that we can now afford to be generous. It is your Father's good pleasure to give you the kingdom. Therefore you can afford to give. You can afford to be generous because you are very rich. Look what is coming to you. The amazing thing is that whatever the Christian gives doesn't go on his debit side in his heavenly account, but on the other side. That is how you lay up treasure in heaven – by giving. God's mathematics are exactly the opposite of ours: whatever you give makes you richer; whatever you get for yourself makes you poorer. That is God's heavenly bank account and you have got an account right now with God as a child of his. So he says, "Lay up treasure in heaven". That is the best of all bargains, isn't it?

The reason is that where your money goes and where your material things go, there your heart will follow. I heard a lovely story of a little boy in a church and one day a missionary came to that church called Mr. Burt. At the end of the missionary meeting, there was an offering to help Mr. Burt and his work overseas. This little boy put a penny in the offering. A year later, Mr. Burt came back to the church and the little boy said to his parents, "I want to go to that meeting."

He was so keen that they asked him, "Why are you so keen to go?"

He replied, "When he was here last time, I gave him a penny and I want to hear what he's done with it!"

Now he was absolutely true to real life in this. Where you have put your money, there your heart will follow. That is one of the reasons for giving to missionary work: giving yourself to it, your heart will go after that gift.

We have looked at four different dangers but is there a thread tying them together? I think there is. I am going to tie them together in two twos. The first two, the hindrances of hypocrisy and fear come because the Christian is thinking too much about the people in this world and not enough about God. The second two dangers, greed and worry, are coming because one is thinking too much about the things of this world. Put them together and all dangers come because the Christian is thinking too much about either the people or the things in this world and too little about God and the next world. This theme carries right on in the rest of the chapter and we are going to see how it is tied up beautifully with our Lord's return in glory.

12:35-59

It is impressive to watch the demolition of a large building. I have seen that done with explosives. In fact, our whole civilisation is to be demolished. We know it, God the Father has said it. He has already marked the date in his calendar. He has not told us when it will be, but those whose eyes are opened to what the hand of God is doing in contemporary events know that the time is drawing near when we shall reach the end of the world as we have known it.

The next great world event is the return of the Lord Jesus Christ to earth. He has been once, but three hundred times in our New Testament the Word of God is that he will come again. On the last night before he died, Jesus said, "I will come again," but are *you* ready? I am afraid that the vast majority of our fellow countrymen are not even watching for it. Tragically, when the building comes down, they will be inside it. Be ready; be prepared. Supposing I could tell you the date, and supposing the date was this week, would you be glad or sorry? Would you make any changes to your life or carry on doing exactly what you had planned to do? That is the acid test of our Christian life. We should be busy doing the things that Jesus wants us to do.

Years ago, Lord Shaftesbury was responsible for getting the children and the women out of the mines. You can read of them going down into that filthy darkness and crawling through the mud, hauling tubs of coal without wheels. They pulled them with chains around their waist in that underground horror – the nearest thing to hell in darkness. Kids were doing that for up to sixteen hours a day, staying down there, opening and shutting the draught doors, and it was ghastly – appalling. Lord Shaftesbury saw that, and his Christian soul was revolted. He said, "I'll smash it." He did – and he smashed so much exploitation of children and women. The Factory Acts began in this country, from which workers still benefit today. We need to remember some of the early battles that went on, but do you know at the head of every sheet of that man's notepaper was written these words: "Even so, come Lord Jesus." That gave him the motive to get on and remove some of the horrors from this nation. Lord Shaftesbury wanted to be found getting those children out of that hell when Christ comes again, and so that motivated him.

Luke 12

Jesus is coming back. Will you be ready when he comes? He said it is like the master of a house who has gone off to a wedding feast and he may be very late home. These things go on quite a time and it may be midnight or even after, but if he has good servants, they will be ready and waiting. In the east they had long flowing cloaks, and when they worked they used to bring up the cloak and tuck it into their belt. They had their loins girded and they were ready for work. We would say: tighten your belt, dressed ready for work – watching and waiting, with lamps lit, everything ready to spring to attention as soon as the master appears. So, there is no hasty gathering of anything, no rushing around in panic but being ready. It is a vivid picture, especially if you know Middle Eastern society and the wedding feasts that go on, and the servants (and even the slaves who I discovered were there even in modern times in the Arabian Peninsula). Good servants are working, watching and waiting, ready for the moment.

Whatever God has given you to do that is right – this is right for you to be doing when he comes. You don't need to be in church when he comes. You could be making love, but then he has given you love and he has given you your spouse, and it is right to be found doing what he has given you to do. You could be at your daily work for the glory of God and it is right for you to be there. It doesn't mean that we have got to be singing choruses every spare moment we can, so that he can find us singing about him when he comes. He wants us to be busy doing what he has given us to do and nothing else. The one thing he doesn't want to find us doing is sinning, but he does want to find us serving. Therefore, when he comes and finds us watching and working, there is clearly reward for those whom he finds like that.

One of the most remarkable things this passage teaches is that if you have been serving Christ and are doing so when he arrives, then he will gird himself and serve you. That is where the story leaves human society way behind. I have not known masters do this, but here this is what he does.

Now let us turn to the bleak side of the picture, because every coin in the Bible has two sides. To those who are alert, active, watching, waiting, working – reward; but to those who have abused his absence – punishment. It is at this stage that Peter got a little worried: was this for the disciples or for all people? Well, Peter asked and Jesus didn't answer him so I'm not going to either. You can apply it as the Holy Spirit leads you. Jesus told another story and left the hearers to apply it to themselves in their own way. There are those who say, "The master's been gone a long time, there's not much sign of his return. So there's plenty of time to get things straight. I can do what I like at the moment." That is the reaction he is now pointing at. It is those who feel there is plenty of time to get ready for the Lord's return – that there is no immediate danger; no immediate sign of his coming.

It is those who say – as is mentioned in the third chapter of the second letter of Peter – "Where is the promise of his coming? All things are just as they are ever since the creation, there's not a glimmer of any sign." It's easy to say that, and it is even easier to jump to the conclusion that we have all got plenty of time to straighten things out, and now we can beat each other, we can hurt others, and we can indulge ourselves and eat and drink and get drunk – after all, there is plenty of time to put it all right. There is not plenty of time, that is what Jesus is saying here. We dare not abuse the gift of time, it is not everlasting time here – it will be in heaven.

When the master comes and finds that a servant is abusing his delay and thinking there is plenty of time to get things straight for his arrival, and finds that things are not straight, that master is going to be very severe indeed with that servant. See how this applies to your own heart. Now we see some of the principles of God's justice – for this is talking about the return of Jesus to judge the living and the dead, and the principles of justice on which God operates. They are not necessarily the principles of justice on which man operates. They are more just, and there are only two principles here laid down that may surprise you, but you need to know because you are going to face this. Jesus is coming again to our world and you will be there even if you were dead beforehand. You will be raised from the dead. At some point everybody will rise from the dead and be judged.

Here are the two principles: first, ignorance is not innocence. I have been in trouble with the police long ago. I attended an event at an Oxford college. Arriving by car I saw a long, straight street outside the college and there were cars parked all down one side of the street. There was a gap, so I parked there. There were no "No Parking" notices and no yellow lines – nothing whatever to indicate that one couldn't park there. When I came out of the college about six hours later I found a parking ticket on my windscreen telling me that I had broken the law.

So I went straight to the police station and said, "What's this?"

They said, "Well, we don't want you to park there."

"You never said so," I replied. "There are no yellow lines, there were no signs."

The policeman said, "That doesn't matter. We could pick you up for parking your own car outside your own front door in a cul-de-sac if we decided that it shouldn't be there, whether there were any signs or not."

I had no idea this was the law of the land. If they decide you shouldn't be in a certain place, it doesn't matter whether there has been any warning or not, you have broken the law.

"I've never heard that, I said. "I just hadn't a clue. I'm prepared to accept it from your lips, but why? What was wrong with that street?"

"We don't feel it's wide enough for cars to pass each other in the middle if there are cars parked in that street," he explained.

"But you're not putting yellow lines or warning signs?"

"No. We can say that is an obstruction and we can say it's dangerous. So you be careful where you park."

I learned the hard way that ignorance is not innocence. You can't plead ignorance. If you have done something that is wrong, then it is wrong.

That ignorance is not innocence comes out in Jesus' prayer on the cross, "Father, forgive them, for they know not what they do." Do you notice that? In other words, you can do wrong and not know it, but you have still done wrong. That is a sobering thought, and when the Judge comes back he will judge us by what is wrong, not necessarily by our knowledge.

To mitigate and offset this principle, those who have been ignorant that they are doing wrong will fare much better than those who knew it was wrong and still did it. In fact, after a quarter of an hour of a fairly pleasant conversation with the police at Oxford, they said, "Since you didn't know, you can go, but it was wrong and don't let us catch you doing it again." So I breathed a sigh of relief – thinking of the headlines there could have been in the Surrey Advertiser!

Here, then, are two principles of judgment: ignorance is not innocence; but in the day of judgment those who have never heard the gospel will fare far better than those who have heard and rejected. If you have known what was right and done wrong you are going to be in a far worse state than those who have done wrong and didn't know it.

Actually, these two principles are acknowledged in British law. On the matter of killing, there is a profound difference between the crimes of murder and manslaughter. Murder is for those who knew what they were doing and did it. Manslaughter is for those who didn't realise what they were doing and the consequences of their actions, and yet did it. They both did wrong but manslaughter carries a lighter punishment than murder. There are therefore degrees of punishment in God's judgment. After all, he wouldn't be a just God if there were not, but do you find that very comforting? I'm afraid I don't. There will be degrees of suffering to be faced by those who have done wrong. Some will fare better than others. Jesus in fact spoke of Capernaum and Chorazin, villages in which he had preached and done miracles. In the judgment, Sodom and Gomorrah and the the men of Nineveh will be better off than those who have had opportunity. Frankly, where does that put Britain today? Think of the opportunities we have had: more Bibles in our language than any other language in the world; more churches and chapels, more people preaching. We have had every opportunity. We know, therefore, that Britain will fare far worse than other nations for rejecting the God of our fathers.

The next point is that in being ready for the Lord's coming, you may have to go through distress and pain of a peculiarly difficult kind: social separation, even within your own family circle. If you are going to be ready for Christ, it is going to mean suffering. For Christ himself, doing the job he had been given to do by his heavenly Father meant distress. He had a baptism of fire to go through – a baptism of suffering – and he said, "How I wish it were already accomplished." It is going to be the same for us because he came to set the earth on fire, and fire is not very pleasant and not very comfortable. Fire is going to upset people, and they are going to run from it. This is not a very peaceful thing. In fact, he went as far to say, "I came not to bring peace but a sword." If you think preaching Christianity is going to bring world peace, have another think! Christ never said it would, he said it will bring division. Even within the family circle – husband and wife, father and son, brother and sister – split right down the middle. I have united many people in holy matrimony, conducting weddings in churches where I have been pastor. Looking back at my ministry, one of the most painful features of it is this: I divided more couples than I have united. How I wish that when one partner comes to Christ, the other would come too. How I wish that when a wife goes to a coffee morning and gets interested in the gospel and begins to seek God and finds him, and she finds a living faith in Jesus, the husband will come along too, but in so many cases it doesn't happen. Sometimes it is the other way around and there is a husband whose wife has no interest and gives him no backing and they split down the middle. They can become estranged because the deepest things you no longer have in common. It is difficult to see.

I have seen children come to the Lord and their own parents oppose them; parents come to the Lord and their teenage children despise them – and families are split right through by Christianity. The sheer joy of seeing a united family in Christ who are all ready to meet the Lord when he comes is lovely, but I am afraid that is not always the case. Maybe you come from a family where not all are ready; the others don't even want to get ready for our Lord's return. They are not interested.

Then Jesus talks about signs. He tells people that they can forecast the immediate future – they are so good at it. He picks up a very well known and simple illustration of weather forecasting which was important in the Middle East, an agricultural community. You can really tell the weather in there. When the wind blows from the west, it comes from the Mediterranean and it brings moisture and coolness, and the soft rain drops on the limestone hills, they turn green as the grass grows. You have got to have that rain to grow because it goes through the limestone so quickly and it dries up so quickly. So when the wind is from the west even though there is a cloud no bigger than a man's hand on the horizon, people are thrilled. But when the wind comes from the desert, hot and dusty, they know that the grass is going to wither and die even in hours. So they became good at discerning the signs in the sky. So Jesus could challenge them: why did they not discern that present time and its meaning?

In our own time, there are experts who are writing for the financial news media to tell you what the markets are going to do. They can say, "Take your money out of this and put your money into that." They have brilliant brains and they forecast things but they haven't a clue that Jesus is coming back. They are utterly blind to the significance of contemporary events. If you ask them what is the meaning of the things you are reading in your newspapers, they would say, "I don't know. It's chance, it's choice, it's chaos – can't see where it's going, can't see any pattern." But if you read your paper with the eyes of Christ, with your Bible in one hand and your newspaper in the other, you will see the signs. They are there for all to read. You see the sign of Israel returning to her own land. Do you see the signs of the breakdown of democracy and its replacement with dictatorship? Do you see the signs of movement towards one world government? Do you see the sign of increasing anarchy and violence? Do you see the sign of growing spiritual interest in all religions? These signs are there for all to see, and the Christian looks and gets excited.

In our Lord's earthly ministry the signs were there for the Jews to see. They should have known he was the Christ because of those signs. I believe that many people were spiritually blind in Jesus' day just as there are millions of people in our world today who cannot see any pattern or meaning in contemporary history and miss the signs.

Finally, Jesus told a simple story which included this: settle out of court if you can. If somebody brought a lawsuit against you, and you were in the wrong and it was going to come up in court, you would be a fool not to try to settle before you got to the door of that court. Once you get in that court and judgment goes against you, then you have had it. You go to prison until you can pay the total fine, which frankly is pretty bad news if you have nothing to pay with. It is a picture, good advice at a human level, but that is not why Jesus told the story. In the context, he is telling us that every man and woman is heading for court. There is a lawsuit against you. It is God's law.

The certain thing is that when you get to that court, there isn't a ghost of a chance of winning the case. How wise you would be to settle out of court now. The glory of it is that we can – that is what forgiveness means. That is what justification means, a term taken from the law courts of two thousand years ago. It means: case dismissed. When God sent his son Jesus Christ to this world, he came with a message: settle now; God is prepared to take your case now and dismiss it before you get to court. One thing is absolutely certain: the court date when your case comes up is fixed on God's calendar. The second certainty is that you are going to lose that case, you don't stand a chance – but my good news for you is that if you repent before God and believe in Jesus Christ right now as your Saviour and Lord, you can settle out of court. All your sins can be forgiven and taken away, wiped out of God's accounts so that there isn't a single one of them left written in there; the lawsuit is over. There is one thing that no-one can afford to put off, and that is getting right with God and settling out of court now, because once God has sent a man to prison (and that is just another term for talking about hell; I know people don't like the idea of hell but we get all of our teaching on hell from Jesus and

Luke 12

here it is again), you won't get out until you have paid every last penny. Frankly, that leaves you there for good because you will never have enough to pay. You haven't enough goodness to pay God for all the bad things you have done. You never will pay and therefore you stay there.

We have been thinking primarily about the second coming of Christ, and that is the big crisis. But you may not have until then to settle. Do you realise that? There is an event that can precede our Lord's return. By that event (your death) you must settle. For one thing, the Bible makes it absolutely clear that at your death the matter is sealed, the great gulf is fixed, and there is no second chance beyond that. That is your crisis date by which things must be right. I had an occasion to go into a mortuary, into the refrigeration room, and there were bodies lying around. I looked at the face of one dead man. He had obviously been big, strong and fit. He looked about fifty, hadn't a grey hair, and there he was lying, stiff and cold. It looked as if he had just died and been brought in. That could have been me or you. For that man, if he hadn't settled out of court it was too late. I am not trying to frighten you, I am just addressing you as Jesus would. If you are not right with God, if your sins are not forgiven, settle now. Jesus' teaching means you are to be ready for whatever comes – so whether his return is the first event or your departure, whether he comes to you and for you or whether you go to him first, whichever occurs earlier, you can say, "Lord, I'm ready." You can tell whether you are ready because if you are then you will love his appearing and long for his return.

13

Read Luke 13

Now we are given two very simple little picture stories in which Jesus describes the kingdom of God. It is like a grain of mustard seed – something so small that you can hardly see it with the naked eye. When some seeds are in your hand they are like little bits of black pollen – tiny specks. Locked inside every one of those specks is the potential for a tree that can grow anywhere between eight and twelve feet tall – big enough for the birds to nest in. Birds like a mustard tree because they love those little seeds in the pods, and they will soon come and find a favourite perch. Jesus teaches that the kingdom of God is like that. It looks a tiny thing. After all, when Jesus ascended into heaven he left behind him eleven men, most of them pretty poorly educated. That is how it began, and that was the tiny mustard seed in an obscure corner of the Roman empire in a despised nation. Two thousand years later there are hundreds of millions of people in this world who acknowledge that Jesus Christ is Lord. That little group of men was like a mustard seed and had within it the potential of a tree that the birds of the air could come and nest in. If you study your Bible carefully, you find that "birds of the air" is a phrase that is often used as a picture of the nations moving around the face of our globe. This little group of men had within it the potential of including all those nations, and that is how it is happening.

As we have seen before, Jesus always bore in mind his

whole audience. When he gave a picture story that was an outdoor story which would appeal to the men, he usually followed up with the same lesson in the form of an indoor story appealing to the ladies: It is like a little bit of yeast that you put in a large lump of dough; once again, that little bit of yeast has the potential in it to spread through the whole lump affecting it and changing it. They didn't buy yeast in those days, they baked their bread fresh every day. They kept just a little piece of the bread and let it ferment and go mouldy. That is what they used to leaven the next batch of baking bread. It was the fermenting enzyme that they used in those days. Once a year they cleared the whole pantry out just before the Passover, and saw that no mouldy bread was left in the house. They had a clean start once a year. One can think of some very obvious reasons at a practical level for doing that. It also was a symbol of clearing out everything that is mouldy, and it became a symbol in the Gospel: clearing out every mould in your heart, leavening your heart, and being wary of the leaven of the Pharisees, but that is another story.

Jesus took this picture of a kitchen. Leaven would spread right through the whole lump of dough. There are certain things that Jesus teaches us about the kingdom and I will give you five that I can see in these two simple stories. First: the kingdom of God comes to our earth from outside the earth. It didn't start here, it has to come here; it has to be put into our society. It doesn't spring from mankind – no human can build the kingdom of God; it is beyond human capacity to build a utopia. We have tried again and again to create a new world for our children, but we can't do it, it has to come from outside. The kingdom of God has to be put in as that seed of mustard has to be put into the soil before it can do a thing, and as the yeast has to be put into the dough. So, when Jesus came to our planet, the kingdom

Luke 13

of God was being planted in our society. It was being put in the soil, put in the dough.

Second, the kingdom of God works from inside, and that is why it is largely unnoticed. When you put a seed in the ground you don't notice at first. Even when you do see something, the growth is imperceptibly slow, and no-one will turn aside to see it. I have never seen anybody standing watching a plant grow, have you? They may notice that it is a little bigger than it was, but it is not a sensational thing. It is working inside; the seed is working in the soil; the yeast is working in the dough – invisibly working from inside, but nevertheless, the potential is enormous.

Outside our old home there was a tarmac drive, and snowdrop bulbs had been left behind from before it was resurfaced. The tarmac would crack – thick, solid tarmac, which had had a steamroller on it – as the flowers came through it! That is like the Kingdom of God in that nothing can stop it now. You put yeast in dough and leave that dough, and there is nothing can stop it leavening the whole lump; put a seed in the soil and there is nothing that can stop it developing. You can concrete it over and it will split the concrete. A living thing has more strength than dead things.

Third, we have already noted that you can't stop it. King Canute placed his throne in the waves. By the way, it is a legend and totally untrue that he tried to stop the waves coming in. What he actually tried to do was to prove that he did not have the power to stop the waves. There were those who thought Canute was omnipotent and wanted him to do impossible things. So to prove he couldn't, he put his chair in the waves and then said, "Now I'll show you that I can't stop them." You can no more stop the kingdom of God than you can stop the tide coming in. You can no more stop Christianity from spreading than you can stop the sun rising.

The fourth thing that comes out of these two little stories

is this: the spread is not very spectacular. No-one would stop and look at it. Every now and again they may notice something has changed, but it is almost so imperceptible that this world that is longing for sensation will crowd after a man who can bend spoons, but will not come and hear the gospel. The world, looking for sensation, does not realise the Kingdom of God is growing at the rate it is and many would be shattered to be told that hundreds of millions of people have acknowledged Jesus Christ. They don't notice it, they don't want to notice it. But lives are being changed in our world by the Lord Jesus Christ. The world is not interested and doesn't notice. It is like the seed growing and the yeast working.

The next thing I notice about the Kingdom of God is that the end product is out of all proportion to the beginning. If the beginning was a handful of men, the last product of it all will be a multitude that no-one can count – a huge number.

Finally, one day the kingdom will be complete; it won't be a bitty thing. The yeast leavens the whole lump of dough, and the mustard seed will go on growing until the tree is of full height. The kingdom of God will go on growing and spreading until God has everybody he wants in it – until people from every kindred, tribe, and tongue are sitting down in that kingdom; until the nations have come from east, west, north and south, and have sat down with Abraham, Isaac, Jacob and the prophets. Do you find that exciting? It is great to know that this is the only kingdom that is like this. Of course it is not as spectacular as things that happen in the world – revolutions and one party overthrowing another. When today's political parties are forgotten, having vanished in the dusts of time, the kingdom of God will be there.

The next thing to mention is that if the kingdom itself is increasing, your opportunity to get into it is decreasing. As it gets bigger, one day the door will shut.

Luke 13

It is amazing how people will discuss everybody's salvation but their own. Many read murder novels, look at the news headlines and take a kind of ghoulish interest and have a morbid curiosity in the latest train crash or bomb outrage, but we are reluctant to discuss our own death. Somebody came to Jesus and wanted to discuss the disaster of a building that had fallen and killed people, but Jesus leads his hearers to think about their own death as the master says "I do not know you...."

Jesus' words of warning echo through the centuries. It is a sobering thought that the door is going to shut. I heard of a Sunday school teacher who was telephoned by a man known to be dying of cancer who said, "Tell me about Christianity." The Sunday school teacher's heart leapt as he thought, "I can help this man." Over the phone he told him what Christianity was all about, then said, "May I come around and see you? I'll gladly call and discuss it further."

"No thanks, I was just curious," came the reply. He had only wanted to hear a bit about Christianity, but wasn't the slightest concerned about himself. The poor Sunday school teacher's heart fell.

Many people are interested in what we do. I remember when I was a chaplain in the RAF, and the number of young recruits coming to services was growing. A Wing Commander came to me and said, "Good for the boys this, more prayers you have the better." That was how he talked. I went to an army camp in Arabia and fell for it the first time. The CO of the camp said to me, "Now padre, you want to serve us, do you?"

"Yes," I replied

He asked, "How many do you want at the service?"

With tongue in cheek I replied, "A couple of hundred."

When I appeared there were precisely two hundred men sitting there, but not one officer and not this CO. So the next time I visited that camp on the south coast of Arabia he asked again, "How many do you want at the service?"

This time I said, "You get the officers there, and I'll go around and invite the men – all right?" You see, it is so easy to be glad that other people are getting religious, glad that these young people are getting sensible ideas, but what about you? Are there few that will be saved? Get in, you be one of the few, because it is a narrow door. You can't get much through except yourself. You will have to leave your pride behind; you will have to leave your sins behind. They are too wide to get through that narrow door. It is sometimes a battle and you have to fight. Some will say, "Lord, Lord, open for us," or, "We ate and drank in your presence."

We all need to make sure we make it our top priority, make every effort, agonise to get in, because one day the door will be shut and people will be left outside. The sober truth, which is often denied today, is that the kingdom will not be open forever. There is a heresy creeping around in Christian circles called universalism. It argues something like this: "If God is love and he loves us, he will never shut the door. Surely, when we all get to hell we will be so anxious to get to heaven he will let us come and there will be a second chance after death. Surely God's love is the most powerful thing in the universe, and therefore it can't fail, and therefore he must get all of us into heaven." Have you heard that kind of talk? I tell you this: Jesus never talked that way. He even said that when people get to hell they will want to get to heaven. There will come a day when people plead with God to let them in, and God says, "No, I gave you an opportunity and the door is shut." Somebody has defined hell as the place where truth is known too late. I suppose the saddest two phrases in the English language are "too late" and "shut out". One of the worst things about hell is that you can see heaven from there. Whenever Jesus spoke of hell he used the word Gehenna, a geographical name from a deep, dark valley on the south and west sides of the city of Jerusalem. It was so deep that at one point the sun never reached the valley bottom. It is down there that Judas hanged himself, as the Bible says, "He went to his own place." In that valley you looked up a sharp escarpment and right on the top you could see the towering walls of the temple and Jerusalem. Jesus taught that is what hell is like. You know what you have missed and know that it is your responsibility and yours alone, and that you are there by your choice because you had an opportunity when the door was open, and you wouldn't take it. Now the door is shut and there is frustration and anger – "weeping and gnashing of teeth." Have you ever seen a person really so bitter and so angry with themselves that they missed an opportunity and knew that it could never come again? That is how Jesus painted hell. That is the tragedy of thousands of people who live near wherever you live. The door is open at the moment and God is saying: repent and believe, come right in, the kingdom is yours. Strive to enter in, agonise to get in; get in if you possibly can now, because when it is too late there is nothing that can be done.

We shall get many surprises you know when we get to the other side of life. There will be some not there that we expected to be there; there will be some very important people in this world who won't be there. There will be many politicians not there who have led millions of people. Some pop stars that youngsters have worshipped will not be there. It is rather sad to see the kind of worship that is offered to men who will just not be in the next world unless there is a radical change. Do you remember that day that John Lennon said that the Beatles were more famous than Jesus Christ? I trembled when he said that, and the decline began that day. For he said it in the presence of the One to whom all authority in heaven and earth is given. The Lord is a jealous

God and he will not share his glory with another, and he won't stand for things like that. One trembles for those who have had adulation in this world, for those who have been at the top of their career in this world, those who have built up a great business in this world, those who have had a big bank balance in this world – those whom this world regards as great and important people.

There is going to be an awfully big surprise when you get there. The last will be first and the first last. People who have been insignificant and unnoticed here will be the important people there. Strive to enter in. Make sure you are there.

My first point about this passage was the spreading kingdom, my second point concerns the closing door, and the third is about the resisting city. Jesus was now in Perea, a strip of land on the east side of the Jordan, down in the deep valley. He was right at the spot where John the Baptist, his own cousin, had been arrested and taken to that castle overlooking the Dead Sea, the rock fortress of Machaerus, where in the dungeon John the Baptist languished until, finally, his head was chopped off. Herod was king over that area and he was scared of another John the Baptist; he was still very uneasy in his conscience about John. So Herod schemed and got hold of some Pharisees, people with whom he normally wasn't on speaking terms. These Pharisees pretended to be friends, and pretended to want to help Jesus, warning him that Herod was going to kill him. Once again our nice little sentimental picture of Jesus suffers a bit of a shock here. We think Jesus always said nice things about people and was always tactful and courteous. As we noticed earlier, Jesus says, "Go and tell that fox...." In calling him a fox, Jesus was speaking the truth, calling him what he was.

Some months later, when Jesus stood before him, Herod said: I have heard you can do wonderful things; do some for me. Jesus had not one word to say to Herod. How would you

Luke 13

like to be in the spiritual condition in which the Lord Jesus has nothing to say to you? You can't talk to a fox.

Here in Luke 13, Jesus testified to the saving work he was doing in Herod's territory, casting out demons, healing the sick. His life was already mapped out and he would finish his work and then go to Jerusalem. Jerusalem had killed the prophets and that was where Jesus would go.

Behind it all is Jesus' sublime faith in God the Father. God knows the day you are going to die, too. Isn't it lovely to be quite sure I am going to live long enough to do what he wants me to do – then he can take me; to know that your life has been mapped out, and that, if you keep in the centre of his will, nobody can spoil that plan. Nobody can bring it to an untimely end. My time is in his hands.

So Jesus went to Jerusalem, the city that was going to kill him, the people who were going to assassinate him at the age of thirty-three, and he wept over it and said, "Jerusalem, Jerusalem...." He has just been talking to a fox and now he uses the picture of a hen. Do you see the connection? Herod was supposed to be the king of the Jews, or at least of part of the Jewish nation, and he was a fox. But Jesus, again with that lovely mind of his, could see pictures in so much, could take a little everyday scene and fill it with spiritual meaning. Have you ever seen a hen gather her chicks and rustle up her feathers, and the chicks "disappear"? You think there is only a hen there, and all the chicks are inside; they are protected, they are "in" the hen. It is a lovely sight – then you just see a little beak peek out.

Here is a literal translation of what Jesus said. "I was willing to do this, but you willed not." In other words, there was a clash between Jesus' will and Jerusalem's will. The very greatest power God has given me is to say no to Jesus, and I have that power. God respects my freedom. The one thing that God will never do is to force his will on me if I will not. That is why he will not get everybody to heaven. That is why there is such a place as hell, and why there will be many who will go there. It is not that God's love is lacking; it is that he respects us as human beings: If you will not, I will not. How often would I have gathered you, and you would not? A parent once said to me, "I feel I have strong will power, but my child seems to have a stronger won't power."

Here is the tragedy of the one city Jesus had chosen for his throne, where one day he will have his throne – the city of Jerusalem. So the kingdom was not established in that city. Jesus wept for them. When he died, the temple veil that hung over the holy of holies, a curtain perhaps forty feet high, gorgeously embroidered, was ripped from the top to the bottom by unseen hands – not from the bottom to the top, not by human hands. When they looked into the Holy of Holies it was empty. God had gone. He said: you won't see me again until I come back as King and you say "God bless the one who comes in the name of the Lord". One day, Jesus is going to come to Jerusalem as King, and they will bless him for it.

You can't stop the Kingdom of God. The only thing you can do is to stop yourself entering it – which means if you are outside it is no one's fault but your own. You have willed not to enter, but praise God, the door of the kingdom is still open now.

14

Read Luke 14

14:1-24
Attending a lavish meal in an Officers' Mess on one occasion, I was amused to see how many of us didn't know which implements to pick up first. There were rows of them, and the first course was diced melon. You could eat it with a spoon, a fork or a knife and fork. Some diners were looking along the row to see someone with better knowledge. I went for a meal once with a Durham miner who had just come off shift work, and I've never seen such a skilful performance in my life. I have never seen so much gravy conveyed to the mouth with a knife only. I want you to use your imagination now. Imagine that you have invited me to lunch, and that you are a vegetarian on principle. You have invited a number of other guests too. I turn up to your vegetarian lunch and it is all very well prepared with nuts, lettuce, etc. You have got it all nicely laid out. The first thing I do when I sit down at your table is to pull out of my pocket some cold sausages, and then point out to you, in front of your guests, how inconsistent you are because I have seen you drink milk and eat eggs, and they are animal products. You say, "Ah, they weren't killed to get the milk or the eggs out of them."

I reply, "Well, you're wearing leather shoes, and obviously an animal has been killed so that you could have them." I deliberately open the conversation at table by making you look silly in front of your guests. Then, since that produces a bit of a lull in the conversation, I say, "This is a funny lot of people for you to have invited. They are all people who are likely to help you on in business. There's your boss sitting next to you, and there's quite a wealthy neighbour further down the table." Having begun to criticise you for your choice of guests, I then look around them and say, "I notice you took the bigger sandwich. I have been counting how many cream cakes you've eaten and it's now five." Then finally, in the horrible embarrassed silence that occurs, one of your guests sitting next to me tries to make conversation and says, "I hear you're going to have a big do at your church fairly soon," and I say, "Well, you're not likely to be there for a start." I guess that by the end of that meal you would be wishing you had never invited me, or you are making your mind up that you will never have me back.

I have in fact been describing how Jesus behaved at a meal table. Do you realise that? A criticism reached me once from someone who felt that I had been over-emphasising the aggressiveness of Jesus. But I have no choice and I must preach the truth, the whole truth and nothing but the truth. I have been trying to show you what Jesus was really like. I know that it shatters some of your notions about the Son of God because it has shattered mine first – having been brought up to believe that Jesus was always nice, always said the right thing, was always courteous, always tactful, charming and gracious, and that if you invited him to your house he would behave beautifully. Brought up on that kind of sentimental view of Jesus, I was left with this horrible problem: "Why did people hate him? Why would anyone crucify such a person?"

The stark truth is that he was an aggressive person, and by modern standards of social etiquette, rude. In fact he seems almost deliberately to have gone out of his way to provoke people when they had invited him home as their guest. For example, he started this meal by making the Pharisee who had invited him look ridiculous, and showed him that his scruples were illogical and inconsistent, and made him an object of ridicule to the rest of his guests. That is not very polite to someone who has invited you for a meal. Then, he looked around the guests and started saying, "I noticed you all chose the best places when you came in, scrambled for the top table" – that is not very polite. Then he begins to argue with his host about the people he has been inviting to the feasts. Then at last, someone trying to make polite conversation says, "I'm looking forward to the Messianic banquet in the kingdom." Jesus says, "Well don't think you'll get there." That seems a bit embarrassing. You would finish up with a horrible silence.

This is the Jesus who was crucified. I just want to tell you this: if you invite Jesus into your home or your heart, don't imagine that he will just come and approve of everything that you are doing. He may well come and start criticising. He may well come and say, "Why do you do that? Why are you doing this?" He will put his finger very uncomfortably on those sensitive points in your life. He is not a very easy guest to entertain. We need to think twice about entertaining him.

Let us look at these incidents. Having given you the feel of the situation – and words that some people might call tactless, discourteous, aggressive – let us see that in fact good morals are better than good manners, and that Jesus was putting his finger on issues that are far more important. The Lord God, when you get to heaven, is not going to ask you whether you used a table napkin or ate peas off a knife. He is going to ask about far more important issues. Did you open your home or were you too afraid of breaking social custom and kept yourself to yourself? Did you open your meals to guests? Were you given to hospitality, or were you afraid of it because you couldn't match up to others' ideals of hospitality – because you were too embarrassed? That is the kind of question he will ask. One of the marks that we know God and that we are welcome to his feast is that our table will be open too.

Now let us look at the first topic of conversation at this meal table. Jesus was invited as a visiting preacher to meet a group of hand-picked guests. There they are at the dinner table, and the first subject that comes up is healing. Remember that the host in this case had a scruple about healing on the Sabbath. He got it from the law of God. God had said, "On my Sabbath you do no work." So I know that the meal was cold. They had salad on the Sabbath, they didn't have roast. There it was, laid on the table, and it was cold because cooking was work.

The Pharisee, trying to do what was right before God, made a long list of what was work and what wasn't work on the Sabbath. One of the things that was work was the work of healing which, if it could be delayed until the next day, should not be done on the Sabbath. A man with dropsy was sitting right opposite Jesus. We don't know if they planted that man there. We could, I am afraid, assume that, because it says, they were watching him suspiciously.

The sick man had obviously had the condition for some time. He could certainly wait until the next day. There is Jesus – he raises the subject and he knows that his host will be horrified if he heals the man. Yet, without consideration for his host's feelings, he challenges him: "Is it lawful to heal on the Sabbath?" He is asking for a scriptural text for that. The host couldn't do it. We have to accept this challenge. How often we confuse tradition with truth. How often we think that we are saying something that is God's Word, but if you look in the Bible carefully it is not there.

Let me give you some examples. The idea that three wise men who came to Jesus when he was born were *kings* is a pure tradition; it is not there in the Bible. Yet it is amazing

Luke 14

how many people think it is. It is also interesting how many people think that the book of Jonah says that he was swallowed by a whale. It doesn't say that. You read it if you doubt me. It is amazing how many people think that Eve gave Adam an apple. It never says that. These are just traditions, but let us go to rather more serious things. It is astonishing how many Christians teach that women should not pray in public, but you show me a text that says that. It is a tradition. It is amazing how many things we have been brought up to think we shouldn't do on Sunday, but you give me a text for it. You will find it very difficult to do so with many of the things about which you have inhibitions. I was brought up with – and accepted – the idea that every Christian had to be a total abstainer, and I assumed that it was in the Bible until I looked for myself and discovered that it did not teach this. In certain circumstances it could be the right course for a Christian, but it is very much dependent on the circumstances and is not an absolute rule.

As you go through the Bible and really study it for yourself you find that many of our traditions are just not the truth. They are our interpretation, but not God's inspiration. We must be very careful. It is amazing how many people think that it is more spiritual to have organ music in church than an orchestra or a guitar. Yet, you give me a text for that and I will give you many texts for stringed instruments. Our traditions build up.

The Pharisee was doing what I have done and what you have done. He had his own list of things that were right or wrong. He assumed that they were scriptural but they weren't. Jesus was asking for a text: "Does our law...?" Notice that he accepted the Commandments. They would not answer. If they had answered, they would have had to say, "Our law doesn't say anything about healing." Jesus healed the man, asking whether those present would have pulled an animal from a well on the Sabbath. The lesson that we should learn is this: check your traditions with the truth. Check the things you think are biblical with the Bible. Check the things that you have been brought up to regard as important against what God says is important. Get your sense of proportion right, for here was a man who would pull his own ox out of a well on the Sabbath, but who wouldn't countenance healing a man with dropsy. One of the dangers of religious tradition is that we get more upset about petty things, and churches can argue about little things and things that don't matter a brass button to God. We can argue about them instead of seeing that God has certain important things for us to be doing. The order of service and what people wear is far less important than whether we are worshipping God.

As far as I can see, what happened in this account killed the conversation. Jesus asked them a question they wouldn't answer, and if you do that you are not likely to have a nice flow of conversation. It was Jesus who changed the subject – from healing to hospitality. Who would you invite to a wedding reception? I can remember the days when we went through the guests. We started off thinking we would have a nice quiet wedding. But then one begins to feel: we ought to invite so-and-so, and cousin so-and-so.... So it went on. I had my relatives, and my wife's mother was one of thirteen so you can guess what a problem we had. Jesus' teaching now shows us that in our hospitality we reveal quite a lot about ourselves. Do you invite people from whom you expect to get something – people who will honour your table; people who will sparkle and enhance your reputation in being able to get them to a meal? Why do you invite a certain person? Is it because they will invite you back? Or is it because you want to help them? Because you want to offer something? An important New Testament word is "giving"– it is about giving yourself in hospitality, not trying to get anything back at all. Therefore you are safer with those who can't invite you back and with those who won't say, "We've been to you, now you come to us in a month's time." Jesus said, "When you give a feast, invite the poor, the maimed, the lame, the blind. And you will be blessed because they cannot repay you; for you shall be repaid at the resurrection of the just."

The real question is whether you want to be repaid by men or by God. Do you want to be repaid now or later? God keeps accounts and he will not be in your debt, and one day he will pay you for every meal you gave. It is quite a thought – that God keeps the bills!

Jesus had noticed that at this meal they were all scrambling to be on the top table next to the visiting celebrity – which was himself. It may even have been that his seat was occupied by an eager person, and that person had been sent right to the bottom of the table to make room for him. Jesus teaches us that if you take the wrong place, and think of yourself as more important than you are, you will have to go to the very bottom. Why? Because all the other seats will be filled up by then. Jesus came out with a statement which is so needed that he repeats it at least five times on different occasions: "Whoever exalts himself will be brought down, and whoever brings himself down will be exalted."

We choose the pews we like in church, we choose the seats that suit us, but Jesus would say: why not just take any seat, start at the bottom with the poorer seat, so that someone else might have a better seat than you? Let God exalt you. This is disturbing and challenging. We point the finger at the Pharisees and say, "What dreadful people they were," and "Thank God I'm not like a Pharisee." Remember that the Pharisee said he thanked God he wasn't like someone else – so it would be mutual. But in fact the Pharisee is very like us. We are all guilty of having a streak of "Pharisee" in us.

Jesus went on talking at the table. You can imagine the

atmosphere was going down. This meal that was going to be such a great social occasion, such a success, and such a feather in the cap for the host, was falling apart at the seams. The host would have been very glad when somebody tactfully tried to get this guest into conversation. Isn't it funny how, when people know you are religious, they desperately try to find some religious connection? You have a meal with a lot of people who don't go near church, and they ask you what your job is.

"Actually, I'm a minister."

"Oh, what kind of a minister?"

"A Baptist."

"Oh yes, we had a second cousin twice removed who used to go to the Baptist church up in Yorkshire."

They desperately try to find some religious connection. This is known as being polite, trying to show interest in the other person's interest.

Because Jesus had said, "You'll be repaid in the resurrection," a guest commented, "Isn't it going to be great when the feast in the kingdom comes, and we all rise, and how happy are those who eat bread in the kingdom of God." Jesus then told a story which called into question that sense of certainty – one of the most devastating parables. He said, "A man gave a great feast." In the Middle East this is how they operate. We might say, "Will you come to a feast on March 20th?" On the day itself we would have all the feverish preparation, set the table, get the food cooked. In the Middle East what happened then was that, when all was ready, the servants of the master would go out to the guests and summon them. It was courtesy to come immediately the call came. This is the picture behind this story – a fascinating social custom.

So you have to be ready, dressed, waiting all that day. In other words, you have already declared your intention of

Luke 14

coming so the master has a right to expect you to be ready at any moment on the day. Now can you see the meaning of the parable as it unfolds? Jesus speaks of two groups of people: those who were invited to the feast and didn't come, and the group that were not invited. This is the message I have for you: *the group that didn't come were those who made excuses*.

The first man's excuse was that something had cropped up in his business. "I've bought a field and I must go and look at it." I would have thought that was bad business. You would think that a good businessman would look at the field before he bought it, wouldn't you? In other words, it is a sheer excuse. Business had more attraction for him than the feast.

The second man had bought some oxen and wanted to try them out. Novelty was more important to him than coming to the feast. He knew that he should have been ready; he knew that was the day in which he would be invited.

The third man said, "I've got married." What was to stop him bringing his wife? It is as if someone says, "You see, I've just got back from my honeymoon, and so I'm sorry I can't come." In which case, natural affection and family ties have become more attractive than the invitation to the feast. All these people are saying that they have something better to do rather than respond immediately.

Preaching the gospel is like this. Not all your hearers belong to Christ yet, and I have to say in his name, "Come, for all things are now ready; Jesus has died, he is risen, the gate of heaven is open; there's nothing more that needs to be done on the host's side." The tragedy is that people say, "Well, you've just caught me at a bad time— I'm going through business pressures; I've got a domestic upheaval on my hands; there is something I've just promised to do with a friend; maybe next Sunday tell me if you're having an evangelistic campaign again. Yes, I would like to come, but you've just caught me at a bad time in my life." Yet you knew that God wanted you to be ready.

I have seen people who know that God has called them to come. I have preached the gospel and I know that God has said, "Come now. All things are ready now, come." They have refused and the result is their place in heaven will be filled by someone else. The whole gospel is in the word "Come". I love that word.

"Him that comes to me I will in no wise cast out."

"Come, buy wine and food without money, without price."

"Come, for all things are now ready."

You will find this word all the way through the Bible.

The master of the feast was furious. Why? Because if people have shown interest in attending a feast, and told you that they intend to come, and you get everything ready and you say, "Now come," and they then make excuses, you know that all along they had no intention of coming if there was anything more interesting, anything they would rather do. That is the tragedy of it. The master is having his feast thrown back in his face.

There are people who would be Christians today if they had nothing better to do! They think they will attend a church. They intend one day to come to heaven. They intend one day to straighten things out with God. When the call comes, when the crunch comes and they don't respond, they are saying, "I didn't really intend to. It was way down my list of priorities, and anything else can put me off: my friends at work, my career, my marriage, my business life." Anything at all can come in between them and the invitation.

The master was furious and said this, "None of those I've invited will come. None of them will be there." It breaks my heart to realise that there are people who have been to a church where I ministered, and got interested, and the Lord has said "Come" and they have refused. The master may well say, "You will not be there. You were not prepared to come when I called. I had everything ready for you, and you wouldn't come. You said you intended to, you said you wanted to be part of it, you said you were interested, but when I said "Come", you stayed." What does God do about those who refuse? He says, "Right, I'll give your place to someone else. Go and get someone else to fill this place. My house shall be full." God has already decided how many people there will be in heaven. The number of the elect is already settled. God will have that number, and if you are not part of that number it is not his fault it is yours. If he has said, "Come" and you didn't come then it may be an awful part of hell's remorse to you that you know that there is somebody sitting in your chair in heaven at that feast and you could have been there, but you didn't come when God was ready. It is a case of whether you come to Christ when he is ready or when you are ready. If you wait until you are ready then you won't come, but if you come to him when he is ready there is a place for you.

The master at the feast said, "Go out; get hold of anybody you can. All right I've invited these people and they've said no, I choose to invite some more. Go and get them." The great Baptist preacher Spurgeon used to pray like this— "Lord, save all the elect and then elect some more." That is a true biblical doctrine of election. If you refuse God's election, if you refuse his call, then frankly he will elect some more.

All over the world people are coming to Christ. Many of them may well be taking the places of those who have refused to come, but "My house shall be full". God's house will be full, so those who refuse his hospitality do not spoil his feast, they just ensure that someone else gets their place.

Now this happened in Jesus' earthly ministry. Alas, he

came to his own people, the Jews, and one of the greatest tragedies of history is that the Jews who were first invited into the kingdom said no. What did Jesus do? What did Paul do in the name of Jesus? Whenever Paul went to a new town he preached first to the Jews, but when they refused to come he didn't go on with them, he simply said, "I turn to the Gentiles" – and they came. So, if you have had the privilege of being in church for many years, if you have shown interest in the kingdom, if you have shown some intention, if you say, "Well, some day I intend to accept. Some day I intend to become a Christian", may I beg you to come now? At this very moment – accept Christ now, rather than leave it until God has already filled your place with someone else. "Come, for all things are now ready."

Whatever feasts you may have on earth, whatever parties you go to, whatever banquets you attend, heaven is presented to us in the Bible as a feast, a banquet, the biggest and best party you ever went to and ever saw. We are looking forward to a wedding reception – not heading for a graveyard but a feast. Therefore, Christians should behave as those who are on their way to a party.

14:25-35

There were great crowds of people following Jesus, but he did not feel that this was necessarily success. He knew that the crowds meant that though the quantity of his followers had increased, the quality had gone right down. It can be the problem in a large church: the more members you have, the less responsible members can feel, leaving things to others. Jesus can do far more with a few who are prepared to go all the way than a crowd of followers who are not really serious.

Were some in that great crowd following Jesus for what they could get out of him? They had high hopes that he was on his way to Jerusalem to set them free from the Romans, to give them joy, to give them all they had ever wanted. Jesus turned around and said something to them calculated to send most of them back home. For he would rather have one person coming after him who has counted the cost and who means real business and is prepared to go all the way than to have a great crowd coming for superficial and selfish reasons.

So the theme now is the cost of being a disciple – and counting the cost. Time and again, Jesus lost a convert by warning him of what a Christian life would mean. Think of the rich young ruler who came to Jesus. He said that he wanted to follow him; he wanted eternal life. Jesus could so easily have said, "Well, we could do with you in our team. Would you like to make a pledge to the funds? Come on in. We're glad to see you." But Jesus told him to go away and get rid of all his money and then to come and follow. The man went away, but Jesus watched him go very sadly. The tragedy is that if you do not count the cost of being a Christian you will travel so far, and then, as soon as the quality requirements come, you will stop. At that point, you are going to be in a worse condition than when you started. You are going to be so useless for your job as a Christian that you will have to be discarded and will be no further use to the Lord and Saviour who called you.

We are going to look first at the *cost* of being a disciple, then at the *reason* for counting the cost of being a disciple. I am just unfolding what Jesus has said.

He mentions two things which hurt very deeply and cause us to want to argue with him. The first is: "Whoever comes after me and does not hate his mother, his father, his wife, his children, his brother, his sister, cannot be my disciple." Many people wish he had never said that. Let me point out straight away, that the meaning of the word "hate" was not quite the same then as it is in our own time. It has become today an emotional word meaning "malice in your heart", "a desire in your heart to hurt someone"; "a desire to do them down, injure them, offend them or insult them". That is not what the word "hate" in the Bible means. It is an example of how we have taken something that can be right and made it horrible by our own perverted emotions. In one of the Psalms, King David says, "Do I not hate them with perfect hatred?" Do you know what *perfect* hatred is? It's a hatred that is free from malice, but it is a hatred that consists of action and choice rather than emotion and malice. That is what you find in the Bible. In Romans 9 God says, "Jacob I loved; Esau I hated." He is not referring to his emotions or feelings towards them. We are so wrapped up in feelings in this age of ours that we can't read the word "hatred" without feeling it. But it means "Jacob I chose and Esau I turned away from." That is what the word "hatred" means. When the psalmist says about the enemies of God, "I hate them with perfect hatred," he means, "I turn away from your enemies; I am not going to be an ally of those who hate you. I'm not going to line up with those who are against you; I choose to go a different way to them; I choose to disassociate myself from them." Now, don't get me wrong. The Bible says that the family is a holy thing and that your relationships within the family are to be kept intact in God's sight. What this text is saying is this: if ever the claims of Christ and the claims of your nearest and dearest conflict, there is no question as to what the disciple of Jesus has to do. He has to love Christ and, in action, hate his nearest and dearest. For you see, sometimes those who are nearest to you are your greatest foes in your spiritual life. Even Simon Peter, who was one of Jesus' closest friends on earth, became at one point his greatest enemy when he said, "Jesus, you're never going to the cross. Whatever else you do, I'm not going to let them kill you." Jesus said, "Get behind me, Satan!" and said it as strongly as that. He was at that moment hating Peter with perfect hatred and saying: no, God has called me this way and if you call me that way I must turn my back on you. One of the tragedies of this world is that when the grace of our Lord Jesus Christ comes into family life there can be divided loyalties and affections.

For the true disciple of Christ there is no choice. I remember a girl called Patty, a nurse in Sunderland, County Durham. She became a Christian and went home and told her parents, "I now belong to Jesus Christ."

Her father said, "Patty, you forget that or you get out of this house." He faced her with a stark choice—"I am not having a Christian live in this family. So you either drop all this, or you get out."

She replied, "Well, Dad, I love you very much, but I love Jesus more and you leave me no choice." She got out. I am thrilled to be able to tell you that Patty, who had a wonderful influence on many people and finished up as a nurse, nursing lepers out in Africa, was sent for by her father some ten years later, "Patty, come back home. I need you."

But earlier, when the choice had come, she – in the sense of the Bible word – hated her father; she turned her back on her own dad. That is part of the cost of being a disciple. The very nearest and dearest relationship to you may have to go if Christ calls. Notice I say *may* have to. It doesn't follow that you have got to cut all links. It is when the claims conflict. I remember a woman I was trying to tell about Christ and encouraging her to accept Christ as her Saviour and she said, "If my husband is not going to be in heaven, then I don't want to go." There comes a point where Jesus says, "I must be first, absolutely top priority."

The second part of the cost is even more frightening. He says that the second condition is to hate yourself as well – to turn your back on yourself. Now I suppose in this age, the pressure is on us to be fulfilled, to satisfy self, to choose a career that will draw the best out of myself, to indulge myself. This is the mood of our age. But read the teaching of Jesus and you find that Christianity means a cross, not a cushion. It is not a bed of roses; it is a crown of thorns: if you want to be my disciple, then take up your own cross.

A cross is not a minor ailment. When a lady talked to me about her rheumatism and said, "That's the cross I have to bear," I cringed. Look, a cross doesn't give you rheumatism, it gives you death. A cross kills you. A cross is an instrument of torture and execution. Jesus isn't just saying, "I want you to take up hardship," he is saying: I want you to take up death to yourself. It is the one thing we find so difficult to do: to die daily.

As I have mentioned elsewhere, when I held a baptism service I used to say to the congregation: "You know, we're going to bury some people today. You're attending a funeral service. Three young people we're going to 'bury' – why? Because they're dead. We're going to bury the life that they've lived, the life they've chosen, the life that's been centred on what *they* wanted to do, and what they found fulfilment in, and what they found satisfying. We're burying that. To be baptised into Christ is to be dead and buried; to have taken up your own cross and to have said, "From now on, I don't care what happens to me. I don't care whether I find a fulfilling job or not. I don't care whether my ambitions are achieved or not. I am dead. I'm on a cross and I've been crucified with Christ."

Here are the two conditions of discipleship. Jesus turned and said these two things to the whole crowd. He said, "Whoever of you does not forsake all that he has cannot be my disciple". Can you see that there is a huge difference between being in a crowd that is listening to Jesus and becoming one of his disciples? How many disciples of

Jesus are there in your congregation? It doesn't follow that because you are in church, listening to the words of Jesus, that you are one of his followers. You may be just one of the crowd and he is saying to you: These are the conditions if you want to be my disciple, not just a follower; if you want to be my disciple, all your nearest and dearest must be put behind you if I call; even your *self* must be put aside as well. It has got to be me and only me, your Lord, in your life." That is the *cost*.

When a crowd begins to follow Jesus, it is so easy to follow along with others without counting the cost – this can happen when there is a crowd of young people getting excited about Jesus and singing Jesus songs. How easy it is to join them because it sounds exciting and good and you are one of the crowd, without sitting down and saying, "What is this going to cost?" The time to count the cost is beforehand, not afterwards. You are not joining a secret society; Jesus has told you all that it will involve before you join, before you commit yourself. It is a bit like marriage – two young people who don't think about the meaning of marriage but rush into it are fools. At the beginning of the marriage service, the minister says, "Marriage is ordained of God and, therefore, it ought not to be entered lightly or unadvisedly or thoughtlessly, but with due reverence and fear of God." It is a big thing you are doing, a costly thing. You are now one person and you are choosing to become half a person. That is a very big choice to make.

If you are going to buy a house together, do you rush off to the nearest building society and say, "Let's have a mortgage"? Do they then say, "Fine, how much do you want? Here it is." No, they say, "Just sit down there for a moment. What's your wage? Have you any other savings? What's your income?" They won't touch a mortgage with you until they have sat down and counted the cost and seen whether you are prepared and whether you have thought it through and can meet that cost and can go on meeting it in the event of rising interest rates and prices. Then we should not tackle a thing like discipleship of Jesus more lightly than we should tackle a house mortgage or a marriage.

We should sit down first and say, "What is this going to mean?" I don't know if you will lose your job because you follow Christ. I don't know if you will lose your money because you're going to follow Christ. I don't know if you will lose your health because you follow Christ. But I know that you should sit down and count the cost. I know one thing: that it will cost you everything. Jesus uses lovely pictures to get across his truth. If you were going to lay the foundation of a tower, wouldn't you count the cost first to see whether you had enough money to finish it? Wouldn't a leader going into a battle first carefully weigh it up? The life of a Christian is on the one hand like a building and on the other hand like a battle. It is hard work and it is a conflict. A person is foolish to start being a Christian until they have sat down and said, "It's going to be a building and it's going to be a battle. Am I ready for that?"

The higher a building goes, the harder it is to build. The Christian life is not easy and it is not just a "building" struggling against circumstances, it is a battle struggling against enemies. The day you become a Christian you have made an awful lot of enemies. Particularly, you have made Satan into one of your most implacable foes. Are you ready for the battle?

Believe me, there are times when a Christian nearly goes under. Have you read *The Pilgrim's Progress*? There are marvellous insights in that book. Don't read it, though, until you have read your Bible right through first – your complete reading of the Bible is the highest priority.

Again and again, "Christian" is nearly lost; he's fighting

for his life; he is down but not out. There are times when the devil knocks you flat. Are you ready for that? Pick yourself up again and go on. Count the cost. It's not a picnic; it's not one big jamboree. It's not going from one big rally of Christians to another, singing on the coach as you go. It is a building and it's a battle. While the Lord will graciously give you lovely moments, there will be other moments when it is a hard, tough fight. It was for our Lord and it will be for us. He says, "Sit down and count the cost first before you go any further. It will cost you everything." Someone has said that "salvation is free, but it's not cheap". That is a very good statement. Salvation is free – you can't do anything to earn it – but it's not cheap. It costs you nothing to begin the Christian life; it will cost you everything to continue it. That is the truth.

When it says that you must forsake everything, and whoever does not forsake everything that he has cannot be my disciple, does that mean that I must give away my car and my house? Does it mean that I've got to say goodbye to my family? There are those who have taken it quite literally like that.

Let me tell you a story of someone who I believe hit the real meaning of this text. A young man in his twenties, who was in show business, read this. He went home to his bachelor flat and he got sheets of paper and wrote down everything that he had. He was surprised to find how much there was. He listed his sound system and CDs, motor bike, camera and his clothes. He finished up with about three sheets of paper. Then he prayed, "Now Lord, I give you my motor bike," then he ticked that; "I give you my camera," and he ticked that. He went right through the items, one by one, and he gave everything he had to the Lord. Then he said, "Now Lord, you tell me which of these things I can keep." He went through the list and the Lord said, "You can get rid of that; you can keep that. You can give that away, but I can use that." He finished up with about two-thirds of what he had written down, but in actual fact he finished up with nothing. Can you see that? He had given everything and only kept what the Lord allowed him to keep. The Lord has used him so mightily since because he learned very early how to be a disciple. That is counting the cost.

We return to the point that Jesus wants disciples of quality. He uses another word picture which gets across this point. He wants *salty* Christians. I have discovered that the greater the cost of discipleship, the greater the quality, and the more costly your Christianity is, the more quality it has.

Some of us had the inestimable privilege of going behind the "Iron Curtain" in the Communist era and meeting Czechoslovakian Christians, and we were touched with their real quality. Why? Because some of them had lost their homes, their jobs; some of them had been in prison. I have not been taken away by police and put in prison because of being a pastor, but I met a pastor there who had been. There is no plain clothes policeman sitting in a church in England taking down every word preached and hauling the minister in to answer for everything said.

I know that many believers in Engand have paid very heavily for following Christ in one way or another, whether in your relationships, in your career, even in your family. That has produced quality. The marks of the nails are in your hands and that produces salty Christians. In other words, if my discipleship has not been costly, then it isn't quality, and if it isn't quality then I really am not much use to my Lord and Saviour – I am like salt that has ceased to be salty.

Verses 34-35 always puzzled me. I studied some chemistry at university. Sodium Chloride is salt and it always will be salty and it always has been salty. NaCl will always taste salty and that's it. So I wondered how salt loses its saltiness.

Oh, how people do dismiss the things that Jesus said because they think he didn't have enough modern knowledge. He knew perfectly well what he was talking about. The salt of those days was scraped up from the Dead Sea shores, as it still is today. It was, therefore, not pure salt. It was a mixture when it was scraped up, but it had enough salt in it to be useful for the purpose for which you bought it. There were two ways in which salt could lose its saltiness. One was if you scraped up too much of the sand underneath the salt. Still to this day, they can do it. A crooked dealer in salt can scrape up a fair amount of the light coloured sand with the salt and mix it up and sell it as pure salt, and in fact a lot of it is sand. It has no taste and no effect, so that you can lose your saltiness from the very beginning by bringing too much of other things in with the salt. The second way is if salt was left exposed and not protected, covered and kept carefully – then the rain could wash through the salt and wash the saltiness away, leaving again only the sandy part. That could happen. That is why, if you are going up the motorway and see one of the service areas, you will see a pile of rock salt to put on the roads when it's frosty, but over the pile you will see a large polythene sheet to stop the rain washing the crude rock salt.

Now here are the two ways that Christians can lose their distinctive quality. One is that when they first come to Christ they bring too many other things with them. They bring too many of their old sins with them; they bring too much of their old life with them. The result is, they will lose it, or at a later stage they can go back and bring more of that stuff in. They can go back to their old life. The more they bring in, the more they will lose their distinctive quality. There is another thing that can happen if this spiritual life that you have been given is not nurtured and protected and kept carefully: the storms of life can wash away the saltiness.

Either way, when you have lost your saltiness you are not of any use for anything else and you are discarded. Paul, the great missionary, had a fear of this lest having preached to others he would become "cast away", which means "put on one side as useless".

Let us look at the two purposes for which salt is used. They are only mentioned here in Luke 14 and they are not the sort of things that you would think of first. He doesn't mention using salt to preserve things, though it was used for salted meat. He doesn't mention using salt as a flavouring agent in food. These were not the two primary uses. The salt that was scraped up from the shores of the Dead Sea was used for these two purposes: as a fertiliser and as a disinfectant. Because it had potash in it, salt was used on the soil to promote plant growth. Good things could grow because the soil had been salted. It was also used in the same way that you would use a modern disinfectant in a chemical toilet, for they didn't have proper toilets in those days. They had a heap of soil at the bottom of the yard and a shovel by its side. You simply used that and you covered the dirt with a shovel. Then, from a bowl or a jar nearby, you sprinkled the salt on as a disinfectant which stopped the evil things spreading – and that is what a Christian is for.

A disciple of Jesus is to be the salt of the earth. So that when he is around, good things grow and grow more quickly because he is there – in the office, in the shop, in the home. He is also there as a disinfectant, to stop bad things spreading. If he is salt – and salt is salt – then bad things will be inhibited by his very presence. If you have lost your salt, neither of these two things will happen where you are. Things will just go on from bad to worse in spite of your presence. So this is why Jesus set the standard high and taught people to count the cost. Don't follow him unless you are going to be a true disciple. Don't just be part of a crowd coming along. To an individual he said, "If any man would follow me, let him take up his cross...." Just one who does this will be more use to him than the whole crowd.

Count the cost of following Jesus and become the salt of the earth. Baptism is all part of this because in being baptised you have counted the cost; you are leaving behind the self-centred life that is not prepared to build or to battle for the Lord.

15

Read Luke 15

Who hasn't heard the parable of the prodigal son? Is there anything new to say about it? The remarkable thing is that it is so well known that people don't know it. The very title we give it demonstrates, as clearly as anything could, that we have missed the whole point of it. For it is not the parable of the prodigal son, it is the parable of the priggish son. I daresay there are more people who have something in common with the elder brother than the younger. If we have, then the parable is for us.

We have got the parable wrong because we think that when Jesus told a parable, he was preaching a sermon and that a parable is – as I was told at school – an earthly story with a heavenly meaning; an illustration of the gospel. Indeed, there are some people who say to me that they believe the whole of the good news of Christianity is to be found in this parable. I can't believe that, because there is no mention of the cross or the resurrection in this passage.

Like every other parable of Jesus, it was not spoken from a pulpit; it was not given as a children's address or a sermon, it was a weapon of words used in the middle of a battle. He used these weapons of words either to defend himself or to attack others. Therefore, if you ask me what a parable is, I would say it is a story with a sting in its tail for somebody who listened to it originally. So the first question you ask if you take any parable of Jesus is: "Who did he tell it to?" and then: "Why did he tell it to them at that time in that place in that situation?"

Therefore, the most important part of this parable is to get a grasp of 15:1-2. In those two verses you are told who was there when he told the story, and then you will understand why he told it, and why it is quite wrong to call it the parable of the prodigal son. When you look at those two verses you find that there were two groups of people in the situation, as there are two brothers in the story. That gives you a clue straight away. The two groups of people there were the friends of Jesus and the enemies of Jesus. If you don't realise that Jesus made friends and enemies, you haven't yet understood him. Wherever Jesus went, he seemed to split the people down the middle. They just couldn't be neutral towards him, they either became for or against. They took sides very quickly. Some people loved Jesus; some people hated him. Some became his friends and some became his enemies.

It is in this setting that the parable was told: where there were enemies of Jesus grumbling about the type of friends he was making. Of course, a man may be told by his friends. Birds of a feather flock together. The kinds of friends a man makes will tell you a great deal about his character, personality and outlook. For one of the free choices we have is this: we choose our friends. We didn't choose our relatives, and they didn't choose us either – we need to bear that in mind. When you join a church, you don't choose all your fellow brothers and sisters in that church. You didn't choose your boss. Maybe you did choose your employees if you have any.

It is shattering to see what kind of people became the friends of Jesus and what kind of people became his enemies. Imagine that Britain had been occupied by a foreign power and some of your fellow-citizens were extorting money for

Luke 15

the occupying forces. Do you think they would be popular in your town? Do you think they would make friends? The people who were the friends of Jesus included the tax collectors for the Romans who were given a free hand to bleed the people dry as long as the empire got the fixed tax from them. They were Jews who had volunteered for the job. Jesus mixed with them, went to their homes, even called one of them to be one of his disciples. They called Jesus "the friend of the tax collectors". Now can you imagine a person who made friends with people like that – traitors, lining their own pockets at their own nation's expense, in the pay of an invading army? Can you imagine them being popular? Jesus was sitting having a great party with tax collectors. This was the one group of people that nobody else would go and have a meal with, and he was there.

There was another group who were friendly with Jesus, called "sinners". They were the ones who had long since given up religion. On the whole, while tax collectors were rich, "sinners" were poor. They included the hard-working, labouring men who had long since given up trying to keep the ten commandments and made no pretence at trying to be religious. One of the greatest insults that was given to our Lord and Saviour Jesus Christ I believe to be one of the greatest compliments that was ever paid – they called him "the friend of sinners".

Because he made friends of that kind of person, he made many enemies of the other kind of person. For one Zacchaeus that Jesus won, he lost an entire crowd, and he chose to do that. To that poor little man up the tree, Jesus said, "You come on down, I'm coming to have lunch with you today." He was the only one that went in to have lunch with Zacchaeus. It says the whole of the rest of the crowd stayed outside. The enemies were made up of the respectable people and the religious people, and those who at least were trying to be good, and trying to keep the ten commandments and to live a decent life. Why did they become Jesus' enemies? Because he became the friend of people for whom they had no room.

It was in that very tense atmosphere that Jesus told the parable. Do you begin to see its sting in the tail now? So there is the situation. Jesus is sitting down and enjoying a party in the tax collector's house with sinners around him. The people looking in through the open archways of the courtyard are the respectable, religious people, and they would have thought: he claims to be the Son of God, claims to be a religious leader, claims to tell us what God is like, and look at him! Here we are, we have lived respectable lives; we have tried to be good, we have tried not to do evil. Whether we have always succeeded or not, we have at least tried, and these people haven't even tried. They just gave way to temptation; we at least tried to overcome it. They murmured. Jesus took those two groups and he began to talk about them in a very subtle and roundabout way, but I guess before he got to the end of the parable they had got the message loud and clear.

We had the two little parables that help us to understand the main parable: the lost sheep and the lost coin – two lost things, one of which was lost far away; the other lost at home. Do you see that clue beginning to prepare us for the main story? Two sons, one was lost far away and the other lost right there at home. It is not the parable of the prodigal son, it is the parable of the two lost sons. One, like a sheep, had rolled right away, had strayed away into a far country, and the other, like the coin, was still within the house and still lost.

Jesus was such a skilful storyteller. He could include everybody in his audience at some point. So he told an outdoor story for the men and an indoor story for the ladies, and the whole audience was with him; his theme was that losing something brings sadness but finding it again brings great joy. He is already trying to explain why he is happy with

Luke 15

these tax collectors, why he is enjoying a meal with sinners, why there is such a lovely atmosphere in there, and why outside there is such a miserable atmosphere. He is teaching that "lost" means unhappiness and "found" means joy.

There is another thing: "lost" puts someone on their own; "finding" makes them want to share with people. Have you noticed in those two little stories that when the sheep was lost, the shepherd went out all on his own to find it, but when he found it, he called his friends and neighbours and the thing was shared together. When the woman lost the coin, she went on her own round the house looking for it, but when she had found it there was a time for getting together. One of the meanings of lostness is this: that when a child of God is lost, there is a dreadful loneliness which comes into that situation, and the Lord Jesus Christ came all on his own looking for that sheep; but when a sheep is found, when a lost child of God comes back home to him, that is the time to get together; that is the time to celebrate.

It is the lost people who say, "I can be a Christian without going to church." If they say that to you, just say to them, "All right, but are you?" It is the lost people who talk about being an individual. It is the lost people who think of a solitary life; but I tell you, when you are found you want to get together with your friends and neighbours. You want to be together in fellowship. You want to celebrate – it is a time for sharing.

So here is the theme. Jesus has been out looking for people but now we are celebrating together. These are my friends and neighbours I have called in to celebrate. He would have done that if only one had come. What happened to Matthew, that scribbling little clerk who collected taxes at a custom post, when Jesus said, "Follow me"? He had been a very lonely man up to that point, but what was the first thing that he did? He threw a party and celebrated.

I remember speaking on this some time ago and that night there was a young man who came back to the Lord in the middle of the sermon. He told me that as he went out of the doorway, saying, "When's my party?" Celebrate together! Seek one-by-one. It is a lonely business getting lost and being found, but once you are found you want to share it. So to a person who says, "I can be a Christian without going to church," I think we should say, "Well, you be a Christian first, and then see what you want to do. You'll want to celebrate, you'll want to get together and say 'Let's share the joy.'"

These two stories have a lot in them that prepares us for the main story. There is only one parable in this chapter, not three: the lost sheep, the lost coin and the two lost sons are all one parable. It says, "Jesus told them this parable" – so, the two little stories prepare for the big one. Now our minds have got certain ideas in them: the sorrow of losing; the joy of finding; the loneliness of being lost and of seeking the lost; and the togetherness of being found and celebrating. So Jesus has prepared his audience. They are with him, listening.

I want you to notice one more thing about the two little stories before we get to the big one: things that happen here on earth affect the feelings of heaven. This is a very important point to grasp. The angels celebrate when just one person on earth comes to the Lord Jesus Christ, repents of sin and makes a fresh start in him.

Now we are ready to study the parable of the prodigal son, or as I prefer to call it, the parable of the priggish son. There are two sons here, and we have to look at both of them. There is a happy ending to the story of the first one, but not to the second. Let us look at the first. I want to paint this story again vividly for you.

Here is a young man who started out in life with the words "Give me" on his lips. He thought life begins by getting hold of things, by grabbing them, seizing opportunities. He had to learn the hardest way, in the school of experience, that life begins when you say, "Forgive me."

The Jewish law was that if a man who died had two sons, his property would be divided into thirds. The elder would get two-thirds and the younger would get one-third. That was the law, but he could also by law give that money to his sons before he died and virtually retire. This was what the youngest son was asking for. "Dad, I want it now." Here again is the second wrong step that he took, and the second wrong attitude that wrecked this young man's life: to want things now rather than later. This is of the essence of sin. It is what ruined Esau's chances of ever inheriting his father's blessing – because one day Esau was hungry and he wanted some of that nice soup now. He wasn't prepared to wait. This is the weakness of our human nature – when we are interested in *now*. Am I going to enjoy it tonight? Tomorrow morning? I am not interested in good prospects in my career in forty years' time, I want a good job now with plenty of money now and plenty of free time now. That is how this young man talked. He was saying, "Give me"; and he was saying, "Give me *now*." The most wonderful thing to me in this story is that the father gave it to him. He must have known what his son was like, and he must have known what he would do with the money. It was perfectly within the father's rights to say, "No, son. When I'm dead you'll have it, and what you do with it then is your business." That is what many fathers have said and would say, but this father said, "All right son, here it is." It takes a big father to let a son ruin himself.

A man had a son who reached the late teens and almost wrecked the family home. He was difficult, he was sullen, he was bad-mannered. He was spoiling the family circle, he was selfish, he clearly didn't want to be under the restraints of the family. So do you know what that father did? They had two cars: one the normal family car and the other an old jalopy that they had kept and just used for a bit of shopping. This man called his own son into his study and he said, "Son, here are the keys to the old car. Here is a sum of money. You don't want to stay, go. Come back when you want to be part of the family." That took courage. It took a good father to do that. The boy went and they didn't know where he had gone, and that man didn't sleep for some nights afterwards, wondering what he had done. The boy came back many months later – changed.

Parents, have you the courage to give your children the chance to wreck their lives, and to welcome them back when they come? There comes a stage in your family life where you have got to do this with your own children. It is what God the Father did. He gave every one of us life and health; he gave every one of us a chance – some gift, some ability – and he gave every one of us some opportunities. He said, "There you are, I've divided to you my substance" – and look what we have done with it. What a bold Father God is, to give us the chance to sin.

I know where that young man went to from Galilee, which was not a very exciting place to live. They used to make for a town about two or three hundred miles to the north, called Antioch, which has been called the "Paris" of the Roman Empire. It was the place for nightclubs and theatres. It was the place where you lived it up. Above all, it was a Gentile city so it was away from Jewish inhibitions; it was away from religious taboos. That was the far country because, though it wouldn't be far today by car or plane, it was a long way on foot then. That is where the young men of Galilee went if they wanted to rebel against their parents and get out of this strict, religious atmosphere. Off he went.

He had plenty of friends because he had plenty of money. If you want to spend money, you will find plenty of people to

Luke 15

help you do it. He went there because he wanted freedom. He went there because he wanted fun. He went there because he wanted friends. Above all, he went there because he wanted life. He had it, and he enjoyed it for quite some time, as you can – the far country is quite enjoyable for a time, and he lived it up. He was a no-good, he was wasting his life, he was wasting his dad's money.

I read a very amusing thing recently of a father who sent his son to take an aptitude test to try and get him into a job. Back came the report: "This boy is best suited for retirement!" One can understand that. That is what this young man wanted. He didn't want a job, he wanted to enjoy himself. He forgot about his dad but his dad never forgot about him. That is the situation.

There are two nagging questions hanging over the far country, which you may forget but which come back. First, what will you have to show for it at the end? Second, how long is it going to last? It can last an awfully long time, it can take many forms, and it can be very enjoyable. Both those questions have to be asked by those who want to get away and live it up, and enjoy life, and find freedom, and be independent of parents. I'll never forget a teenage girl I once saw stamping her feet and saying to her parents, "Just you wait till I can get a flat of my own and be away from here! I can't wait to go." She was so angry with some restraints which were being put on her by her parents for her own good, but that was her attitude. Those are the two questions and it came pretty quickly for this young man for two reasons. First, there was a famine. He hadn't bargained on the economic depression that was coming. The famine began to hit him as well, and he began to be in want, and the money was running out. He hadn't asked, "What will I have to show for it?" This little expression "riotous living" means that he wasted his substance on it.

There are so many people for whom life is a roundabout and you get on, and you have a great time; you go round and round while you are on it. You get off just where you got on, and you have nothing at all to show for your money – no lasting benefit. So he wasted it all, and he had nothing – his father's hard-earned property had been dissipated with nothing to show for it, and the end had come.

I don't know if you realise how Jews feel about pigs. Orthodox Jews will not even mention the word "pig". It is an unclean animal in the Hebrew law. Here is this young man sitting with the pigs. What does that tell me? It tells me that all his self-respect is gone, for when a man will do what once he would never have done, when a man who once had scruples about a thing will do it and not think twice about it, when a man loses his principles, he will lose his self-respect. He will get to the point where he no longer looks up to himself and when a man does that he is finished. Yet when a man gets to the end of the road, he might just be beginning. Isn't it strange in human nature that we have got to get to the bottom before we look up? We have got to get in a real mess before we will call on God. When all other things have failed we are prepared to try him. It is sad that we go to him last.

On the other hand, even if he is the last resort, he is a wonderful resort. God doesn't even turn anybody down who has put him at the end of the line and tried him last. This man got to rock bottom and then he came to himself. I don't like the translation "came to his senses". I prefer "came to himself". We do dress ourselves up. We do cover ourselves up – not just with clothes that we try to use to impress people with what we are or how we want to be. We do express ourselves with social veneers and etiquette. We cover it all up. You know, the greatest and most dangerous ignorance in the world is not to know yourself. On the Parthenon temple in

Athens you will find above the main portico there two words inscribed which the ancient Greeks said were the heart of all wisdom: *Know yourself.* The tragedy is that very few people do know themselves, partly because we don't want to. We prefer to know the outside and not the inside. Sometimes we have to get to rock bottom and go through disaster before we take a good look in the mirror and say, "So that's what I'm really like – I am an utter fool."

That is what this young man thought. He would have said to himself: "Look what I've given up to get this," and he would have pushed into his mouth if he could those husks, carob pods – and they are pretty rough stuff to chew. There he is, stinking of pigs – and they do stink. He was wanting to get in the trough and eat the swill, and at that moment he got through to himself. Did you know that you can't come to God until you have come to yourself first? That is why many people can't get through to God: they have never been to themselves. This man came to himself and knew he was an absolute fool. Then he realised two more things: the blessedness of those who stayed home and the unworthiness in himself ever to go home. These were real truths. Now, for the first time in his life, he was facing reality. He was a fool, he had done wrong, and he was prepared to say, "I've sinned in the sight of God" – and he had. He was breaking the law of God about pigs for a start, but he had sinned in other ways too.

He realised that good thoughts never saved anybody. This man's realisation of his true condition and true folly and true sin would not have done anything for him unless he turned the thoughts into action. He did. You may have certain thoughts now but those thoughts will do nothing whatever for you unless you do something about them. He said, "I'm going to go back."

His thoughts and motives were still very mixed. On the

one hand he wanted to go back, which was good. On the other, he thought he could still bargain with his own father. He thought, "Now, I can't be a son any more, I am not worthy of that. But surely he might want a hand on the farm, he might want an extra labourer. Surely he would give me a wage, just give me a bit of bread to eat instead of this swill." He still never thought about the father's feelings. What would the father feel with his own son in the kitchen? So he still wasn't thinking about his father, but anyway, however mixed his motives, he got up and went. I tell you, I don't care how mixed your motives may be, but if you will get up and go back to God, he will have you. He has a way of straightening out the motives. He doesn't mind why a person comes, as long as they come.

This is what happened. As soon as the father saw the son, he ran. Maybe we would have got the young man to clean himself up first, but the father ran, and he fell on his neck, which would have been grimy with dirt, and he kissed that neck. That is God's love.

The boy didn't even get his bargain out. He said, "Father, I've sinned against you and against God – not worthy to be called your son...." and that was as far as he got. Father wouldn't hear another word. There was no rebuke for the past, no advice for the present, no demands for the future. The father didn't say, "If you'll promise to try and be better, you can have a second chance." He said, "Bring the robe, bring the ring, bring the shoes." If you have never been in a country where poor people don't wear shoes and where slaves don't wear shoes, you won't understand that bit. It is a sign of sonship.

Now why did the father do all this? The son hadn't promised to be better. The son hadn't proved himself; he hadn't been on a probationary period. I'll tell you why: because the son had done the one thing necessary to receive

Luke 15

all that. What one thing had he done? He had left the far country, that's all. The one thing that God asks us to do when we come to him is to leave behind that self-willed, self-indulgent, self-centred life that we thought was life. He says, "You've got to leave that behind. Just come home." You can't come home and stay in the far country. If you leave that, sonship is yours. No wonder they began to dance.

There are millions today who think that if you want to get real life, get as far away as you can from Christianity, get as far away as you can from God. If you want real life, forget religious scruples. Forget all these things that you were brought up to regard as right and wrong. Get away! They will come back I trust some day before it is too late and they will find that the very place where they thought it wasn't, there it is. "I am come that they might have life and have it abundantly."

Shall I tell you what I find is the greatest fear among young people today? It drives them to do extraordinary things and try extraordinary experiences and watch extraordinary films. It is the fear of missing something that would make life fuller and more abundant. Of course you can't do everything, and if you go to see this film, you can't see that one. If you go to this country, you can't go to that country. All along there is this dreadful fear, "Am I missing out on life? Am I missing something?" While you are running to try to catch up, you are running away from it. Life is to be had in Christ. You can drop everything else and lose everything else, and if you have Christ you have found real life.

So he came home, and found at home that joy and celebration that had no hangover because it says, "They began to be merry." The happiest person that day was not the boy but the dad. "My son was dead, my son was lost" – do you know you can be lost even though you know where you are, and you can be dead even when you are living it up? That is the message of this chapter. If you don't know Christ now, you are dead and you are lost, whether you know it or not. When you find Christ, you are alive and you have been found.

We still haven't come to the point of the story. Said a Sunday school teacher to the class, "Who was sad to see the prodigal come home?"

"The fatted calf," said a child, which I suppose was true! Of course, there was somebody who was not. Wouldn't it be lovely if the parable finished at the point we have just reached? What a happy ending! But the only happy ending there can ever be is in the next world. Very few of Jesus' stories have a happy ending. Most of them face people with the facts of life. The truth was that this was not a happy situation because there was another brother. When you look at him, it is shattering. Almost every sin in the book is seen in him. Pride! He says, "What's going on?" Can you hear the tone of voice? "I was not told." Pride is there, anger is there too. He was angry and wouldn't go in. Resentment is there: "You never gave me a party, Dad." Malice is there, "He's wasted your money on prostitutes." How did he know? That had never been mentioned.

Malice, pride, anger, resentment, but you know the real problem with this boy was one of the things that is wrong with a lot of us who have been brought up in Christian circles. We have lived respectable lives, but we haven't had life. We have been sons and yet we have been slaves. You know, the prodigal became a slave when he sold himself to the pig owner, but the elder brother was a slave, too. He shows it in what he said. The things he had done on that farm were a duty not a delight. He had been doggedly loyal, he had done everything his dad wanted done; he had been lovingly or lovelessly faithful. He had kept going, he had lived as his father wanted him to live, but there had been no joy, no love there. This is the tragedy and it is a very real point of tension in a church fellowship when there are older Christians who have been doggedly loyal and come to every service and kept the place going when there were only a few in it. Then some people come in from right outside it with no church background, who had never been loyal. There they are shouting "Hallelujah!" and dancing in the aisles and so thrilled to be in, and there is resentment and anger. There are two things that the elder brother didn't like: number one, that the prodigal was getting things so easy; and number two, that he was enjoying it so much.

This is the resentment that we can have if we have been brought up respectably, if we have been brought up that you must go to church and that it is right to be doggedly loyal and that you must keep trying to be good. Then somebody gets it all so easy, and it is just handed to them on a plate. We resent that it has been for us a long struggle, and it has been for us a weary business, and that we have had to keep ourselves to it. Here is this person that gets everything handed to them, and they haven't done any of this, and we resent that it has been so easy. Then we resent that they enjoy it so much, because in our dogged loyalty we didn't enjoy it as much as that, and we didn't want to shout "Praise the Lord!"

I think of a dear woman who went to an Anglican church in London and shouted, "Hallelujah!"

People suddenly came rushing over and said, "You mustn't do that here."

"But," she said, "I've got religion."

"Well, you didn't get it here, Madam."

That kind of attitude! I tell you today that there is a new wave of God's Spirit throughout the world. People who have had no church background are coming into church and they are wanting to dance in church, and they are wanting to shout in church, and they are wanting to enjoy their religion. People who have been going loyally for forty years through the ages find it very difficult to appreciate: "Why should they have it all so good? Why should they enjoy religion more than I do, and I have been so loyal all these years?"

It is not easy, is it? But one of the acid tests of our relationship to our Father is this: are you thrilled when a person gets it easy and enjoys it? Or are you angry and resentful? I want to read something now which will test this in your own heart. It tested it in mine. It is written by an American chaplain to the forces:

> [In 1945] I was appointed chaplain to the high Nazi criminals during their trial at Nuremberg. Before having to visit these Nazi leaders in their cells, I asked myself the question, "Must I greet these men who had brought such unspeakable suffering on the world and the cause of the sacrifice of so many millions of lives? My two sons had been victims of their misdeeds. How should I comport myself before such men so that they would be willing to perceive their need of God's Word?" First of all, I went into Göring's cell; the former air marshal took a military attitude, clicked his heels, and gave me his hand. Then I made them all a short visit.
>
> This was on November 20th, just before the trial began. The night I passed in prayer asking God to give me a message for them. From this moment God gave me the grace, after the example of Jesus, to hate the sin but to love the sinner. These men must hear something of the Saviour who suffered and died also on the cross for them. There were twenty-one prisoners, six of them chose the Roman Catholic Church for their spiritual aid, fifteen others desired Protestant ministry. Four out of the six were Roman Catholic; seven of the fifteen were members of the Lutheran church. Striker, Yodel, Hess and

Luke 15

Rosenberg never attended a service. A double cell of the prison was made into a small chapel where we could hold services, and a former lieutenant colonel of the SS was the organist. Towards the end of my service in Nuremberg, this organist trusted in Christ. The simple gospel had changed his heart. Frank, Seyss-Inquart, Kaltenbrunner and von Papen attended the Roman Catholic service. Keitel, von Ribbentrop, Raeder, Dönitz, von Neurath, Speer, Schacht, Frick, Funk, Fritzsche, von Schirach, Sauckel, and Göring formed my congregation. We used to sing three hymns, read portions of the Bible, and then give a short address, closing with prayer. There was never any trouble or difficulty.

Sauckel was the first to open his heart to the gospel. He was the father of ten children and had a Christian wife. After a few visits, we knelt down by his bed, and he prayed the publican's prayer: "God, be merciful to me, a sinner." I knew that he was sincere. Then Fritzsche, von Schirach, and Speer asked if they could take communion. As I saw these three men receiving the bread and wine, I was seized with an emotion, for God had worked mightily through his Word and Spirit in their hearts. As repentant sinners, they had accepted pardon through Christ. Raeder, the chief of the German Navy, read zealously his Bible and often came to me with difficult passages. Keitel, the chief of the German Army staff, asked me to convey his thanks to those who had provided for their spiritual welfare, being criminals. With tears, he said, "They have helped me more than they could've imagined. May Christ sustain me." With von Ribbentrop at first, I found no response, but later on he started to read his Bible. Then followed the promulgation of the sentences: Göring, von Ribbentrop, Keitel, Kaltenbrunner, Rosenberg, Frank, Frick, Striker, Sauckel, Yodel, and Seyss-Inquart were condemned to

A COMMENTARY ON THE GOSPEL OF LUKE

death by hanging. Hess, Funk, and Raeder to prison for life, von Schirach and Speer to twenty years. For Neurath to fifteen, Dönitz to ten, Schacht, von Papen, and Fritzsche were acquitted.

The greater part of the remaining time I spent in the condemned cells. Through a favour of the prosecution, the condemned men were allowed to see once more their wives. It was a very sad meeting. I heard von Ribbentrop ask his wife to promise to bring up their children in the fear of the Lord. Sauckel asked his wife to vow to bring up their numerous family beneath the cross of Jesus. Göring asked what his little daughter Etta said when she heard his sentence and was told that the child hoped to meet her daddy in heaven. This affected him, and it was the first time I saw him in tears. Day and night, I remained with those who had committed their souls to God. I visited some of them five times daily. Von Ribbentrop read his Bible the greater part of the day. Keitel was most moved by the portions which spoke of the redeeming power of the blood of Christ. Sauckel was very upset—said many times that he would collapse before the execution of the sentence. He prayed out loud continually, "Oh God, be merciful to me, a sinner." These three took the communion for the last time with me in their cells. God had changed their hearts and now in the presence of death, having lost all material things and their unworthy lives, they were able to rely on the promises of God for lost sinners.

On the evening before the execution of the sentence, I had a long interview with Göring. I put before him the necessity of preparing himself to meet with God. In the course of our conversation, he ridiculed certain Bible truths and refused to accept that Christ died for sinners. He made a conscious denial of the power of the blood. His last words were, "Death is death." As I recalled to him

Luke 15

the hope of his little daughter to meet him in heaven, he replied, "She believes in her manner and I in mine." An hour later I heard agitated voices and learned that he had taken his life. His heart was still beating when I entered his cell, but when I questioned him there was no answer. A small, empty glass tube lay on his breast, and he had gone into eternity, a frightful end.

As the hour of the execution of the sentence approached, now that Göring was dead, von Ribbentrop was the first to mount the gallows. Before he left his cell, he declared that he put all his confidence in the blood of the Lamb that made atonement for sin, and he asked God to have mercy on his soul. Then came the order to proceed to the execution chamber. His hands were bound. He mounted thirteen steps to the gallows. I uttered a last prayer, and he was no more. Keitel also went into eternity confiding in the pardoning grace of God. Then Sauckel went to his death. With a last greeting to his wife and children and a last prayer, he exchanged his earthly life for an eternal one. Frick assured me before his death that he believed also in the cleansing blood, and during our simple gospel services he had personally met Jesus.

Of the last group was Rosenberg, who had constantly refused all spiritual aid. To my request, if I might pray for him, he replied with a smile, "No thank you." He lived and died without a Saviour. Now came Striker's end. At first, he refused to give his name, but as the moment of execution came, he mentioned the name of his wife and went into eternity with a cry of, "Heil Hitler," a dreadful end.

What do you feel about that? People in my family were killed during both the wars with Germany. Aren't you thrilled? Aren't you so glad? Can't you be so excited that these men

I have mentioned are celebrating with the Lord Jesus? They came home. Oh yes, I know what they had done. God knows even better what they had done, but God accepted them. They are your brothers and they are going to be in heaven with you, and you are going to be celebrating with them. Do you see how we react as the elder brother? Oh, I hope you don't. I hope you say, "Dad, I'm thrilled they came home because those men were no worse than me. I am no better than them and I need your grace." Your heart will have told you whether you have got the Father's love in your heart or the elder brother's reaction.

This is the meaning of the parable, and the sting is in the tail. I want to tell you that I believe more of us have more in common with the elder brother than we have with the younger. We may not have been a long way away from God, though some have been. We may not have painted the town red. We may not have lived it up. We may not have thrown overboard all the religious scruples of our upbringing. We may have stayed at home and lived religious, respectable lives, but I want to finish by telling you this: the father in the story was as loving towards the elder brother as to the younger. He came out to the elder as he had run out to the younger. He dealt so tenderly: "Son, this is your brother ... you've nothing to lose by welcoming him. All that I have is yours. You could have had a party anytime you wanted."

This is the tragedy – that those of us who are so respectable but so lacking in the exuberance and vitality of knowing the Lord – we could have had it all along. That elder brother could have had the fatted calf for just asking. It was his already; the father had already divided things to his sons. The opportunities we have missed to have real life and to enjoy God to the full – but the father pleads and says, "Oh, my son. This is your brother. He was terribly lost, but he's home." It is right to celebrate, it is right to praise the Lord, it is right to sing and dance, it is right to be excited that more and more people are coming to the Lord now, more than have come for some years.

Let us ask the Father to give us his love, and let us stop being slaves to duty, and delight in grace. Two things the elder brother couldn't stand were grace – giving everything to a person who didn't deserve it – and gratitude.

This, like many parables of Jesus, is not finished. There is no happy ending. There are questions I want to ask. Did the younger brother stay at home? Did he make good? Did he not think about the far country ever again? I don't know. Did the elder brother make it up with the younger brother? Did they become friends? I don't really know because Jesus told the story and then stopped suddenly, as much as to say: you finish the story. Because in the situation in which he spoke he was inviting those religious, respectable people to come and join the party. Come on in, write your own ending to the story.

The BBC, when they broadcast this parable in a dramatised form, made the fundamental error of finishing the story with the elder brother saying, "Sorry, Dad, I'll come on in." But that did not happen. Do you know what really happened? Those people who murmured at Jesus being friends with sinners – corresponding to the elder brother of the story – wrote this ending: The elder brother glared at his father and said, "I'll kill you for this." That is what they did. For the father in the story is Jesus. The Father was in him, but that father in that parable was Jesus. The elder brother was the Pharisees and the scribes and the religious people who got Jesus onto a cross and killed him because of who he is.

I ask you at the end of this solemn message: what ending have you written to the story? Are you a younger brother, and have you been a long way from God? Then will you write in the ending now and say, "I don't understand fully what it's going to mean. I just know that if I come back to God now, then that is where I ought to be and that is where it is going to begin." You write that end in your own heart, but I want to plead with those who are more tempted to be the elder brother. Would you write this ending? "Lord, I'm thrilled that there is new life surging, and that people with no church background, and who aren't used to ways as I have known them, and who aren't used to the kind of loyal service that I have given or tried to give you over the years, have come. Lord, I am thrilled that they are back home, and I am looking forward to meeting those German Nazis in heaven. I belong to them, and we have all received grace together. Lord, I want to be part of the celebration. Count me in, kill another fatted calf for me because I'm coming to the feast."

Write your own end to the story. Jesus invites you to do so.

16

Read Luke 16

16:1-18
The theme of Luke 16 is money, and it comes as a surprise to learn that Jesus said more about money than any other subject – more than about prayer, about heaven, even about salvation itself. He did this because it plays so great a part in our life. This chapter is largely made up of two stories which begin with an identical sentence: "There was a rich man...." The two stories are very different. One I want to call "The Story of the Good Bad Man", and the other "The Story of the Poor Rich Man".

We will take the second story first, but there is a connection between chapter sixteen and chapter fifteen which we ought to discover before we move on. This Gospel was one continuous narrative. Therefore, these stories were told in the same situation as the parable of the prodigal son. The connection is this: here are men who have had plenty of money but finished up with no friends. That is such a common occurrence and such a terrible possibility that our Lord develops the theme in another story. The prodigal son had a third of his father's estate, went away and spent it all, and when the money was gone he was left without a single friend. The elder brother had two-thirds of his father's money and yet there he was, complaining, "You never gave me a young goat that I might make merry with my friends." The simple fact is, reading between the lines, that he had no friends to make merry with, and that he wasn't the type who liked parties anyway. He too would finish up as the younger brother had done, but with lots of money, and lots of possessions, and no friends. That is a condition in which most of us can finish up, for all of us are heading for bankruptcy. There will come a time in every life when we become penniless, when we will have to leave to other people everything that we have. All of us will come to the point where money fails us and cannot buy us a single thing. One of the crucial questions then will be: will you have any friends when all your money has gone? That will depend on how you have used your money while you have had it. There is a direct relationship between our possessions and our relationships, which we are now going to explore in a most extraordinary story.

Scholars have wasted a lot of time discussing this from so many angles because it seems at first sight a thoroughly immoral story. For one who claimed to be the truth, to be talking like this and to be telling us a story in which every single character is a thoroughly dishonest rogue, has raised many questions in the minds of the hearers and readers of our Lord's teaching. This story of a number of rogues all twisting finance around and all coming out of it fairly well raises questions in our minds.

I divide the story into two little parts: a man's predicament and a man's prudence – how he got into a jam and how he got himself out of it by astute wit. The first stage in the story is his predicament. The man is in financial difficulties and it is his own fault. He is the manager for an absentee property owner. This is a common situation in the Middle East and here is the man fiddling the books so that he is lining his own pockets – managing someone else's property so that he is the one who is benefitting. Sooner or later that kind of thing will get out, at first in the form of rumours, and the rumour reaches his boss's ears. The boss says, "I'm going to audit your accounts, and if they are not straight you are out on your neck." The man is in the predicament of losing his job, his whole career. Everything is tumbling around his head because he knows that he is not fit for other employment. He has not worked with his hands and labouring is not something he is strong enough to do. He has been a pen-pusher all his life, but who will employ him after he has been sacked in this kind of dishonest situation?

Since there is no social security, the only other alternative in those days was to beg. He was too humiliated to do that; he couldn't sink low enough to go around asking people for help. So the man sits down, and in his predicament he thinks, "Is there any way out?" With great intelligence, he sees a brilliant way out of dealing with his predicament. It is thoroughly immoral, it is dishonest but it is quite an astute move. There were two courses open to him: one short term and the other long term. He was still tidying up the accounts, or he was still in the job until the audit had been made, so the two things he could have done were these. One, he could have made off with all the rest; he could have embezzled it. But that was a short-term policy because that money would run out and he would only postpone the day when he would be destitute and couldn't do anything.

But he took a second course, which was clever. There were a number of debtors to his boss. He was holding from them certain IOUs signed by name. In those days, a lot was paid in kind rather than in money – some was for wheat, some for oil, and so on. What he did was to interview each of these debtors and say, "I'm prepared to let you have this IOU back and let you write it down. The whole accounts are going to be audited and I can help you in this situation. If you owe a thousand bushels of wheat, here is your IOU, write eight hundred and when the account is audited you are going to be two hundred to the good." Now it says something about the debtors that they eagerly accepted the scheme. They were as much rogues as he was. We shall see later that his boss was a rogue too.

It was just a jungle, this whole business, and everybody was out to make a quick deal and get ahead of the other chap, and come out of it alright. So his debtors rewrote the IOUs. Do you see what he had done with them? He had made them fellow criminals. At the very worst, he could always blackmail them later. But there is honour among thieves and he was now one of them, and they were part of his whole set up. So in fact, when he did lose his job there would be many people who would think kindly of him. "Alright, he did us a good turn, now he's down on his luck, we'll do him a good turn" – and you can see that he has lined his own nest for the future. He has done a long-term thing that is going to ensure that when his money fails there will be people who think kindly of him. That is an astute move. The man has done something very clever indeed. When the audit is finally made and the thing crashes and he is penniless, he simply walks down the road to the homes of those whom he has helped. They will say, "Well you helped us, we will now help you," and the man is alright.

Now when the boss heard about that, one of the most surprising things is that with a cynical and grudging admiration he praises the man, as much to say, "Well, if I'd been in his shoes, I'd have done the same thing. I've got to take my hat off to him. That's a very astute thing to have done." Which shows that the boss was up to these kind of tricks too, and that he had to recognise a man who had stolen a march on him and got in first. So the whole story is full of rogues who are doing dishonest things to line their own nests.

The most surprising thing of all is that Jesus commends this dishonest rogue as well – which tells us something quite profound: that Christians can learn a lot from those who are

Luke 16

not believers. The Church can learn from the world. There is no one so degraded that you can't learn something from them. Christian young people, your parents may not be believers but that does not mean you can't learn something from them. Employees, your bosses may not be Christian but that doesn't mean that you can't learn a great deal from them. As Jesus says, sometimes the children of darkness, who don't know God and don't love God, are a good deal more sensible, and a good deal more astute, and a good deal more prudent. That is a pretty startling statement. Remember that Jesus was talking to his own disciples when he said it.

Now let's ask: what are the lessons we can learn from this story? What was he being praised for? Let me make it clear: he was not being praised for dishonesty. He is labelled a dishonest manager and no one must ever use this story as a justification for dishonesty in business practice. He is not being praised for his intelligence, though he certainly was a clever man to have spotted this way out of his problems. But he was being praised for his good sense. Even in this immoral situation, there is a certain amount of good sense from which Christians can learn a great deal.

What was the good sense he showed – or, if you like, shrewd, astute, prudent, even in the Authorized Version "wise" – for this man was wise? In what way was he wise? Just two things show his good sense. Number one, to this man facing the future, people mattered more than things. If he had embezzled the money that was left he would be saying things matter more than people. But facing the future he realised that people matter more than things, and that in the future it was going to be far more important to have friends than to have a bank balance. That is the real security in life – it is not in how much money you have made but in how many friends you have made. That is the first thing and we can learn from that, quite profoundly, that *people matter more than things.*

The second thing in which this man showed tremendous good sense was this: *the future is more important than the present.* By embezzling money he would have solved the problem of the immediate present, but he had enough sense to look beyond that, to the distant future, and to see that the future is more important than the present.

Now here are two ways in which this man has something to teach everybody. For in everyone's life people matter more than things and the future matters more than the present. Whereas we live in a society that seems to have gone overboard the other way and is saying, "Things are more important than people, and the present is more important than the future." True wisdom is the other way round, as Jesus made clear in this story. So far, somebody may feel that Jesus is being terribly worldly, and he now goes on to draw out the moral clearly by saying, "Use your money to make friends". But isn't that a very worldly principle?

We lived very near to someone at one stage in our married life who would spend huge sums of money in one evening on cocktails, and have loads of people round. He used his money to make friends. You would say, "Well, surely that's not a Christian thing to do. Surely, that's not what God wants us to do." But that is precisely what Jesus says here is good sense. "Therefore, make to yourselves friends by means of your worldly wealth." It is surprising advice coming from the lips of Jesus Christ, the Son of God, isn't it? But there is one dimension that makes his advice totally different from the man who spends large sums on cocktails to make lots of friends among his neighbours. There is one huge difference between our Lord's teaching and the worldly attitude to this principle: he puts this advice in the dimension of eternity. We can learn from the world and use our money to make friends who will receive us into an *eternal* home. That one word "eternal" alters the whole meaning of what he said. The world uses its money to make friends who will receive them into their earthly homes. Jesus is teaching: learn the same principle but put it in the dimension of eternity and use your money so that there will be friends waiting for you when your money fails, which will be the moment you die.

One minute after your death you will be unable to sign a single cheque, or draw a single penny from your bank. One minute after you are dead you are an absolute pauper; you possess nothing. Your clothes, your property, your house will be left behind, your bank balance will be divided among others; everything will go. That is the future that is more important than this present. That is the time when people matter more than things. How many will welcome you into their eternal home?

In other words, Jesus is using a very worldly principle and applying it to another world, and showing that worldly people apply it to a wrong time scale. It means: will there be people the other side of death, who will rush up to you and say, "Welcome! I'm so glad to see you because some of your money helped me to get here; some of your money made it possible for me to have this eternal home"? Is a proportion of what you give going elsewhere and buying a Bible, or sending a missionary somewhere? Someone may listen or read and become a Christian, and their future life opens up to them. There is a place in glory for them, and they will be in heaven. Some day, when all things are revealed and all is known, they will find out who gave the money that made it possible for them to have a home there.

You see, the world can only see to the grave and can't see beyond. So the world responds very readily to such appeals as Shelter, and Christians should be interested in helping people in this world to get homes—I'm not decrying that for one moment. But the most the world is interested in is giving people a temporary shelter here. A Christian should be far more deeply interested in providing shelter beyond for people. Money spent to help people to get to heaven, to help those who are going there, is money invested in eternity. Those who say "you can't take it with you" have not read our Lord's words about laying up treasure in heaven.

Now lest you get the wrong impression at this point and think that Jesus is actually commending dishonest management, he immediately goes on to say, correcting that impression, what honest management is. He compares the wealth of this world and the wealth of heaven in three separate ways. There is going to be wealth in heaven and it is not a socialist state. Wealth will not be evenly distributed; it will be distributed according to merit. We know how it is distributed on earth, often very unfairly. But how will it be distributed in heaven?

Here are the three contrasts. Contrast number one: on earth, however much wealth you have it is little; in heaven your wealth is much. In other words, the riches of heaven are beyond our imagination. People in heaven are going to be multimillionaires, but it will depend on what they have done with the little they have had here. Those who have been faithful in the little they have had here will be given much.

The second contrast is this: wealth here is always dirty wealth. The adjective used is "unrighteous mammon" or "dirty money". This tells me something that I didn't always realise. I used to think that money was neutral and that you could use it either for good or bad purposes, but I have now come to see that Jesus said money itself is bad. It was invented in a fallen world and it wasn't the will of God that we should have money. Money has some inherently wrong things in it. Therefore, to use money aright is a real battle, for money can appeal tremendously to you. If you are going to use it for the Lord you have got to fight a battle with it and redeem it because it is part of our fallen world. The money that you bring for your offering in church may not only have been used for wrong purposes already, and may be used for wrong purposes after it has passed out of the church's finance account – it is, in itself, a wrong thing. It is, in itself, something that carries inherent temptations to people. If you have been faithful with "unrighteous mammon" then you can have true riches. There will be no money in heaven, but there will be true riches there.

The third contrast Jesus draws between wealth in this world and wealth in the next is that all wealth in this world belongs to someone else. Nothing you possess really belongs to you. The proof of this is that you cannot keep anything for yourself. There isn't a single thing that you possess in this world that you won't have to say goodbye to. It is only on loan to you; it has only passed through you so that if I pull out my wallet at this moment, that money in it came to me from someone else and it will go to someone else – just passing through. Therefore Jesus is teaching us that in this world everything you have is another's; you are stewards of something that is on loan to you but you can't keep it. Whereas in the next world, true riches are yours to keep. This is the contrast between wealth in this world and wealth in heaven. Wealth in this world is little, it is unrighteous, and it is another's; wealth in the next world is much, it is true riches, and it is yours to keep.

Have you heard of Jim Elliot, the missionary to the Auca Indians who was martyred? Do you know what he said, throwing away his life in that way? He said, "A man is a fool who will not give up what he cannot keep to gain that which he cannot lose." Businessmen, there's a proposition for you. In fact, Jim Elliot exchanged all his worldly wealth, including life itself, for something he will never lose. He got the best of that bargain, undoubtedly. That is true stewardship.

Having drawn the lesson from the dishonest steward, and having said what true stewardship is, Jesus now lays down this principle: "You cannot live for money and for God." These are two incompatible rivals. You cannot have them both in your heart. It is impossible to live for money and to live for God. That is a categorical statement which many don't believe, but Jesus made it in as simple a way as that. Something will happen to your feelings, your thoughts and your motives if you try. They are bound to put one of these two above the other. They are bound to put money or God first – you can't love them both. You can't live for them both. You can't direct your ambitions to them both. There is just no room for both in your life.

At this point Jesus was rudely interrupted by laughter by some religious people, Pharisees, who thought: we worship God and we make money; we are successful businessmen and yet we are religious people. They thought what Jesus was saying was ridiculous. Deep down in the human heart is this philosophy planted: that wealth is a blessing and poverty is a curse. That is so deep in our hearts, even among Christians, that we can get to the point where we regard material wealth as a sign of God's blessing. The claim is sometimes made: "We are the proof that God blesses financially."

Now before we accept that claim, without examining it very deeply, let us realise that our Lord's philosophy was the opposite of that kind of thinking: "Blessed are you poor ... Woe to you rich!" In other words, he said wealth is a curse and poverty is a blessing. Now these two philosophies can't mix. The Pharisees taught that their material wealth was a sign of God's blessing on their spirituality, but Jesus taught that wealth is a curse and poverty is a blessing – sobering words indeed. Jesus proved to them that living for money and living for God were incompatible in their own lives.

They may have impressed others that they were wealthy and godly, but they had not fooled God. They loved money, they lived for it; but first, their attitude to the gospel of Christ was wrong, and second, their attitude to the law of God was affected also.

Jesus said that until John the Baptist, the law was preached. Now the good news had come and he, Jesus, was preaching the gospel, and the kingdom was being thrown open and people were snatching. That is the word he uses: seizing, snatching, grabbing the opportunity of the kingdom, and rushing to the gospel. But it is not the money lovers who are snatching this opportunity. By and large, though there may be exceptions, those who live for money don't snatch the opportunities of the gospel. Who were drawing near to Jesus – the rich or the poor? Who were seizing this kingdom, the Pharisees and Sadducees, who were the wealthiest groups in that land and very religious people, or the simple poor? When Jesus told John the Baptist what signs of the kingdom were coming he finished with this: "The poor have the gospel preached to them." Prostitutes and tax collectors were seizing the kingdom and leaving behind their love of money.

I have lived in one of the wealthiest parts of England where there are more millionaires within fifteen miles than in the whole of the rest of the British Isles put together. Are these the people who snatch the gospel, who seize the opportunity of Jesus Christ? Are these the people to whom it is so easy to preach, who eagerly take the kingdom by force and say, "This is the biggest opportunity of my life! This gospel of Jesus Christ is like the best pearl I've ever found and I'm prepared to get rid of all the other pearls and seize this one"? Is this the area where people are as eager to read the Bible as they are to study the pages of the Financial Times? Is this the area where the gospel is being welcomed, and being forced, and being seized and snatched as the greatest opportunity that has ever been presented? No, it is not. The church is struggling in this affluent country. You can go to Southeast Asia, you can go to Latin America where there is appalling poverty, but the church in Latin America is growing at two and a half times the rate of the population growth. Jesus found wherever he went that money lovers do not seize the gospel.

A rich young ruler came to him and said, "Lord, I want eternal life." Jesus said, "You can have it. Just drop everything and follow me." The gospel of the kingdom was there. Did he seize it? Did this rich man snatch it? Did he say, "That's just what I've been waiting for"? He turned around and went away sorrowful. That was Jesus' experience and those who are eager to snatch a business opportunity are far from being those who are eager to snatch the gospel. Try to win them. There are glorious exceptions and the Lord in his grace has touched some businessmen and some successful ones – very few. When they try to reach their fellow businessmen and those who have got everything that money can buy, and nothing that it can't, they find it one of the toughest jobs on earth to get through.

The second thing was that rich people, lovers of money, tend not only to ignore the gospel, but to bend the law of God. One of the most extraordinary views about Jesus that has become popular today is this: that Jesus bends the laws of God; that he came to make love the guiding principle, and was prepared to relax standards. In fact, this characteristic appears in those who love money, rather than in Jesus. Jesus makes it quite clear now he says "not one jot or one tittle...." A jot is a little dash that changes one Hebrew letter into another and a tittle is the smallest letter in Hebrew. He is saying that it is you lovers of money who bend the laws, and who bend principles. It is one of the effects of being affluent.

Well, be specific Jesus. Tell us what you mean, give us

an example. He gives an extraordinary one. Their attitude toward marriage and divorce was revealing. When I began my ministry, divorce and remarriage was hardly heard of in Christian circles. Now it is such a common problem that ministers and clergy regularly meet in conference to discuss how to cope with breakdown of marriage – not just outside church but within. It is one of the marks of an affluent and acquisitive society that the marriage laws of God get bent and that the standards of God get relaxed.

Why should those who love money develop a lax attitude to marriage? I can see why and I can see it happening. It is this: when you have got a lot of money and love it, then you can buy what you want and discard what you don't want. It gives you the power. You don't have to live with that old suit; if you don't like it you get rid of it and buy another. You get into a habit of mind where you put things on and put them off, or you buy what you want and buy your way out of what you don't want. Marriage becomes simply a business deal, a contract. If it doesn't work out, you write it off as a loss; you buy your way out and simply try again. If you don't get out of the contract what you expected then you write it off and you make another contract. In our Lord's day this was the picture. I don't know if you realise just how like our own day it was then, but even the rabbis were saying that really, in this matter of marriage, if there is incompatibility then the two should divorce and each find a more compatible partner and then they should just get together. People were divorcing their wives because they had a loud voice or because they burnt the toast. I am being quite literal here. This was actually being debated by rabbis Hillel, Shammai, and Akbar. This is what they were coming up with. In fact, divorce was rife among the wealthy, the affluent and the acquisitive.

Into that situation Jesus came and said that not one jot or one tittle of God's standards can be altered. Divorce and remarriage may be legal in man's sight but it is immoral in God's sight, and he made that utterly clear. You see, he was saying that this love of money, affluence, acquisitiveness dulls your sensitivity to the opportunities of the gospel. You are so busy looking for opportunities to make money that you miss the opportunities to receive grace.

According to the standards of Jesus, most of us in many UK congregations are rich. When you read the phrase, "There was a rich man", who did you think of? We should have thought of ourselves. Compared to someone in first century Israel, I am fabulously wealthy. Most are rich and therefore we need to listen to these words of our Lord very carefully. We need to ask how we are using our money – whether we are using it to make friends in heaven. We need to ask whether our desire for things, possessions, affluence – our acquisitiveness – is dulling us to the opportunities of the gospel that are there; is it the case that we are not seizing, not snatching, because we are comfortable? We are so concerned to get our home and garden and car nice that we are neglecting the opportunities of the kingdom. We need to ask: are we being tempted to bend God's standards, to lower his laws, because we are so affluent?

It is a tough passage, isn't it? Jesus was putting his finger on this spot. Whether you are a prodigal son or an elder brother, you can finish up when your money fails with no friends, and that is tragic. Jesus is saying, "Lay up for yourselves treasure in heaven." How wealthy will you be when you've left everything behind? How much will you be worth five minutes after you die? That is the question, and by the grace of God you can answer that. He who was rich, yet for our sakes became poor.... When he died, he had nothing to leave but his clothes, and those were taken from him. But through his poverty we might become rich. There are some who have very little in this world who will be multimillionaires in glory. What a shock that will be; what surprises we shall have! The world looks at a man who has made a lot and looks up to him, but Jesus' teaching reveals that it is your bank balance in heaven that is going to be the important thing.

16:19-31

Are you finding the central portion of Luke's Gospel challenging, stirring and very humiliating? Luke knew what he was doing when he wrote this Gospel. He knew that no one is ready for the account of the cross and the resurrection until God has broken down every bit of self; until he has shown us ourselves as we really are.

The Gospel takes away our pride, breaks down our obstinacy and shows us so clearly that all of us, respectable and renegade alike, are sinners in God's sight. We are being humbled and brought low so that we can then come to the foot of the cross. When you do, the message of the cross will mean so much to you. By nature we would rather go straight to the cross and hear about the love of God but that is not the way to appreciate his love most fully. So these chapters are very stirring. The story of this poor rich man is one of the most devastating in the whole of the Bible. It is the only passage that describes the feelings of unconverted people after death. If someone asked me to give a title for Luke 16, I think I would want to call it, "How to take it with you when you die." It is a chapter that tells you how to turn your money into real wealth; how to use your material possessions on this earth in such a way that when you die you are rich.

This story which begins in exactly the same way as the other story at the beginning of the chapter, "There was a rich man..." is a story to tell you what not to do with your money in this life if you really want to know the good life after you have died. There are many people today who I think are making no preparation for the future whatsoever. I know they have taken out life insurance; I know that they are getting into a pension scheme if they can; I know they are trying to hedge themselves against inflation by tying themselves to the spiral, as one man put it to me. He was changing his job because, he said, "In my present job I'm going backwards and I want to tie myself to the inflationary spiral and keep my head above water." But when I say there are many people not making any preparation for the future, I am not thinking of the rest of this life, I am thinking of the life after death. There are those who live on earth as if they are going to live here forever, and if they think about death their understanding is that death is the end – extinction; that the day you die you cease to think, you cease to feel, and therefore you cease to *be* as a self-conscious identity.

Now we have our Lord Jesus Christ instructing us about life after death. I believe he is the only person who is in a position of authority to tell us exactly what does happen to a person when they die. There are three facts which come out here, which I want to state clearly. Fact number one: you will survive death. After death you will have thoughts, feelings, memory and conscious existence. Every single one of us will survive death. That is part of the teaching of the Lord Jesus, who was the only one ever to choose to be born into this world, and the only one who came from the other world into it. His teaching means that you will survive death, and you will know that you do, and you will be conscious afterwards.

The second fact that comes out clearly is that not everybody is going to enjoy a better, more comfortable and happier life after death. For some it will be much better than this life; for others it will be a good deal worse. The idea that all of us are going to finish up in much the same kind of circumstance is totally alien to the whole teaching of the Bible. Fact number three: the life you have lived in this world is the deciding factor as to whether the life after death is going to be better or worse; the decisions that all of us have made here and now are the decisive factor for how we shall be living then. Every one of us has the opportunity in this life to decide our own future destiny, and to prepare for it. We each have our destiny in our own hands. It is our decision which will settle what life after death is like.

Before we look at the details, may I ask this question: Is this story fact or fiction? Is this another of Jesus' parables? I am afraid I can't answer this question. Some people feel it is very important. Is he simply telling a story, the details of which we cannot press because it is fiction? Or is he describing an actual event when he said, "There was a rich man...." Was there a rich man? When he said, "There was a beggar called Lazarus," did he know of a beggar called Lazarus? I honestly don't know. It certainly doesn't say it is a parable, and it would be the only parable in which Jesus ever named one of the characters. So he may well be thinking of a real person. Whether it is fact or fiction, it is true. Even those matchless parables, like the one of the prodigal son, though they are fictional they are always true to life. There is nothing that happens in a parable of Jesus that is not true to life. You study his parables and you see that he was not given to fantasy. "A sower went out to sow..." – you and I may have seen that very thing happen. I certainly have, out there in the Middle East. "A woman looking for a lost coin," "A shepherd looking for a lost sheep" – these are true to life situations. Therefore, I believe that the one story Jesus told about life after death would be as true to life beyond as all the other parables are true to life here. We cannot get round this story, as some commentators try to do, by saying that this is fiction, and therefore you don't need to worry about the details. There are those who try to evade the challenge of Jesus' teaching on the suffering in the world beyond by saying it is all pictorial – as if the symbol of fire and unquenchable thirst are more horrible than the reality behind the symbol. In this way people say, "Oh well, it's only symbolic language. You don't need to worry about it." If it is symbolic then the reality is just as terrible as the symbol. I believe that here in this story we have got something that is true to the next life, and the details are true if the story is a parable.

It is about two people, and the contrast between their circumstances in this world and in the next world. The total reversal of their circumstances is such that the gulf between them in this life, great as it is, becomes even greater in the next world – only they have changed places. The man who is on the top in this world is then at the bottom, and the man who was at the bottom in this world is then at the top. The gulf between them in this world is narrow enough to cross, but in the next world it is widened and so is uncrossable. This is the heart of the story.

We look first at the contrast in this life. Great inequalities of wealth were rampant in the days of Jesus – there were a few very rich and many very poor, and the gulf between them was huge. In many countries today there are huge gaps between the few rich and the many poor, with very few people in the middle. We have lived in a country which has created more and more in the middle.

Here was a rich man in his house. He was a glutton. Nowadays he would be called a gourmand, that is the polite word for it, but he was a glutton. He wore fine, expensive clothing. He had a beautiful ornamental gate outside his house, for the word for "gate" here means a beautifully worked wrought iron one. The man was living in the lap of luxury and enjoying himself to the full. He had a good chef and he ate well every day. Another human being was carried to that gate every day at the time when they threw the scraps out, emptying the dustbins from the rich man's table. In those days they didn't use napkins when they wanted to wipe their hands, they took a piece of bread and they rubbed it on their hands (bread is a very good cleansing agent). Then the filthy bread was thrown under the table and that was swept up and thrown out of the gate, and the beggar was carried to pick it up.

That is the contrast. Two human beings are within a hundred yards of each other, and their ways of life were so totally different. The beggar was a sorry sight. The word is that he is covered with open running ulcers. The dogs in the Middle East were not kept as pets; they are wild, mangy stray dogs that wander the streets. He hadn't the strength to keep them off licking his ulcers. I make no apology for using that kind of language in painting the picture – that is the picture that Jesus painted.

What a contrast! For the rich man, no name is given. Some people have called him "Dives", the Latin word for rich, but the name is not given by Jesus. Jesus did give a name to the beggar and the name is significant. Jesus never gave a name unless it corresponded to either something that a person was by nature or something that they could be by grace. So when Jesus gave a name to anyone, that name signified far more and told you something about the person. The name Lazarus is related to the word "Eliezar", which means "God has been my help." It means that though this beggar got little or no care from human beings at all, he had a faith that God would see him through, and that is all he had. So here are two men living within sight of each other and they knew about each other. The rich man reveals in his memory in hell that he knew about the beggar and that he even knew his name. Here is one man who had everything but God, and another man who had nothing but God. That is the contrast and it is an appalling picture.

They both died. Suddenly the stuffed body of the one and the starving body of the other were dead. It was inevitable. Of course, it matters not whether you live in a palace or a hovel, that is the end to which we must all come. In the dust we are equal made. They both died, but it says, "One of them was buried." That means that the beggar had no funeral. His body was carted off the streets and probably tipped into the Valley of Gehenna, where such things were left – a corpse to rot and be picked at. But the rich man had a funeral. It was reckoned that if you managed to get through life with a nice house, good food, good clothes, and a good funeral to top it all, you'd had everything that life could offer.

Now we turn from the contrast in this world to the much greater contrast in the next world. Where was that rich man? How was he feeling at the time of his funeral? Was he at peace as his body was? No, he was not. Both survived death and, for both, death fixed finally their future destiny as it does for everyone. The moment we die that has settled the rest of our existence one way or the other. The gulf at death cracks wide open so that those who wish to cross from one state to the other afterwards are not able to do so.

We look first at this poor man sharing paradise – a man who had never been looked after at all on earth was looked after one minute after death, and looked after superbly. Death is a lonely journey – we must make it on our own, and we must say goodbye to those who would wish to help us, but for those who die saying "God is my help," for those who are ushered into the presence of God himself, if God is their help, then angels are his helpers. I believe in the reality of angels. One of the most exciting things will be the first five minutes of death, to be looked after by God's helpers. This poor beggar, who had been carried by maybe a few of his friends to that gate to pick up scraps, was now carried by angels to meet the most famous believer of all time: Abraham.

It is a tremendous moment that for this poor beggar he is being given the place of honour at the right hand of Abraham – in Abraham's bosom. The angels are there serving him! For in glory those who know God is their help on earth will be above the angels, and the angels will serve them. Here is this beggar surrounded by servants. Can you imagine it? I think he had to keep pinching himself to find out if it was real. He, a beggar, being waited on hand and foot by angels, and sitting down at a feast! No crumbs under the table now, a feast on top of the table for the beggar and the chief seat at that feast. The memory of his earthly sufferings would fade very quickly, and indeed would now make his present joy even more wonderful. Like a bad dream after one awakes, he would look back at the days when he scraped dustbins to get a little bit to eat.

He is feasting but where was the rich man? What was he doing? What was he feeling? I have to be true to the scripture and say that these are some of the most important words Jesus ever uttered. He would not have told us anything that would mislead us. I believe that he who said "I am the truth" would give us the detailed truth about life after death. He said that rich man was in pain. None of his relatives thought so; none of the mourners at the funeral guessed that this was so. As a symbol, if you like, of that pain, or it may be just a straight factual description of the reality, the pain was that of unquenchable thirst in a very hot climate. I wonder if you have ever had that kind of pain. I have only once had it in my lifetime when I was stuck in the Arabian Desert with a Land Rover that broke down, and we had no water. You begin to imagine water. You would do anything for water. It is horrible to be really thirsty. In this country we hardly know what that is. That is how it is described – hell is a very thirsty place. The prophet Zechariah says there are no rivers there. That is why when Jesus died on the cross and went through hell for my sins, how did that show itself? He cried out, "I thirst." He was going through hell at that point: until your tongue swells and is like a great dry wad of blotting paper in your mouth.

Now the rich man becomes the beggar – the roles are reversed. He is asking that Lazarus may just dip his finger in some water and come and touch his tongue. "Send Lazarus" – so he knew his name and he knew all about him. Here he is asking, "Just send the beggar to me with a little bit of water." What a reversal, an incredible state of affairs! You see this man has memory beyond the grave, and part of the torment of being separated from God is memory – to remember all the lost opportunities, all the missed chances and all the times that God was trying to get through to you. To have to live with the memory of all that and know that now it is too late.... Somebody said hell is truth known too late. Do you know that everybody in hell will be a believer in the kingdom of heaven? Do you know that everybody in hell will believe in God? Do you know that everybody in hell will believe that Jesus Christ is the Son of God? It will all be too late to do the right thing about it – imagine the torment of knowing that you could have been elsewhere, and by your own choice and by your own fault you are where you are.

Abraham's words to this son of Abraham – and fancy he was a son of Abraham and can't be with Abraham: son, remember all the good things you wanted you got. Everything you thought was good you got. You never thought of the good things beyond the grave. You wanted it now. You wanted good clothes, you wanted good food, you wanted a fine house – you had it! Everything you wanted, you got." In other words: your ambitions and your desires were all centred on another world than this and you got what you wanted. Whereas this poor beggar centred his thoughts on this world, and now he has his good things that he wanted. In other words, you get what you want. What you have really wanted before you die you can get. In this world, if you want the things of this world, if you want them badly enough, you can get them. If you want the good things of the next world badly enough you can have them. It is a sobering thought: son, you had the good things; Lazarus didn't. Now he is having them. It depends where you set your heart, for where your treasure is, there will your heart be also and that is where your life will follow.

Why was this rich man where he was? Why was he suffering? What was his crime? There is no list of sins given, there are no vices mentioned, there are no crimes which now confront him. This man is where he is not because of what he had done but because of what he had not done. That is the shattering thought. Trying to understand why he was there, I listed three things. I started by asking: Was he there because of indulgence of self, because he just looked after number one, and just enjoyed himself, and just satisfied himself? Partly, but I don't think that was the deepest reason. Behind indulgence of self I found indifference to others. Was that why he was there? That the only thing he gave to that beggar were the scraps that he didn't need or want. But behind that, I detect a life of independence from God – that is the real thing. That is one of the perils of being well off, that you don't need God. One of the perils of being comfortably fed, clothed and housed is that we think we don't need God – we don't say, "God is my help," because we don't need help. "We are getting along very well, thank you."

The deepest reason why the rich man was there was because until he got there he felt no sense of need, but when he needed help it was too late to ask for it. This is really the deepest thing. Not just that he didn't feel the needs of others, but that he didn't feel his *own* need. Therefore, he lost all his good things. It was at that point that he began to be religious. Here is the man praying – but it is the only case in the Bible of anyone praying to a saint and it was pretty useless so it is not a practice to be encouraged. "Father Abraham..." and Abraham gave a reply to his prayer but didn't answer it. He couldn't answer it. The man had fixed his destiny and nothing now could change that.

The man then became filled with missionary interest. For the first time in his life he was concerned about saving other people – and again it was too late. The man is saying, "Well, can't we send a missionary? Can't we do something to save my five brothers?" I guess his motives were mixed. I think he was a bit worried about the thought of spending the rest of eternity with his five brothers. I mean that, because in the agony he was in, what is worse than that is to have a lot of your relatives around you in the same agony – maybe even reproaching him too, and saying, "You were the older brother. You led us this way. You brought us here." He couldn't face the thought of that. He asked, "Will you send a missionary? Send Lazarus!" Here he is begging the beggar to go and save his brothers. Can you imagine the brothers' reaction to the beggar walking through the gate and saying, "I've come back from the dead and I've come to tell you your brother is in hell and suffering"? Do you think they would have listened? Abraham understood human nature, and though times have changed, human nature hasn't. Abraham said that they have the scriptures (Moses and the Prophets); let them hear them. That was all they needed. While they were eating and drinking and enjoying themselves, there lay the scriptures on the shelf, untouched.

There is enough in the Bible to save you from any suffering at all in the life beyond the grave. All the truth you need to know about the future is there. There are many

Luke 16

things about the future I don't know, many questions I would like to ask, many details I would love to be able to pass on to you and I can't – but I tell you that in the Bible there is enough for you to know all you need to know about how to be right with God, and how to be able to look forward to a bright future beyond the grave.

The rich man knows that his family wouldn't listen to the Bible. You've got to give them proof – a miracle. Look, send someone back from the dead and they'll believe. Abraham knew human nature. If someone should rise from the dead, that wouldn't convince them.

The sad truth is that human nature will not be convinced if it doesn't want to believe. If someone will not accept the greater witness of God's Word, they will certainly not be convinced by the lesser witness of man's word. That is true to life. The real thing we need is not more evidence, but more willingness to believe. If a man is not willing to believe, even miracles don't convince him. How do I know that's true? Because this was in fact what happened. A few weeks after this story was told, a man was raised from the dead. His name, as it happens, was the same as that of this beggar. His name was Lazarus. He was raised from the dead. Did the nation of Israel turn to God and say, "Praise be to God; we believe it! We'll prepare for the future." No, they said, "Let's kill Jesus for raising Lazarus." They even plotted against Lazarus too.

So those who demand proof, miracles and evidence, and say that if they are given that they will believe – don't you believe it. If they don't want to believe God's Word now, they will not be convinced on any other ground. The only ground we have for preparing people for the future is to say, "This is what God says your future is going to be. This is how you may prepare for it." Praise be to God that so many millions are believing God and taking him at his word, preparing for that future and getting right with him, and therefore right with their neighbour too, and allowing the grace of Jesus Christ to put them right.

Once you have been born, it is inevitable that you go on to death and to judgment. That process cannot be stopped or avoided. At some point in the road there is a fork in the road, and those two roads continue in different directions, and there is a great gulf fixed between them. The gap appears even in this life. There is a crack running through the human race between those who say, "God is my help, I'm a sinner needing his grace and I come to the cross and accept him" – and those who will not take God's Word for the future.

As long as you are alive that gulf is narrow enough to cross. Even in the last moment of life people have jumped that chasm, and by the grace of God have woken up in paradise. A dying thief did – a man who had never done a good thing in his life as far as we know, and was executed for his criminal acts, yet that man in the last moment crossed the chasm, and heard the Lord's Word, "Today you will be with me in paradise." How important it is to jump across before we reach the end of our earthly pilgrimage, for none of us knows when that will be, soon or late. It is what we do in this life that prepares for the next. If we regard this life as something for our enjoyment and our satisfaction, to look after number one, to live it up, to get everything out of life that we can regardless of others and regardless of God, then I tell you one day Abraham will say to you that you have had your good things; you have had your good time. Those who are having a tough time here and may not be having the opportunities that others get, if you will by faith trust in Jesus Christ and say "God is my help", then you will wake up among the angels.

17

Read Luke 17

17:1-19

It took Jesus three years to turn fishermen into fishers of men – three full-time years of training. There is no short cut to Christian service. Yet the training was not given in some cloistered monastery or a Bible college. Most of it was given quite incidentally as they lived among others. There were some formal sermons, and that was a vital part of Jesus' teaching, but a great number of the lessons he taught sprang out of life situations. Other lessons were given in just a few sentences as they walked along the road. That is the ideal way of training.

If you have not been able to study at a theological (or Bible) college, don't necessarily envy those who have. They are not the best places to learn to be a Christian – I speak from experience. The teaching that Jesus wants to give us is the kind he gave the disciples. If you are walking and talking with Jesus as you go through life, three years of living with him can train you to be a fisher of men. There will be sermons that you hear, formal discourses on certain truths, but if that is the only training you get from the Lord Jesus it is not enough. You will become a listener, a passive sermon taster only. You need to let life situations on weekdays become a channel for Jesus telling you something about yourself and about other people.

Remember that Jesus is now on his way to Jerusalem. Time is very short. He knows he won't have much longer to teach these disciples, and so he is giving them lessons in how to follow him. Some of them spring out of life, others he slips in a sermon that is only five sentences long and gives them a profound lesson in how to be a Christian. There are three lessons we are going to learn from Jesus in this passage: one on sin, one on faith and one on thanks. These are three very simple lessons that all of us need to learn if we are going to be good followers of the Lord Jesus, and become fishers of men, able to help other people.

First, a little lesson on sin. I am sure you realise how serious it is for a Christian to sin. But there is one thing that God regards as far worse than sinning yourself, and that is to make someone else sin. Indeed, it would be better for you to be dead than doing that. This word comes very deeply to us and challenges us all. Jesus said it is inevitable that this will happen in our world – occasions for such things must occur. Why is it inevitable? Because we copy each other. It is inevitable because, crowded on this planet, we are not living each of us on a desert island. No man lives to himself, and all of us, for better or worse, influence other people. We cannot help it. Others will copy us; others will take a cue from us. We do that with dress, we do it with language and in other ways. I suppose that the outstanding example of this is the relationship between parents and children. How much your children pick up from you as parent – they learn most of their vocabulary and their habits from you. But it is not just between parents and children. Our behaviour affects other people. Therefore, one of the saddest burdens all of us have in our conscience is this: how many other people have sinned because of me? It is a sobering thought.

Where do people learn to swear? Do they think that up themselves? No, they copy other people and they think it is big to do this. You think of most of the sins you have committed – did you not learn most of them from someone else? We are not that original, even though we have got original sin in us. We are not able to think up new things so easily. We pick them up from the media, from our personal friends, and when we get in a gang of friends then we all influence each other, and we either lift each other up or we drag each other down. We are all like sheep.

Have you ever watched sheep? If one finds a hole in a fence all the others will follow. They really follow each other; "All we like sheep have gone astray," says the Bible. It just needs one to do something and the rest will do it. So Jesus taught that it is inevitable that this will happen. We are so made that we can't help influencing other people, and we can't help copying other people. Therefore, such things are bound to happen, but woe to those who do it.

How do we lead other people astray? I can think of a number of ways. First, by example. They see us doing a thing and they say, "It must be all right so I can do it." Second, in teaching. In what we say we might alter the standards of God and say, "Oh well, we're modern now and the standards of God are old-fashioned, so we don't now need to observe these principles." That kind of teaching, which is very widespread today, is causing people to stray. Jesus had some very severe words for those who relax one little bit of God's laws. Funnily enough, we can also cause them to sin by tightening God's standards, and by making stricter standards for them than God made. That is the opposite way of doing it, but the Pharisees did it this way. They had such traditions that they were narrower than God's laws. The result was that most people just gave up. Giving up on the traditions, they gave up on the principles, and they became technically known as "sinners". That was the label given to them in the Bible days because some people had made the standard so strict that some were just giving up, and therefore sinning in all ways. Next, we can do this by provocation. I may say to or about someone, "You know, I can see their besetting sin, it's bad temper." What I may not be aware of is that I provoke them to that bad temper, and that I stimulated it, and that it was really my attitude or action which caused them to lose their temper. So in a host of ways, as we go through life we can be making others sin, and Jesus said that it would be better for you to have a millstone around your neck.

Millstones can be seen in Galilee – black basalt rock about a yard across with a hole in the middle, and if you had one of those around your neck you wouldn't even get to the seashore, never mind get in. But if others took you to the seashore, tied that around your neck and threw you in, you wouldn't stand a chance. Jesus is teaching here that there is a fate worse than death. There is one thing worse than dying and that is to live with the knowledge that you led others astray, and to know that one day God will face you with that responsibility.

Now that is the negative side of the lesson on sin. The positive side of the lesson is this: are you one of those who is a little centre of life, neutralising sin, reducing it, dealing with it, and removing it? Every one of us in the church is either a person who is adding to sin by encouraging it, by leading others to do it, or we are reducing it and removing it from the scene. How do you remove it? The answer is by rebuking it and forgiving it. Let us take the first: rebuking it. One of the most awful dangers is this: when we see sin we talk about it to everybody but the one responsible for it. That is an unspiritual and an unchristian attitude. The Bible makes it quite clear that if you see sin there is only one person you should talk to about it and that is the person himself or herself. You shouldn't go to anyone else; you shouldn't gossip about it, you shouldn't criticise them behind their back. You should go to them and – in love –

rebuke it. Someone who has the courage and love to go to the individual direct is the person who will remove sin from the scene and not add to it.

Secondly, when they repent: forgive. I have noticed in life this simple fact and I pass it on to you as an observation of Christian fellowship: those who have enough love to forgive are those who have enough love to rebuke. Those who don't have enough love to rebuke don't have enough love to forgive; the two go together. Both are demonstrations of love. In fact, those who don't speak to a person but talk behind their back are those who will be resentful and unforgiving in spirit; the two go together again. This is the lesson Jesus wanted people to learn: he did not want them to be adding to the sins of other's lives, but taking the sins of other people away – reducing the heap of evil in the world, not increasing it; not causing sin, but curing it.

It is very difficult to forgive someone else because it involves forgetting it, and putting it right out of your relationship, right out of your mind. Jesus gives us some guidance about how many times we may have to do this. It says something for our lack of spirituality that a person who may have offended us three times is somebody we then can't forgive. In fact, Jewish rabbis of those days used to say: "If you can forgive your brother three times in one day then you are a perfect man." Jesus said seven times in one day. I think that pretty well covers every relationship you have. I would be surprised if you could tell me that somebody has sinned against you more than seven times a day. I have done a little mathematics and that is forty-nine times a week. I once heard a Christian say, "Just wait till he does it the 491st time," because he had been reading "unto seventy times seven" – he had been working that out – that is 490. But what Jesus is teaching is this: don't count; even if the same person sins against you seven times a day, you still go to him seven times, and if he says "I'm sorry", you say, "Right, that's forgiven and forgotten, and it's dealt with."

The reason for doing this is of course that is how you hope the Lord will deal with you. When we say the Lord's Prayer there is only one thing in that prayer we say about ourselves, have you noticed that? There is only one profession that you make about your own Christian life in that prayer. There is only one ground on which you pray the Lord's Prayer: I have forgiven those who have trespassed against me. It is the only thing you claim when you ask for God's mercy: that you have been merciful. It is a sobering thought, but insofar as you have been merciful to others then God is able to give you mercy. It is not because it is a bargain, nor because showing mercy deserved God's mercy.

In the last verse of Romans 1, having described some pretty horrible features of social life in the Roman Empire which are very common today, Paul writes: "And these people who do such things not only do them themselves, but encourage others to do them also" – as much as to say that is the depth of depravity, not when you have reached rock bottom and wallow in the mud yourself, but when you want to drag everybody down to your level. That is more serious. Far better to be out of this world altogether. To be drowned in the depths of the sea; it really would be better for a person to be at the bottom of the sea, dead, than to be living and doing that kind of thing. But the positive thing that we are to be doing is rebuking sin and forgiving it. We are to forgive and forget. Then we are reducing the sin around us – being a follower of Jesus.

The second lesson is about faith. I can guess the reason why the disciples said to Jesus, immediately after lesson number one, "Increase our faith." Who is sufficient for these things? Who is as good as this? Lord, we'll never make it. That kind of standard is too much for us. Seven times a day

– the same man? Oh Lord, we just don't have enough faith to do that. Lord increase our faith. Now at first sight, this is a prayer we would all want to pray. It is a very beautiful prayer we think, a prayer that is right and good. Surely that is our very need, surely the whole basis of the Christian life is faith. Surely the one thing we need is more and more faith. If we are ever going to reach the standard of forgiving each other and rebuking each other, give us more faith. Make us stronger believers. Yet you know, there's something seriously wrong with the prayer "Increase our faith".

It is not that you can't have bigger faith. There are degrees of faith. Paul in Romans 12 says, "Let everybody think soberly according to the measure of faith given him," and Jesus said, "You of little faith," and, "I have not met such great faith. No, not in Israel." Yes, there are degrees of faith, and what is wrong when you are conscious that you are only a little believer and saying, "Lord, make me a big believer"? You read the life of Hudson Taylor, you read the life of George Mueller and you say, "Lord, these were men of great faith! Lord increase our faith." Surely that is a lovely prayer and valid prayer? Yet our Lord rebuked the prayer and corrected it because there is something profoundly wrong with it. It is a prayer that seeks to shift the responsibility from us to God. It is declaring: Lord, we are inadequate, so you do it. If we are not careful our prayers get into this habit of thought, passing the responsibility over to God and saying: you do it. The Lord's rebuke comes in this simple lesson on faith. It is not enlarging that your faith needs, it is exercising. A lot of our prayers need serious examination at this point. Are we trying to make him do what we should be doing in our prayer? It is maybe so in this matter of faith. Jesus would say use the little faith you have. It is not a bigger faith you need, it is to exercise the little faith already given to you. That is the way to a stronger Christian life.

Jesus said, "Your faith may be no bigger than a mustard seed," and that is the tiniest thing; we would say a speck or a pinhead in our language. If in their days they wanted to say something was tiny they would always say "like a grain of mustard seed". If you look at it on your hand you can only just see it with good eyesight. If somebody gave you a mustard seed and you said, "But I'm asking for a tree", the answer would be: "I've given you one; take that tiny thing I've given you and do the proper thing with it. Put it in the soil, that tiny thing has life in it – use it! Put it in the soil and you've got your tree." It is one of the most profound spiritual principles that you get stuck spiritually if you don't use what you have. There is no use praying for more. If your faith was only tiny and you were prepared to use it, you could speak to a mulberry tree – which by the way has the strongest roots of any tree in Israel, "Get up and go," and it would go and plant itself in the sea. All you would need to do would be to speak.

Let us not water down what Jesus said. Let's not spiritualise it and say he's speaking of the mulberry tree of worry or the mulberry tree of this, that and the other. Let us take it as he said it, quite literally. People sometimes accuse me of being a literalist. Well, there are some things in the Bible I don't take literally because the Bible itself doesn't take them literally. If I was a literalist through and through I would believe there would only be animals in heaven because it says that in the last day he will divide the sheep from the goats and take the sheep to heaven and send the goats elsewhere – that is literalism, and I am not a literalist. On the other hand, where a simple straightforward statement of fact is made, I am a literalist and I take it literally. I am not going to spiritualise this text because Jesus said you could talk to a tree and tell it to go and it would move if you exercised faith that big. I wonder what your reaction to this is.

Luke 17

James 2 says, "Faith without actions is dead." I believe that the real reason why Christians get stuck and we do not see more is not necessarily the lack of earnest prayer that God will do more, it may be that we are not exercising the little that God has already given us. I believe this applies to the gifts of the Spirit. I believe it applies to the graces of the Spirit. "Lord, give me more patience."

"Are you using what I've already given you?"

"Lord, give me more love."

"Are you using what I've already given you?"

"Lord, we need more money."

"Are you using the money I've already given you as I want it used?"

"Lord, give us revival."

"Are you using the revival I've already given?"

Do you see what I mean? It's a lesson in faith. Not just to pray big, but to act big. Not to throw it back on the Lord and say, "Lord, you do more with us," but to respond to the Lord's challenge: You do more with what I've given you, and see what happens. The glorious thing is that your faith increases as you use it. Your gifts increase as you use them. Your graces increase as you use them. Your spiritual muscles get bigger as you exercise them, and faith is a kind of spiritual muscle.

The third lesson that we have to learn from this passage is about thanks. It follows from this one because supposing we do enlarge our faith by exercise and do more in the name of the Lord, supposing we do see things happening, supposing we are doing more ourselves – the greatest danger then is that God, having thrown the responsibility back on us, and we having accepted it and exercised ourselves, that we then expect thanks for it. Here is one of the most subtle dangers. The little Jack Horner syndrome, who put in his thumb and pulled out a plum and said, "What a good boy am I." For plum, substitute some gift or grace and you have got the picture.

There are two things we need to learn about thanks. On the negative side, don't expect any. On the positive side, learn to give thanks to the Lord. Let's take the negative side first. A most extraordinary story that Jesus tells here is quite shattering, and we are going to have to work out the practical implications of it: never expect to be thanked for what you do for the Lord, because if you receive thanks for what you are doing for him it assumes that you have been doing a favour and not a duty. You are not thanked for doing your duty, you are only thanked for doing favours. Therefore, it is a most dangerous thing to be thanked for doing something that was your duty.

Some people after a sermon have sometimes made a comment to me, beginning by saying, "I know you don't like to be thanked, but...." Now can I say that they've got me wrong? The real problem is I *do* like to be thanked. It is by nature that I like to be thanked; it is by grace that I don't like to be and ought not to be. I preach because it is my down to earth duty. If I wasn't doing it as a duty to the Lord I shouldn't be doing it. If he told me to be in a certain place preaching then I am just obeying orders. If he didn't tell me then I shouldn't be there. Can you see the simplicity of that?

Jesus taught us to think like this and beware. Now let me say straightaway that there is a ministry of encouragement we are told in the scriptures to exercise. We are to encourage one another. That is different from thanking one another. To encourage one another is to say, "The Lord has used you to bless me," and in that way you are giving glory to the Lord and you are encouraging the person. But to thank the person for doing it is to put them in a dangerous position spiritually. The Lord speaks of sending a servant out to look after sheep or to plough. Ploughing is evangelism –

breaking up fresh ground; looking after the sheep is pastoral work. All Christian service work comes under ploughing or shepherding. If you have a servant and you send him to plough or look after your sheep, when he comes back do you shake his hand and say: thank you so much for looking after my sheep, thank you so much for ploughing? Does your boss say that to you regularly? 'Oh, I'm really so grateful to you for doing me that favour. Sit down let me get some food for you. No, a master who has a servant says, "Now you've finished ploughing, get my meal ready." Only after he has finished all the duties can he sit down and enjoy the meal himself.

It is a very hard saying and a difficult one to accept and apply. Jesus has a feast prepared for us in heaven, but that is at the end of the day. Our duty at the moment is to serve him. We can sit down at the feast when we have finished our duty. But Jesus is teaching: even when you have done your level best, don't think you have done God a favour, and don't think you have got him in your debt. He has still spent more on you than he has got back from you. You are still unprofitable servants. So, even when you have put your very best effort into it, be encouraged in the Lord, but don't allow yourself to be thanked.

Is there any place in church life for votes of thanks? I know we are given to this. We thank the ladies for preparing the meal; there are thanks at the AGM of every organisation to those who are going out of office – but should we do it? Or should we praise God that they have done their duty? Should anyone be in any job in church if it is not their duty as a servant of the Lord? If they are doing it as a duty to him, should they be thanked for it? Or should they say, "Even though I've done my best, I know it is still not good enough, and it still doesn't repay the Lord for all he has done for me"?

Have you ever noticed that throughout the Bible neither

God the Father nor Jesus the Son of God ever thanked anybody for what they asked to be done? There is not a recorded case to my knowledge of God ever saying, "Thank you so much for doing that for me." There is not a recorded case of Jesus ever asking for something and then saying, "Thank you so much for doing it." Jesus said, "Go and you'll find a donkey; I need that donkey. Just say, 'The Lord needs him.'" That was all that was needed. That is the relationship between us and the Lord. If we do our duty as servants, don't expect thanks. Otherwise, you've got a mental outlook that is saying, "I've been doing the church a favour in doing this. I've been doing the Sunday school a favour; I've been doing the choir a favour; I've been doing someone a favour." You haven't. You've done your duty to the Lord. There will be a feast; one day he will say: you have now finished your duties to me, now sit down and eat and drink. Great is your reward in heaven.

On the other hand, let us learn the positive lesson because if we stopped at this point we could become unthankful people and that would be devastating for us. We are to be full of gratitude, but the thanks should go where they belong. Praise the Lord for those who do their duty. Praise the Lord for those who faithfully serve him in your church. Praise the Lord for it because it is the Lord who told them to do it. Praise the Lord that he supplies workers in his vineyard.

It comes out in a little story of ten lepers. I have never had much to do personally with people suffering from leprosy though I have heard missionaries speak of this dreadful condition where the body is not only in a very sad condition which becomes more and more grotesque, but where this very physical condition is going to cut that person off from social contact, even from their own family, and make them an outcast. Thank God that so many Christians have done so much to support missionaries who have gone out to relieve this condition. But then there were no drugs to meet this need, there was no cure, lepers were just pushed out and had to live away from others. They tended to live on the borders between different countries, so that if one country rejected them they stepped over that border. That is why when Jesus was walking along the borders between Galilee and Samaria, he met a bunch of these people, both Jews from Galilee and a Samaritan in a common tragedy, together living on the borders so that they could jump one way or the other when they were not liked. They kept a hundred paces away from Jesus – that was the regulation. They called to him, "Jesus, have pity." They were people of prayer. They prayed as hard that day as ever before because Jesus was passing. They must have heard that he could heal lepers, and not just remove their physical condition but put them back in their families and society.

They weren't just saying prayers, they were pleading with Jesus to have mercy on them and heal them. Jesus healed them in a way that he heals so many: he made them exercise the little faith they had. On this occasion he didn't say, "Right come here and I'll touch you." He told them to go and have a medical inspection in Jerusalem. That was the procedure then. "Go and show yourself to the priest." As they walked along, one of them looked at his hands and said, "Look!"

In other words, the faith that he made them exercise was to walk in the direction of the medical inspector. As they obeyed Jesus and believed, something happened. That is how faith operates. They obviously had a little faith in Jesus or they wouldn't have asked him to help them, and so Jesus made them exercise the faith they had. When Jesus met a man lying on the floor he didn't say, "Look, let me take you by the hand, lift you and pull you up." He was teaching him to exercise his own faith. "Get up and pick your bed up." You see the principle of faith coming through. It is not more

A COMMENTARY ON THE GOSPEL OF LUKE

faith we need, exercise the bit you have got. Act on it and as you go you are healed, and as you act on it, it happens. So they were healed.

It is a lovely story and we could finish it there, but it has a sad ending. All ten lepers discovered that their flesh was healing, and that the discolouring of their skin was going, and nine of them began to run in the wrong direction. They went heading on for the medical inspector. One stopped, watched the other nine running ahead, and came back. He fell on the ground and praised God with a loud voice. When you have really had the touch of the divine on you, you tend to be much louder – you lift up your voice. I think one of the reasons for our soft praying, quiet worship and our so dignified approach is that we haven't had this kind of touch. People do tend to get louder.

He praised God with a loud voice, uttering thanks to the God who had touched him. He was the only one of the ten who hadn't been brought up within the people of God. It is a sad fact that those of us who have been brought up in the people of God are sometimes less full of praise and thanks than those who haven't had that background who have come to it fresh and had a touch of the divine. We tend to take answers to prayer for granted. Jesus said, "Where are the other nine?"

There is a lovely psalm:

Oh that men would praise the Lord!
They go into the desert, they're parched, they're dying of thirst and they pray and the Lord meets their need,
and saves them in their distress.

Oh, that men would praise the Lord!
They're in dungeons, they're chained, the gates have closed on them, and they pray in prison to God and he

releases them and answers their cry.

Oh, that men would praise the Lord!
They go down to the sea in ships and great waves rise up, and they're tossed to and fro like drunken men. They cry to the Lord in their distress.

My, how people pray at sea in small boats. I have seen big strong fishermen in the Shetland Isles cry out to God when they battle with the sea. God sends peace and brings them to their desired haven but, "Oh, that men would praise the Lord." It is people of praise God wants. Don't expect thanks, but do give thanks. Getting thanks should not be our concern. We have really touched rock bottom in spirituality if we are resentful or hurt because we weren't thanked when we gave up the job. If you are doing a job, give thanks that you have been given a chance to do it. When somebody else takes it over, give thanks that somebody else is going to have the privilege of serving the Lord. But in everything give thanks. Let the Lord know your needs by prayer and supplication with thanksgiving.

The people who are the best servants of the Lord are not those who are looking for thanks, but those so full of gratitude that they can serve – that they can do it whether anybody sees it or not, whether anyone shows appreciation or not.

We have been given three very simple lessons in this passage. From them we can draw this contrasted picture. On the one side we see a Christian, a follower of Jesus, who is misleading his fellow Christians and causing them to sin, and adding to their troubles. We see a Christian who is constantly praying great and noble prayers, "Lord, increase our faith. Lord, do greater things" – but is not exercising what he has. We see a Christian who will be offended if he isn't extended a vote of thanks that's minuted by the church when he gives up the job. You see a Christian who is not going to be a very good disciple. On the other hand, I see another Christian who is a forgiving Christian, who is curing sin in other people, removing it from others' lives. I see a believing Christian who is not praying a lot of startling prayers, but is getting on and exercising the things that God has given. I see a Christian who is always thanking God and grateful for the privilege of serving. I know which Christian I would like to be, and I know which Christian I would like to work with, and I know which Christian is going to glorify the Lord.

17:20-37

The title for this study could be "How *not* to look for the Lord." The passage is full of negative instruction for Christians, and for others – because if you are looking in the wrong way, you will miss him. If you don't know what to look for or how to look, the Kingdom of God might pass your front door and you wouldn't be aware of it.

The whole thing started with some Pharisees, not followers of Jesus, asking Jesus a question about their own understanding of what they were looking for when they talked about the Kingdom of God. They had a great conception of what would happen when God really stepped into their world and situation, as some people today have an idea as to what he should be doing and how he ought to be operating and say, "Why doesn't God do this?" and "Why doesn't he sort out the Middle East?" and "Why didn't he stop that war?" We have got all these ideas as to how God should be acting in our world and we tell him what we think he should do and we complain when he doesn't do it. But we may be missing what he is doing.

The Pharisees had an idea that when God's Kingdom came, it was going to be spectacular, with a whole lot of

Luke 17

pomp and ceremony. God would really come in power and glory, and everybody would know about it. The Pharisees would have chief seats in the main grandstand. They expected great nationalist pride. They expected a spectacular overrunning of their enemies. They expected a kind of six day war, only preferably one or two days.

Of course, Jesus kept talking about the Kingdom of God. His sermons in the early years were nearly always on this theme. So they naturally said, "Well, when is it going to happen?" Jesus realised that their ideas were wrong in two particulars. One, they were looking for a visible kingdom; something that was spectacular, sensational, that everybody would see and notice – unmistakable signs of the presence of God. On the other hand, therefore, they were still expecting something in the *future*. Their very question reveals that they were assuming it was still to come.

Jesus corrected both ideas. When the Kingdom of God works on this planet, it is not in the kind of spectacular way they expected. It is not the kind of nationalism that is so characteristic of our world – as soon as power comes, glory has to follow and, therefore, there has to be a great display of power. Jesus said that the Kingdom of God is among you. They should not have been looking for a great visible display of fireworks. In fact, it is already happening. It was there and they had missed it. On one occasion when Jesus cast out a demon he said, "If I, by the finger of God, cast out demons then the Kingdom of God has arrived" – It has already come upon you; it's here.

If one person is born again and becomes a child of God and starts living the Christian life, the Kingdom of God is present. It could have been happening to a person sitting in your church. It does happen time after time: God is touching lives and changing them.

When Jesus came to Bethlehem, there was just a baby in

a stable. The Kingdom of God was coming and they didn't see it. Later, when the baby was taken to the temple, the crowds only noticed a teenage girl cuddling a little baby, but Simeon and Anna, just two people, realised the Kingdom of God was breaking in and they praised God. Later, people saw a man wandering around the shores of Galilee with a few fishermen and wondered what they were up to, but it was the Kingdom of God breaking through. Later still, those men, now increased in number, went out two by two to the towns and villages. The power of God was with them and great things happened, but the Kingdom of God was coming. This is God's favourite way of working – not in the way that would catch the attention of the media, but the Kingdom of God is operating and things are happening. Praise God, they are.

That was Jesus' correction of the Pharisees' notions of how God should operate. We say we want God to do the spectacular things but he would say: Let me straighten out your life; let's get *you* into the kingdom; let's demonstrate the kingdom in power in *your* life. For the kingdom is righteousness, peace and joy. Where God is doing that, the kingdom is coming. We are so often tempted to try and turn the Kingdom of God into a publicity stunt. With our gimmicks we are tempted to try and impress men in the way that we think they can be impressed – but the Kingdom of God goes on working like leaven in the dough; like seed planted secretly in the soil – nobody sees it germinating, nobody sees the first roots go down, but something is happening – all over the world. There will probably be many thousands today who will come to know Jesus Christ and enter the Kingdom of heaven – and it will be unreported. Today many are entering the kingdom and seizing it by force, snatching it and saying, "I want to be in this thing and I want Jesus to be my Lord and Saviour."

Luke 17

What used to affect the ancient Jews affects Christians also. We are vulnerable to the same thing: wanting to look for too many spectacular signs of our Lord's coming. That exposes us to all kinds of difficulties and dangers. For the rest of this passage, Jesus is speaking to his own disciples and warning them not to get like the Pharisees; not to look for his coming in the wrong way. Don't be vulnerable to those who tell you where to look and how to look. He gives us some wonderful advice on how to be prepared for his return to this planet. Because just as the Pharisees looked for the Kingdom of God coming, so Christians look for that great event predicted three hundred times in the New Testament –the reappearance of our Lord Jesus Christ on the earth.

The Bible has promised that he will make two visits to our earth; he has already made one and he is going to make a second. That is so clear. The Old Testament is packed with promises of his first coming and some hints of his second, but primarily packed with promises of his first coming and they were all true and he came. The New Testament is packed with promises of his second visit and they will come true equally. But how are we to look for this and be ready – not to panic, not to become vulnerable to false predictions and to those who say, "This time and this place." It is very important that we should look for the Lord's return in the way that he told us.

At one time in my ministry I had a considerable number of phone calls from people who asked for the pulpit, saying, "The Lord has revealed to me when he is going to return and I ask you to let me tell your church. If you don't, your blood is on your head"—that kind of conversation. In a sense it was encouraging that they were saying this, even though it was false. It means we are getting nearer, because Jesus did say that the nearer we get, the more misleading prophets we would get, because Satan wants us to get confused about this.

How are we to look for his return? In a sense, we are a bit like a bride. We are not right there yet, we are waiting for this marriage of the Lamb. So there is tension and waiting. In that tension we can begin to look in the wrong direction and in the wrong way. Here are the three bits of advice, as I see it, which Jesus gives: don't look around, don't look back, and don't look ahead. Take the first: don't look around. As we get nearer to the Day and as the Bride gets more excited looking for her Bridegroom, there is a restlessness apparent among Christians who, more and more, are moving from church to church, place to place. It is a disturbing symptom of a little over-excitement about our Lord's return that we would like to be in this or that group of Christians when he gets back. Jesus would say: stay right where you are; I will pick you up where you are. You don't need to rush around. It doesn't matter where you are. When Jesus comes, you will know about it as soon as anybody else does. I find this rather exciting.

When he first came, there was one star in the sky that pinpointed one place on earth. There is to be a sign in the sky at his second coming but it is the sign of travelling from east to west. Lightning travels at 186,000 miles per second and the circumference of our earth is 27,000 miles. That is as quickly as you will get the message when Jesus comes back. You work it out for yourself. The whole world will know immediately Jesus is back.

When it will happen is the Father's secret. Don't look around at other people. It will be utterly unmistakable and you will know the minute Jesus gets back wherever you are. There is a sober word which we need to remember. There must be a time of suffering before the time of sovereignty and we must be rejected before we can reign.

The second thing Jesus teaches us is that his return will not be gradual but cataclysmic. There will not be a lot of advance publicity. In the days of Noah people were getting on with the business of eating and drinking, marrying and money-making, then suddenly the day came and the rains came. In the time of Lot in Sodom, all the people were carrying on – food, drink and sex just as usual, and then suddenly it came. Minutes before Jesus returns to earth, people will be getting meals ready, making love, going to the office. In other words, life on earth, as far as the world is concerned, will be going on as usual. You cannot expect any great change in social behaviour before the coming of our Lord. Therefore, to look around too much for signs in the world is rather foolish.

I believe that there are scriptures that tell us that Christians will know approximately when Jesus is coming, but not exactly. There are scriptures that say he will come like a thief in the night, which is unexpected, but then they go on to say, as in 1 Thessalonians 5, that you will not be surprised if you are alert and watching. You will be waiting up and you will be watching for the burglar coming; you will be there. You will be alert and we are children of the day; we won't be caught out if we're watching for this.

Christians see the signs of the times. They see the fig tree budding and they look up, for they know the day of their redemption is drawing nigh. We shall know the approximate time, but of the day and the hour, no man knows.

The next point is: when he comes, don't look back. I don't know where you will be. I have assumed that you may still be alive. If you have gone to be with the Lord first, you are not going to miss a thing; you will get a front seat. That is 1 Thessalonians 4 – they got very worried about those who died and were going to miss all this. Paul taught: Don't grieve as others do, or have no hope. The dead in Christ will rise first, they will be in the front seats; you will follow them; they won't miss a thing.

When the call comes, you will know absolutely certainly the he is calling you away. When that call comes, don't think of another thing, just go. It means that you will be free to respond and free to hesitate and free not to go. It means that you will know that he has come and he wants you with him. Your reaction at that point is going to be crucial. It is going to reveal so much. Jesus said first, "When that comes and I come back...." When he comes, we go. The first thing is: don't give any thought whatever to any material possession you have at that point. Don't go into your house and find a suitcase. You are leaving everything behind. There must be no thought whatever of your house, your garden, your car or your bank balance. Drop it, come straight to Jesus. On that day, let him that is on the housetop not even go down the stairs into his house, just take off straight from that roof and come. Quite seriously, I am trying to imagine this. I really find it difficult. I know, in that moment when he comes back, he wants me with him and I have just got to take off and go. Those who have got thoughts of their material possessions show that their heart is still bound to the things of earth. Don't look at anything you possess – it can't help you anyway. It can only hinder at that point. It tells me this: you must sit so lightly to your possessions now that the Lord could call you at any moment and you wouldn't even have a moment's regret at leaving any possession behind. It is one of the ways in which you get ready for his return. Sit very lightly to your property.

The next things is: don't be concerned with leaving behind the life you have lived. In a sense, when Jesus comes and he calls me to join him, that will be for me a moment of death – leaving behind the life I have lived, the same as happens when you die. At that moment, whoever would want to save his life will lose it; and whoever will lose it, will save it. In other words, there is to be no thought of preserving your life, no thought of holding on, and no thought of trying to follow that very deep instinct of self-preservation which even at that point could take over. If the call to go home to be with the Lord in death comes to you before he returns to earth, then at that point you can do the same thing: not one glance back at property left behind; not one bit of hanging onto life, just: "Jesus, here I come." He is waiting for you. The two strongest links we have with this world together with our relatives are our property and our life itself. We have a deep instinct to preserve these, but when Jesus calls, his call has precedence over everything else.

Don't try and work out all the details. Be ready for a totally unexpected departure. In that day, people will take off for Jesus so unexpectedly that they will be busy doing something else, and indeed that is what we ought to be doing. It will be a different time for Christians around the world. For some it will be night; for others daytime. You may be in bed and it is right that you should be. You shouldn't be staying up all night because you think the Lord is coming, you should be asleep. Don't panic, and don't be too ready. No earthly ties have any relevance at that moment. The only relationship that matters then is your relationship with Jesus.

The disciples asked the question "Where, Lord?" Jesus answered, "Wherever the body is, there the eagles [or vultures] will be gathered together." You won't need to know where. You will have a homing instinct as to where you ought to be, as those birds have. From every part of the planet you will see people coming with Christ, until there is a great crowd of Christians gathered around him. The dead in Christ will rise first. Then we, who are still alive, will join them. What a moment! For further discussion on the signs of the End, please see my book entitled *Living in Hope* (Anchor).

18

Read Luke 18

Most of Jesus' teaching was as he walked, as he travelled, and that is how the disciples learned so much from him. I tried the same when I took a group of church members to Israel, and as we walked around, I talked and preached to them as it were, and one church member said, "David, we've learned more from you in eight days here than in six months at home." I don't know how that was, but I was able to point to things. We watched a shepherd separating the sheep from the goats and putting the sheep in the sheepfold at night and leaving the goats out in the dark. Then the group understood what Jesus meant.

As he and his disciples walked up to Jerusalem it is all getting a bit dark; there are shadows beginning to fall across the whole situation. He is still preaching, still healing, but somehow already the shadow of the cross is looming over the whole story.

Let's look at the two parables which he addressed to the disciples – and these weren't told to hide anything from anyone. He was using them as illustrations to the disciples and both were about prayer, which in its simplest form is talking to God. The two parables tell the disciples: first, how to get through to God with something which he seems not to be interested in; and the second parable, which is one of my favourites is about the kind of prayer that God hears and the kind of prayer he doesn't hear. And we need to know all this. It will affect us in our praying.

A COMMENTARY ON THE GOSPEL OF LUKE

The first parable is of the persistent widow, and her prayer was to a judge, asking for justice. Obviously, something unfair had happened to her and she appealed to this judge to vindicate her and do justice for her. She had been treated badly. Unfortunately, she went to a bad judge and we are told only two things about him. He didn't believe in God and he didn't care about people. What a judge! But then he got the position. And so she asked him: "Grant me justice against an adversary; defend me against this neighbour who is doing me harm." He seemed quite indifferent; he didn't fear God and he didn't care for people. However, she knew the secret of getting what she is asking for, and that was to bother him so much that he would get tired of her. And Jesus said don't give up praying for something because you don't seem to be getting an answer. Go on "bothering God" until he does it for you. But the difference is that you're dealing with a very different judge. God is a just judge. The judge on earth was reluctant to hear her prayer. God in heaven is ready to hear our prayer. There is a big difference there. Nevertheless, Jesus is really saying 'keep bothering God and he will give you your justice.'

We know from the Book of Revelation that early Christians found themselves praying for justice. The world was treating them unjustly and there seemed no end to their suffering. Now this applies to Christians in many parts of the world today who are crying out to God for justice, because they are persecuted and it is unfair, and it shouldn't happen.

You can imagine the Jews in the holocaust were praying to God for justice. So there is a difference between the human judge and his reluctance and a heavenly judge and his readiness because the heavenly judge is ready to give us justice and will do so. But there is still the lesson to go on asking until you get what you are asking for. It is so easy to give up. People tell me, "I prayed to God for this and it didn't happen so I gave up." And they maybe only prayed once. But Jesus says go on.

At one stage my children said "We want bicycles – everybody at school has them and we don't." They didn't ask once, they asked almost every day, they wore me down and we got them bicycles after telling them to be very careful along the main road – don't take any risks because it's very dangerous. It is the same with God. If you want justice from him, keep on asking until you get it, and he is more ready than any earthly judge to give it. Life is unfair; that is the underlying assumption. All people will experience the unfairness of life. In fact, our children learned very early to say "It's not fair." And their faces used to screw up. It is tragic that some people go right through life saying that. I get adults saying to me – Why should God let this happen? Why does God do this to me? It's not fair! But keep on, said Jesus; don't give up – because you've got a judge who is really on your side. If we only ask for something from God once, I would question whether we really want it. It is those who *go on* asking who get through, and they don't give up. So that is the first parable Jesus told to the disciples as they walked up to Jerusalem.

The second parable is also about prayer and it is a contrast between two people who went to the temple in Jerusalem to pray. But although they were both in the same building, there was a stark contrast between those two. One was a Pharisee, a good man, a religious man, a man who had really tried his best to be what God wanted him to be; the other was a tax collector. As we have seen, a tax collector in those days was virtually in the protection racket and you can imagine that they were squeezing people hard and were threatening them if they didn't pay up.

When I was in Warsaw going through the Jewish ghetto remains, they told me that happened there during the war.

A COMMENTARY ON THE GOSPEL OF LUKE

The Jews were squeezed in to a very small area – walls were built to keep them in – and then the Germans got Jewish tax collectors to collect the money from their own people. You can imagine how popular the tax collector was when he was lining his own pockets and getting very rich and squeezing people by threatening them with Roman punishment – or German punishment in the case of Warsaw. They were traitors to their people; they were lining their own pockets at the cost of their own people, and they were raking it in. The other man who went into the temple to pray was a tax collector – horrid man; everybody hated the tax collectors. Zacchaeus was one such man, and Zacchaeus was charging people four times too much for the Roman taxes. He admitted that. There were the two men – one was heard by God and the other wasn't, and it is the opposite of who we might think. The Pharisee went right up to the front of the temple and stood in front of God and said, "God, I thank you that I am not as other people" (robbers, murderers, adulterers, even like that man at the back. I thank you that I am not like *him*.) And did you notice one word that he used five times – which meant that his prayer got no higher than the ceiling? *I* thank you that *I* am not like everybody else. *I* give tithes. *I* fast twice in the week. Jesus said that the man prayed thus *with himself*, or *to* himself. A prayer full of 'I' doesn't get up to heaven. God doesn't listen to that kind of prayer.

The man at the back was quite different. It was a "me" prayer. God be merciful to *me*. I'm a sinner; I've been living a wrong life. I've been deceiving my fellow Jews; I've been raking in money by telling lies to them about what they should pay. He knew it. And it is interesting that the first parable of the persistent widow was asking for justice, but here this man is asking for *mercy*. Since God is full of mercy, if you want to get through to him, appeal to his mercy. Now I have listened to hundreds of prayers and attended many prayer meetings but I have rarely heard a Christian pray for mercy. Isn't that strange, when that will get the prayer straight through to God? It is one prayer that he is bound to answer – he is so full of mercy. If somebody asks him for mercy, he immediately answers that prayer. Why do so few Christians pray for mercy? I have heard prayers for health and wealth and happiness, for safety, for healing, for all kinds of problems we have, but rarely ask for mercy.

Why not? The church teaches us to in ritual and that is the only time I have heard Christians pray for mercy – "Christ have mercy. Lord have mercy." It is because you don't ask for mercy unless you don't believe you deserve anything. To ask for mercy is saying "I don't deserve anything from you Lord"; and only people who are desperate, who know they are so bad that they don't deserve a thing, will pray for mercy. That opens up the heavens straight away. This tax collector with all his badness, all his sin, simply said, "God be merciful to me" – and Jesus said that God heard his prayer and not the other man's.

This reminds me of a sequel to the account of the Nazi criminals which we thought about earlier. One after another, many of those Nazi leaders came to the Lord and said "God be merciful to me". He was merciful and those who asked for his mercy were forgiven and found salvation. There is a book about it entitled *Mission at Nuremburg*. I told this story to the church in Guildford and an architect came to me with tears streaming down his cheeks, and he said "I was in Germany, part of the British occupying army during the time of that trial, and some of us who were Christians spent a whole night in prayer begging God to have mercy on the criminals. Until tonight, I have never heard that our prayer was answered. Now you tell me that most of them came to Christ through Padre Gerecke*" [*the chaplain who ministered to the prisoners].

I was speaking in Newbury to a house group and told this story there. A young couple burst into tears and were laughing and crying at the same time. I thought they had lost control of themselves and I stopped speaking and asked the couple if we could pray for them. They said, "No, carry on." I said, "Well look, you can go into the next room with my wife and she will help you." "No," they said again, "carry on." As I continued, they went on weeping and laughing. Afterwards I went straight to them and asked, "Tell me, why were you so almost hysterical when I told that story?"

The wife said this: "Keitel, the chief of the army, was my uncle and wherever we've gone in this world and they've found out that Keitel was my uncle they will have nothing more to do with me." She said to get away from it they had emigrated to Australia. People found out there and made their life a misery. They went from there to Canada and they found out and they had now gone to live in Newbury and the people there had found out too and said "You're Keitel's niece."

She continued, "Now you tell me this story I can lift my head up; a cloud has rolled away from my life. Now when anybody points to me and says 'You're Keitel's niece', I will say 'Yes, and he's in heaven with Jesus – will you be?'"

She said the whole situation had now become different. I mention all that because it makes that parable so real.

As soon as a Nazi criminal who's responsible for killing so many people says 'God be merciful to me, a sinner', God hears that prayer and answers it. Even von Ribbentrop who was in charge of Hitler's propaganda and who would spread Hitler's lies on the principle that the bigger the lie the more that people believe it, when he mounted the scaffold to be hanged, he said 'I trust in the redeeming blood of Jesus'.

Now I don't know how you feel about that, but I have had people resent deeply my telling that story because they can't cope with God's mercy when it is offered to people like that – and especially people who say "Here am I and I've lived a good life and I've done my best, I've gone to church – and yet it seems as if God and his mercy went straight to those dreadful men and saved them." It is always an offence to those who think that they do deserve something when they hear that God does something for those who don't deserve a thing. When, in the 1960s, I first heard that account, I couldn't cope. It was such an amazing example of the grace of God.

Having told the disciples how to pray, and the kind of prayer that gets straight through, Jesus took a little child and gave them an object lesson. Fathers – not mothers – had brought their children to be blessed by Jesus, and the disciples took a very adult position and said he hadn't time for little children – and Jesus was very cross, and he called the little children to him, sat one on his knee, and said 'unless you become like a little child you don't get into the Kingdom'. He meant by 'a little child' not an innocent, because little children are not very innocent. He meant that kind of trusting attitude. If you treat little children rightly they will trust you and obey you. And unless we become like a little child to our heavenly Father we are not going to get in.

We move on to the two people he met on his way to Jerusalem. First, the rich ruler stopped him in the street and said, "Good master, what must I do to inherit eternal life?" That is a good question. People rarely ask it, because it's about the next world and the next life, and people today rarely ask how they can be good for the next life.

I was invited to speak at the Stock Exchange in London. They asked me for my subject before I went, in order to advertise it, and I gave them this: "You Can't Take It with you and if you could It Would Burn". They didn't like that subject and refused to take it, so I changed it to: "How to Invest your Money Beyond the Grave" – and they did advertise that. I spoke to stockbrokers and staff – it was quite an ominous crowd – telling them what Jesus said about investing your money beyond the grave, because all of them were investing it in the life *before* death – how to retire to a nice bungalow and how to have plenty of income before you die. But Jesus talked about how to have income *after* you die and how to ensure that you will be rich in the next world. There will be many surprises.

To this rich young ruler, Jesus' immediate reaction was: "Why did you call me good?" He was really saying there is no one good but God, and he was testing the man to see if he was really recognising that Jesus was God. There was a lesson. We have spoiled the word "good". We say, "Did you have a good holiday?" "Have you had a good meal?" We even say, "Good dog". We have robbed this word "good" of its real meaning. When you say goodbye to someone, you are saying, "God be with ye." But we have robbed these words of their significance. And the word "good" we apply to anything: the weather; anything we enjoy we call good. It is the wrong use of the word. We do use it of people – he was a good man or she was a good woman – but in fact Jesus was right in saying you shouldn't call anyone good except God. He is the only really good person. Everybody else is capable of doing good things and being good in some ways, but none of us is good through and through. Why do you call me good? – Jesus could have added: you recognise that I'm God? It was a rebuke. Jesus ran through the Commandments and this man said, "I've done all those since I was a boy." Jesus looked at him and said there was one thing lacking, and then told him what he needed to do: to go and sell all his possessions, give the proceeds to the poor and then, "Come, follow me." Then the man looked very sad because he had great possessions. It wasn't that he had great possessions –

the possessions possessed him, and he could never let them go. He went away sad. His possessions possessed him. Then Jesus said it is very hard for rich people to enter the Kingdom of God. That is a startling thing to say but, as we have noted, by comparison with people in Jesus' day, we are all rich. Just to afford to be in our houses we need to be rich, and it is hard for rich people to enter the kingdom. Why? Because somehow rich people can buy anything they need and it's very difficult for them to come and say: God, without you and without your mercy, I'm nothing. It is hard for rich people to admit they need something when they are used to buying everything they need. I have to confess I am rich and I can pay money for everything I need. I don't need anything because I can pay for it. Hard for rich people... but not impossible. With God, all things are possible. That was his reply to "Who then can be saved?" If rich people can't enter, who can?

Peter said to Jesus, "We left everything we had to follow you." It was rather naughty to say that, but then Jesus said no-one has lost family or brothers or money or land or anything for the sake of the kingdom who is not repaid many times over – in this age and in the age to come. In other words, those who have given up anything for the sake of Jesus will be rewarded. I can bear witness to that. For every friend you lose, you get a dozen, even in this world. Jesus has a way of repaying which is lovely.

Now let us look at the other man that they met on the way to Jerusalem – a blind beggar. If you were blind in the ancient world, you couldn't make a living, you just had to beg. They were passing through Jericho and there was a blind beggar on the roadside and he could hear this crowd making a huge noise and he asked what the noise was about. He was told: Jesus of Nazareth is passing through. The blind beggar shouted out, "Son of David, have mercy on me."

And the people nearest to him told him to be quiet. That made him shout even louder – "Son of David, have mercy on me." Jesus heard him and said, "What do you want me to do for you?" What a wonderful moment! He said, "Lord, that I may receive my sight." Jesus said, "Receive your sight; your faith has made you well." Immediately, the man received his sight.

"Son of David" was what he called him, and he *was* the Son of David. He was descended from David and that was the title of the Jewish Messiah but he was so much more. When the Messiah came, every Jew knew that he would be related to King David.

I have missed out verses 31-34 where Jesus says that everything prophesied of him in the Old Testament is going to happen now. He would be delivered into the hands of the Gentiles. That is something Christians have forgotten. *Gentiles* put Jesus on the cross – Romans, not Jews, yet for two thousand years the church has blamed the Jews for the death of Jesus. That has got such a deep root in Jewish hearts that they have been anti-Christian, and if you mention Christ to a Jew, the memory of the crucifixion comes up, and the accusation of Christians through the centuries.

Jesus said all that is prophesied they will do; they're going to humiliate me. They will spit on me. They will mock me. They will flog me and they will kill me. All those things happened, and they were all foretold centuries earlier. But then Jesus adds one thing that is also prophesied: on the third day he will be raised up. The disciples couldn't take it in. They couldn't think of their Jesus being spat on, flogged and mocked, and they certainly couldn't think of him being killed. Above all, they just could not grasp that death would not be the end for him, but that he would be raised up. Well, all that happened – as we know.

19

Read Luke 19

19:1-27
If there is one theme in the Bible we don't like by nature, it is the theme of the Day of Judgment – with the thought that one day our past will catch up with us. It is so obnoxious to us that we will find any reason for denying it. One of the most popular beliefs is that there is nothing after death: "Don't worry, if you get away with it till the day you die, that's it; that's curtains for you. You will never have to face your past because you're dead; you're out of it; you've escaped." That is not true, because no one ceases to exist when they die.

Then there is another common idea that people keep telling me when I speak about heaven or hell. They say, "Well, I think you make your own heaven or hell here." Of course that gets away from Bible teaching. Believe me, no one has tasted hell here except Jesus. The very worst experience of life is still not to be compared to hell because nobody on earth is so separated from God's influence that he is tasting hell. Likewise, thank God that the finest experience on earth is still nothing compared with heaven.

It would be dreadful news if it were the case that what we have got down here is heaven and hell. I want something better than this, of course – who would want to live eternally if the best that we know is all there is? It is when you have tasted just a little bit of heaven that you want to live forever.

There are others who say, "Well, God's a very tolerant old boy. He won't judge you, he won't ever condemn you – he is really rather nice and you can get round him." All these things are saying, "No judgment" – but when I read my Bible there are certain things said so clearly that I have either got to agree with them or burn my Bible.

One is that judgment is not now, it is future, and God has already put a cross on the date on his calendar when it will be. A second fact that is utterly clear is this: that God himself has delegated the task of judging us to Jesus. I don't know if you find that a comfort or not. Personally, I don't. I know that being human he knows our circumstances and he will understand, but I know that nobody had such a devastating insight into human nature as Jesus, and that when he looked at you he saw the lot.[1]

We now turn to the story of Zacchaeus. Jericho, to this day, is a lovely town with trees and flowers. It owes its prosperity to a spring of water, which is mentioned way back in the Old Testament and which you can see for yourself today. There it is in that deep rift valley, the Jordan Valley, and that water has turned it into a garden. It was a very rich city, and furthermore, placed as it was on an important road, it was the post for the customs and excise for entry into the country. Therefore, it was somewhere a tax collector really could make a fortune. Zacchaeus was not a man that you would like to have around, not a man you would think of asking home to Sunday lunch, not a man who was very popular. He had made a lot of money at the cost of losing all his friends and had sold out to the occupying enemy forces, swindling his fellow countrymen. He really had exploited the situation for his own good and he had no moral principles. He was a bad man, yet I expect to see him in heaven.

How did it happen? I have tried to ask what it was that started Zacchaeus off in his quest for truth and reality. Why did he want to see Jesus? I don't know but I am going to speculate – the only answer I can come up with is the memory of a godly mother and father. The reason I say that is the name they gave their little boy. Whatever your children turn out to be, the names you give them are important because you hope that name will fit them and influence their character. Do you know what "Zacchaeus" means? It means, "A good boy; the just, the righteous; the upright man, the straight and honest person" – and can you imagine the parents when they got this little baby boy choosing that name?

A Methodist minister who served in Poplar, London for many years, tells how one day a couple came with their little boy and asked to have him christened. When the minister said in the service, "Name this child", the parents said, "Genius".

He whispered to them, "Can't you think of another name? That really will be a handicap to him all his life; fancy being called 'Genius'!" The father said, "You call him 'Genius', I want to give him something to live up to." Can you imagine having to live up to that sort of a name? Zacchaeus – good man – fancy having to live with that name, especially in view of his career! I believe that his parents had so planted deep within his heart a desire to be right, a desire to be good, that when the chance came he took it. That is speculation, and we must leave speculation, get back to scripture and see what did happen. I want to ask why it was that this man was so changed. It is a total and most dramatic conversion, changing his total outlook, character, personality and way of life. How could it happen? Let's look at how salvation was welcomed into the house of that lonely, bad man.

I believe there were two secrets. One was that he was absolutely determined to get through to Jesus, and I tell you that anybody who is determined to get through to Jesus will have their life changed. Here was a man who had got everything he wanted because he had a single track mind, and all through his career he had made it his job to get what he wanted, and had gone to the very top of his profession.

When he had made up his mind to do a thing, he did it. Thank God for men like this, even men who have done it in the wrong way and gone hard after a bad life – when they become Christians they really do go hard after the good life.

This man was so determined to get through that he wouldn't let anybody get between him and Jesus. That is the first secret of this man's start on the road to real salvation. One of the things that happen so often when somebody gets interested in Jesus is that they allow someone else to get between them and him. Sometimes they look at the church and instead of being determined to find out what Jesus is like, they look at what the church is like, and they say, "Well, look at so and so, and so and so, they are Christians...." Some say, "Well I'm interested in Jesus but I've just fallen in love and I've got a boyfriend or a girlfriend" – and that friend comes between them and Jesus and they lose interest. He was determined to find out what Jesus was really like. A person who is as determined as that will begin on the way of salvation. So he climbed the tree and he ran ahead of the crowd. A mulberry tree has a short straight trunk and a lot of horizontal branches. It is a fairly easy tree to climb, but the man looked a fool; ridiculous. "Look at him. Who's that climbing that tree? It's Zacchaeus." Can you imagine it? But he is so determined that he doesn't even mind looking a fool.

There were some surprises that Zacchaeus got at that point when he was up the tree. The first was that Jesus noticed him – though he thought he was well hidden in the branches, That could happen to someone in any congregation. You may think you are one of a crowd, that you are inconspicuous, but Jesus notices you.

Secondly, he was surprised that Jesus addressed him – actually talked to him.

Thirdly, Zacchaeus was surprised that Jesus knew him. They had never met, and I suppose the biggest surprise you get when you accept Jesus is that you have come to someone who knows you inside out.

Fourth surprise: Jesus called him. Nobody would have anything to do with him, yet Jesus called him.

Fifth surprise: Jesus accepted him as he was. He didn't make any conditions. He didn't say, "Now Zacchaeus, if you promise to change your way of life I'll come to your house." He accepted him as he was.

Sixth surprise: Jesus befriended him: "Today I must stay at your house."

The seventh surprise, and the most disturbing of all, was that Jesus preferred him to all the others, because when Jesus went into that house he lost the friendship of that crowd. This must have touched Zacchaeus at a very deep level. How had he heard about Jesus? Maybe he had heard about the conversion of Matthew, another tax collector. Maybe some of Zacchaeus's own staff had been following Jesus and they had been changed, and now here, suddenly, all these surprises totally reverse his life. He was probably converted before he had come down the tree.

Zacchaeus hurried! He seized the opportunity. If you hear the Lord call, that is the moment to seize. I remember a Scottish engineer coming to see me once. "Pastor," he said, "years ago in the war I was in the middle of a battle and I was in danger of losing my life. I said, 'O God, if you'll get me out of this, I'm yours for the rest of my life. Just bring me back to my wife and kids and you can have me.'" He had been given something of a Christian upbringing. He knew what it was to follow the Lord, and he made that promise. The Lord saved his life in that battle, and he came back and he forgot the promise, and for years he went on. Then he said, "I've just one question: Can you have a second bite of the cherry?" I could only say, "I believe you wouldn't be here unless the Lord was giving you that chance of a second bite. Now he is giving you another call."

He said, "Right," and went away. He didn't say anything more, but the next Sunday he came into church looking like a cat with ten tails, and he was so full of the joy of the Lord. But only twice in that man's life had he had that opportunity, when God said: Come, I want to come into your life. Come when you are called. It is those who hurry down the tree, who hear Jesus say, "I'm coming to you today" who respond – no delay, no questions of what it may mean, no worrying about the changes that will follow, just: He wants to come, I must hurry and fling the door open. If you miss those opportunities, there is no guarantee they will come again. If Zacchaeus had not hurried down that day he would never have had another chance because it was the last journey of Jesus to Jerusalem and he would never pass through that town again. He had come through it frequently, but this was the very last time. He was going to his death in a few weeks and Zacchaeus's last chance was there.

So he hurried down, he got on with it, and he accepted Christ while he could. When salvation is welcomed in, then it is also worked out, and we move now to the other side of salvation. If a man is really converted, it begins to show very quickly and it showed in Zacchaeus. These were not things he was doing to earn his way to heaven. These were things he was doing because he was now on the way there. The things that you could not have persuaded Zacchaeus to think of doing before, he now did gladly of his own free will.

The first thing we see is benefaction. Instead of being a greedy, grasping man, he began to give. He began to share; he began to think not of his own wealth but of other people's poverty. Fancy that – the poor must have been astonished. He didn't say, by the way, "I will give to the poor." He used the present tense, "I give," which means he was already doing it.

The second thing that happened was restitution. Even

Luke 19

though you have been forgiven all your sins, this may lead you still to try to put things right. You are right with God therefore you desire to be right with men – it follows. One of my dearest friends is a farmer in Northumberland, a man called Peter. I remember the day he was converted. It was in a tiny stone-built Methodist chapel. It was a young farmer's club service, and I found myself speaking to all them, and that night Peter came to the Lord. We had some great times after that. We used to hold harvest festival services in his fields when he got the crops in and it was tremendous. One day he came to me and said, "I've just had to do something. I've just been reading Luke 19. As I read it I remembered that I had sold a cow to the neighbouring farmer, and I had lied about its age, and the farmer should have known better, looked at its teeth or something, but he didn't. He bought the cow and therefore he paid more for it, as you would pay more for a cow that was wrongly dated." So Peter had been back to him and given him the difference in value and said, "I've got to do this," and the farmer said, "You're a fool, I've never noticed."

Peter replied, "No, I'm not a fool. I'm a Christian." There is proof: if salvation is worked in, it works out.

This was the proof that something radical had happened. It is the best evidence of all – a life that has changed. I remember a fourteen year old girl called Sandra who said to me, "I want to be baptised."

I said, "Well Sandra, would you mind if I asked your parents what they think of your Christianity?"

"They're not Christians."

I replied, "They'll really tell me. And would you mind if I asked your schoolteacher if you're a Christian?"

"But she's not a Christian."

"Never mind, would you mind if I asked?"

So I asked the parents: "Hmm, if she'd help with the

washing up I'd think she was a Christian!" That was the mother's response.

Teacher's response: "Hmm, I don't see anything in her at work, and her attitude to homework doesn't show that she's a Christian." That was her reaction.

So I said, "Sandra, it's not showing yet, so I think perhaps we'd better wait a bit."

Do you know the outcome of that? One year later I baptised Sandra, her father and her mother. It showed, and that is one of the few occasions when I have baptised a household, for that was the complete family. Sandra is now serving the Lord overseas. It shows.

"Today," said Jesus, "Salvation has come...."

Zacchaeus taxed himself very heavily. To repay fourfold was the heaviest penalty of the law for robbery with violence. Straight robbery – you had to pay much less. It was usually twenty percent interest if you restored it straight away. It went up to maybe fifty percent if you didn't or if you had lost what you had stolen.

One of the loveliest statements in the Bible comes now. You will not find it in any other religion: "The Son of Man came to seek and to save that which was lost." Do you know what, "lost" means now? You can be lost living in a fine home with a big bank balance; you can be lost to God.

An evangelist was speaking to students in Cambridge and one of them said to him, "I've been looking for Jesus for so long and I can't find him," to which came the reply, "Isn't that strange? He's been looking for you for so much longer than that. However did you miss each other?"

The real truth is that I am only a Bible teacher because Jesus went looking for David Pawson. You are only reading this because Jesus went looking for you.

Does that mean it doesn't matter how I live now? Does that mean I can do what I like? "I'm on my way to heaven,

Luke 19

Hallelujah! It's all-great! Everything's going to be mine one day in Jesus, so who cares anyway! I'm saved." Does it mean that? I'm afraid it doesn't. We begin to have eternal life now in Jesus, but that does not mean that we can sit back and say, "It's fine. I'm saved, everything's going to be great." No, there is still judgment to come.

What Jesus taught here is based on historical fact. In the year AD 6, King Herod the Great died. He was a horrible man – he had killed the babies at Bethlehem. He was the one who hated Jesus at his birth and wanted to get rid of him. This Herod had wanted his son Archelaus to inherit the land and to be king, but the Romans were then governing, so Archelaus had to go all the way to Rome to ask the emperor for the kingdom. While he was away he delivered his castles and his treasury to his servants to look after and to do business while he was gone. It would be a long journey to Rome and back. While he was gone, some rebellious Jews who didn't want the son of Herod on the throne, got together a petition and sent a protest separately to the emperor, to stop him being king. The emperor decided to give Archelaus half the kingdom, and his two brothers the two other quarters.

So Archelaus came back in AD 6, and asked how his servants had managed his wealth during his absence. Those who had done well he gave posts in his cabinet to govern. Those who had not done anything with his wealth he removed from office. He allowed them to go on living in the place but they had no responsibility. Those who had sent that protest and deputation saying, "We don't want this man as king," he had executed. Jesus took this historical event and taught us that it is how he will act when he returns.

There are those who will have used gifts and opportunities faithfully and continued loyally in his service, and have something to show for what they had been left – they will be given a position of real honour and responsibility in the world to come. But there will be those who have done nothing with what they were given. There will be the judgment seat of Christ for Christians. What a motive that gives you for getting on with the job. Note that he only gave them a gold coin. It was not much to entrust. He is teaching us that even the smallest gift matters.

There will be those who do not want Jesus as King. He has gone away to receive a kingdom and he will come back as King, and he will reign on this earth. One day all the kingdoms of this world will become the kingdom of our Lord Jesus Christ. Hallelujah! At last, a worthy ruler of the world. One day he will come back, let no one be in any doubt. Whether the people believe the Bible or not makes no difference, he will return. When he comes back, those who didn't want him to be King will have to die. That doesn't mean that they become extinct. You don't cease to be when you die. It will mean they cannot live in the new heaven and the new earth that he is coming to bring.

In other words, if you don't want Jesus to reign in your life now, there's no place for you in his kingdom then. How could there be? Which makes this life what Keats called "the vale of soul-making". It makes this life the valley of decision.

19:28-48

The triumphal entry which has been celebrated by generations of believers in the commemoration that is called "Palm Sunday" was a day of tremendous emotion, because although it started fairly quietly it became a very joyful day then suddenly, in the middle of all the joy, there were tears shed publicly. The whole atmosphere changed and then there was hatred, envy and malice stirred up in the excitement. The whole day is a kaleidoscope of human feelings. I want you to enter into it in heart as well as in mind, to try to understand what was happening.

Luke 19

So let us paint the scene. Jerusalem is like a nightlight in a bowl. It stands on a hill which would be quite dramatic by itself but it is overshadowed by a ring of hills all around it, higher than itself. The rim of the bowl is only broken at one point in the southeast, where the brook Kidron breaks through the rim to get down to the Dead Sea. Here on the eastern side of the city, the high point of the rim of the bowl is the Mount of Olives.

So you go from the city of Jerusalem, from the temple, down into the Valley of Kidron, up past the Garden of Gethsemane, over the Mount of Olives, and from there you look fifteen miles due east and the land drops away from you all the way down to the deepest point on the earth's surface, Jericho, through a barren wilderness. Just over the top of the Mount of Olives, nestling on the eastern side, out of sight of Jerusalem which is the other side of the Mount of Olives, there are two villages: the one nearest the summit is Bethphage, and just a little below it, Bethany. That was the nearest place that Jesus came to having a home during the three years of his public ministry. Two sisters and a brother lived in that place and Jesus spent the night with them whenever he could when he was passing through.

On this occasion in the month of Nisan—the fourth month of the year, which roughly corresponds to our month of April, they had all made the long journey from Galilee in the north, across the Jordan, down the Rift Valley to Jericho, then up that long climb of three thousand six hundred feet over fifteen miles to the little village of Bethany. From there they were within striking distance of Jerusalem and they had come for Passover. Something like two million people would be camped on the hills around the rim. They would be facing inwards, camping where they could wake up in the morning, and look out at the temple and look on Jerusalem. The whole thing was so exciting; it was the biggest event of the year.

There were crowds waiting, and one of the things they were discussing was whether Jesus would dare to show his face in Jerusalem this Passover – especially those pilgrims from the north where Jesus was so popular, where they wanted him to be king, were wondering. They would be camped on the slopes of the Mount of Olives debating this. Do you think he will take the throne? Do you think he will unite our land again? Do you think he will throw out the enemy occupying forces?

On that day, Jesus and the disciples got up and began the journey to Jerusalem to go and visit the temple. As they left Bethany, Jesus said that he was going to ride. It is the only occasion in the whole of the Gospels as far as I know when Jesus rode on land – the only time he asked for a mount – and the disciples, knowing him, would be aware that something special was in his mind because Jesus would never have ridden on the back of an ass and let the disciples walk. He wasn't that kind of person. If he had felt tired, he would have thought of getting them an ass too – I am quite sure. So the fact that Jesus declared his intention to ride meant that something special was going to happen, for when you ride into Jerusalem it is always for a purpose, and usually a military purpose.

Many have ridden into Jerusalem to conquer – coming in power to reign. The crowds would quickly have become excited that he was riding, but the tragedy was that they did not notice the animal he had chosen to carry him. They had eyes only for the one who was riding. An ass would have been seen as the wrong thing to ride in on if you were coming as a conqueror. An ass is no use in battle and is never used in that way.

In the First World War, Jews offered to fight with the British Army to remove the Turks from Jerusalem. In a barracks in Egypt, the first Jewish legion was formed. The

British Army was asked if they could become a crack unit that would really be able to fight in Palestine. They wanted to become a commando unit and to be cavalry. The British authorities gave them some mules and the two Jewish leaders were very much exercised about this. One of the Jewish leaders, Jabotinsky from Russia, said, "This is an insult, to give us mules." So he refused to take them on but the other man, Trumpeldor, said, "It's the beginning of our forces so let's start with the mules." They were then sent to the bloody battles of Gallipoli, where they were simply engaged in taking the supplies to that ill-fated expedition, driving their mules over the mountains. Finally, of course, after nine months, that disaster came to an end. The British had to withdraw. The Jews slit the throats of their mules and thus came to an end the first part of the modern Israeli army, the Zion Mule Corps. But a mule was half a horse, it was only half an ass – and yet they felt it was an insult to go to war with mules.

Jesus said, "Go into that next village and you will find an ass. It's not even broken in yet, nobody's ridden on it but bring me that ass." The tragedy is the people didn't look at the animal; they missed the whole message of that day. They should have known the scriptures better. When Jesus did anything, he nearly always referred to the scriptural background, quoting a text. When he cleansed the temple, he quoted Jeremiah. Here he is going back to the prophet Zechariah who, hundreds of years earlier, had said, "Jerusalem, Jerusalem, your king is coming to you but he'll come meek and lowly, riding on an ass."

At this point I notice that Jesus exercises his divine authority over men, over animals, over everything. Only one who is God has the right to say to a person, "I need your property." Only one who is God can control an animal that has never had someone on its back. The authority of the

King comes through: "the master needs him." It might just be that the Lord Jesus will say to you, "I need something from you." He doesn't say "please", he just says, "Tell him the Master needs this." If he says, "I need you, I need your house, I need your car, I need your job, and I need your money" – the master needs it and there is nothing more to be said. He takes complete control of the situation.

Now the procession is winding up over the top of the Mount of Olives and they come within sight of the crowds. Already the disciples know it is a royal procession. Already they are taking off their jackets and putting them down in the road, and you only do that for royalty. Over the top Jesus comes, and the crowds in the camps would have seen and understood – and suddenly it was all happening.

Suddenly people realised that the day they had been awaiting for a thousand years had come. It is very difficult for us to realise how long Jews are prepared to wait for something. We tend to want things straightaway. We tend to get very impatient if we don't see the answer to our heart's longings quickly, but the Jews are prepared to wait century after century after century. Parents are prepared to tell their children about a hope in their hearts and say, "It might come in your time or your children's time or your grandchildren's time, or your great-grandchildren's time but don't let this hope go." For two thousand years now the Jews held the hope that they would get back to Jerusalem. Their greeting at Passover time to each other was, "Next year in Jerusalem." Now they have got Jerusalem.

I recall VE day, 5th May 1945. I can remember the singing and dancing in the streets, and the crowds in London. We had waited just six years for that day to shout, "Freedom and peace." What an excitement! That was only six years but when you have waited one thousand years for something and it happens, you just take off. You rip the trees to pieces, you

Luke 19

wave the branches about, and you lay your hands on anything you can. The crowd ripped branches off and waved them, and they began to shout. I want you to get the excitement of this great day.

What had they been waiting for? They had been waiting for another king as good as David – the king who a thousand years earlier had given them peace and prosperity, under whose reign the kingdom had stretched to its limits; the king under whose reign they all felt secure because he was a humble man of the people and a man after God's own heart; a man with wisdom, who could kill giants and could lead them to victory; a man who had suffered as they had suffered; who wrote hymns of praise for the people to sing; a king who was musical, who pulled out his stringed instrument and sang songs about the Lord to them. He was a king who was ideal. For a thousand years, they had had a very sad history of civil war, invasion, and deportation. They had a history of being a little country overrun by Assyrians, Babylonians, Persians, Egyptians, Syrians, and by Greece and Rome. They had never had their land to themselves again since David – never such peace and prosperity.

Down through that millennium there was passed from father to son, and son to grandson, this hope: one day there will come riding into Jerusalem a king. Now do you understand why on that day the crowds took off? Do you understand why they got so excited when they saw this man who was already rumoured to be fit to be a king, when they saw him riding in to crowded Jerusalem? So they began to shout and sing and let off all the steam that had been bottled up through those centuries. Of course, Jesus would have made the perfect king for them. He was a wonderful teacher, he could always decide the right thing to do in difficult situations, he loved children, he was fair, he was wise, and he loved the ordinary people. He would have put those hypocritical religious leaders firmly in their place. He could even raise the dead. If you had the chance for a prime minister like this, how would you vote in the next election? If you could get a hold of a man like that to rule over our country, wouldn't you vote for him straight away? There was no doubt in their minds what was happening. Again I must remind you that everything they said and did revealed their minds and hearts. The crowd shouted, "Hosanna!" That doesn't mean hello, it doesn't mean hail, hosanna means "save now" – get on with the business now, get us out of this mess now, get on with it. Hosanna, hosanna – it is a plea; it is not praise, it is a prayer. All the things they said, "Blessed is he who comes in the name of the Lord...." "Son of David" –do you notice all the language is saying the same thing? What they did was significant.

The last time they had broken off palm branches and spread them on the roads outside Jerusalem had been well over a hundred years earlier for a man called Simon Maccabeus and his son Judas Maccabeus, who set them free from the Greeks for just about fifteen years. The last time they had taken off their coats and thrown them down in the road was when a man called Jehu came to Jerusalem to be king and drove furiously down the streets. There is no doubt what they were thinking at that point. They thought: at last it is all coming true and at last we have got the king. The throne of David is no longer vacant. At last, we are going to get rid of all the quislings and the underground movement. At last we are going to get rid of all the violence in the streets. At last we are going to get rid of all the cruel punishments. At last we are going to get rid of those hated enemy soldiers patrolling the street corners. At last, we're free. On that day it was stark nationalism – and Jesus knew that he had to let that steam out. He knew that there had been so much bottled up for centuries, he just had to take the cork out of the bottle.

Luke 19

The Pharisees didn't like it one bit and Jesus said, "You cannot tell these men to be quiet." If he had tried to keep them quiet there would have been a riot. The very stones on the road would have started shouting. At best, maybe the Pharisees feared that the Romans would come and stamp it out – or maybe it was sheer envy that they had never been received like that themselves. I don't know what their motive was but they tried to stop it.

Jesus told the Pharisees he was not going to stop it, even though they did not understand what was happening. How few of them looked at the ass, but every one of the four Gospels tells us very clearly in detail that it was an ass and running alongside was its colt. They emphasised this detail. Why? Because it shows that the people didn't understand what was happening. Jesus had not come to fight the Romans, he had not come to use physical force to regain the throne. If he had, he would have chosen a horse.

When Jesus comes back the second time he is going to come riding on a horse. You will find that in Revelation 19. That is because he is coming to stamp out evil, using force to do so. But when he rode in that day, he was not coming to do that. Jesus came in on an ass, and a more peaceful animal you cannot find. Can you imagine going to war sitting on the back of an ass? It is not even dignified. You jog along and you look too large for the beast, your legs hang down so that your feet nearly touch the ground. It is not used in royal processions.

Study the ancient monuments in the British Museum and you will never see a conqueror on an ass. You see plenty of cavalry, plenty of fine chargers snorting down the great wide procession way but never an ass. How simply Jesus came that day, winding down the lane that comes from the Mount of Olives, on an ass, and they missed it. So Jesus bursts into tears. This is an extraordinary moment. The term used in the

Greek is the strongest word – it means sobbing your heart out. As he comes towards Jerusalem, Jesus shook with sobs. Why? Thousands of people were welcoming him, praising God. At his birth the angels in the sky said, "Glory to God in the highest and peace on earth to men in whom he is well pleased." Now that is echoed back and the crowd is shouting, "Peace in heaven and glory to God here." They turned it all around and they are sending back an echo of praise. Isn't Jesus thrilled? Isn't he happy about this? No, he is very sad. Jesus didn't mind showing his feelings in public. We do, but he didn't. He wept and he sobbed and he shook. People must have thought he was being overcome. Sometimes at weddings I notice people cry. It is a funny mixture of joy and sadness, isn't it? But people are crying out of joy. Maybe people thought he was so happy, so moved; so touched by all the Hosannas that he was weeping with joy. But no, he wasn't. Let us realise that Jesus often sees things totally differently from us. The things that may excite us and get us all worked up may cause him deep sadness and we have got to ask why that is. What did Jesus see that other people didn't? What was wrong? The answer is that they thought it was a day of triumph but he saw it as a day of tragedy. They thought it was the end of their troubles but Jesus could see it was the beginning of their troubles. Why? The reason is very simple: they did not understand what makes for peace. What is your idea of peace? What picture does that word bring to your mind? A sunny Sunday afternoon in a deck chair, in a garden with high hedges and birds singing – is that your idea of peace? Two artists were commissioned to paint a picture to be called "Peace" for the foyer of a political building. One of them painted a draft picture which showed a woodland scene with the sunlight streaming through the branches onto the bluebells below. There was not a leaf stirring in the wind and he called it "Peace". The other artist painted a cliff, and the waves were beating against the foot of this cliff and the gale was blowing it and blowing the grass and the shrubs on the top of the cliff sideways. The whole picture was in turmoil and movement. Right in the middle of the picture, halfway up the cliff, was a bird sitting on a nest.

When that great Indian Christian, the Sadhu Sundar Singh was converted, a gang of his enemies took him and tied him to a stake and covered his body with leeches to suck his blood until he died. They found him still alive three days later. They set him free and the leader of the gang asked him, "Why is there such peace on your face?" If only we knew what made for peace. The things we think make for our peace: our comfort, health, enough money to live on, a pleasant home, family around us, children who love us and whom we love, security, our old age provided for, a bungalow down in the West Country – these are the things that we think make for peace. During wartime we think: if only we could stop the war, stop fighting and stop bloodshed.

Something that makes for peace is when you have got the wrongs put right in your own life. There will be wars and rumours of wars yet.

So the crowd has the wrong idea and it is no accident that this same crowd that shouted "Hosanna", a few days later shouted, "Crucify". Why? Because a crowd always turns on those who will not give them the peace they want. That is the tragedy. So Jesus saw what that nationalism would lead to. Jerusalem would be under siege. Enemies would be all around it, striking down into that city. Every single detail of that vision came true forty years later. Titus marched on Jerusalem. He camped on the next hill round from the Mount of Olives, another hill from which you view the city and he called it Mount Scopus – the Latin for view. From that viewpoint he surveyed the city and deployed his troops around it. Finally there were Jews jumping into the flames of the burning buildings to avoid being captured by the Romans. The city was pulled to the ground.

The reason why the crowd missed their opportunity was that they did not realise when God came to save them. He had come to save them. Up the hill the little ass went, down the road to the Kidron Valley – just the Garden of Gethsemane there – up towards the Golden Gate which is now bricked up and will remain bricked up, the only gate that is bricked up in the whole of Jerusalem but it was open then. It is the gate of the king, and up that slope he came towards the gate, and when he came through the gate, the crowds all expected him to turn right. Instead he turned left. Now what is the significance of that?

To the right was the fortress where the Romans were garrisoned. To the left was the first court of the temple, the Court of the Gentiles, where anybody from any nation of the world could come and pray – but in Jesus' day you couldn't pray there at all because there was noise, there was smell and there were animals all around. There were money-changers. There were people sitting at tables who were selling items for sacrifice at exorbitant prices to the pilgrims. The one place that should have been a quiet place of prayer, where anybody in the world could come and pray to the God of the Jews, was so busy and you could not pray there. It was then that Jesus used force. Dismounting from his ass, he picked up a whip and he used it on Jews. Now that is the surprise of that day; that is the shock to the people. Jesus is teaching, in effect: I came not to deal with the other people, not to deal with all those you think are to blame for your troubles, not to deal with those who you think have robbed you of your peace; I have come to deal with *you*.

My message is a very simple one. The Lord wants to deal with his people first. We are very conscious of the troubles of the world. It is very easy for us to blame this group and that

Luke 19

group for throwing bombs and causing trouble. But the Lord would say: I have come to save you. There is something in us that wants to be saved from everybody else but not saved from ourselves. There's something in us that says, "Jesus, don't change *my* life." He meant your life to be a house of prayer. What have you made of it? He came to save us from that which is robbing us of peace with God, and peace within ourselves. Let the Lord deal first with anything that may have removed your peace; to remove not the problem first but a self-life that robs us of peace in every situation, that has not been quiet before God, that has wanted to be free from trouble but not free from sin – a life that has been more concerned about physical health than spiritual health and holiness; a life that has been more concerned that things should work out as well on earth as we expect them to in heaven; a life that shrinks from the cross and wants a cushion.

Jesus comes to save us from our sins – then we can tackle the other problems and begin to talk about putting the world right and consider all the matters of our circumstances – that difficult boss, that house that is too expensive or inadequate for your family. Then we can deal with that physical handicap you are struggling with, but first let us deal with that inner temple of your spirit. Let us get that clean. Let Jesus put his people right.

We are not so excited about that and I can guess that that is the point at which the hosannas began to fade – as soon as he turned left, as soon as he picked the whip up, and as soon as he began to attack Jews with it, the hosannas would die away, all the excitement would go, and the crowd would be puzzled and sullen, turning away and saying that he was not going to do it – that he was not going to bring them peace, but upset and disturb them.

Very patiently, Jesus cleared out of the temple what should not have been there, and what dynamism he must have had.

One man with a whip to get rid of all those people! Then he taught morning after morning after morning, trudging over the Mount of Olives to that temple. He taught the people because teaching is what we need if we are to be saved ourselves. Day after day, he taught them, answered their questions and tried to show them that the real fault was in them. He didn't talk about the Romans, he didn't talk about Herod, he didn't talk about Pontius Pilate but about the good news.

Invite him to cleanse the temple that is you. Ask him to put you right so that you may be a centre of your peace in the world and let him reign on the throne of your heart. Don't shout with the world to be free from this, that, and the other trouble – rejoice in the peace that you have been given. Have peace in your heart – whatever is troubling you, whatever hopes and dreams you have that maybe you have thought were going to come true and haven't. Whatever disappointments you may have had, Jesus is talking to you quietly about the things that need to be put right – that is what he really wants to do.

Note

[1] There are many facts about judgment that the Bible states clearly. I have dealt with some very important questions about salvation in my book entitled *Once Saved, Always Saved?* and about the doctrine of hell in *The Road to Hell* (both published by Anchor).

20

Read Luke 20:1–21:4

The moral of this passage is: never argue with the Lord – you will lose. Habakkuk the prophet is a classic case. He argued with God and got completely tied up by the Lord in reply. We first have three attempts by other people to challenge Jesus; indeed, to trap him so that he would say something that would get him into trouble; then we turn to Jesus himself, who three times initiates something. So we have three things said to him and three things said by him. All this took place in the temple, where he was bound to be reported on to all the leaders of the nation.

The first question they asked Jesus was, "By what authority do you do all these things?" He had just cleansed the temple and single-handedly cleared all the money changers out. This was because there were Roman coins and Hebrew coins in circulation and most people had some of both. Only Hebrew money was allowed in the temple and therefore they had to change their Roman money into Hebrew money to put some in the temple treasury – that is the background.

Now he responded to the question with a question in return. That is a clever device if you are discussing anything. Jesus asked, "By what authority did John the Baptist work? Was he authorised to do what he did by man or by heaven?" His questioners dared not answer, because if they said heaven gave him authority he would immediately ask them why they didn't believe him – because they certainly didn't. If they said human authority, they would be trapped by their own words.

In fact, God the Father had sent both John the Baptist and Jesus. Jesus then told them the parable of the vineyard which showed them what they wanted to know, because Israel was often seen as a vineyard, and the owner of the vineyard is God. This parable really accused them of killing the Son of God because, Jesus said, the owner of the vineyard sent servants at the time of harvest because he expected some of the produce as rent. Each of the servants he sent was cruelly treated, killed and sent home with nothing. So, Jesus said, the owner of the vineyard finally said instead of the three servants I sent to collect the rent and they were badly treated, I am going to send my beloved Son. Surely they will respect him. Of course the answer was they didn't respect the son any more than the servants, and they said: If this is the son, we'll kill him and we'll inherit the vineyard – there will be nobody else to inherit it so it will be ours. Jesus was saying: God sent me to you, his vineyard, and you are planning to kill me already so that you can have the vineyard to yourselves. That was the answer to their question: God had given him authority to cleanse the temple of the money changers.

He then quoted Psalm 118:22 – "The stone which the builders rejected has become the capstone" – the most important stone of all which holds the arches together at the top. It is the top stone. The builders won't have it, but he has become the most important stone of all, and anyone who falls over it will kill themselves, and anyone on whom the stone falls will be crushed. In other words, he is saying to the tenants: the one you have rejected will become the most important person in your life.

By the way, in discussing all that Jesus was saying, we are discussing the one who will decide *our* future, and that is why your attitude to the stone the builders rejected – to

Jesus – is going to decide whether you go to heaven or hell. That is why we study the life of Jesus – to get to know the person who is going to decide our future.

The next question he was asked was a really tricky one – What do you think about paying taxes to Caesar? That was a red hot question: if he had said they shouldn't be doing that, they would report him to Rome and he would have been in trouble. If he approved giving taxes to Caesar, his popularity with the people would go to zero. He asked for something; our translations say he asked for a penny but he asked for a denarius – a silver coin which was a day's wage then. It bore the face of the emperor. He held it up and asked whose face and inscription was on it.

"Caesar's."

He taught them: "Give to Caesar what belongs to Caesar and give to God what belongs to God." He was throwing the challenge back – are you giving to God what belongs to him? Well then, give to Caesar what belongs to Caesar – his money, his wages which you are using, and give to God what is God's. Again, they had no answer to that one.

Another group listening to Jesus were the Sadducees. They were the liberal leaders of Jerusalem and they didn't believe in resurrection – they didn't believe in the supernatural side of scripture. They denied the miracles. They came to Jesus with an invented problem intended to trap him. They referred to a practice called Levirate marriage which was started by Moses: if there were a number of brothers and one of them married and he died, another brother had to take over the wife and raise up children for his name, to preserve the line. An old Jewish custom, today it doesn't apply except among some really conservative Jews. Their artificial problem was this. They said there were seven brothers in a family. The first brother married, he died, so the second brother took over the wife, and again he died childless, and she went right through the seven brothers, was married seven times, all childless. They asked: in the resurrection – which they didn't believe in – whose wife will she be? It was as much as to say: now we've set you a problem; you believe in the resurrection as the Pharisees do, then whose wife will she be?

One of the most difficult questions I was ever asked came when my elder sister was dying of cancer, her husband having died of cancer not long before, and the question my sister asked me was: "Will I soon be with my husband again?" I really got tied up in my answer because marriage is only for this world and only for life. In my marriage, my wife and I vowed "until death us do part", and that is something that many husbands and wives refuse to face when their spouse dies. So my sister's idea of heaven was: "I'll be with my husband again." But in heaven we shall not be married. We shall be brother and sister with a lot of other brothers and sisters. The marriage relationship only survives until one partner dies and then the marriage has gone. I remember fumbling for an answer with my dear sister because I couldn't go along with what she was really asking about. She was longing to be with her husband again but her marriage to him was over and all our marriages will be over when one partner goes and the vows we took no longer apply. You will not be reunited as a married couple and that needs to be thought about. The things we say in a marriage service are big vows: for better, for worse; for richer, for poorer; in sickness and in health. That is a big promise to make "until death us do part". Then you will no longer be held to that promise. That is why, for example, you are free to marry someone else as soon as your first spouse dies – not before.

I remember a Baptist pastor whose wife died. On her deathbed she told him who he should marry as soon as she had gone. I conducted that marriage just three or four months later and they were a lovely couple and were very happy indeed. Why did people question me as they did for conducting a marriage so soon after the first wife had died? I was happy to do it. The lady the pastor married was a granddaughter of Spurgeon – who was one of the greatest preachers in London. So that is something that we should think very honestly about.

Jesus told the Sadducees that we will be like the angels, we won't marry or be given in marriage and we won't die; we will live forever – but not as husband and wife. Then he turned it back on them by saying, "Have you never read in the Book of Exodus that God, when he was introducing himself to Moses at the burning bush, said, "I am the God of Abraham, and the God of Isaac and the God of Jacob." He did not say I *was* the God of your fathers, I *was* the God of Abraham and Isaac and Jacob – but I *am*! Jesus was teaching that those three are still alive. God is not the God of dead people but of living people. He is the living God and so he is the God of my elder sister. He *is* her God, not *was* but is. *I Am* is the name of God and that is present tense: not I was – but I Am.

I once asked the Lord: "What's the nearest English equivalent to your name in Hebrew?" I wanted a word I could use when I spoke to him, and immediately to my mind came the word *Always*. God is always; he will always be your God; he is always your helper, always your fortress. It is a wonderful English equivalent. The Hebrew word is Yahweh, which is related to the verb *to be*. It is a participle of to be, and therefore it is usually translated in your Bible as I Am. Jesus took that name and used it for himself and every "I Am" said (seven times) was really saying "I'm God". Those first two words are doubly emphasised in the Greek New Testament – *ego eimi*, and ego means "I" from which we get egotism and *eimi* is "I am", so that when Jesus said "I am" he was virtually saying "I, I am". They took up stones to stone him to death when he said that because they recognised what he was claiming. Only God has the right to say that.

We turn from three things that other people said to Jesus and he now says three things to them, and this is all going on in the temple in one week. Now he challenges others – first about their belief in the Messiah. They all believed as good Jews that one day God would send the Messiah to rescue them from their troubles, and many of them believed this would be a direct descendant of David – a "son of David" – which Jesus was, but he was more than that. This is what he is challenging them about.

He quotes Psalm 110:1 which is more quoted in the New Testament than any other verse from the Old Testament, and David writes, "The Lord said to my Lord, 'Sit at my right hand until all your enemies are your footstool.'" Now he said David calls the Messiah "my Lord". It was the practice in those days when a king defeated another king he insisted that the other king lay down on the ground and he then put his feet on him as a footstool. Some of the Egyptian monuments my wife and I saw when we went up the Nile portrayed the Pharaohs sitting on a big throne and under their feet were images of all the kings they had conquered.

God has promised the Messiah, calling him Lord. Now Jesus points out: how can David call the Messiah "my Lord" if he is only a son of David? You don't get fathers talking to sons like that. He is really saying: you are missing the point of that verse, and the point is that the Messiah is God's Son as well as David's son.

The teachers of the law recognised that this was a very clever treatment of scripture and in the course of this teaching they flattered Jesus. He responded to their flattery by insulting them – an extraordinary thing to do. Remember where Jesus was when he did this. He issued a warning about these teachers of the law with their pride and greed. He pointed out they were proud, loving their status – they loved walking around in their long robes. They loved the chief seats in the synagogue. They loved the seats of honour at banquets. They loved being treated as top people. They were greedy, taking money from widows by promising to pray for them. That is a terrible thing. They were deliberately making money from the most vulnerable in society, because a widow was really vulnerable.

We come to the most famous story of all – the little gift put by a widow into the temple treasury. Jesus was watching people who put their gifts in and he was not asking how much their gift would *buy* but how much it *cost*. That tells you something about Jesus. He said that widow has put everything she has to live on in the temple treasury, and that is the biggest gift of today. He said that is more than all the others have put in – and all the rich people had been pouring money in. That tells you how he values money. He looks not at what it will buy, but what it cost to give, and the widow put in "two mites" and together they would make up a farthing in English money. We don't have farthings now but a farthing was a quarter of a penny.

One famous preacher in the City Temple, High Holborn, London was Dr. Parker, and he once preached on this. A widow in his congregation came up after the sermon and gave him a big cheque. She was a wealthy widow and she said, "The widow's mite". Dr. Parker said to her, "But the widow gave two mites", and she reluctantly wrote out a second cheque for a large amount and gave it to him. Then he said, "But madam, the widow gave everything she had," at which point she turned around and stamped her way out of the church. He was right to remind her that to use the term "the widow's mite" was flippant unless you were giving everything you have.

I think it is rather lovely that the widow in this chapter is known now all over the world because she was so generous.

Have you noticed that Jesus uses the Old Testament on a number of occasions? That is scripture, the Word of God, and if scripture said something, the Lord was saying it. That is why he quoted Psalms – 118 first and then 110. If we follow Jesus, then we too take that same attitude to scripture. It is God's Word, and behind all these studies I share with you my conviction is that scripture is God's Word, and that to quote it properly is to quote absolute truth. It makes a huge difference.

Jesus spends his very last few days of his earthly ministry arguing with people, and the moral is: never argue with the Lord, you are not going to win. He is too clever for you. Many have learned that to their cost. If you argue with God, you are going to lose the argument.

21

Read Luke 21:5–38

Over a quarter of the verses of the Bible contain a prediction about the future. It is a book of prophecy from beginning to end, and altogether there are 735 future events predicted in the Bible! Of those, 596 have already occurred. So just over 80% of all the predictions of the Bible have already happened; and since most of the others are about the end of the world and that clearly hasn't yet happened, it is understandable why. But that is astonishing accuracy in prediction.

We call the passages of scripture that look into the future "apocalyptic". That's from a Greek word *apocalupsis* which means *unveiling, uncovering, revealing what is hidden*. Of course the future is hidden from all of us – our personal future is hidden and so is the future of our land and indeed the world. But there are predictions in the Bible about the future of the world and its end, and Jesus himself has engaged in apocalyptic revelation where he pulls the curtain back and we look into the future. The Bible does say that the test of a true prophet is that what he predicts happens. The mark of a false prophet is that what he predicts doesn't happen.

So now I want to look at nine prophecies that Jesus makes in this apocalyptic chapter – we shall look at the things he predicted, some of which have already happened, others of which have not happened yet but are going to.

The first extraordinary prediction he made was about the temple in which he was teaching. He said that one day every stone would be thrown away and not two stones would be left on each other. The temple was built on a huge platform which extended either side of a hilly ridge called Mount Moriah. Herod built a stone platform on high walls to either side. That platform was so big that you could build thirteen English cathedrals on it and still have room to spare. One side of it is what we used to call the Wailing Wall – where you can still see where they go and pray and stuff prayer requests into the cracks between the huge stones. I measured one of them and it is forty feet long by three feet high and three feet deep. It must weigh a hundred tons – solid limestone. How they ever lifted that into its place in the wall I don't know, but these huge stones were quarried in a cave underneath the temple. You can go into that cave today and see the limestone, which is very soft until it is brought out of doors into the atmosphere, then it oxidises and becomes really hard. You can imagine workers in that cave under the temple carving out these huge stones and then wheeling them out on rollers, then lifting them up to thirty or forty feet, on top of each other. It was an amazing achievement but Herod was a great builder and he was building them a new temple to try to please people and get on their right side.

When the disciples spoke about this magnificent building, Jesus said that the day was coming when not one stone would be left on top of another. That was an extraordinary prediction because it was not yet complete at that time, yet in AD70, the whole thing was pulled down. The Romans were pretty good at demolition. When they decided a building should go, it went, and they literally threw the temple over the edge of the platform. Now you can see the fulfilment of this prediction today because the Jews have excavated the south-west corner of the platform and they have found the first century main street which runs alongside the bottom of that Wailing Wall – which is not the temple, it is just its

Luke 21:5–38

foundation. They discovered that street is paved with huge flat stones and even today it can be seen that the large blocks they used to build the temple up on top of the platform have crashed down onto the street, breaking the paving stones. It is astonishing to see that today, and it is proof that Jesus' prophecy was correct – the whole temple has gone and all that remains is that huge platform and the wall at one side of it. It is one of the most unusual prophecies Jesus made.

Then the disciples asked him when all this would happen – and what signs they would have that it was going to happen. Jesus warned them not to be deceived. Many would come in his name, claiming to be him, claiming that the time was near. If our only interest is getting prophecy fulfilled, if our only interest is in the future and how will we know when it is going to happen, then we are very vulnerable to deception and I am afraid it is happening to many Christians today.

Israel has a history of false messiahs and the last of them was Bar Kokhba in 135AD. He led Jews to rebel against the Romans, who finally wiped Israel out and wiped Jerusalem out. That was the end of the nation of Israel until 1948.

So the second prediction was that there will be deceiving people, dangerous people who will try and cash in on your anxieties and on your speculation about the future.

Thirdly, Jesus moves on to his predictions about the world and he says there will be two kinds of bad news: first of all, national disruption. There will be wars and rumours of wars – wars between nations and wars within nations, and you know that since 1945, which I foolishly regarded as the end of war, there have been many major wars, either within nations or between them. We hear also of many natural disasters – things like earthquakes, tsunamis, famines and pestilence, disease.

Now Jesus here is warning against worrying when all you hear is evil events, both human and natural. You are not to let them get on top of you because all these things are going to happen. On Jesus' lips there is a sense in which they are inevitable. So that tells you what the world news is going to be like until the end of the age – a combination of natural disasters and human conflicts.

The fourth prediction he made concerned his followers, and he said: you are going to be arrested and brought before the courts. You will stand before kings and governors and they will try you, and it will all be for my sake, for the sake of my name. For the first three hundred years of church history, this all came true. And when you study that part of church history to about AD300, the church was constantly persecuted and there were many court cases in which the disciples had to be the defendants. So far, all his predictions have come true.

The fifth prediction he made concerned Jerusalem, and one thing the Bible makes quite clear is that the nearer we get to the end of this age, the more Jerusalem will figure in the news; and we are seeing that. There is something about Jerusalem, and it is the focus of the world. Many people believe that when there is peace in Jerusalem the world will know peace, and certainly it is true that the Middle East is a kind of reflection of the dangerous situation we are all in. "Jerusalem" means the "city of peace" – "salem" is "peace" – shalom means peace. Although it has been called the city of peace, it has been attacked and invaded seventeen times. No other city in the world has been subject to that number of invasions. Time and again, armies have come against it including the Crusader armies from Europe. It has been the subject of Muslim attack; it has been attacked again and again, and you can still trace the ruins of these occupations in the stones of Jerusalem.

So Jesus is saying that they are going to see their capital captured, and it will be trampled on by Gentiles – non-

Jews – until the times of the Gentiles are fulfilled. Again, we have seen that. It has been under Gentile trampling until 1967 and in that year it was liberated by the Israeli Army from the Arab occupation. When the times of the Gentiles are over, then Jerusalem will no longer be trampled down. That is the prediction.

It was of course trampled down by the Romans finally in AD70 and there were many Christian Jews in Jerusalem by then and they believed what Jesus said here: "When you see armies besieging the capital, get out, escape as fast as you can; don't bother to pack your luggage. Go!"' And it would be tough on nursing mothers and pregnant women. They will just have to get up and go. In AD70, all the Christian Jews in Jerusalem left when the Roman armies were surrounding the city, and they escaped to a town on the other side of the Jordan called Pella. In other words, those who believed Jesus' predictions escaped and got away free.

It is clear when we read all the apocalyptic passages of scripture that the fall of Jerusalem in AD70 was a kind of foretaste of the end of the age when Jerusalem will again come under that kind of siege. Zechariah 12–14 tells you all about that final siege. It is going to come and therefore Jesus' counsel is still relevant – get out! Don't stay anywhere near the city when you see the armies around it. Zechariah predicts that an international army – a united nations army – will one day camp around Jerusalem, and when you see that happen, you know that their desolation is near, says Jesus. It is interesting to read Zechariah's predictions of what will happen. Jesus confirms it with his own apocalyptic uncovering of the future.

The sixth prediction (in vv. 25 to 28) is of signs in the sky, when the sun, the moon and the stars are shaken. Jesus' prophecies about the future are also in Mark 13 and Matthew 24 and the three passages illuminate each other and should be studied together. There is no doubt that the final signs of the end of the age are the shaking of the heavenly lights, and of course everybody on earth will be aware of that – when the sun goes dark and the moon no longer reflects the sun, and the stars are shaken. Jesus says there will be terror on the earth. We forget that God is in control of the whole universe, and when Jesus was born a special star was sent to point the way, and when Jesus died, the sun went out for three hours – no ordinary eclipse there. The heavenly lights will reflect what is happening on earth, and when they are shaken, you will know that is the last sign of all – and therefore you will know that the next thing you will see is the Son of Man coming in the clouds back to Earth. That is the one most exciting thing that Christians look forward to: Jesus is coming back here. He promised that again and again. Actually three hundred times that is mentioned in the New Testament. The last sign of his coming will be the shaking of the sun, moon and stars.

When I was a boy, I was taken to a pantomime in a big theatre. I had never been to the theatre before, and I sat there with an excited crowd waiting for it to start, and the first sign that it was about to start were the house lights going out. And I remember my little heart beginning to thump as the house lights went out and as soon as they had all gone and we were in darkness, the curtains parted on a brilliantly lit stage and the action began. That is what it is going to be like. The house lights (as it were) will go – sun, moon and stars, all the natural light will go; and the next thing is the stage is lit up from east to west – more than by lightning according to Jesus. Right in the centre will be the Lord Jesus himself.

Jesus then gave the parable of the trees. He was speaking to people who knew that when the trees begin to bud, summer is near. In the same way, when we see the things he has foretold begin to happen: lift your heads up; your redemption is near, because the Son of God is near. You have seen the last sign of all when the house lights go out, and you know the next thing will be the Son of Man coming in the clouds.

Now this parable of the fig tree has been misunderstood very badly in our day. The fig tree is only mentioned because it is the first of the trees to bud in Israel.

My wife and I were once in Salisbury and we were looking at the trees there. Most of them had not even begun to bud. The willow trees by the river were green. They were the first trees to tell us that summer was near. So if Jesus were telling this parable to us he would say when you see the willow and all the trees begin to bud you know that summer is coming. It wasn't the first time that Jesus appealed to common sense in relation to the natural world. He earlier had appealed to the fact that when you see a red sky in the morning you know it's going to be bad weather – "red sky at night, shepherd's delight; red sky in the morning, shepherd's warning". It is common sense. We have seen it happen so often, we know what is going to result. And Jesus is simply appealing here: when you see the fig tree – the first one – and the other trees begin to bud, you know that summer is near. So when you see these predictions that I have made happening, you will know that your final redemption is near and you won't be caught out and surprised.

The way in which this parable has been misunderstood is that fig trees are thought to be representative of Israel, and this has led many preachers to say that Israel budding – as it has in 1948 and 1967 – tells us that the Son of Man is near. However, that is not what Jesus said. He said when you see the fig tree and all the trees budding, you know that summer is near. He was not picking out the fig tree on its own. If you can look at the trees and know that summer is coming, you should be able to see all these things happening and know that he is coming. And so he turns to a phrase which is a common term for death – so and so has *passed away*. Jesus uses that expression three times now. First: "this generation won't pass away until all these things have happened."

Now of course, if "generation" there means a single generation – thirty years – then he was wrong because it didn't all happen in that single generation. But we realise that the word *generation* in scripture means a number of possible things. It can mean *this breed, this issue, this race* and indeed that is the alternative in my Bible at the bottom of the page. It says there "or *race*". Now some people have found a gleeful delight in suggesting Jesus was wrong, that the generation passed away and it all didn't happen. But when you realise that he was referring to the race of the Jews – he is saying now this race, this breed – *this* race will not pass away until all these things have happened – and of course, he was right and has been right all along. The Jewish race has not passed away, it has survived. All the attempts to wipe out the Jews have failed and some of us have lived through the biggest attempt of all to wipe out the Jewish race – the holocaust – and it failed. It wiped out six million of them but there were twelve million still left, mostly in America. They have survived; and Jesus is saying that Israel will not pass away before all these predictions have come true.

Then he says heaven and earth *will pass away*. The Bible talks about the heavens being rolled up like a carpet. One day you will see that, and everything on earth is going to pass away, so don't get too tied up with those temporal things. Jesus' words will never pass away. That is why it is so important to study them – get to know what he said. His teaching will always be relevant, even after all the dreadful things have happened.

Jesus now teaches on how to survive all this, and he gave some very practical advice: Don't be weighed down with dissipation and drunkenness. That is the world's very

Luke 21:5–38

understandable reaction, but if we simply dissipate our lives and get drunk, that day will close on us unexpectedly like a trap. When people face horrors, one of their reactions is dissipation and drunkenness. He also warned about the anxieties of life. If you get so anxious about the future, you will be caught in a trap. But the way out is to watch and pray. Those are two words that frequently occur in Jesus' teaching. What are we to watch? Be watching what is happening in the world around you; watch for these signs. Some of them have already come and some haven't.

Keep in touch with God – that is the point of prayer. Pray that you may be able to escape all that is about to happen. That is a legitimate prayer. Don't be worrying about it – worry is a dead end. Keep in touch with God. He is still in charge of everything. This is the secret: watch and pray, keep your eyes open and keep your heart open, and if you are in touch with the Lord in charge of it all, that will keep you from falling. So don't become escapist, but stand. That is a favourite verb throughout the New Testament – "having done all, stand." Stand firm!

The last few verses of this chapter tell us Jesus' schedule – his routine programme in the last week of his life: each morning in the temple, teaching; each evening he escaped to spend the night on the Mount of Olives; and all the people came early in the morning to hear him at the temple. Jesus has only days to live and yet he spends those days teaching and his words are very important. Anybody's last words are important, but his last words are more important than anybody else's. That is why we have studied the chapter in which he has made those predictions. And if we watch, we shall see them happen. When you see them happening, don't worry; don't let the anxieties of life get hold of you, but say, "Jesus told me this was coming. Why should I be worried? He knew it all, and he has told us to expect it, so let's believe him and get ready for the future, not try to ignore it.

It is extraordinary that we Christians know enough about the future not to be worried about it, and not to go crazy about it but to wait for it and expect it. This world is not here for ever. Heaven and earth are going to pass away. Just make sure that you don't pass away with it. Watch and pray and you can escape and stand.

22

Read Luke 22

22:1-38
It is interesting that all four Gospels spend a third of their pages on Jesus' death. No biography would ever do such a thing. This tells us his death is more important than all his life and that is why you get snapshot after snapshot of things that happened, almost inevitably leading him towards his death.

The first such "snapshot" concerns Judas – who nearly jeopardised the whole thing. There are two questions we have to ask about him: *how* was he going to betray Jesus, and *why*? This has puzzled commentators for many centuries. Take the how. That is fairly simple: he was reporting to the officials about when they could catch Jesus alone, given that he was very popular, and many loved and supported him. If he had been arrested in front of a huge crowd a riot could have started. The authorities had to find out that week when they could catch him without the crowd, and that is how Judas would betray him. He was the inside man. The officials consented to give Judas money and that is why he did it.

I am afraid there are three things that Satan can offer a man to corrupt him – sex, power and money. That is how men have been corrupted through the ages. With Judas, it was money. He was the treasurer – self-appointed, no doubt; he would have offered to look after the money for the rest. We know from another Gospel that he helped himself to some of the money that came in, and therefore that was his weakness. When the authorities knew him, they said, "We'll give you money." Thirty pieces of silver was the price of a slave, and you moved up socially when you had a slave of your own to do all the dirty work for you. So they were offering Judas enough money to move up to the middle class of people – those who could afford a slave. That is how they got hold of him, so we have answered the how and the why.

It is also intriguing that he was the only one of the twelve from the south of the country, from a place called Kerioth and he was known as Judas Iskerioth – "Iscariot" we call him. The rest were all northerners, Galileans, and the north is where most of the rebels against the Romans came from. Anybody who was from up north was under suspicion, but here it is the man from the south. Jesus had chosen him and he had preached and healed in the name of Jesus.

It is interesting that in the New Testament, of twelve apostles one was a traitor, and in the Old Testament, of twelve tribes one was a traitor – the tribe of Dan. Dan was originally one of the twelve but disappears and is replaced by one of the other tribes being divided into two parts.

In the next snapshot, Jesus tells Peter and John to go and get ready for the Passover, and that is for every Jew the highlight of the year. Still to this day, almost every Jew celebrates Passover – when the angel of death passed over the Jews in Egypt and killed the firstborn of every Egyptian family but not of Hebrew families. But when Jesus sent them to prepare the Passover they had to do it secretly, and Jesus had arranged all that somehow. I don't know when or how he had done it, but he said go into the city and when you see a *man* carrying water.... That is the first clue. You never see a man carrying water in the Middle East, the women do it. That was the first unusual sign. Jesus had told Peter and John to follow the man to the house where he lived and then ask him for a room, and he would show them an upper room, fully furnished. All this shows that Jesus prepares

Luke 22

thoroughly and had already made arrangements; and he said I've *longed* to have this meal with you before I suffer and so I have arranged everything for you. They went and found it just as he had said. They found the upper room fully furnished and ready.

In those days, they didn't have chairs around a table. They had cushions on the floor and reclined at table. That meant your feet were next to your neighbour's head. Your feet might be hot and sticky because you picked up a lot of dirt on them, so whereas nowadays we offer guests an opportunity to wash their hands, it was washing feet that was important then.

So they lay down on the cushions around the big table. Leonardo da Vinci's picture of The Last Supper is wrong. He has them sitting at the table, but they *leaned* and therefore John was leaning with his head on Jesus' breast. He was the favoured one to whom Jesus told secrets, and somewhere round the table all the rest were also reclining.

It is interesting that at that point Jesus talked about a banquet that was coming, which would be in heaven. Jesus always spoke of heaven as a banquet, a big feast. And here we have Jesus telling the disciples that he had longed to eat and drink this Passover with them, and he would not touch it again until it was fulfilled in the kingdom. That is why, every time we have the Lord's Supper, it is done "until he comes". It is a reminder of the meal we are going to have as well as the meal that they did have, so it has a past reference and a future reference.

One puzzling thing is the timing of all this because they were eating the Passover a day early. The first day of the Passover was the following day, and it is interesting that on the following day they killed the lamb and shed its blood specifically at three o'clock in the afternoon. That was the instruction in the book of Leviticus. It was exactly at three o'clock on the following day that Jesus died, and that is why all the language of the Passover lamb is transferred to Jesus in the New Testament. His blood was shed – the Lamb of God was killed at the exact hour when hundreds of lambs were having their throats cut.

Now the next little snapshot, which I call "The Eucharist Established" because Jesus took bread and said, "This is my body", and he took wine and said, "This is my blood". Now the word Eucharist is used in many churches to describe what other churches refer to as The Last Supper or The Lord's Supper – there are all sorts of names for it. But the word Eucharist has come because in Greek "eucharisteo" means "I give thanks" and Jesus gave thanks over the bread and the wine. What is he doing? He is giving them something to remember him by, and you can imagine someone who is about to die doing just that.

The next snapshot is pretty disturbing. He says: "the hand of my betrayer is with me on the table." You can imagine what a shock that was to the other disciples. They realised then it was going to be one of them, so they began saying, "Is it I?" This was now the second or possibly the third time he had warned Judas that he knew what he was going to do, and this was the most pointed warning of all yet.

Jesus was constantly appealing to Judas not to do it, and in this way he was getting very near to exposing Judas to the other eleven. You can only imagine what they would have done if he had told them. They realised that any one of them could do it. But they were already disputing something else. I find it extraordinary that at this late stage they were arguing about who was greatest, and Jesus knew what they were thinking and what they were talking about, and he taught them who is the greatest: whoever serves. "Who is greater – he who sits at the table or he who serves at the table?" And he was saying true greatness among them was going

Luke 22

to be the opposite of true greatness in the world. Worldly greatness is seen when someone who has climbed up the ladder is in control of others – not to serve them but to rule them, like the kings of the Gentiles. The kingdom of Jesus is the opposite of that: you are not to lord it over people, you are not in authority, you are to serve humbly.

Then Jesus has a word for Simon Peter. The name "Simon" means "a reed", which is something that would shake in the wind; it has good roots but it is very slender and flexible above the roots. "Simon" was the disciple's name when Jesus called him. "Simon, Simon ... Satan has wanted to sift you." What does that mean? To sift you like wheat is to separate the wheat from the chaff. It is a simple synonym of setting someone apart, of separating them from others, and Satan wanted to separate Simon from the other apostles. Jesus had prayed for him. What must Peter have felt at that point? Just try to imagine Jesus saying that to you. It is an insight into Jesus because it means that he hadn't been praying for Judas. He had been praying for Simon and that's what helped to make Simon a rock – "petros" (Peter). The reed became a rock under Jesus' help, and Jesus prayed for Simon and he is interceding for us right now. If nobody else is praying for you at any time, remember that Jesus is praying for you now.

Peter was very disturbed by the idea that he would be separated from the others – that horrified him and he said: Jesus, I would go to prison for you, I would even go to death for you. That to me is an amazing insight into Peter – even if everybody else were to go, Jesus would still have Simon Peter. But Jesus said to Peter, "Before the cock crows tomorrow morning you will have denied me three times."

Twice in this chapter we have read about Satan. Satan is in the background here, trying to take the disciples one by one, getting hold of Judas. Satan had entered into him. That is a horrible phrase. So from now on, Judas was controlled by Satan from inside.

Now Jesus has a very strange thing to say. The whole situation was changing. He reminded them that when he had sent them out to go and preach and heal and announce the kingdom, telling them not to take a bag, not to take any food, but to depend on the people they went to, they had never lacked anything. Now, he says to them: when you go out, take a bag, take provision. They were going to need it because the whole situation was now different. He would now be "numbered with the transgressors". They too would now be regarded as guilty of treason, so would need two things they never needed before: provision and protection, if necessary selling something to get enough money for a sword. From now on they would be hunted and hated too.

Readers have not always realised that Jesus was flexible in his advice to the disciples, depending on the circumstances. He could tell them to go out and depend entirely on the Lord for provision and protection, but only in certain circumstances; and in other changed circumstances he tells them to take their own provision and protection. Many have latched on to the first situation and said you must go in faith and the Lord will provide for you and the Lord will protect you. But that doesn't always follow, and we need this flexibility. The danger is that you take Jesus' counsel in one situation and apply it to every situation, and that is a difficult and dangerous thing to do. Jesus was flexible and now he advises them to take a bag of food and to take a sword to protect themselves. That is when one of the disciples said, "Lord, we've already got two swords", and Jesus said that's enough – meaning that's enough of that. We see later that Peter used a sword to slice someone's ear off, and Jesus had to heal it.

Luke 22

22:39-71

So began the most radical injustice in history. The Jewish court should not even have been meeting in the early morning, long before sunrise, because it should have met in daylight, not in the night. Jesus is central to each of the situations which are now described, and the people decide for themselves what their attitude toward him is going to be. That is the shape of the passage.

The first part of the passage shows Jesus agonising in Gethsemane, and we notice three things here. First, he was shrinking from a cup which he was to drink. That is a very interesting phrase because it tells us that Jesus was not as brave as the others who were going to be crucified apparently. He was shrinking from it. Now many people were crucified in those days, including two thieves as we shall see, and many of them went bravely to their death. They did not shrink from it as he did, and he was really in terrific torment about the whole idea, and we only realise why when we look at the word "cup". What was this cup he was so reluctant to drink? As with most things in the New Testament, the clue lies in the Old Testament, where the cup was always a symbol of God's anger and God's wrath – a cup that sinners needed to drink to the dregs. This was surely the cup that Jesus was shrinking from. He realised that for the first time ever he and his Father were going to be separated, and for the first time ever his Father would be angry with him, and he knew what that would be, so he shrank from it. He had enjoyed his Father's company all the way through, and everything he said, the Father was telling him to say. Now there was to be a break in their relationship, and this is due to the fact that the Father was going to desert him. As soon as our sin was put on Jesus, his own Father was going to have to turn his back. That is the secret of the cross and it is a secret that many are reluctant to accept because it tells us that God the

Father himself was going to turn his back on his own Son.

He was under such pressure that the sweat became drops of blood on his forehead, and doctors will tell you that is a sign of extreme stress. Blood was falling on the ground. The first blood of Jesus to be shed for you actually was in the Garden of Gethsemane. What added to his problems was that the disciples were all asleep. They were exhausted with sorrow. They also knew that something terrible was about to happen, and it is again the body's response that when we are really facing horror, a sleep is very welcome. He went back to them and said "Why are you sleeping?" It was the one time he needed companionship, help and support and it tells us here that an angel came and gave Jesus strength. If you don't believe in angels you will have problems with the whole Bible and particularly with the story of Jesus. The angels are there at his birth, at his temptations in the wilderness, and time and again they step in. The only point where they don't, and where they didn't support him was when he died on the cross. But in Gethsemane an angel was standing by him when the disciples were not.

The arrest of Jesus was carried out by the temple soldiers not Romans. Jewish soldiers came to arrest him, led by Judas. So we see Jesus the Jew betrayed by a Jew, arrested by Jews. These were his fellow countrymen. After his arrest in the garden, he rebuked three people.

First he rebuked Judas – "are you betraying the Son of Man with a kiss?" That was the secret sign that Judas had arranged with the authorities of the temple. What a sign to choose because it was an expression of love, a profound expression of loyalty.

Then he had to rebuke Peter. Remember that Peter was one of those who said they had got a sword and Jesus had said that's enough, and Peter now used the sword to slice a man's ear – one of the guards who had arrested Jesus. Peter

Luke 22

remembered what Jesus had said – you now need to take a sword – and Jesus had meant to protect themselves, not to protect him. He never told them to use a sword to protect him. He was talking about their future when they would need protection. Jesus healed the ear and the name of the healed man was Malchus, and he later became part of the first church. That is not in the scripture but we know it from elsewhere.

The third rebuke on Jesus' lips was to the leaders for coming in darkness. He pointed out that he had been openly teaching in the temple daily in full daylight. They could have come and arrested him anywhere, but here they were, coming in darkness. He was shaming them too, because it is only when you want to hide from people what you are doing that you choose darkness rather than daylight. They should not have been doing this, but this was their hour when darkness reigned, and certainly there was a moral darkness here.

Then comes the most tragic story of all I think, when Peter denied that he had anything to do with Jesus, and Jesus had told him that he would do this. That shows that Jesus had the pre-knowledge of God, and so it turned out. In the courtyard of Caiaphas where they were waiting for Jesus to go on trial, a fire had been kindled and people were warming their hands around it. A servant girl said that Peter was also with him (Jesus). Peter denied that connection. Then someone else standing by said: "You also are of them."

"I'm not!"

From another Gospel we know that Peter began to swear that he did not know Jesus. Then, thirdly, somebody noticed that Peter had the accent of Galilee. Peter responded: "Man, I don't know what you're talking about." Then the cock crowed. Three times he had denied Christ.

Three things happened in succession. One, the cock crowed and two, the worst thing of all, Jesus himself, who was there bound and awaiting trial, turned and looked at Peter. That look must have been terrible; it can't have been a look of triumph – I was right Peter, now you see I predicted this. I don't think Jesus for a moment would gloat over being right. I think it must have been a very disappointed look: Peter, you too? The other disciples had all gone. Peter was the only one who had followed and was now in the courtyard of the house of Caiaphas.

That is where I stood with some of our own church members on one occasion, and we all heard a cock crow, and it was a most significant moment. I think all of us were thinking: "Lord, would I have done that?" The answer, of course, is yes.

Why did Peter deny him? I think the only answer is cowardice, and that he was so scared for his own skin now that he was afraid and could not bring himself to acknowledge that he was with Jesus.

The third thing that happened was that Peter went out and wept bitterly. It must have been a dreadful moment for him when Jesus had looked at him sadly.

There is an interesting sequel to this which we get from another Gospel. Just a few days after Jesus' resurrection, Peter went fishing. Typically, Peter couldn't stand hanging around in Galilee waiting for something to happen. They toiled all night and caught no fish. When the sun rose, there was Jesus standing on the shore, though they didn't know it was him, and Jesus told them to throw their net the other side of the boat. It is interesting that this unknown figure on the shore after the resurrection said throw your net the other way – and they did and they caught 153 fish in one throw. Then they realised that the man on the shore was Jesus, and Peter jumped over the side of the boat and splashed his way ashore. On that pebbly shore, which I have visited, Jesus healed Peter's heart. There are only two occasions in the

Luke 22

Gospel where a charcoal fire is mentioned. One was where Peter denied the Lord and the other was after the resurrection where Jesus lit a fire and cooked breakfast for them. When Peter came dashing ashore, all wet, he looked at the fire and remembered, and then Jesus said three times to Peter: do you love me? He was deliberately going through the three denials at the other fire to put it right with Peter – and it must have done that.

There is something even more interesting. There are different words for "love" in the Greek language, and the first time Jesus said to Peter: "Do you love me more than these others?" Peter's reply meant: You know everything; I'm not going to say what is not true, I like you enormously. He wouldn't use the word "love" and so Jesus came down to Peter's level and said: Peter do you like me? Peter said you know everything Lord; you know I like you. He wouldn't say the word "love". Peter was told "feed my sheep" and was made the first pastor of the flock. That is another story after the resurrection, but it is interesting that Jesus said three times to him, around this fire: Do you love me; do you like me? What a master Jesus was at picking people up and healing their hearts.

Let us return to the arrest of Jesus in the Garden. The temple soldiers took Jesus away for trial and one of the perks of being a soldier was that they were free to do anything they liked with the prisoner. It was their privilege to mock prisoners and so they began to mock Jesus, beating and insulting him. The Jews did not torture a lamb before they sacrificed it. So all this was extra. God did predict Jesus' death, and indeed demanded it, but he didn't demand the torture beforehand.

We come to the first part of his trial. Remember it is the Jewish court still that is trying him, not yet the Roman court, and the Jews were determined to find Jesus guilty of blasphemy, for in the Jewish law that was a capital crime. If they could find a blasphemous remark of Jesus he was a dead man. He was being tried by Jewish law, and so three of his titles came up for discussion.

The first was the title "the Christ", and they demanded of him: "Are you the Christ?" Christ is not a surname of Jesus. It is almost the word "majesty" – it is the Messiah, the expected King who would deliver them from all their enemies, and for centuries they had looked for the Messiah to come. There were many false claims to be the Messiah and Jesus warned us about them – those who say "I am he", "I'm the one you're looking for". Jesus was being asked: are you the Christ? Tell us. He said: "If I tell you, you will by no means believe."

Jesus said: "From now on the Son of Man will be seated at the right hand of God." That was the truth. "Son of Man" is a title that was used over eighty times in the book of Ezekiel where it simply means human being, and whenever God spoke to Ezekiel he always addressed him as son of man. But there is one verse in the Old Testament (Daniel 9:27) where there is another Son of Man who is going to come in the clouds of heaven and who will return to heaven after he has been here – that is the Son of Man that Jesus picked up on – not the eighty times in Ezekiel but the one time in Daniel, where it refers to a divine person.

Jesus' saying you will see the Son of Man seated at the right hand of God was a direct claim, so much so that all of them asked, "Are you the Son of God then?" This time he said, "You are right in saying I Am." We have already seen that this was claiming to be the Son of God – "I Am". So at last they had evidence from his own lips, and they said, "What further testimony do we need? For we have heard it ourselves from his own mouth" – which was again illegal. You could not condemn a man out of his own mouth. You could condemn him out of other people's mouths. But we know from other Gospels that they could not find witnesses to agree, and Jesus was put to death not for what he was, not for what he had done, but for what he said about himself. On the charge of blasphemy alone, they thought he deserved to die. As far as the Jewish trial was concerned, it was over. But then they had a big problem. Blasphemy was a capital crime under Jewish law – the law of Moses – but it was not a crime under Roman law, and the Roman occupation of the land had forbidden the Jews ever to execute. They could only execute a person by reporting them under Roman law and this was the greatest injustice of Jesus' trial. The Jews tried him for blasphemy and found him guilty, but that would not have washed with Pontius Pilate who was there as a Roman to govern with Roman law. So they now had to go to Pilate and persuade him that Jesus deserved death. They had now found him guilty out of his own mouth, which is illegal and they could not execute him, for that was illegal in the Romans' eyes. So they had to transfer him to Pilate and not only transfer him but change the charge, and they changed it to treason. We shall see next that they charged him with treason – that he was upsetting everybody and that he was forbidding the payment of taxes to Caesar (which he had not done) and that he was claiming to be the King of the Jews, which of course was seen as treason.

As you can see, these are all incidents building up to the cross, which was the greatest miscarriage of justice in human history. Never was an innocent man put to death as Jesus was, and you can see how they had made up their minds before they tried him that he was going to die. They were determined to get rid of him and that is the real truth of the cross. Yet it was not just men who were doing it, but God. That is the biggest mystery of all until you realise that Jesus who was without sin was dying to pay for everybody else's sins.

23

Read Luke 23

If we were writing this we would have dwelt on the pain of Jesus as those nails were driven through. We would have given a harrowing description of the horror and the blood and the crowds. Yet here we have the Word of God and it is a matter of fact, simple, straightforward account of what happened. There is really not a word of feeling here – no description of the emotions. There are just the facts of what was done and what was said. Though you can't help but have very deep feelings when you read this account, it is faith in the facts that is the important thing.

"We may not know, we cannot tell, what pains he had to bear, but the fact is we believe it was for us that he hung and suffered there." The emphasis in this chapter is on individuals and how they reacted to the facts. There was Jesus on a cross but all that is said is pointing our attention to the various people in the narrative and how they were responding to it or reacting to it—coming towards that cross or running away from it; deeply moved or making jokes.

At some point the Holy Spirit is going to tell you where you would have been that day; that is the group you would have been with; that is what you would have been saying and doing. I want you to be wide open now to the Holy Spirit, and as I take you through this story again, look at each of the people and say: "Lord is it I?"

Not one of us would have had the courage to say, "I'm a follower of his and so you can put me on a cross too." The only others on crosses had been put there against their will. So we won't see ourselves on the cross as we study this chapter. It is a deep truth that we were crucified with him. Jesus is there on the cross alone but you are somewhere else in the crowd.

The charges against Jesus were false. He was being slandered through human lips by the prince of lies himself, Satan.

There are two people that I want you to look at now. One is Pilate and the other is Herod. Pilate is a strange contradiction: a man who wanted to do right but didn't; who knew what he ought to do but couldn't bring himself to do it. We have to ask this question about this enigmatic character: why? Why did this man who had no one above him in that scene, who was the person with power of life and death in his hands, fail to do what he knew he ought to do? He could not plead that he had been given orders. He had no excuse at all. Why then did he collapse? Why did he fail at the crucial moment and become a moral coward?

The answer is very simple: he had a past and he was blackmailed. The crowd was blackmailing him. You see, this man was in his first position of power. He had risen from the very bottom. He had been born a slave but had earned his freedom and he climbed up the social ladder. We know he did it by licking the boots of the man above him and treading on the face of the man below him, and he climbed up. Now he was a governor. I know it was in a tiny little province away at the end of the empire, but he was a governor. He was getting up the ladder and it was as high as he would go. On his way up he had made some very silly mistakes. Twice already since he came to govern these Jews just three years prior to these events, he had blundered.

First he had marched into Jerusalem and into the temple carrying the Roman eagle. I don't know whether he was

Luke 23

aware of the Jewish law about graven images in the worship of God, but it was a blunder. It started a riot and he quelled that riot with bloodshed. It was a bad beginning for a man who showed little sensitivity. The second blunder was when he tried to improve the Jerusalem water supply and built an aqueduct into the city which you can still see today. To finance this expensive project he stole money from the temple treasury. When this was discovered, another riot broke out. He disguised his soldiers in civilian clothes and sent them in with swords underneath their coats. When the crowd became ugly, he let his soldiers loose on them but it turned out far worse than he intended and the blood of Galileans was mixed with their own sacrifices.

Word of these two blunders got back to Rome and Pilate had already had an ultimatum: one more blunder like this, one more mistake in governing these people and you're out of a job. Pilate was on the edge of a precipice and the crowd could say, "We'll tell. You don't give us what we want now and you will be reported straight to Caesar, we'll start another riot, you're finished." This man, because of his past, became a moral coward and he has gone down in history as that. He had a good wife and she had had a dream about a good man, and she said, "Pilate don't do this, it'll ruin you." But he went ahead and did it.

When we say the Creed, apart from Jesus we only include two human beings when we state our faith. We remember the woman who brought Jesus into the world and the man who put him out of it. Pilate eagerly passed the buck to Herod, learning that Jesus had been brought up in Galilee in the north which wasn't really his territory. Actually, Jesus had been born in Bethlehem, Pilate's territory, but that was not known at this stage. So over to Herod he went.

Now Herod was a man of the senses and loved sensations, show and entertainment. He wanted to see Jesus do a miracle;

to see amazing things happen. Herod was prepared to see but not to believe; he was prepared to have his senses titillated but not his faith stirred. He was prepared to have things in this world but not to think about the next. We know from his past and we know from his life that he was a man who lived purely for material things. Jesus was sent over to Herod by Pilate, and Herod was there, full of entertainment, full of material possessions, full of this world.

Do you get the feel of Herod? There is something about him that is disturbing. He is thoroughly worldly. So when Jesus stood before Herod, Jesus kept his mouth tight shut – no answer, just total silence. It is a sad fact that if you are so worldly and so tied up with worldly entertainment, with the things that this world offers, that in fact, you won't hear anything from Jesus. He can't talk to a person like this who only wants the sensation, the exciting thing. Jesus didn't come to bring novelty to people.

Next there is the journey (vv. 26-31) through the streets, the Via Dolorosa. It is a winding road and it puzzles you why, and the answer is very simple. They took the longest possible route through the city so the whole population would see what happened to those who disobeyed the Romans. Marching in front of the poor prisoner there would be a soldier with a big board, and on it would be written his crime so that the crowd might see.

They turned out much as happened three centuries ago when people used to turn out at Marble Arch to watch children being hung for stealing five shillings' worth of bread. Did you know that? There is still a triangle of stones where the gallows of Tyburn stood and where the crowds turned out to see people put to death. It is not long since England had that and I am afraid now we are getting it back again because violence on the screen is just another way of enjoying that and seeing people getting hurt, and getting a thrill from it. We are reverting to the kind of business that happened here – when the crowd enjoys seeing violence. It is only one step from seeing it on the screen to seeing it in reality.

So the crowd turned out and followed. Winding through the streets they went with a soldier, and on that placard was written Pilate's last desperate measure to salve his own conscience: THIS IS THE KING OF THE JEWS. It is a defiant word from Pilate.

Now we notice two more people. First there is a man from north Africa. I don't know why he is there – has he come for the Passover? As Jesus carries the very heavy beam, he can't do it because he hasn't had anything to eat. His Last Supper was his last meal. He has been flogged to within an inch of his life, he hasn't had any sleep, and he falls, and the Roman law was that a Roman soldier could compel any civilian to carry a load for one statute mile – one thousand paces. It was a very gracious man who would go two miles, but the Roman soldier could say, "One mile, one thousand paces, carry this." The soldier, looking around, tactfully thought he had better not use a local person as doing so could cause trouble. So he saw an African, a man called Simon or Simeon. I can see him grabbing him by the scruff of the neck and saying, "Pick that beam up; carry that cross." The African picks up the cross, and starts carrying it. Jesus would come first and so Simon (or Simeon), as he carried the cross, would see the back of Jesus all the way, staggering. I guess he began to wonder what Jesus had done. They had really treated him roughly. The African got interested in Jesus – so interested that he is mentioned twice elsewhere in the New Testament. He is mentioned by Mark in his Gospel and it says, "Simon who was the father of Rufus and Alexander" – obviously known to the early church, Christians. So this Simon became a Christian and his two sons became

Christians. He is mentioned in Acts 13 where he is now in a place called Antioch. There he is part of a prayer meeting that is going to send Saul and Barnabas out. It says that five people were praying and among them was Simon the Niger (meaning "the black") and there he is again. Here is a man who, against his will, was brought into the picture. He came out of curiosity but found himself involved – and so involved that he got related to the man staggering up the hill in front of him, becoming a Christian and a Christian father, and a father of Christians.

They turned a corner and there was a group of women weeping and wailing. They had known Jesus away up in the north. They looked at him now at thirty-three, and they wept for him. Now the one thing that is out of place at the cross is pity for Jesus. We are not told the story of the Passion in order that we may take pity on him. That is what these women were doing as they wept for him. He said: weep for yourselves, not for me.

Then Jesus said this very strange thing which many people have found difficult to understand: If they do these things when the wood is green, what will happen when it is dry? It is the saying of a carpenter. You have to understand woodwork to understand why these words of carpentry burst out from him. After all, there was a beam of wood and a soldier near him was carrying a hammer and nails. These were the tools of his trade, and here he was and he was back in the carpenter's shop. He was imagining and remembering how he would take a piece of wood and it would not be quite dry. It would not be seasoned, as we say. It would still have green sap in it and he would be trying to cut it. As soon as he brought the blade to bear, it wouldn't get through; the wood was green. So you discard that piece and then you take a piece that is dry and seasoned and ripe, then you shape and cut that.

I take this meaning from his words: You are looking at

me and you are looking at a piece of green wood that is not ready to be cut down, not ready to be pierced; I am innocent (green, as we say); what do you think will happen to you when you are ripe for this? What do you think will happen to this city and to you and your children and your husbands and your grandchildren – what will happen to you when you are ripe for the Roman judgment? You see me surrounded by these soldiers with these hammers and nails. They are going to attack my body with those tools but I am green wood. He was looking to the day when their rebellion against Rome would be so ripe that Rome would cut the city right down. He was looking further ahead to the days when the whole world would be so ripe for judgment that people will literally call to the hills and to the mountains, "Fall on us and hide us from the wrath of the Lamb." If they would do this to Jesus when he was innocent, what will happen to those who are guilty? If they would do this at that stage of history, what will happen at the end of history? That is what these words of Jesus are teaching us: Don't think of me, think of yourselves; think of your future, weep for yourselves.

Turn the cross back into your own heart and ask: am I ready for the future, or am I ripening for judgment like a piece of seasoned wood just waiting for the axe to fall? So are we among the women who have had sympathy, or are we like Simon, who has been pulled into it somehow and found himself responding?

I suppose crucifixion is the most terrible death that has ever been devised. I have never seen anybody crucified, I don't know that I could stand it. Crucifixion leads to death but it doesn't kill. Very briefly, it is so to nail a person up that they are torn between two terrible alternatives. One is to ease their breathing by pressing on their legs and taking the weight of their body on their feet and hands so that they can breathe. But that causes such excruciating pain through the nails that it is preferable to relax in which case the lungs are stretched by the weight of the body and breathing becomes difficult, and they fill up with liquid and a man can choke. So he is stretching and bending: trying to ease the pain; trying to breathe. It is a horrible death which usually took three or four days. The record was about seven days a man survived on a cross. For Jesus, it was six hours, which was very short. Pilate was surprised when he found out it was only six hours and that Jesus was dead by three o'clock. But of course Jesus died at the precise moment that God the Father chose for him. In that six hours he went through worse agony than anybody ever went through in seven days on a cross – because he went through hell.

At ten minutes to three he has been on that cross since nine o'clock in the morning when they had put him up with two common criminals to humiliate him. They took off his clothes and they nailed him to a cross.

Now there are two more groups of people. One group is full of mockery and makes a joke of the whole thing and laughs. They include the rulers, soldiers and people in the crowd. The devil had taunted him years earlier when he was painfully hungry: "Save yourself, turn the stones into bread." Now this group were taunting him. We might think that if Jesus had given way to the devil's temptation three years earlier, he would have given way now when the devil, through people's mouths, said, "Save yourself." Jesus could have stepped off that cross easily because he had almighty power. He could have wiped all of them out with one word. There were ten thousand angels hovering above his head that he could call on at any time. Yet Jesus stayed on the cross.

So they went on laughing at his weakness because they thought he was helpless. There are still people today who laugh at Christ, not directly all of them, though some do. I have heard people make mockery of Jesus, and it goes through you like a knife. But they laugh at Christ now by laughing at Christians. They laugh at the weakness of Christianity and they laugh at the poverty of Christians. They laugh at the helplessness of Christians in the world and that is the same mockery: "Save yourself." So the world still treats it as a joke, something to laugh at, something to treat with contempt, slight amusement, ridicule.

One of the criminals laughed too, but the other one didn't. He was convicted of sin – his own. He was convicted of righteousness – Christ's. He was convicted of judgment to come. He felt he deserved it all. Here was a man who had seen the truth. He was the only man in the whole crowd to realise what was happening; the only person who understood the sign above Jesus' head, because when they nailed the body to a cross, they also nailed the label of his crime above him. You may have seen little crucifixes with INRI: Jesus of Nazareth, King of the Jews, in Latin. It was in three languages: Latin, the language of the greatest system of administration the world has ever seen; Greek, the language of the greatest culture the world has ever seen; Hebrew, the language of the greatest religion the world has ever seen. In those three languages, his crime was there: this was the King of the Jews.

The criminal on one side read that notice and believed it: you are a king and you are going to have a kingdom. The faith of this man is incredible – to look at a dying man pinned to a cross and say, "Lord, remember me when you come into your kingdom." There is tremendous faith—the only person who believed that this was the beginning, not the end; the only person who could see through the cross to the crown. And he got a beautiful reply. The word "paradise" is not a synonym for heaven or kingdom. It means a very special part of the kingdom. It is a Persian word meaning "the king's garden", "the palace garden."

This could be your story – if you have seen beyond the cross to the crown, and seen the kingdom that this king is going to have. Lord, remember me.

Every word and phrase is important. The sun went out at midday. It wasn't just an eclipse because it lasted three whole hours – in pitch darkness. Jesus died at three o'clock which was the very hour that knives were raised in thousands of tents and kitchens. A knife was drawn straight through the throat of lambs on that day, the fifteenth of the month Nisan in that year. It was Passover day. The lambs were killed at three o'clock so that they could be prepared for the Passover meal, skinned and gutted to be roasted in the evening. So at three o'clock, the very minute when thousands of Passover lambs were having their throats cut, Jesus died. The Lamb of God that takes away the sin of the world—that was not a coincidence. Jesus had said, "I have power to lay down my life." Believe me, it was Jesus who decided to die at three o'clock and committed his spirit to the Father. He had finished everything he had come to do. He had gone through all the suffering required of him by the Father and more, for there was suffering given to Jesus that the Father never ordered. God required his blood, and that blood was shed.

The veil of the temple was a gorgeously embroidered curtain, forty feet high and many feet wide, which had hung in the temple for centuries, and which veiled God from the common gaze and kept people out. Only once a year did the High Priest go through that curtain and see where God lived and see the glory. It was ripped from the top to the bottom, not by human hands but by divine hands. When it was ripped apart, the priests stared in and there was nothing there. God had gone. He had forsaken the whole scene. That is why it went dark of course – where God is, there is light; where God is not, there is darkness. Hell is dark, it was hell on earth for three hours and the Father had forsaken even

Luke 23

his own Son. He had planned this for our salvation but he had left Jesus alone. So the temple was seen to be emptied.

Now we see the Centurion (our equivalent would be a regimental sergeant major), a big, tough chap in his uniform. He has been in charge of the execution squad. It has been a difficult time with the crowds but he has got his job done. He doesn't like doing it, he is a good man basically. You have to get these things over with. So he got these three on their crosses and he saw them up. He sat down to watch and he had to stay there until they were dead to see that nobody came and pulled the nails out. As he watched he came to a conclusion. As he listened to that man in the centre talking, he began ever so slowly, step by step, to realise the truth. The first step was when he realised that Jesus was a good man. There is innocent blood on our hands; we have actually put to death a man who was innocent. Then from another Gospel we know that he took one more step and said, "This was the Son of God." A Roman soldier was the first Gentile to feel the effect of the cross.

There we see Joseph, a man who had always been afraid of coming right out for Jesus. He had spoken for him in the council, he had voted against his death, he had done what he could but he would not come right out. He is a man who, in a sense, came out into the open when it was too late. He stood up to be counted when Jesus was dead. After Jesus was dead, he asked for the body. Joseph had a tomb and wanted to give him a good funeral.

It is a pity when we realise after someone has died that we wanted to do so much for them. We spend on flowers which the dead person can't appreciate. The nice things we say about people when they are gone – what encouragement there would have been if we had only said them while they were still around. So the funeral was the point at which Joseph of Arimathea came right out. He was a man who didn't like to face the cost. He was a man who would rather talk by night. He didn't want his colleagues to know that he'd had chats with Jesus. So he kept it well hidden. Are you a bit of a Joseph of Arimathea – not shining for the Lord where you work or at home – you have secret talks with Jesus by night? Sometime in the future you are going to come right out for Jesus, but why not now? Why leave it until it is too late? Joseph of Arimathea at last did identify with Jesus, burying him.

We missed out one person from earlier in the narrative. His name is very interesting: Jesus Barrabas. He was guilty of every one of those charges that Jesus of Nazareth was being accused of. Jesus was being accused of rebellion, insurrection, setting himself up as a leader, and Barrabas had done all these things. Barrabas deserved to die but suddenly found himself free. He had been certain to die and now he found himself out in the streets. I often wonder: did he find his way up the hill to Calvary? Did he go and look at the cross that should have been his? Did he touch that cross and say, "I should have been nailed to it"? For Barrabas is like all of us who believe in Jesus. Barrabas was the one man who could stand at the foot of the cross and say, "You're in my place. You're where I should be. What I have done deserved what you're getting."

If you haven't seen yourself anywhere yet, I hope that you will see yourself there now. For the truth is that for what I have done with the life that God has given me, I don't *deserve* to live – and neither do you. But Jesus sealed my pardon with his blood. Hallelujah, what a Saviour! He died instead of me.

24

Read Luke 24

24:1-12
In the 1920s, two Oxford men, Lord Littleton and Gilbert West, decided to spend an entire summer holiday studying the records of the resurrection with a view to proving that Jesus never rose from the dead. Separately they went into the matter in depth. When they met, they embarrassed each other by having to admit that the evidence had convinced them that Jesus rose from the dead. They published a book, a typical long-winded title of that period: *Observations on the History and Evidences of the Resurrection of Jesus Christ*. About ten years later, a young man called Frank Morrison, who was studying law, decided to do exactly the same, realising that if you could once prove that Jesus was in a grave somewhere, Christianity as a religion would collapse. So he examined the evidence, started writing his book to prove that Jesus was dead, and finished up by having to write a totally different book: *Who Moved the Stone?* Morrison, too, was convinced that Jesus is alive.

I have heard Professor of Modern History in Cambridge Herbert Butterfield say that the resurrection narratives convinced him also of the historical accuracy of those who have given us the story of the resurrection.

Dr Arnold of Rugby was also convinced by a study of the stories of the resurrection that Jesus Christ is alive.

If a person does not believe that Jesus is alive, there is only one reason for that: they want to believe that he is dead. They cannot have studied the evidence; they cannot have studied the narratives of those who were there at the time. One of the most striking features of the stories of the resurrection in our Bible is that there are discrepancies between the accounts of Matthew, Mark, Luke and John. It is those very discrepancies which convince us of the truth. If men are making up a story, if they are concocting an alibi, one thing that marks out such an invention is that their stories agree in every detail. Any detective, any magistrate, any judge, any jury will tell you this. But when you study the four Gospels, the very kind of discrepancy that occurs when you have different people witnessing the same sequence of events occurs.

J.B. Phillips, who translated the New Testament into English, produced a book entitled *Ring of Truth* and in it he says that, as he translated these stories, every one of them had the ring of truth in them. Real people, real reactions, real events – he too was convinced.

These discrepancies are not contradictions. When looked at closely, they fit together into a sequence of events which you can reconstruct. The kind of discrepancy is this. Luke says that Peter ran to the tomb. The Gospel of John says that Peter and John ran to the tomb. There is a discrepancy there but not a contradiction. It is clear that both statements are true but the ring of truth comes in that one person noticed Peter and someone else knew that there were two. That is the kind of "discrepancy" that if this story had been invented would not have occurred.

Another one is that Mark says that when the women came to the tomb a shining angel spoke to them. When Luke recorded these events, he says two shining angels came. Discrepancy yes, but naturally one of those two would be the spokesman. Luke mentions both, and Mark mentions the one who spoke. There is not a contradiction there but there is the kind of discrepancy that true witnesses would record. So as we read these accounts the thing that hits us again and again is that this is straight history. These things actually happened and the way the people behaved is the way that we would have behaved in the circumstances.

Have you ever seen a ghost? Have you ever confronted a visitor from the supernatural world? If you have, then I bet you were as afraid as these people were. You would behave just like those women.

If some women came to you in an excited condition and said they had just been to the cemetery and they had seen an open grave and had seen somebody who had walked out of the grave, would you say, "I believe you, thanks for telling me"? No, you would have been excited, maybe overwrought; that is how the men behaved here.

We are reading about real facts. Our faith is squarely based on history. I am so glad that it is because unlike every other sacred book in the world, the Bible is simply a string of historical facts – things that actually happened. We don't follow flights of philosophy, we don't let our fancy take us into the clouds of mysticism. We base our faith on what has happened in this world of ours; things that once done can never be undone. They put Jesus in the tomb and put a stone over it and sealed the stone and guarded the seal, but once Jesus is out of that tomb, they can never put him back into it. History cannot be unwritten.

Now we are going to look at two groups of people. First we are going to look at the women and how they reacted. Then we are going to look at the men and how they reacted. The ladies had the honour of being the first to know that Jesus had risen. In a sense, that offsets and balances two other firsts for women. First, it was through a woman that sin entered the human race. It was through Eve, a woman, that the darkness of Satan first entered into human thinking and relationships.

It is as if God wanted to do something appropriate to respond to that: it was through a woman that salvation first entered the human race. It was two women, Mary and Elizabeth, who first knew that the Son of God was coming to earth, and had come. A woman brought salvation into the human race in the person of the Son of God; and it was to women first that the news of the resurrection was given – to the women who were there because they had plucked up enough courage to come and do something that needed to be done but which was distasteful and unpleasant to do.

I must mention the funeral customs in those days. I want you to understand how the women felt. When a person died, if he was to be given a funeral of honour, his body would be semi-embalmed. Special spices with aromatic and antiseptic qualities would be strapped to the body to counteract the natural process of decay and corruption that sets in so quickly, particularly in that climate. That process of decay really set in on the fourth day in a cool tomb there. Therefore, there was a limited time in which you could counteract that process and try to stop it or try to delay it or try to fill the grave with a sweet smell. So as soon as a person was dead, they would take forty yards of long linen bandage and anything up to a hundredweight of these sweet spices. They would wrap the body round and round, tipping in the spices as they went. It was a loving act, the final thing that you could do for someone. It had been done when Jesus died, but it had been done in a hurry.

When Jesus died, we are told they did wrap his body and we are told that the rich man who gave his own grave had also given some spices which no doubt he had in a cupboard for his own corpse. They had hastily wrapped the body but they only had three hours between Jesus' death and the beginning of the Passover. Jesus died at three o'clock in the afternoon and the Passover began at six, at sunset. In that time they had

Luke 24

to go to Pilate, persuade Pilate that Jesus was dead, persuade him to release the body, take the body from the cross, carry it to the garden, wrap it up in spices, put it in the tomb, put the stone there, seal it, and do everything before six o'clock that night. They had three hours in which to arrange the entire funeral and the job was not properly done.

I believe Jesus died on Wednesday afternoon at three o'clock. That is the only time that really fits everything said in the Bible, but I would not be too dogmatic. It might have been Thursday, I am almost sure it wasn't Friday. He was three days and three nights by the Jewish calendar in the tomb. Yet by the Roman calendar he rose on the third day, which means that he rose sometime between six o'clock on the Saturday and midnight. It is difficult for us to get into the thinking of Jews whereby the day begins at six o'clock in the evening. So anytime after six o'clock on Saturday evening, Jesus could have been raised. We know he had risen long before dawn on Sunday. The grave had been empty long before the women got there, and they arrived before the sun was up, just at the first light of day, so sometime between 6 p.m. and midnight.

The Sabbath that followed Jesus' death was a high Sabbath, a special holiday for Passover. That would be followed by the weekly Sabbath, the Saturday. So the women were kept from doing the job properly until first light on Sunday morning. It was the very earliest opportunity they could do this. During the Passover, you couldn't touch a dead body or you would be defiled. During the Sabbath you must do no work. So as soon as they could, they got out of bed early that morning and went to complete the embalming. They would only just be in time.

Do you realise that by this time rigor mortis would have set in, and the task of wrapping those bandages around the body would have been very difficult? Do you realise that, having had to wait that long, the process of decay would have begun? Those dear women loved the Lord so much that they were prepared to come even while it was just the beginning of the day and still dark, and to come to an eerie place, without men, and to come with spices and be prepared to tackle that job. What courage and what love! That is what they did, and because of that they were the first to know that Jesus was not there.

You can understand that their nerves would be in a state of tension. They would already be pulling themselves together to do the job. They would be wondering what they would find in there. No wonder then that they were perplexed and puzzled to find things totally different – to find the soldiers gone, to find the stone which must have weighed many hundredweight pushed aside. It probably weighed a ton and a quarter – that is the average weight of these rolling stones that you can still find in the Middle East; to find that rolled away and to go in and find the body gone, on top of the tension in them that had been building up to do this thing – to find all that! They were now thrown off balance. They were bewildered, their minds had come to a full stop, and they didn't know where to go next.

Do you know that is usually what God does just before he is going to show you something wonderful? He brings your plans to a full stop, he throws you into a turmoil; he brings you into a place where you don't know where to go next, and that is a lovely place to be. It is a place where God is going to step in and say something new. To a lesser degree, we have all had experiences like this with the Lord. We have made plans to do something, we thought we were doing it for him, and we thought it was right to do it. We went ahead and somehow it all fizzled out, it all came to nothing. It seemed as if we had come to a dead end and we didn't know where to go next.

Luke 24

So they were well-intentioned, they were bewildered and their minds were in a bit of a turmoil – and at that point two angels stepped into the picture. That was the last straw, it really was. They were terrified, that is the word, and it is the strongest word for fear in the Greek language. They were, it says here, "Bowed down to the ground." That is putting it mildly. Their knees turned to water and they collapsed. They were so terrified, and ladies will understand exactly that. They just collapsed and it was the way that nature in their bodies relieved the tension. There they crouched, on the ground, with wide, staring eyes, open-mouthed, panting breath and rapidly beating hearts, wondering what on earth was going to happen. Do you know there are people who don't even believe angels exist? There are people who don't realise that we are surrounded by myriads of intelligent beings other than human beings, and that they are watching what goes on here on earth. It is not just childish to think about the angels guarding you while you sleep. The hosts of the Lord encamp around those who fear him. The angels are there. We don't need to think of this universe as an empty place – that away from earth there is no life. There is life right through the universe. The skies are full. With angels and archangels, we praise God today.

At point after point in crises in Jesus' life, the angels are there, helping and speaking, ministering in some way, doing something positive. They were there at Jesus' birth putting it right with Joseph, explaining to him what was happening, preparing Mary for this event, warning Joseph and Mary to take the little child down to Egypt. They are there with our Lord in the wilderness when he is tempted by Satan and desperately needs supper. The wild beasts were around him and the devil was tempting him but the angels came and ministered to him. They were there when Jesus desperately needed company in Gethsemane. Jesus said to his disciples,

"Will you stay here and watch and pray?" When he came back they were all asleep and an angel appeared to him and strengthened him. When there is no one else to help you, remember the angels.

Here at this point, the angels came. They were just tidying up the grave, that is all. It was an angel who came and rolled that stone away. They were God's messengers releasing that tomb. The stone was rolled away, I believe, not to let Jesus out – for in his resurrection body he could pass through closed doors and through the very grave clothes – it was to let the world in. So the angel rolled the stone away and sat on it. What a lovely picture of strength. Jesus had ten thousand angels as his personal bodyguard. It only took one of them to roll that stone away, and a couple of them came to meet the women; it was a frightening experience.

Now I want you to notice what the angel said to the women, "Why do you seek the living among the dead?" If the women were surprised to meet the angels there, it seems that the angels were surprised to meet the women. Why were the women seeking the living among the dead? Do you realise that half the human race is dead and half is alive? There are as many people alive on earth now as there are lying in their graves. It is a sobering thought, but in which half do you look for Jesus? The answer is that you will find him among the living. If you want to find the Lord Jesus, the last place to go is a cemetery. Go where there are living people because he is not among the dead. He is not to be found in a crematorium or a graveyard. It is crazy to think of Jesus as dead and gone. To class him with all those great people whose bones lie in our earth is just silly. Why seek the living among the dead? What on earth were they doing there wasting their time, wasting their money, wasting everything else? Why had they come? I want to give you two reasons why the women were there that day and show you that the church today is guilty of the same two faults.

First: those women were there at the grave because they were letting common sense dictate their action. Common sense says when a person's dead, they are dead. Natural reason assumes that what happens naturally is normal. Therefore the normal thing to do is to go to a cemetery if you want to find Jesus. But death is not the normal end, decay is not normal. Sickness is not normal. These things are invaders, intruders, abnormalities in God's world. He never intended people to be sick and to die. These things have come in with sin and spoiled our world, so in this world common sense can be mistaken. Common sense can't believe the resurrection because common sense says it's not *natural* for dead people to rise. But I tell you, it's normal. There was one person who came to our world who lived a normal life, and his name is Jesus. He lived a normal life because he lived a good life, a pure life; he was God's holy one. That is the life you were meant to live. When you are living a holy life, you are living normally, properly, you are living as God intended you to live. God had said in his Word that a person who lived a normal life would not see corruption (in Psalm 16). Let us never accept the state of the world as it is. Let us never accept sickness and death as inevitable natural events. Even the scientist has no biological explanation for death. Whilst the scientist can point to the immediate cause of a death, he can't point to the ultimate cause: that it is not normal. You weren't made to die, you were made to live. You weren't made for sin, you were made for goodness.

The second reason why they came to the graveyard that morning was that they had forgotten the word of the Lord. The angel said to them, "Remember how he spoke to you when he was still in Galilee." Jesus had indeed told his disciples that he would be handed over to wicked men, and that he would be killed, and that he would rise on the third day. As we have already observed, the Bible contains many predictions, and if you remember the words of the Lord you can be assured that its remaining predictions will happen. Common sense might say there will be a tomorrow and a tomorrow and a tomorrow. The Bible says it is going to come to an end, and the heaven and earth that we know will pass away. Are you going to believe common sense or the Word of the Lord? Common sense says human nature will always be sinful, we will always be imperfect, no one's perfect and you can't make bad people good. But the Word of the Lord says that if any man is in Christ he is a new creation. These women were rebuked by being reminded of what Jesus had predicted.

Let us see what the men did. Those women took the rebuke and then presented the men first with the evidence and second with their own testimony of supernatural experience – and the men wouldn't believe. I am now going to make a point to men. These women came and they said they had seen the empty tomb and the grave clothes, and the stone had gone, they had seen angels and been reminded of the words of the Lord. It was a totally convincing case they put, but the men would not believe. I find this both comforting and challenging. It is comforting for this reason: that the resurrection was not put out as a story by a group of men who wanted to believe it – credulous fools who believed anything they heard. These were a group of tough, down to earth, realistic men – tax collectors, fishermen – and they would not believe. Of course, therefore, do you realise that there would have been no preaching of the resurrection unless it had been true, because only the truth would have convinced these men. The resurrection must have happened to convince them. Nobody else could have convinced them. Jesus must be alive or these men would not have gone out as flaming apostles to spread the news over the whole world.

Luke 24

But I find it challenging for this reason: after three years with Jesus, they still didn't believe his words, and that is sad. They were letting common sense dictate instead of the word of the Lord, so they made the same mistake as the women. No wonder Jesus, later on that day, called two of them, "Foolish ones, and slow of heart to believe all that the prophets have said." They had it in writing; they had it from Jesus' lips. They had heard the testimony of the women. How much more did they need?

Do you know that it is literally true that the evidence for the resurrection of Jesus is far stronger than the evidence for the existence of Julius Caesar? There are many more documents and far earlier documents about the resurrection than about the existence of Julius Caesar. Yet I never met anybody who didn't believe that there was a man called Julius Caesar who once invaded this country.

For the resurrection of Jesus, what more evidence could we ask for? There were promises centuries before it happened, records as soon as it happened, a testimony for two thousand years – what more do people want? The men didn't believe but there was one among them whose heart and mind were in a real turmoil. I want to try to get inside Simon Peter's mind. As Peter listened to these women whom he thought were hysterical, I believe his mind was saying, "Supposing it's true and I denied him? Supposing he is alive – I've got to get to him. I must meet him before he tells the other apostles about me. I must get right with him, I must meet him first." Peter decided to find out straight away if it was true. He set off for that grave as fast as he could go. At least he could check the evidence.

He went to the tomb and he found the wrapped-up grave clothes collapsed, laid as they were with the head turban. He found nothing else, no angels. So he went off home by himself. What someone has called the greatest untold story in the Bible occurred. Some time that morning, Peter was alone and suddenly a voice said, "Hello Peter." We don't know what transpired in that conversation. It is too sacred to repeat so the Lord has not told us. I guess that Peter poured out his soul and said, "Lord I denied you." Between those two was forged a bond so deep that Jesus chose Peter to be the first pastor and look after the first church, to feed his lambs. Peter and Jesus met that morning because Peter was going to follow this through – look at the evidence and think it over. The meeting with Peter is mentioned later in this very chapter (at v. 34) because that evening, when the two from Emmaus got back they said to the disciples: "The Lord has risen indeed, and has appeared to Simon." That is how we know it happened.

You should know that Jesus is alive. I want to plead with anyone who does not know. The evidence is there – study the evidence. Read the record, listen to the testimony of those who have had supernatural experience of the Lord. But then you get away by yourself and you think it through; let Jesus come into your life. I know it sounds crazy but you can meet today a man who died two thousand years ago. I know that common sense is all against it. But I want you to believe the word of the Lord because that is how people meet Jesus – when they leave common sense behind and say, "If God says it, it's true. If Jesus is willing to come into my life then I'm going to ask him, and when I ask him I will thank him for coming because he keeps his word. I am going to believe in his word." When you believe in his word, you find that he is real. You can say, "I serve a risen Saviour. He walks with me and talks with me." You will have a real relationship with him.

How gently these people were introduced to the risen Jesus. I suppose that Jesus could have stood outside that tomb and waited for them to come. I suppose that he could have come to them first thing on that morning but to most of them he didn't come till the evening. Do you see that God gently leads people? He showed them the stone rolled away first, then the grave clothes, then that the body had gone. Then he sent them an angel, then they shared testimony, then the Lord Jesus appeared to Mary by herself, then to Peter by himself, then to two walking down the road to Emmaus, then to eleven, and then to five hundred at once. Do you see how gently it grew? The evidence, the testimony, the direct relationship with one then two then eleven then five hundred, and that's how it happens today. Quietly, unnoticed, Jesus is making someone take the Bible and read the record and study the evidence. Then he is introducing them to other Christians who testify of their relationship and what God has said to them. Bit by bit he prepares them and draws them until the great day comes when they meet Jesus. I think of a young man who got hold of a Bible and started reading it and then came and talked with me, so I gave him my testimony and told him what I knew and had experienced. Then he went off, and two or three days later he said, "I was just walking down the High Street and I met Jesus." That is when it really means something.

I could spend a lot of time going through the evidence – it is very convincing. You might agree intellectually that it is a sound case, but that wouldn't make you a Christian. I and countless others could give you our testimony and that wouldn't convince you either and it would not make you a Christian, even though you would say, "Well, I envy them their experience, it seems real to them." But one day you will meet Jesus. Then you will have no doubt about the resurrection. You'll just say what a friend of mine said. He was a converted bookmaker in county Durham. Somebody said, "How do you know that Jesus is alive?" He said, "Well, I was talking to him only this morning!"

24:13-36

"The road to Emmaus" has been described as the most beautiful story in the world, and it is all the more beautiful because it is true and because it happened to two ordinary folk, just like you and me, on a dusty road eight miles long that goes down the hill from Jerusalem, westward, to a little village which even today is called Emmaus.

We are going to look at the five stages through which this pair passed as they came nearer and nearer to a living experience of Jesus; and every single one of us is at some point in one of these five stages.

Stage number one we could call "the blind eyes". You can fail to see that Jesus is very near to you, nearer than the person sitting next to you. Now there are six possible reasons why they did not recognise him. I will leave you to take your pick from them.

First, they were walking west into the sunset, and when your eyes are looking straight into a vivid sunset it is not easy to see the features of people; that may have been it, and it certainly was about half past five in the evening and the sun was going down in the west over the Mediterranean Sea. But I don't think that's the reason.

Somebody has said that their eyes were too full of tears. I think their tears had probably dried up by then. It was three days after they had lost Jesus. I don't think that is the reason either.

Some people have guessed that these two had never seen Jesus close to, and people always look very different at close quarters, as compared with seeing them at a distance. These were not two of his most intimate disciples. They were two people who had seen him, heard him preach, but never got close to him and maybe that was it. Now he was walking alongside. But I don't think that is the reason.

It has been suggested that their last memory of him had

been so different that they didn't recognise this face that was now relaxed – that when last seen, Jesus' face was torn, pinched, a face that was being changed by pain, suffering and loneliness, and faces do change. At the moment of death the facial muscles relax and a face nearly always assumes an expression of peace at death. Maybe they didn't recognise him because his face had relaxed and was full of peace instead of pain. But I don't think that is the reason.

Some people have felt that his glorified body was somehow different from his previous body and that this was why they didn't recognise him.

But I will tell you the reason I think they didn't see him: they didn't *expect* to. And if you don't expect to see someone, you are likely to miss them. If you attended someone's burial, you wouldn't expect to meet them in the high street three days later.

Little children would never have done this. They don't have their minds closed by the finality of death, and if these had been a little boy and a little girl running down the road to Emmaus, I am quite sure that they would have turned round and said, "It's Jesus!" Children have that openness to any possibility, but we grown-ups decide what can happen and what can't happen. We have all our scientific, logical reasons laid out. They had too, even in those days, and they were as sceptical of the resurrection then as many are today. Their minds being closed to the possibility, they never saw him; they didn't know who it was – this "stranger" who just walked alongside them and began to chat to them.

It could be that you have no idea that Jesus is alive now because your mind has never been open to the possibility. You might be thinking he was a great man but dead and gone these two thousand years and that's it. Yet you could be so near to him.

I call the second stage "the burdened faces". They began

to talk, and Jesus asked them why they were so sad. They explained that it was because of things that had happened to Jesus in Jerusalem.

Isn't it ironic? What a situation – they were talking to him about himself. As they walked down this road, they gave Jesus six reasons why they were sad, any one of which would have been enough to depress – but these were six reasons piling up on top of each other until they were overwhelmed with grief.

The first reason was that they had lost the best person they had ever known. It is always sad when a good person goes, a person of whom others think highly.

Second, it was a great prophet who had gone – and there had been an absence of great prophets for four hundred years. This had been a man who could speak from God and could do mighty miracles, a man in whom the supernatural became the natural, in whom the heavenly became the earthly. To lose a prophet as well as a friend was tragic, and at the early age of thirty-three.

Thirdly, this man had not died in an accident, he had not died of a disease, he had been subject to judicial murder. He had been assassinated. There is no other word to describe this death – he had been crucified, innocent as he was.

Fourthly, it had been their own leaders who did it. No gang of bandits, no bunch of criminals, but the respected leaders of the nation, priests and rulers.

Fifthly, their hopes for the future had been dashed with Jesus' death. They had hoped that he was going to save the nation – to redeem Israel. Hopes pinned on Jesus had gone.

Sixthly, beside all this, something had happened that very day which seemed to have made it even worse. Their hopes had been revived a bit. Jesus had always said that on the third day he would come back, and they thought it was going to happen because some women had gone to his grave

Luke 24

and his body had gone. So their hopes that had been raised had crashed again. No wonder they looked sad.

The first reaction when you begin to be aware of Jesus and to talk to him is to become unhappy – because all sorts of questions are raised in your mind and all sorts of things begin to happen. I remember watching the face of one man who started coming to a church of which I was pastor and he came along very cheerfully the first time; the second time, he looked a bit serious. The third time he had a long face. The fourth time he looked as if he was sitting on drawing pins and he began to get more and more unhappy. I said to my wife, "Mr. So-and-So is getting near to Jesus." Of course you begin to get unhappy, it is disturbing. All your life is being upset. All sorts of things are going to change and the future seems so confused, and you don't know how to adjust to it and you begin to be aware of all sorts of things in your own heart that are disappointing. There may be some confusion and bewilderment. But it is a better step on from simply being blind to his presence. You are beginning to think about him, even if you are not yet ready to talk to him consciously.

The third stage I call "their blundering minds". Jesus said, "foolish ones" and he didn't call anybody a fool lightly. If you study the number of people he called a fool, you will come to some interesting conclusions. He says a man who builds a bigger and bigger business and plans a retirement with everything that money can buy is a fool, if he has never got ready for the day that God will say to him, "I require your soul of you now." How rich is that? A man who only looks after his body and neglects his soul is a fool. How foolish these people were, who were "slow of heart to believe in all that the prophets have spoken." Why didn't they believe it all? Anybody can believe bits of the Bible and it doesn't make that much difference to them. But to believe it *all* – that is when you begin to make sense of life and you begin to see God's purpose unfolding. That is when you don't despair. That is when you begin to see the mighty will of God being worked out in history and in your own life – when you believe it all.

Then Jesus gave them a Bible study. One of the things he did – after he rose from the dead and before he went back to heaven six weeks later – was to give Bible studies. He took people through the scriptures, through the books of Moses, through the Psalms, through the Prophets. If ever you are going to understand God's purpose for the world and for you, then you have got to get into the scriptures. Someone has got to take you through it. You need to understand the things that are said there which are predictions for the future. Jesus knew the Hebrew Bible from end to end. Indeed, according to the New Testament, Jesus wrote the Old Testament. The Spirit of Christ was in the prophets, predicting beforehand the sufferings of Christ and the glory that should follow them – says Peter in his first letter in the New Testament. So Jesus took the scriptures that had been written centuries before and explained that, as it was written there, it was necessary for the Christ to suffer.

You know some of the scriptures – "He was wounded for our transgressions, he was bruised for our iniquities, the chastisement of our peace was upon him and by his stripes we are healed. All we like sheep have gone astray and we've turned every one to his own way and the Lord has laid on him the iniquity of us all." I am quoting Isaiah, written 700 years earlier. Can't you see? Can't you believe it? They listened and they began to realise what utter fools they had been; that the cross, far from being a tragedy, was a triumph; far from being a disaster, it was the climax of God's purpose; far from being the end, it was the beginning. They began to see it in an entirely different light.

What do you see in the cross? If you know your Bible,

Luke 24

you can see in it the greatest thing that Jesus ever did – for you and me. So they began to listen, and they saw that it was necessary; that men had not spoiled God's plan but that God had overruled men's plans and used wicked men to fulfil what he wanted done.

They passed on to the next (fourth) stage: "the burning heart". There comes a point when your heart begins to burn. What were they burning with? Two things – first of all, they were burning with shame. They had been so dense. Wouldn't you be ashamed if somebody took your Bible and showed you things that you had never even realised were there and made you realise that you had never even read it properly – that you had just picked up a few stories at Sunday School of Noah's Ark and Adam and Eve in the Garden and feeding the five thousand and you thought you knew it? As an adult, you have got to humble yourself and realise you have hardly begun to know the Bible, that it is written not for children but for adults. It is the book that will need to be studied every day if you are even going to begin to understand its lovely message. They were burning with shame, but burning too with excitement; beginning to get all excited inside because it was all making sense.

Do you feel any excitement that it makes sense, that it begins to fit together, that it begins to be meaningful and real, and the most important thing you have ever listened to? When you have reached that stage, there is one more thing needed. When your mind has been instructed from the Bible, when your heart has been inspired by the touch of Christ, one more thing is needed – that your *will* should act! That is so simple, yet that is the thing that floors many. They listen with their minds and they understand it. They see the truth of the Bible. Their hearts get excited – and yet they don't meet Jesus. He is not real to them. Why not? Because they never get to the point of saying, as these two said, "Abide with us. Come on in. We'd like you in" – and he went in.

How did they recognise him? How did he become known to them? They sat down to a meal – but still they didn't realise who it was. They sat at the table and then he broke bread for them. Now I think I ought to explain. At an eastern meal, the bread comes as large, round, flat, pancake-like things, and the guest is allowed to break it so that he can have the biggest piece for himself. The western custom is to hand the food to your guest first so that they have first pick, but the eastern equivalent is to say, "You break bread." In a devout, religious home, the guest would also be asked to say grace and to give thanks for the bread.

Did they think of the Upper Room and the Last Supper when he took bread and gave thanks and broke it and gave it to them? No! They hadn't been in the Upper Room. Had he a special way of breaking bread? No. There is only one way to break bread. How did they recognise him? It is the simplest and most amazing thing of all. When you are talking to someone and walking with them, you glance at their face, but when they are handling your food, you look at their hands. And the hands that had been below the table came above the table and there were holes in them – and they knew! They had been talking with him for half an hour, and their hearts said it was the third day – and he had come as he said he would. Their first thought was that the others didn't know. They dropped everything, and even though it was dark and even though it was an eight mile journey, they ran uphill – in darkness and in danger. The others must be told.

They had reached stage number five: "their bounding feet to go and tell". They ran up the hill to Jerusalem, ran in and said, "He came."

They replied, "We know! Simon has seen him." Even as they talked, a well-remembered voice said, "Peace be to you!"

Thousands upon thousands of people every day come to know Jesus and move from the spiritual blindness where they can't see him to the stage of longing to go and tell people who don't know.

24:36-53

Strictly speaking, we should not say that Jesus "came back to life". If that was all he had done then he would have died a few years later of old age, and that would have been the end of him. Lazarus came back to life and therefore died again. The widow of Nain's son came back to life and so he died again. Jairus's daughter came back to life and so she died again. But Jesus was raised from the dead and lives to die no more. There was a big change therefore, between the life he lived before his death and the life he lives after the resurrection. It was a new body. It is a body that becomes no older, and that body is in highest heaven today. When Jesus comes back, it will be that risen, glorified body that we shall see. The resurrection appearances occurred during a period of six weeks. He had not come back to do the same things he had done in his earlier ministry. He didn't preach any sermons to the crowds, he didn't appear to multitudes. He did appear once to five hundred, but that was the maximum. The days of five thousand were over as far as Jesus on earth was concerned. He didn't do any healing miracles after his resurrection, he didn't cast out any demons, he didn't cause any blind people to see, at least not those who were physically blind. He didn't unstop deaf ears or make the lame walk. Why did he come back then, for that six weeks? Why did he not just go straight from the grave back home to his Father?

As I read the story of what he did during that time of the resurrection appearances, I get the impression that he was putting the finishing touches to his disciples. He had trained them for three years; they would "graduate" in another couple of months. He is now teaching them certain lessons. For example, and this is a lesson you have got to learn too: Jesus is just as near and just as real when you cannot see him or touch him as when you can. This was the reason Jesus kept appearing and disappearing. One minute there he was, the next minute he had gone. One minute he was breaking bread for the two at Emmaus and the next minute there were just the broken crumbs on the table, and the chair was empty. One minute there are just the disciples in a room, the next minute, even though the doors are locked, there is Jesus. One day Thomas is saying things about Jesus behind his back (as he thought) and a week later Jesus is revealing that he had heard what Thomas had said.

As Jesus kept appearing and disappearing over that six weeks, they got the message – that you don't need to see him to know that he is there. Wherever we go, we may not see Jesus in the room, we may not be able to put out a hand and seize his arm for some comfort, but he is there, he is listening and watching.

Luke, in his Gospel, summarises this six weeks and condenses them into just a page of writing. In that summary Luke singles out four things which Jesus did with the disciples.

First of all, he had shown them his body. All through the previous three years he had drawn a lot of attention to himself. He was always talking about himself. Yet he was able to say: "Learn of me, for I am a humble man." No one ever felt there was a contradiction in that. "I am the Bread of Life"; "I am the light of the world"; "I am the resurrection and the life"; "I am the good Shepherd"; "I am the way, the truth, and the life." Who does he think he is? The big I am? Yes, that's exactly who he is: Yahweh. No great religious teacher has ever been so bold as to claim that. In anyone other than the Son of God it would be offensive. As he drew attention to himself he did it with such truth, love and humility that nobody has ever considered Jesus proud. But the difference is this: before he died on the cross he always drew attention to his *spiritual* qualities. After his resurrection he drew attention to his *physical* qualities. Before he had drawn attention to those spiritual truths which could not be seen and handled, but after his resurrection he showed them his hands and feet.

It is extremely important that we must never confuse our fellowship with Jesus and contact with spirits. The Bible forbids us ever to try and hold séances and contact spirit worlds through a medium. We are not to do this. Our fellowship is not with ghosts. There is only one Spirit that we need to have full fellowship with and that is the fellowship of the Holy Spirit. But Jesus was anxious that they should realise that the future which God has for us is a bodily future. We are not going to float around as spirits for eternity, passing through each other and missing each other. We are going to have bodies that can be touched, bodies that have hands and feet, bodies that are free from the limitations that we know here, but are real bodies.

When Jesus appeared he took pains to show that it really was him. Here is a very profound truth which we need to remember. Some people make Christianity too spiritual. When God saves, he saves all of you – not just your spirit, but your body also. The redemption of our body is part of our salvation. Thank God that Christianity is so real. Archbishop William Temple used to say, "Christianity is the most materialistic of all the world religions," and it is – it is the one that is concerned with bodies as well as souls. It is the one concerned with the whole of man, with the material as well as the spiritual. For God is Creator as well as Redeemer, and God made matter. God made your body as well as your soul, so he wants you to have a new body; he wants to save your body as well as your spirit. The resurrection assures us that he is preparing a place for us, and a place is where a body is.

So Jesus came back and allowed them to see and touch him. I can imagine them crouched up at one end of that room, wondering what on earth was happening. He said, "What have you got for supper," and they had fish and some honeycomb to give him. Then they watched their supper disappear – and that convinced them! There is a lovely human touch here: that was *real* fish.

He taught them that it was necessary for the Christ to suffer and to rise from the dead the third day, and that repentance and remission of sins should be preached in his name to all nations, beginning at Jerusalem.

Let there be no doubt about Jesus' view of the Bible – if the scripture said it, God said it. Before his death we do not see Jesus expounding long passages from the Word. But now, after his resurrection, there has been a change. Now he takes them through the Old Testament. Here is a very profound lesson for Christians: Jesus taught them the Old Testament as the Word of God and as the book about himself. There is a popular notion abroad today that Christians need not bother with the Old Testament, that it is a sub-Christian book in its morals and in its teaching – and that if you want to find out about Jesus, read the New Testament and you have all you need. Don't you believe that. If you want to understand Jesus it is the Old Testament you will need to learn. If you want to understand why Jesus had to die on the cross it is the Old Testament that will tell you. If you want to understand why Jesus had to rise again it is in the Old Testament that you will have to look.

He opened up the scriptures to them and told them what it was all about. He taught them that the Bible is full of predictions, and that every single prediction in the Bible must come true. That was the kind of Bible study he took them through: prediction after prediction; showing that the cross and the resurrection were not a tragedy but a triumph – not something that man had planned, but something God had planned; not something that was the end of the story, but something that would be the beginning because it had all been thought through centuries before and it is all there in the Bible.

I don't know if you have ever done Bible studies of the Old Testament with a view to reading about Christ. A book that had a profound influence on me some years ago is *Christ in All the Scriptures* by Mrs Hodgkin. She takes every book of the Bible and says, "Look at this book and let's see what it tells us about Jesus." About ninety percent of that book is about the Old Testament. When you see how much there is in the Old Testament about Jesus Christ, it becomes to you a Christian book.

So Jesus gave them Bible studies and it is very important that we should be able to find in the scriptures everything we can about him. There is really no point in reading the Bible for any other purpose than to find more and more about Jesus Christ, the Son of God, and how God in his love sent him to earth and made this earth to be a family home for other brothers to Jesus, his only Son. It is all centred in Christ, from beginning to end.

He showed them his body, he taught them his book, and thirdly, he promised his backing to those disciples. The message of Jesus' death and resurrection was to go out to the whole world. That is God's will and intention—that every nation on earth should have Christians in it; that every tribe on earth should hear the gospel, that every tongue should praise the Lord. So this is God's purpose.

It is a frightening thing to go out as a witness. We know

what we have got to do as witnesses. A witness must not embellish; a witness must not say what isn't true. A witness must stick to the facts whatever he does. A witness must simply tell what he has seen and heard, and must pass on what he knows to be fact. But who has believed our report? Who will listen to us? Who is convinced, unless God promises his backing? Unless the Lord works with us confirming the word, nothing will happen.

Now here is Jesus in that six weeks, telling these witnesses to wait in the city of Jerusalem until they are endued with power from on high. If you are going to spread the Word you have to be clothed with power from on high. If God does not clothe with power, then words are mere words and nothing happens. It is not enough to have the book. It is not enough to know the Bible. It is not enough just to say what is in it.

Finally, Jesus took them to the place which had been the nearest thing to a home during the three years of his earthly ministry – Bethany, nestling, as it does, on the east side of the Mount of Olives. There, in a sense out of sight of Jerusalem, he used his hands. When Jesus said farewell he used his hands to bless them. They were nail pierced now. They were the hands that had touched rotting lepers. They were the hands that had stroked children's heads, and they were now the hands that had been nailed to a cross. He used those hands and he gave them his blessing. Because they had his blessing they didn't mind the separation. There wasn't sorrow, there wasn't heartache.

Six weeks earlier the apostles were broken when they thought they had said goodbye to him, but not now. Now he was going back home. Were they sad? No, not in the slightest, because he was going to prepare a place for them. They would go and join him later and they looked forward to the reunion, which of course every Christian may do.

They had learned their lessons and Jesus now ascended.

He went up into those clouds, and as he did so he would have been able to see Jerusalem laid out below him. He would see that little band of men and as he went higher into the sky he would seen something like the astronaut's pictures that we have now seen. Have you seen them, of the Middle East? Have you ever felt what an angel's eye view of our planet would be like? As he went up he would see the continents. As those few little men became too small to see, Jesus would know that from them the gospel would spread all around the globe – to continent after continent, until millions would be saved.

**For more of David Pawson's teaching,
including DVDs and CDs, go to
www.davidpawson.com**

FOR FREE DOWNLOADS
www.davidpawson.org